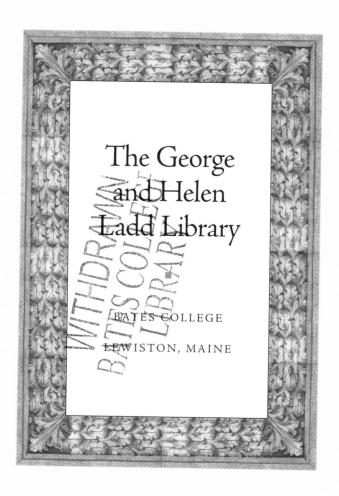

The George
and Helen
Ladd Library

BATES COLLEGE

LEWISTON, MAINE

ENGLAND'S INTERNAL COLONIES

EARLY MODERN CULTURAL STUDIES

Ivo Kamps, Series Editor

PUBLISHED BY PALGRAVE MACMILLAN

ENGLAND'S INTERNAL COLONIES

CLASS, CAPITAL, AND THE LITERATURE OF EARLY MODERN ENGLISH COLONIALISM

Mark Netzloff

palgrave
macmillan

First published 2003 by
PALGRAVE MACMILLAN™
175 Fifth Avenue, New York, N.Y. 10010 and
Houndmills, Basingstoke, Hampshire, England RG21 6XS
Companies and representatives throughout the world

PALGRAVE MACMILLAN is the global academic imprint of the Palgrave Macmillan division of St. Martin's Press, LLC and of Palgrave Macmillan Ltd. Macmillan® is a registered trademark in the United States, United Kingdom and other countries. Palgrave is a registered trademark in the European Union and other countries.

ISBN 1–4039–6183–2 hardback

Library of Congress Cataloging-in-Publication Data
Netzloff, Mark.
     England's internal colonies: class, capital, and the literature of early modern English colonialism/by Mark Netzloff.
        p. cm.—(Early modern cultural studies)
     Includes bibliographical references and index.
     ISBN 1–4039–6183–2
        1. English literature Early modern, 1500–1700—History and criticism. 2. Imperialism in literature. 3. Capitalism and literature—England—History—16th century. 4. Capitalism and literature—England—History—17th century. 5. England—Social conditions—17th century. 6. England—Social conditions—16th Century. 7. Social classes in literature. 8. Working class in literature. 9. Colonies in literature. I. Title. II. Series.

PR428.I54N45 2003
358820.9'—dc21   2003051799

A catalogue record for this book is available from the British Library.

Design by Newgen Imaging Systems (P) Ltd., Chennai, India.

First edition: December, 2003
10   9   8   7   6   5   4   3   2   1

Printed in the United States of America.

CONTENTS

ILLUSTRATIONS

ACKNOWLEDGMENTS

Perhaps appropriate given its topic, this project has entailed a good deal of labor over an eight-year period. I would first like to thank Lois Potter, who helped shape this study in its earliest stages. I am also grateful to Don Mell, Charlie Robinson, John Montano, and Mark Amsler for their help.

This book would not have been realized without the support and resources of a number of institutions: the Folger Institute and Folger Shakespeare Library, the Huntington Library, the Graduate School of the University of Wisconsin-Milwaukee, and UWM's College of Letters and Science. The completion of this study was enabled through a year's fellowship at the Center for 21st Century Studies at UWM. I would like to thank the Center's interim director, Kristie Hamilton, as well as members of the Center community. My thanks also to the staffs of the Newberry Library, the American Geographical Society Library, the British Library, and the Public Record Office.

I have benefited from the comments of audience and seminar members in a number of venues, and I would like to acknowledge the organizers of some of these conference sessions: David Baker, Richmond Barbour, Jonathan Burton, Mary Fuller, Linda Gregerson, John King, Willy Maley, Hassan Melehy, Paul Stevens, Virginia Vaughan, Dan Vitkus, Chris Warley, and Linda Woodbridge. I am particularly grateful to Nabil Matar and Alison Games for their early reviews of this book.

My thanks to those who helped with the final stages of production at Palgrave, especially Kristi Long, Ivo Kamps, and an anonymous reader. Earlier and abbreviated versions of chapters 4 and 5 appeared in *ELH* and *The Journal of Medieval and Early Modern Studies*. I would like to thank Johns Hopkins University Press and Duke University Press for permission to make use of this material.

The University of Wisconsin-Milwaukee has been a supportive intellectual environment over the course of this project, and I would like to thank the Chairs of my department during this time, Mickey Noonan, Jim Sappenfield, and Alice Gillam, for their advice and encouragement.

I have had the benefit of an active and interdisciplinary set of colleagues. In particular, I would like to thank Gwynne Kennedy for her years of mentorship. I would also like to acknowledge my gratitude to a number of present and former colleagues: Herb Blau, Vicki Callahan, Jane Gallop, Greg Jay, Mark Kaplan, Jeff Merrick, Chuck Schuster, Dan Sherman, and Kathy Woodward, as well as my colleagues in the early modern group at UWM.

Gratitude of a different order must be reserved for my family, especially my parents, Richard and Linda Netzloff, and in memory of my remarkable grandmother, Kathlyn ("Nan") Wickham Bowles. I would also like to acknowledge my wife's parents, Probal and Susmita Banerjee, who have always made me one appreciative *jamai*.

This book is dedicated to Sukanya Banerjee. My debt to her is inestimable.

And Speranza and Jhumpa provided their own feline contributions to this project, of course.

S E R I E S   E D I T O R ' S
F O R E W O R D

It continues to be the aim of the Early Modern Cultural Studies Series to usher into print studies that examine cultural exchanges, both within the culture of a given nation or among the cultures of different nations. For the study of intercourse between distinct nations, authors generally turn to the discourse of colonialism or pre-colonialism. Mark Netzloff's *England's Internal Colonies: Class, Capital, and the Literature of Early Modern English Colonialism*, as the title suggests, surprisingly calls on these same discourses to analyze England's relation not to the East, the Ottoman Empire, or the Americas, but to its own "internal colonies," the marginal cultures and underclasses of England, Ireland, and Scotland.

There is no question that this approach yields striking insight into early modern modes of thought, and that it provides a useful extension of, or counterweight to those recent studies that have elucidated ways in which England sought to construct for itself a national English and/or British identity. In the early years of his reign as king of England, James I surely longed for a union between his birth nation Scotland and his new kingdom. And we should not underestimate the ideological appeal of Shakespeare's classless band of Welsh, English, Scottish, and Irish brothers, which invades France. "For he today that sheds his blood with me / Shall be my brother; be he ne'er so vile / This day shall gentle his condition," so Henry V tells his soldiers. In the euphoria of victory, however, Henry suppresses the fates of the so-called low-life characters, Pistol, Bardolph, Nym, and Falstaff—all of whom are vilified, killed off, and/or alienated from the band of brothers. And it is this process of vilification and alienation in early modern culture on which Mark Netzloff focuses. In particular, Netzloff is interested in the way the concerns of class and foreignness are blended into a exclusionary discourse, as when a seventeenth-century pamphleteer, commenting on the poor in Britain, derisively asserts, "We have Indians at home.... Indians in

Cornwall, Indians in Wales, Indians in Ireland." Rather than draw these poorer inhabitants of various nationalities into a wholesome British whole (as does, e.g., the beehive metaphor of the Archbishop in *Henry V*), the pamphleteer associates them with the supposedly inferior racial others of distant lands. The aim appears to be to fuse class prejudice with racial prejudice, possibly in an attempt to transfer the "naturalness" of the other's racial inferiority to the economic conditions of the poor.

England's Internal Colonies scrutinizes the economic and social conditions that underpin this type of analogy. It draws on the work of such familiar names as William Shakespeare, Ben Jonson, Thomas Heywood, John Donne, Francis Bacon, John Speed, William Camden, and Thomas Dekker, but also on an extensive body of texts that deal with issues of piracy, vagrancy, the expulsion of the poor to the colonies, the status of gypsies, and the colonial settlement of regions within the British Isles and Ireland. To supplement his readings of literary representations, Netzloff also inspects early modern material practices, and explores the role of various economic, legal, and social institutions such as the Royal Exchange, labor and poor relief statutes, and the State Paper Office. What Netzloff's impressive study amounts to is nothing less than a new kind of "history from below" rising from the underclasses and subcultures of early modern "Britain."

Ivo Kamps
Series Editor

INTRODUCTION

INTERNAL COLONIALISM IN EARLY MODERN ENGLAND

We have Indians at home—Indians in Cornwall, Indians in Wales, Indians in Ireland

The Hireling Ministry None of Christs *(1652)[1]*

But you may save your labour if you please,
To write to me ought of your Savages
As savage slaves be in great Britaine here,
As any one that you can shew me there.

Michael Drayton, "To Master George Sandys, Treasurer for the English Colonie in Virginia" *(1622)[2]*

As hauyng, emungst sauuages, y' chardege of wylde menn of myne owene nacione, Whose vnrulynes ys suche as not to gyue leasure to y' goouernour to bee all most at eny tyme from them.

Ralph Lane to Sir Philip Sidney, from Roanoke, *August 12, 1585[3]*

England's Internal Colonies addresses the mutual constitutiveness of internal colonialism in early modern England and early English overseas colonial ventures, exploring the ways that colonialist relations within England, Scotland, and Ireland provided interpretive and institutional models for colonial expansion abroad. My discussion situates both internal and overseas colonialism within a history of proto-capitalist development, a process that affected not only the position of England's growing underclass but also the status of the peripheral cultures of Britain and Ireland. Emphasizing the domestic influences on early modern colonialism, I explore how English social institutions and conflicts—especially contentious relations of class and labor—shaped colonial projects and settlements. In addition, I trace the impact of colonialism on English national culture, analyzing expressions of English nationhood as responses to the centripetal threats to community posed by colonial migration and imperial expansion.

This study considers the effects of class relations and a history of internal colonialism in relation to several geographic contexts of early modern colonialism, commerce, and travel. My first three chapters examine the importance of class relations and capital formation to English commercial and colonial ventures in the East Indies, the Mediterranean, and the Americas. In these chapters, I discuss the place of labor in competing mercantilist and capitalist formulations of value and commercial expansion (chapter 1), the Jacobean state's regulation of piracy in the Mediterranean and Levant (chapter 2), and the Virginia Company's policies of "venting" laborers to the colonies (chapter 3). While these initial three chapters are primarily concerned with the impact of class relations, labor, and economic ideology on early English colonialism, the latter half of my book examines specific sites of internal colonialism within Britain and Ireland. Chapter 4 addresses the role of the Anglo-Scottish Borders, and the communities of gypsies and vagrants who populated this region, in early constructions of British identity. Chapter 5 discusses the Ulster plantation, analyzing how technologies of knowledge production (cartography, archival documentation) helped erase the process of colonization from historical and cultural memory. In the conclusion, I critique a traditional approach to issues of class and nation that has viewed these categories solely as products of a later period of industrialization. Throughout this study I emphasize the necessity of situating the interconnected development of the English nation and the British empire in reference to domestic contexts of class relations and capital formation.[4]

In the early modern period, England's underclass was increasingly represented and legislatively codified as a distinct and unruly culture, a seemingly alien group whose status necessitated more intensified mechanisms of social control in the form of anti-vagrant statutes, the creation of workhouses, and recommendations for overseas transportation. These practices of internal colonialism extended as well to the peripheral cultures of Britain and Ireland, nomadic and kinship-based cultures inhabiting regions such as the Anglo-Scottish Borders, the Scottish Hebridean Islands, and Ulster, the northern province of Ireland. The first epigraph prefacing this section comes from a statement made by a mid-seventeenth-century Protestant missionary and pamphleteer. Frustrated by his inability to proselytize the "natives" of Wales, the writer calls upon authorities to reform those subjects populating the margins of the nation, a project that he deems of greater necessity than the conversion of Amerindians in the colonies. Despite his emphasis on the proximity of these groups at "home," this anonymous writer renders them as "Indians," thereby confirming their status as culturally and geographically removed from metropolitan English culture.[5]

This passage, as well as the references by Michael Drayton and Ralph Lane to their fellow English as "savages" and "wild men" cited earlier, points to the interconnections between discourses of class and race in the early modern period. As Benedict Anderson has noted, racial categories "have their origin in ideologies of *class*."[6] Whereas Anderson traces the influence of aristocratic notions of purity of blood on the formation of racial discourses, I will examine the institutions and social practices through which class itself became an increasingly racialized category in the early modern period. I wish to argue that this codification of class difference was formulated in response to the disruptive effects of capital formation and colonial expansion on domestic social relations. Lane's letter, one of the first documents in the archive of the English colonization of the Americas, illustrates how even at its inception the Virginia colony was beset by fundamental anxieties due to problems of social control and class conflict. As Edmund S. Morgan argues in *American Slavery, American Freedom*, the rhetoric of colonial liberty depended, in fact, upon the exclusion of the rights of laborers.[7] The potentially disruptive avenues of social mobility enabled through travel, commerce, and colonial migration necessitated intensified forms of surveillance and control over subaltern class groups. Yet these official efforts also prompted the resistance of those groups subject to that authority, particularly in a colonial environment characterized by an inevitable transformation of social constraints. As Étienne Balibar notes in "Class Racism," class groups became racialized only once they had begun to claim rights for themselves.[8] Michel Foucault therefore concludes that discourses of race emerged out of an early modern context of "social war," a process wherein the social struggle between classes was reinscribed as a conflict between distinct "races."[9]

The representation of early modern England's lower classes as "savages" was predicated upon their lack of amenability to social control, a resistance that was explained through the linked frameworks of class and race. As I will discuss in chapter 3, anti-vagrant laws in early modern England constructed a racialized class among laborers who refused to adapt to the regime of workhouses such as Bridewell, consequently designating these groups for forced transportation to the colonies. This reconstitution of class also served to justify emergent policies of indentured servitude, labor practices that abetted a centralized control over capital and land ownership.[10] Nonetheless, although class and race functioned as mutually constitutive categories in the period covered in this study (ca. 1576–1624), the later seventeenth century witnessed a historically significant separation of these terms, a process that emerged alongside the expansion of racialized slavery in the American colonies.[11] As Theodore W. Allen argues in *The Invention of the White Race*, a corollary part of this process entailed a recuperation of the status of subaltern classes, who were recruited to the service of the state due to a common racial and national identity, an emphasis upon their position as both "white" and "English." According to Allen, "primary emphasis upon 'race' became the pattern only where the bourgeoisie could not form its social control apparatus without the inclusion of propertyless European-Americans."[12]

Early modern colonialism transformed social relations in England, creating a colonial frame of reference that was employed to analyze forms of cultural difference within the body politic and thereby providing an analogous colonial solution to problems of class relations, social control, and regional cultural difference.[13] This process is evident in Michael Drayton's poem to Sir George Sandys, cited earlier. The colonial encounter enables Drayton to reflect on the cultural difference of England's own laboring classes, "savage slaves" whose status he defines in terms of both race and class. Samuel Rid's anti-vagrant text, *Martin Markall* (1610), similarly extends the analogy of "Indians at home" to England's lower classes, describing how the earlier pamphlets of Thomas Dekker and others have succeeded in "discovering ... a new-found nation and people" among the seemingly foreign population of England's own underclass. In a comic treatment of the position of England's poor, Rid explains that this recently discovered and colonized culture has been forced to emigrate to a more hospitable setting, the utopian commonwealth of "Thievingen."[14] Illustrating the influence of the colonial analogy on domestic class relations, Rid's comic depiction of vagrant culture also demonstrates the complexities of this frame of reference: vagrants are figured as the displaced victims of internal colonialism as well as aspiring colonizers hoping to travel to a better life abroad. The image of "Thievingen" thus alludes to the liberating possibilities made available to England's laboring classes through travel and colonial migration. Drawing on Rid's analogy, several early modern literary texts described England's poor as a colonized culture by likening an exploration of the domestic underclass to travel to a distant, foreign country.[15] In Jonson's *The New Inn* (1629), for example, Lord Frampul describes the years he had spent among "those wilder nations" of vagrants and gypsies populating areas of Wales and the North Country: "For to these sauages I was addicted,/To search their natures, and make odde discoueries!" (5.5.94, 99–100).[16]

As England began to formulate theories and practices of colonialism in the late sixteenth and early seventeenth centuries, texts consistently employed a form of analysis that emphasized the resemblances between different colonial contexts. In *The Order of Things*, Foucault describes this mode of analogy, a "knowledge based upon similitude," as a primary medieval and Renaissance form of knowledge production, an episteme progressively displaced by a model of taxonomy and classification, "a knowledge based upon identity and difference."[17] The congruities between domestic and foreign contexts were reinforced upon the assumption that no single colonial site was distinct and could therefore be analyzed on the basis of precedents elsewhere. Sir Humphrey Gilbert, whose career spanned colonial projects in both Munster and Newfoundland, organized a reading group in 1570–71 that studied Livy's *Histories*, which chronicled the Roman conquest of Britain, as a way to analyze contemporary Ireland.[18] When Sir Thomas Smith established the first English plantation effort in Ireland in 1572–75, in the Ards region of northeastern Ulster, he also looked for precedents in Roman colonization. Through his use of Roman colonial models, Smith was the first to apply the term "colony" to an English context.[19] Colonial officials also turned to contemporary examples of internal colonialism to determine appropriate policies. Sir John Davies, poet and attorney general of Ireland from 1606–19, the period of the initial settlement of the Ulster plantation, justified efforts to transplant reivers (cattle raiders) from the Anglo-Scottish Borders based on Spain's expulsion of Moors from Granada.[20] The deportation of Borders reivers in the first years of James I's reign served as a precedent not only for the transplantation of populations in other peripheral regions, particularly Ireland, but also for the expulsion of England's own displaced and vagrant poor.[21] Colonial discourses and practices were thus formed through the use of historical and cultural analogy, demonstrating that early modern commentators thought of the colonization of Ireland and the Americas as part of the same project, policies that additionally encompassed forms of internal colonialism within the nation.

In *The Ideological Origins of the British Empire*, David Armitage notes the long-standing inability of historians and literary critics to discuss the linked formation of the English nation-state and the British Empire.[22] Only a small number of historians have begun to take up the project of analyzing the relevance of English domestic contexts to colonial and imperial experiences in the early modern period. Nonetheless, this research has had surprisingly little impact on literary studies of early modern English colonialism, which have generally neglected to recognize class as an important factor in early English colonial projects. Even in early modern historiography, dominant critical models have largely overlooked issues of class or economics, including the "Atlanticist" approach inaugurated by David B. Quinn and Nicholas Canny, which emphasizes the conceptual and administrative links between English colonialism in Ireland and the New World. These accounts have also failed to consider how the emergence of overseas colonies in both Ireland and the Americas was influenced by forms of internal colonialism.[23] Karen Kupperman's *Settling with the Indians* is one of the few studies that has emphasized the formative role of class relations in the early history of English colonialism. Kupperman discusses how the early modern English employed categories of class and status as an interpretive framework in their responses to Amerindian cultures and, consequently, often compared indigenous cultures to England's own underclass.[24] Nonetheless, Kupperman's analysis does not address the underlying causes prompting these class-based anxieties. I wish to argue that the representation of England's laboring poor as "Indians at home" must be seen in the context of changing class relations resulting from an early history of capital formation in early modern England.

This project employs the term internal colonialism in order to emphasize the domestic foundations of early modern colonial discourses and practices. The term, with its origins in the Marxist critique of imperialism, also foregrounds the interconnections between histories of colonialism and capitalism. Vladimir Lenin was the first to articulate this mode of analysis, which he formulated through a critique of European high imperialism of the late nineteenth century.[25] Whereas Lenin was concerned with analyzing the domestic roots and effects of a particular stage in capitalist development, Antonio Gramsci adopted Lenin's approach in "The Southern Question" in order to examine the geographic divisions instituted through capitalism, which, in early twentieth-century Italy, imposed regional and class relations of colonialist stratification between the industrial Northern and the agrarian Southern regions of the country.[26] Studies of postcolonial Latin American and Chicano/a cultures have extended Gramsci's analysis in order to discuss the forms of internal colonialism embedded in domestic class hierarchies that persist despite nominal decolonization. Mario Barrera describes internal colonialism as "a form of colonialism in which the dominant and subordinate populations are intermingled, so that there is no geographically distinct 'metropolis' separate from the 'colony.'"[27] The model of internal colonialism undermines the typical association of colonialism with geographic and cultural distance. Indeed, internal colonialism blurs the boundaries imposed between seemingly domestic interests and foreign relations, thereby destabilizing the representation of metropolitan culture's imputed stability, insularity, and integrity. By emphasizing the colonialist relations existing within a nation, analyses of internal colonialism expose the intersection of class relations and colonial practices.

Michael Hechter was the first to apply the concept of internal colonialism to the British Isles and Ireland, presenting an overview of the gradual incorporation of the "Celtic fringe" into English economic and national life from the medieval period to the mid-twentieth century.[28] For Hechter, internal colonialism is defined by an "unequal distribution of resources and power" between the core and peripheral regions within a nation. Hechter's analysis counters a "diffusion model of national development," an argument which assumes that a gradual and unimpeded spread of core culture and values to the periphery will enable a modernization of these regions, creating economic equilibrium and thereby canceling out residual cultural differences. By contrast, Hechter's model of internal colonialism emphasizes how the political incorporation and enforced assimilation of peripheral regions are accomplished through the economic dominance of metropolitan culture. An inadvertent effect of this process, however, is a consequent "development of distinctive ethnic identification" among both core and peripheral cultures. Thus, while economic hegemony abets the construction of notions of "Englishness," it also enables peripheral cultural groups to recognize domestic social relations as a form of colonialism, thereby producing an opposition to increasingly centralized national bodies of power.[29]

My analysis of internal colonialism, class relations, and nascent forms of capitalism situates these issues in relation to their impact on what Immanuel Wallerstein has described as the early modern world-system.[30] This study explores the effects of internal stratifications on the early modern world-system, inquiring into the foundational interconnections between domestic transcultural and class relations and an emergent global proto-capitalist economy. Drawing on the work of Hechter and Wallerstein, I also analyze how the early modern English nation created its own peripheries—regions and classes that functioned as providers of extractable resources and labor. However, I wish to offset the overly schematic character of world-systems theory, with its relatively stable positions of core, semiperiphery, and periphery, by emphasizing the complexities of class, region, and cultural difference in early modern Britain and Ireland.[31] I also wish to distinguish my own approach to internal colonialism from the macrological scope of Hechter's analysis, which fails to acknowledge the distinct and divergent histories of internal colonialism in regions such as the Hebrides, the Anglo-Scottish Borders, and Ulster. In addition, unlike Hechter, my analysis will focus on the social practices and agency of individual subjects, emphasizing that the workings of internal colonialism were inevitably mediated and even resisted by those subject to its power. Through my discussion of examples such as the alternative currencies used by laborers and artisans (chapter 1), maritime communities' protection of "renegades," returning sailors who had converted to Islam (chapter 2), the oppositional uses of discourses of colonial "liberty" (chapter 3), and the alliances made between gypsies and vagrants against repressive state legislation (chapter 4), I attempt to locate the narratives and expressions of agency of the subaltern classes and cultures of early modern Britain.

This study also emphasizes the limits to the correlation of internal and overseas forms of colonialism. Nicholas Canny has noted how internal colonialism "hindered and distorted as well as stimulated" English colonial ventures in the Americas.[32] An advantage to the concept of internal colonialism is that it undermines a rigid division between domestic and foreign contexts, exposing the disjuncture as well as alignment of categories of class, nation, and colony in the early modern period. However, forms of internal colonialism did not merely serve as a training ground that enabled more successful and permanent colonies abroad. When texts evoked a domestic parallel or rationale, internal colonialism also functioned as a symptom of historical crisis, marking a breakdown of residual foundations of national and class cohesion. In particular, the effects of internal colonialism were registered in observations noting—and even recommending—a subversion of holistic, integral notions of a body politic, the model of the "commonwealth" advocated in sixteenth-century humanist political thought.[33] This book attempts to foreground the struggle between classes and cultural groups in competing formulations of nation and empire in the early modern period, an era that sees residual embodiments of community profoundly destabilized through the emergence of capital and colonialism.

This study, particularly in chapters 4 and 5, will situate emergent discourses of a "British empire" within a context of internal colonialism in England, Scotland, and Ireland. Definitions of empire, I argue, derived from and were primarily concerned with a domestic consolidation of power and social control. Consequently, representations of empire or British identity did not necessarily entail an advocacy of overseas expansion. In my references to a British empire, I am attempting to analyze British imperial identity and rhetoric in an early modern context, one that is radically distinct from the high imperialism of the nineteenth century. Henry VIII's declaration of England as an empire in the 1533 Act in Restraint of Appeals (24 Henry VIII, c. 12)—"this realm of England is an empire"—witnesses the inward-turning, centrifugal force of early modern English imperialism, which focused more on consolidating domestic power than overseas conquest.[34] References to a "British empire" were first made in order to justify English interventions in Scottish affairs during the 1540s and were therefore tied to English hegemony within the territories of the British Isles.[35] It was not until the 1570s that John Dee first applied the term to refer to the prospect of overseas expansion.[36]

The idea of a British empire first gained currency during James VI and I's joint rule of Scotland and England from 1603–25.[37] As Michael Hechter has noted, because nation-states emerged out of formerly distinct cultures, "Nation-building in its earliest stages might better be thought of as empire-building."[38] James's failed Union of the Realms of England and Scotland (1603–07) proposed a regal union that attempted to conjoin the nations' monarchies, legal systems, and economic policies, offering the mutual naturalization of the subjects of each nation along with an erasure of cultural borders. In its efforts to reconstitute English and Scottish subjects as British and redefine the contentious Borders region as "the Middle Shires," the Union of the Realms demonstrates the constructedness of the nation as an imagined community, to use Benedict Anderson's terminology.[39] The Jacobean Union also served as a countercurrent to expressions of English nationhood; after all, the Union intended to replace national identification with affiliation to a composite monarchy ruling over distinct kingdoms. This study therefore explores the disjuncture between representations of "British" imperialism and "English" nationhood, a topic overlooked in the best-known study of the early modern English nation, Richard Helgerson's *Forms of Nationhood*.[40]

To combat the critical tendency to subsume the constituent cultures and histories of "Britain" within those of England, J.P.A. Pocock, in a landmark 1975 article, called for an analysis of "British history" in order "to denote the plural history of a group of cultures situated along an Anglo-Celtic frontier and marked by an increasing English political and cultural domination."[41] Pocock invokes the need for a reconceptualization of the cultural model upon which "English" history and literary study are based, one that acknowledges the profound differences between an English and British (or in Pocock's terms, "archipelagic") model: as Pocock adds, "the fact of a hegemony does not alter the fact of a plurality."[42] As Pocock notes, the dominance of English sources in the archive, in the form of historical records as well as literary writing, creates an inaccurate view of English hegemony.[43] Pocock's call for a New British History has been taken up by a number of historians, including Steven Ellis, Jenny Wormald, and Brendan Bradshaw.[44] And, although comparatively fewer literary critics have begun to analyze the transcultural relations between the constituent cultures of early modern Britain, the important work of David J. Baker and Willy Maley has helped introduce the New British History to early modern literary studies.[45] Baker and Maley have each emphasized the pervasive degree of cultural hybridity found in the complex cultural landscape of early modern Britain and Ireland, analyzing the ability of subjects to create and perform new identities in this environment. This study extends the work of the New British History, exploring the links between British transcultural relations and early modern colonial contexts, and situates the "British question" in reference to contexts of class relations, economic production, and capital formation.

In order to explain the development of English colonialism, *England's Internal Colonies* argues that one must examine the emergent practices of capitalism in early modern England and, in particular, the evolving mechanisms whereby surplus was extracted from agricultural production. The links between English colonialism and agrarian capitalism are evident even in the earliest colonial project: Sir Thomas Smith's proposal for the settlement of Ulster in the 1570s.[46] Smith formulated a military model of colonization that emphasized social control through the establishment of military fortifications and a systematic division and plantation of the land. Yet the classical rubric upon which Smith based his idea of colonialism used military troops as a means to an end, to secure and stabilize the colonial region so that it could be converted into profitable agricultural property. Smith's notion of colonial husbandry would become a primary concern of English colonialism in Ireland and Virginia. Thus, England's colonies were initially devised as a form of social organization intended to extract surplus from agricultural production. In addition, the means through which these colonies were formed, the confiscation or "escheating" of tracts of land, originated in capitalist practices of agriculture and land management in England. As John Norden explains in *The Svrveiors Dialogve* (1607), the term escheat referred to the recent practice wherein land could be acquired as a marketable commodity without reciprocal feudal duties and services binding landlord and tenant. Land could also be obtained by escheat if landholders committed acts of felony or rebellion, a stipulation later used to justify land confiscations in Ulster, the Anglo-Scottish Borders, and Virginia.[47] The term escheat thus united the practices of agrarian capitalism, and the conversion of land into a marketable commodity at the expense of the customary rights of tenants, with those of colonial settlement, the plantation efforts made possible through the state's acquisition of lands deemed forfeit as a result of their owners' political actions.

The failure of historians and literary critics to trace the mutual construction of "domestic" issues of class and nation and "foreign" concerns of colonialism and empire has resulted, in part, from an inability to gauge the economic interdependence of domestic and foreign contexts in relation to emergent forms of capital in the early modern period. Critical approaches to the history of early modern capitalism often provide a selective reading of Marx's initial formulation of the genealogy of capital from volume one of *Capital*. Marx famously locates the "starting-point of capital" in the emergence of "world trade and the world market" in the sixteenth century.[48] Although international commerce and exchange served a foundational role in the creation of nascent forms of capital, I wish to emphasize how the expansion of capital through international trade was dependent upon and motivated by domestic economic crises and social anxieties. As Marx argues in volume three of *Capital*, the early modern expansion of commercial capital, "taken by itself, is insufficient to explain the transition from one mode of production to the other," in other words, of solely establishing the conditions necessary for the creation and expansion of capital.[49] Robert Brenner similarly notes that one must therefore look at the underlying class relations that enabled capital formation for any origin of capital.[50]

A more productive point of access to the genealogy of capital is provided by Marx in his section, "The Secret of Primitive Accumulation," from volume one of *Capital*. Marx counters the problematic search

for origins implicit in discussions of capital formation by analyzing
not the "starting-point of capital," as he does in his earlier analysis of
commodity circulation, but the necessary preconditions for capital,
which he locates in terms of the erosion of laborers' customary rights
to title and property over the land. As Marx declares, "So-called primitive accumulation, therefore, is nothing else than the historical
process of divorcing the producer from the means of production."[51]
Marx critiques the equation of capital with commerce found in Adam
Smith and other political economists, taking issue with Smith's assertion that the accumulation of capital as merchants' "stock" preceded
and created the conditions for a capitalist division of labor. For Marx,
this notion of a "primitive" or "prior" accumulation of capital is an
ahistorical myth that reverses economic cause and effect. Marx therefore examines how the formation of a capitalist mode of production
depended, instead, upon the existence of "free" wage-laborers, a class
that was created in an early modern "pre-history of capital." This
process not only abolished monopolies and feudal forms of domination but also eliminated the customary rights and protections that
helped ensure the maintenance of a self-sustaining peasant class
through agricultural production.[52]

The formation of capital in early modern England was contingent
upon a multifaceted erosion of the rights of laborers. While agricultural prices rose by more than 600 percent during the period, the
position of tenants and laborers became increasingly vulnerable.
Changes in leasing arrangements, with landlords reconstituting their
holdings so as to maximize profits on the market, left more than half
the population of small tenant farmers in England without any security of land tenure and protection from eviction. The customary
rights and protections available to laborers and tenants were sharply
curtailed and often eliminated in the early modern period, ranging
from those available to tenants (stable freehold possession of land,
access to commons, protection from fines and eviction) to those provided for apprentices and laborers (with penalties for employers who
imposed changes in wages or work hours or who arbitrarily dismissed
workers from employment).[53] In addition, the enclosure of nearly
one-fifth of the agricultural land in England, removed from cultiva-
tion by capitalist improving landlords, further limited the ability of
smallholding tenants to survive through subsistence agriculture,
forcing them to turn to the market and wage-labor.[54] As this population of dispossessed peasants became transformed into a mobile body
of unemployed laborers, these groups found themselves subject to
increasingly draconian anti-vagrant legislation, statutes that contained

the initial formulation of practices of colonial transportation.[55] Thus, while the expanding profits of agrarian capital served to fuel the growing outlets of merchant's capital in the form of overseas trade and exchange, the excess labor of the English countryside provided the human capital and necessary labor for England's colonies.

The idea of a primitive accumulation of capital is an aspect of Marx's historical commentary that has largely been overlooked by economic historians as well as literary and cultural critics. Richard Halpern's excellent analysis of Marx in *The Poetics of Primitive Accumulation* has helped recuperate the value of this concept for studies of early- or proto-capitalist social formations, particularly in reference to the sixteenth and seventeenth centuries. As Halpern points out, primitive accumulation is analyzed most productively not in any rigid chronological framework but, instead, as a structural stage in the formation of capital.[56] My study appropriates Marx's notion of a primitive accumulation of capital in order to undermine the narrative of the inevitable ascendency, consolidation, and emergence of a capitalist mode of production. As Halpern notes, Marx's historical overview of primitive accumulation emphasizes the discontinuities and disruptions inherent in the process of capital's formation. The early modern period has often been characterized as a transitional stage between the dispossession of the peasantry and the subsequent reincorporation of this class into the national economy as wage-laborers in an emergent industrial system.[57] However, for early modern commentators, primitive accumulation represented the limits of economic causality, forms of change that threatened to undermine residual definitions of community and nation. The recent work of Andrew McRae, James Holstun, and David Hawkes has addressed the degree of opposition to capital formation found in early modern texts, which often asserted definitions of a "moral economy" to counter capital's destabilizing effects on social relations.[58] This study will similarly discuss a number of figures who articulated a critique of capital, emphasizing the plurality of opinions and extent of dissent formulated in response to the social and economic changes of the early modern period. Nonetheless, one must recognize the implicit conservatism cf many examples of this critique, whose arguments attest to an inability to conceptualize the modernity of emergent class relations. Moreover, I certainly wish to distinguish the position of my own Marxist-inflected critique of early modern capital from a nostalgic embrace of pre-capitalist social relations, an approach that both Marx and Raymond Williams have cautioned against as well.[59]

Emergent forms of capital enabled increasing possibilities of social mobility and advancement for the "middling sort," including urban

merchants and capitalist landowners, whose social positions testify to
a fluidity of status in the early modern period. However, this study
will insistently use the term "class" rather than "status" in order to
emphasize the profoundly eroded position of laborers during this
period, who were in the process of being converted into a permanent
underclass.[60] My terminology does not overlook the fact that early
modern social formations were described in more porous and less
dichotomous terms such as "ranks," "estates," "degrees," and "sorts."
And, as Raymond Williams has noted, the modern application of class
as a category of analysis derives from the social relations of industrialism and was first coined in the late eighteenth century.[61] Nonetheless,
as I will discuss further in the conclusion, postindustrial class relations
were themselves the product of a much longer history, one that was
predicated upon the reconstitution of the social position of England's
laboring classes, an erosion of customary rights and protections
that enabled these groups to become subject to the labor practices
of both colonialism and industrialization. Furthermore, to quote
E.P. Thompson, "class, in its heuristic usage, is inseparable from the
notion of 'class-struggle'"; despite the historical imprecision of
"class," no alternative term is able to account for the process of agency
and resistance that ultimately produced the historical formation of
class consciousness.[62]

The methodology of this project differs in a number of ways from
previous studies of early modern English colonialism. These studies
have primarily addressed discursive or representational questions,
often without sufficient attention to the material conditions and economic factors that shaped the formation of colonial discourses. By
contrast, my discussion of discursive formations, such as the language
of "venting labor" analyzed in chapter 3, examines this rhetoric in the
context of material practices, including labor regulations, the economy of the English workhouse, and the Virginia Company's second
charter of 1609. The central texts considered in this book include
Shakespeare's *The Merchant of Venice* and *The Tempest* (chapters 1 and
3), Heywood's adventure play, *Fortune by Land and Sea* (chapter 2),
Jonson's masque, *The Gypsies Metamorphosed* (chapter 4), and John
Speed's atlas, *The Theatre of the Empire of Great Britain* (chapter 5).
In my approach to these texts, I have attempted to place them within
a larger cultural field and examine their relation to a range of social
practices and institutions of economic and knowledge production.
I have also chosen not to discuss some texts that have become
traditional objects of analysis in studies of early modern English
colonialism and nationhood, particularly Spenser's *A View of the*

Present State of Ireland and Shakespeare's Henry IV plays and *Henry V*. The large body of criticism devoted to these texts reveals the need to consider a different selection as well as broader range of texts, as I have attempted to do, for example, with discussions of the pamphlet literature on piracy (chapter 2) and Virginia Company textual production (chapter 3). In addition, my analysis also incorporates archival research to a greater extent than many literary studies of early modern English colonialism, giving due attention to material from the State Papers such as correspondence and prose treatises.

This book emphasizes the tensions between such frequently conjoined terms as nationalism and imperialism, mercantilism and capitalism, and nationalism and colonialism, concepts whose distinct and complex histories are often elided in some studies of the early modern period. Chapter 1, for example, will establish an economic foundation for this project's analysis of internal and overseas forms of early modern English colonialism by delineating the differences between mercantilist and proto-capitalist formulations of value and labor. In addition, the following three chapters each consider examples that demonstrate the possibilities of social mobility, cultural hybridity, and alternative communities made possible through internal and overseas colonialism, exploring the ways that these strategic alliances challenged dominant expressions of nation or empire. As these examples demonstrate, one of the chief concerns of this study entails an attempt to locate the textual traces left by expressions of agency and forms of resistance to capital and internal colonialism, providing a history from below of the subaltern classes and cultures of early modern Britain.[63] I wish to associate this book with a more general effort to resituate the study of early modern culture in relation to a Marxist framework of historical analysis. *England's Internal Colonies* presents a critical method that foregrounds questions of class conflict, capital, and labor, a form of analysis that is attentive to the inextricable links between the domestic and the foreign, "home" and "the world," inquiring into the formative domestic impact of early English colonial enterprises as well as the global repercussions of class relations in early modern England.

CHAPTER 1

"THE UNIVERSAL MARKET OF THE WORLD": CAPITAL FORMATION AND *The Merchant of Venice*

THE "ENGLISH" POUND

An abiding feature of constructions of English nationhood lies in the attempt to provide a stable foundation for national identity based upon the consistent, unchanging value of the nation's currency. The hagiography of the English pound, in fact, constitutes a surprisingly large body of literature.[1] Many of these arguments construct a narrative that links the early modern period with the present, presenting a causal connection between Elizabeth I's recoinage of 1560, which stabilized the value of the English pound, and the nation's subsequent rise as a commercial empire.[2] Although this chestnut of traditional economic history has been rebutted by arguments that emphasize the crises inherent in the early modern world-system, the mythologization of the English pound still retains a striking ideological "currency."[3] In a *New York Times Magazine* piece analyzing the state of Britain at the turn of the millennium, for example, essayist Andrew Sullivan locates among other forms of nostalgia a longing for the nation's (and empire's) once-dominant pound, now threatened to be displaced by the Euro.[4] The mythologization of the English pound, the assertion of continuity from the early modern period to the present, creates a nostalgic undercurrent, a perceived loss of value, prestige, and national essence, in which the contemporary nation is presented as a debased remnant of past glory. Although Sullivan, like other recent essayists, conjures this nostalgia to combat the malaise he finds characterizing present-day Britain, his argument is strangely reminiscent of comments on economic change in early modern England. Far from seeing their own moment as a point of origin for economic continuity and commercial imperialism, what typified the first generation of economic thinkers was a panicked response to the economic changes endemic to the sixteenth century.

In one of the earliest examples of an economic treatise in early modern England, Sir Thomas Smith wrote *A Discourse of the Commonweal of this Realm of England* in 1549 (published 1581), using his dialogue to put forward an economic program of reform in a period following the repeated debasement of the English pound and an ensuing, unprecedented inflation of prices.[5] Smith points to the unstable economic system created under the Tudor regime, evidenced in particular by the fluctuations in value of the realm's currency. Smith critiques policies that had manipulated the silver content of the pound in the 1540s, commenting,

> for though the King's Highness may have what coin he will current within his realm, yet the strangers cannot be compelled to take them. And I grant, if men might live within themselves altogether without borrowing of any other thing outward, we might devise what coin we would; but since we must have need of other and they of us, we must frame our things not after our own fantasies but to follow the common market of all the world, and we may not set the price of things at our pleasure but follow the price of the universal market of the world.[6]

In contrast to later mythologies of the stability of the English pound, Smith casts desires for economic insularity as "fantasies." The national economy, as defined by the value of its currency, is not arbitrarily controlled by the monarch at its center but follows, instead, from a "common market." The English pound is rendered as merely one commodity circulating in a global market, not as an iconic object of intrinsic value. The signification of value is thus based upon a system of differences, adjusted according to money's relative abundance or scarcity and gauged only in relation to other currencies. And, rather than flowing from the center, value is created by the margins, the foreign merchants (or "strangers"), whose acceptance of the coin truly confirms its status as currency. Smith accurately casts England as a debtor nation, one whose monarchs had attempted to improve their position and create a greater degree of economic self-sufficiency through manipulation of the exchange rate. Yet the English cannot "live within themselves," for the domestic economy is propelled by foreign merchants whose loans are essential to the nation's economic survival.

In his formulation of "the universal market of the world," Smith embraces the possibilities of the global market, using the prospect of the wealth accrued through circulation and exchange to offset the threat to ideas of sovereignty and hierarchy resulting from the economic power of foreign merchants. Whereas the early Tudors' debasement of the English pound undermined a residual sense of the intrinsic ability of coin or sovereign to signify value, Smith recuperates value by accepting its separation from such iconic and material forms. He thereby posits an alternative model to the dominant mercantilist conception of value as embodied exclusively in the material form of bullion and coin. Smith creates alternative paths in which disembodied and immaterial forms of value might emerge, anticipating not only the arguments of later economic thinkers such as Sir Thomas Mun but also the expressions of value found in Shakespeare's *The Merchant of Venice*. However, this conceptualization of capital is predicated upon an underlying abstraction of labor, an obfuscation of the uneven patterns of development upon which this expanding global market depends. Smith, like other early modern defenders of capital, additionally effaces the forms of surplus extraction that occurred within England during this period, the practices of internal colonialism that had developed concomitantly with a primitive accumulation of capital and, consequently, enabled the colonial aspirations of English commerce.

I begin with this passage from Smith because of its interplay between the domestic and foreign in determinations of value, anxieties shared by a dramatic text of the following generation, Shakespeare's *The Merchant of Venice* (1596). There is also a more direct historical connection between Smith's economic text and Shakespeare's play: Smith's *Discourse*, first published in 1581, at one time was actually attributed to Shakespeare.[7] This chapter examines two tropes that illustrate the mutually constitutive elements of foreign trade and domestic class relations in a period marked by emergent forms of capital: "the lead casket" and "the Royal Exchange." The first section will analyze the casket choice scenes in *The Merchant of Venice*, examining how the play counters the instabilities of mercantilism with a representation of the abstracted forms of value and disembodied mechanisms of exchange that enable the formation of capital. My discussion also traces the effects of anxieties concerning the English domestic economy—particularly those relating to the status of England's currency—on emergent discourses of colonialism. Shakespeare's *The Merchant of Venice*, Mun's *A Discovrse of Trade* (1621), and other early modern texts attempt to differentiate the forms of capital found in the "golden fleece" of domestic manufacture from the taint of Spanish imperialism, associating the disjunctures of mercantilist economics with the abuses of Spain's colonial empire. By contrast, these texts represent capitalist forms of exchange as the means to reinforce the threatened integrity of the national economy. Extending my analysis of the effects of currency policies on class relations and foreign trade, the final section of the chapter discusses the institutional practices of the Royal Exchange, the center of international commerce in London. The efforts of early modern texts to dissever the Royal Exchange from its history as the site of a cosmopolitan population of resident alien merchants marks a transition from Sir Thomas Smith's acknowledgment of the crucial role of strangers in "the universal market of the world." In tracing the movement toward the cuonstruction of a national economy buttressed by foreign trade, I will also foreground the role of England's laboring classes in the expansion of international commerce and formation of domestic capital. And, whereas early modern defenses of capital were predicated upon an abstraction of labor, I wish to examine the history of social struggle that accompanied the production of value and capital in the early modern period, addressing the interconnected histories of internal colonialism, class relations, and the early modern global economy.

***

THE LEAD CASKET

A number of recent discussions of *The Merchant of Venice*, including essays by Walter Cohen, Thomas Moison, Michael Nerlich, Lars Engle, and Michael Ferber, have emphasized the range of economic contexts that are evoked in the play. Despite their differences, these readings generally follow the precedent established by Cohen and link the play's economic language and commentary to the institutions and social relations approximating that of "capitalism."[8] Cohen asserts that the play, and the character of Antonio in particular, can be seen as "the harbinger of capitalism." Yet, in the same passage, Cohen also describes   the   ethos   represented   by   Antonio   as   "native [i.e., European] bourgeois mercantilism."[9] I wish to highlight two important problems implicit in Cohen's statements: the presentation of capitalism as a unitary object of analysis and the conflation of capitalism and mercantilism. This chapter attempts to complicate the use of the term "capitalism" in critical accounts of the play by noting the important differences between early modern forms of capital and capitalism as a mode of production. As Fernand Braudel points out, descriptions of capitalism as a coherent economic system derive from the mid-nineteenth century, and even Marx does not refer to "capitalism" in this sense at any point in his writings.[10] In the early modern period, capital represented an unsettled, semantically flexible array of ideas and objects encompassing "wealth, money, funds, goods, principal, assets, property, patrimony."[11] Despite the varying applications of the concept of capital, these definitions nonetheless deal with tangible objects and economic assets, actual sums of money or moveable wealth rather than more abstracted forms of value. In the early modern period, capital possessed multiple incarnations, yet it was defined in relation to its material forms. Marx appropriately terms the economic thought of the early modern period the "Monetary System," a set of economic assumptions that represented value only in terms of the circulation of money.[12] In other words, even when manifestations of capital became increasingly ubiquitous in the early modern period, these forms of capital were nonetheless conceptualized within the residual categories and practices of mercantilism.

I also wish to emphasize the significant distinctions between capitalism and mercantilism, the latter of which represented the dominant economic ideology of the early modern period. Mercantilism is seen more accurately not as a coherent economic system but as a set of ideas shared by many early modern economic thinkers. One of the primary assumptions underlying mercantilist economics was an equation of value with its material embodiment in bullion and coin. Later political economists, including Adam Smith and Marx, would critique mercantilism for its conflation of value and material wealth, an overdetermined attention to foreign trade that failed to recognize the social relations and conditions of production that serve to enable the creation of value. As a result of its bullionist conception of value, mercantilist economic philosophy advocated state policies that functioned to bring about a balance of trade, attempting to increase the nation's exports while also preventing an overseas drain of the nation's precious stock of bullion and coin. Of course, as Sir Thomas Smith had recognized, the balance of imports to exports necessarily alters based upon the fluctuating value of the nation's currency in other markets.

Thus, these two mercantilist principles—a materialist or bullionist conception of value and a desired balance of trade—were intrinsically competing factors in the national economy, a tension that exposes the ways in which mercantilist economic ideology failed to represent a unified system of economic thought. Nonetheless, mercantilism made an important contribution to the construction of a national economy, recommending the state's intervention in currency valuation, exports, and other economic matters, a statist approach that differs sharply from the laissez-faire policies advocated in subsequent centuries by capitalist political economists.[13]

In contrast to the inherent contradictions and tensions that are held to characterize mercantilist economics, the analysis of early modern capitalism consistently emphasizes capital's increasing and unproblematic ascendancy. Marx's discussion of "The General Formula for Capital" in volume one of *Capital* establishes a precedent for this narrative, focusing on the role of commodity circulation as the "starting-point" and "first form of appearance of capital" (247). In Marx's historical analysis, the sixteenth century serves as a point of origin for capital, a development that he links to the creation of "world trade and the world market" (247). However, contrary to the sense of inevitable emergence and consolidation in this narrative of origin, Marx emphasizes the disjunctions inherent in the process of early modern capital formation. In his discussion of commodity circulation, Marx notes how increasingly complex networks of international commerce undermined the mercantilist alignment of value with its material forms. Through circulation, the money-form (coin and bullion) disappears in exchange, as goods are exchanged for other commodities; in this process, the money-form is even replaced by immaterial forms of credit and bills of exchange, demonstrating the blurred boundaries between commodity exchange and money exchange. Contrary to a mercantilist conception of value in which money functions either as an objective measure or transparent medium of exchange, the money-form itself becomes a commodity of relative and fluctuating value. Furthermore, in emergent capitalist forms of commerce, the goals of exchange extend beyond a single direct transaction and are predicated upon a constant process of circulation that exceeds identifiable markers set by participants or objects, thereby becoming an untraceable, disembodied process, a "limitless" movement that enables the creation of surplus-value through circulation (253). The formation of capital is thus accomplished not only through a process of materialization, in terms of the commodification of the money-form, but also based upon an underlying abstraction, the disappearance of material goods and money through exchange, which may reappear in the form of profit. Because mercantilist economic ideology associated its desired goal of a balance of trade with national wealth in the form of a stock of "treasure" (reserves of bullion and coin), the results of commodity circulation potentially undermined a dominant economic expression of early modern English nationhood.

Early modern texts frequently commented on what they perceived as the pervasive infiltration of the rules of economic exchange into the realm of social relations. The increasingly impersonal, disembodied, and abstracted character of early modern exchange challenged the ability of texts to define social relations in the language of the market.[14] The "intellectual confusion" so often ascribed to early modern mercantilist thought might have resulted from the contradictions inherent in efforts to render disparate and even contradictory economic phenomena as a coherent, systematic whole.[15] The dominant economic language of *The Merchant of Venice* inherits these disjunctions, evincing the congruencies as well as divergences of mercantilist and proto-capitalist economic ideologies and conceptions of value in the early modern period. Part of the play's strategies to recuperate value entail a blurring of the distinctions and tensions between material currency and the forms of representative currency, such as credit or bills of exchange, which increasingly facilitated international trade and domestic borrowing. The "credit" that Antonio advises Bassanio to seek in his name—"Try what my credit can in Venice do" (1.1.180)—contrasts with the materiality of the types of surety Antonio mentions earlier: "fortunes," "money," "commodities" (1.1.177–78).[16] Antonio's "credit" possesses an economic and semantic flexibility that allows it to take both material and abstract form. The power of Antonio's "credit" is indicative of early modern economic practice, as Craig Muldrew has shown, wherein most market relations were informal and "done on trust, or credit, without specific legally binding instruments."[17] In the language of early modern economics, "credit" functioned as both a measure of value and commodity. Antonio's "credit," for example, serves as the means and medium of exchange, representing his ability to transmute abstractions into the material substance of a lent sum of money. Yet credit also acts as a commodity in Antonio's metaphor of making credit "be rack'd, even to the uttermost" (1.1.181). Here he gives the abstraction the properties of metallic currency in terms of its ability to be figuratively "racked," or stretched. The lending of hard currency's material form to immaterial types of exchange and credit therefore serves to regularize disembodied mechanisms of exchange by making them follow the rules of "real" currency. Yet, by embodying the value of his credit, Antonio also makes it susceptible to debasement and devaluation, a position comparable to the unstable status of early modern currency.

The Prince of Morocco, the first of Portia's suitors, attempts to condense value into material form; yet he does so in order to have this material embodiment of value—gold, precious gems—reflect an objective standard of value that lies outside exchange, use, and potential manipulation. In this sense, he reflects the contradictions of early modern mercantilist thought, which similarly attempted to embody value in coin or bullion so as to retain these objects as measures of value. Passing quickly over the lead casket, which he associates with motives of profit ("Men that hazard all / Do it in hope of fair advantages" [2.7.18–19]), Morocco tries to choose between gold and silver, metals that serve as intrinsic indices of value and, by extension, reinforce social markers of distinction. Morocco uses language applicable to the adjustment of specie in his effort to "weigh" and "rate" his value by his own "estimation" (2.7.25–26). Yet he realizes that without an outside measure he cannot adjudicate his own value, despite the intrinsic worth bestowed by his status as a "noble prince" (2.7.2). Morocco therefore designates Portia as the measure of value, claiming in his rejection of the silver casket that her value exceeds that of "tried gold" (2.7.53), the distilled essence of the metal after it has been rubbed on a touchstone or melted in a fire.[18] In early modern economic practice, the melting of precious metals also served as the means to take coins out of circulation and hoard this wealth for oneself, actions allowing one to "gain what many men desire" (2.7.37) in a literal and material sense.[19] Even as he attempts to distill a purified material form of value, Morocco's comments evoke the inevitably manipulable and commodified status of value in the early modern period.

Morocco contrasts Portia's "mettle" with numismatic forms of value, determining Portia's worth in opposition to that of engraved coins bearing the image of Elizabeth: "They have in England / A coin that bears the figure of an angel / Stamp'd in gold, but that's insculp'd upon" (2.7.55–57). His comparison is an appropriate one with which to emphasize Portia's value since the angel was one of the few coins whose rate of valuation remained stable, and even increased slightly, during the Tudor period.[20] Elizabeth was frequently praised for forestalling the debasement of English currency and restoring it to its "natural" value with her 1560 recoinage.[21] William Camden blamed devaluation on Henry VIII's desire for quick profit, and he praised Elizabeth for her ability to call in and remint base metals, thereby restoring the purity of the currency.[22] Yet, although Elizabeth's recoinage may have stabilized the English pound, the £40,000 profit that it produced for the crown surpassed the profit of £30,000 gained through Henry VIII's 1544 debasement of the pound, which Sir Thomas Smith believed had profoundly destabilized the nation's currency, a fact that reveals the economic motives underlying efforts to restore the integrity of England's currency.[23] Thus, there are contextual reasons for Morocco to distinguish Portia's intrinsic value from the unstable and commodified form of the English coin.

Whereas Morocco emphasizes the quality of the metal, Arragon determines value on the basis of the casket's inscription, the "stamp of merit" (2.9.39), or social forms, in which value is figured. But Arragon's choice of the silver casket illustrates how numismatic and social forms fail to indicate "weight," or intrinsic value. Arragon castigates the "undeserved dignity" (2.9.40) of newly acquired social privilege most of all because of its creation through processes of exchange, the fact that "estates, degrees, and offices" are "deriv'd corruptly" (2.9.41–42). He therefore proposes to adjust social hierarchies through "use," to have honor "new varnish'd" (2.9.49). But to test one's "mettle" in this way, like that of the "metal" of specie, serves to efface the "stamp of merit," the insignia of the monarch that establishes the legitimacy of value, the coin or aristocrat's ability to signify worth. In fact, the debased testons of Henry VIII, which were copper coins thinly covered with a silver surface in order to pass as currency, became known as "copper noses" because their silver portraits of King Henry wore away through use, revealing an interior base metal.[24] Thus, while signifiers of rank may be susceptible to the corruption of economic factors, efforts to penetrate to some underlying essence ("th' interior" beneath the "show" that attracts the "fool multitude" [2.9.28, 26]) only efface the stamp of authority that authorizes merit and value, without whose insignia even the noble venturer fails to distinguish which caskets are merely "[s]ilver'd o'er" (2.9.68). Although Arragon attempts to polish the coin of honor in order to expose the difference between its true and counterfeit incarnations, his recommendations mimic the practices of early modern "coiners," who would illegally melt, heat, clip, or treat coins with chemical solvents in order to extract precious metals from the currency.[25] Thus, while Morocco and Arragon attempt to embody value and choose their caskets according to codes of nobility and status, their positions are rendered as analogous to those of the hoarder and counterfeiter, figures who served debilitating and illegal roles in a mercantilist system of value.

Unlike Morocco's definition of value as an objective measure removed from the realm of exchange, or Arragon's embodiment of value in social hierarchies, Bassanio's choice of the lead casket endorses "a dynamic of exchange" and conforms to the dependence of Elizabethan mercantile practice on "a velocity of circulation" achieved through the increased circulation of money and commodities.[26] Yet, despite the proto-capitalist implications of the lead casket, its acquisition is nonetheless linked to the landed property of Belmont, not the commodity circulation of the Venetian Rialto. Bassanio appropriately refers to his recently confirmed union with Portia as his "new int'rest" (3.2.221). In contrast to the ability of Portia's estate to generate riches, Bassanio's status is compared to the devaluation of specie, as he is "abridg'd," or reduced, "From such a noble *rate*" (1.1.126–27, emphasis added).[27] Although Bassanio can claim intrinsic value because of his status as a gentleman—"all the wealth I had / Ran in my veins" (3.2.254–55)—his status is dependent upon a supply of capital to keep that bloodstream circulating; the written words reporting the bond's forfeiture are appropriately said to issue forth Antonio's "life-blood" (3.2.266). In this self-characterization, Bassanio distances himself from a class-specific attitude toward value best represented by Morocco, which attempted to embody value in its material forms, a stance similar to mercantilist thought's own limited conception of value in terms of its accumulation in coin and bullion. Bassanio instead adjudicates his value in relation to a circulating body of capital that is represented—not embodied—by the letter indicating Antonio's losses. This disembodied paper, similar in form to credit or a bill of exchange, is nonetheless likened to Antonio's body and depicted as bleeding capital in the form of lost "ventures" and shipwrecks (3.2.266–71). In the early modern proto-capitalist credit system, Marx argued, material forms of money are not so much transcended as re-embodied in human form, a process that "humanizes" capital while also forcing social relations to follow the rules of the market.[28]

In this process of capital formation that transforms and commodifies social relations, the language of economic exchange becomes an increasingly crucial means to regularize disruptive social change. As Fernand Braudel comments, "any active economy will break away from its monetary language" and necessitate more innovate representational models to conceptualize emergent economic phenomena.[29] In *The Merchant of Venice*, we witness the incomplete status of this project in the early modern period, which is reflected in the complex economic role assumed by each character, including Bassanio. Similar to both Shylock and Antonio, Bassanio's economic survival is dependent upon both credit and "thrift" (profit) (1.1.175–76). Bassanio's status as a gentleman defines him in terms removed from production, a position resembling that of the usurer. As a "venturer," he is also situated as a middleman in the circuits of exchange. More than the consummate "prodigal" consumer in the play, Bassanio also operates as an investor. Like the members of the gentry engaging in commercial ventures in Elizabethan England, he utilizes the capital provided to him by Antonio to turn a profit, to win Portia.[30] Bassanio is able to displace the stereotypical image of his prodigality assigned to him by Shylock (2.5.15) by becoming less like a young member of the gentry and more like a member of the merchant class. His final lines in the opening scene—"I have a mind presages me such thrift / That I should questionless be fortunate" (1.1.175–76)—reflects this new role as a merchant adventurer to Belmont. Marx, in his discussion of "Pre-Capitalist Relations," describes how the early modern adaptation of usury to a capitalist mode of production resulted from the credit system's ability to transform borrowing from its role in an economy of "extravagant consumption" to capitalist conditions wherein the borrower was given a loan based upon his new role as a "potential capitalist."[31]

As demonstrated by the transformation of Bassanio into a "venturer," *The Merchant of Venice* is situated within a contemporary debate that attempted to justify England's entrance into a colonial economy by uniting the heroic dimension of colonial expansion, a chivalric discourse appealing to England's gentry, with the interests of commerce and capital. Antonio's "wealthy *Andrew*" (1.1.27) shares its name with the Spanish galleon captured by Sir Francis Drake in 1596, the same year as the play's initial performance. The comparison of Portia to the golden fleece (1.1.169–72, 3.2.241) also refers to an image frequently used to represent the precious metals of the Americas.[32] In Marlowe's *Doctor Faustus*, Valdes praises Faustus's power to bring "from America the golden fleece / That yearly stuffs old Philip's treasury" (1.1.130–31). Similarly, Henry Roberts, in a poem dedicated to Drake and Sir John Hawkins, commends the privateers, who, "Searching with paine, the Confines of the earth, /…/…fetch more woorth, than Iasons fleece."[33] But most English voyages searching for American gold, such as Martin Frobisher's, proved futile.[34] Particularly in its representation of Morocco and Aragon, *The Merchant of Venice* distances its economy from an older chivalric model of "adventure," one still evoked in the literature of English privateering of the 1590s, foregrounding, instead, an emergent ethos of capitalist "venturing."[35]

Due to English adventurers' constant failure to find precious metals in the Americas, English commercial ideology attempted to differentiate English colonialism from Spanish imperialism by locating the sources of England's own wealth in more traditional, stable, and perhaps mundane networks of commerce. Many early modern texts, for example, applied the metaphor of the "golden fleece" to domestic woolen and cloth industries in conscious opposition to the quick profit of New World gold.[36] The character of Merlin in Jonson's *The Speeches at Prince Henry's Barriers* (1610) points to the employment of the poor in the cloth trade to justify calling it England's "golden fleece," due to which they "need no foreign mine, / If industry at home do not decline" (189–90).[37] As Marx has argued, the historical development of merchant's capital through trade and exchange occurred in opposition to capitalist manufacture and industry.[38] Domestic industry and foreign trade were thus seen as competing forces within the national economy. *The Merchant of Venice* reconciles tensions between these economies by reinscribing the mercantile pursuit of the money-form, the "golden fleece" of specie, as a courtship of a source of wealth—Portia—that is severed from the taint of merchant's capital and associated, instead, with landed property, the most traditional form of domestic production.

Nonetheless, it is extremely misleading to connect Portia too literally to any set of social relations. Although her role as the mistress of Belmont would seem to associate her position with the landed property of the rural gentry, she does not represent domestic production so much as forms of wealth that transcend economic circulation and exchange. Despite her suitors' commodification of her as the embodiment of value (Morocco), status (Arragon), and capital (Bassanio), or even the self-commodification expressed in her statements to Bassanio following his casket choice (3.2.152–67), Portia's economic resources remain noticeably absent from representation, devoid of evident origin, production, and circulation. Whereas the capital running through the circuit of Shylock-Antonio-Bassanio is overly conspicuous, Portia's resources remain outside the play's frame of analysis because they are not tied to the same forces of scarcity and devaluation as those of the characters situated in the economic realm of Venice. In this representation of Portia and the Belmont estate, Carol Leventen notes, "patriarchal power is deftly, unobtrusively posited as existing independent of time and space, independent of history," unlike the inextricably historicized economic realm of Venice.[39]

In contrast to the doubtful resources of both Shylock and Antonio, Portia instinctively dismisses the news of Antonio's forfeiture with the proposal to pay off Shylock, even to six times the debt owed (3.2.298–302). At the play's conclusion, Portia also serves as the messenger of the news of the return of Antonio's argosies (5.1.275–77). This ultimate recuperation of Antonio's fortunes is not subject to the same economic, legal, or even natural rules that circumscribe characters' actions throughout the play. Significantly, the final *deus ex machina* is associated with a reflux of capital, a closure to circulation and exchange as merchant's capital finally returns home. In this sense, Portia serves to domesticate the threat of capital formation to the national economy, translating economic innovation into the residual categories and hierarchies of landed property and the patriarchal household. The play's closure also serves to transform its Venetian setting, where women possessed significant legal and economic rights in the early modern period, to an English context in which women's rights to property and legal representation were more narrowly defined.[40] The "domestication" of the play's setting serves to "domesticate" Portia, ultimately annulling the possibility of her own economic and sexual agency and effectively translating her role from virago to angel of the house. The increasingly abstracted and ubiquitous qualities of economic phenomena thus produced a compensatory emphasis on the domestic economy in its most literal and immediate sense, as "household management."[41] This focus on the stability of the household offered a means to manage the potentially disruptive possibilities of social and economic change.[42]

The romantic comedy of the play's fifth act expands the analogy of economic and sexual forms of circulation and exchange.[43] By enabling the play's closure through the resolution of the ring plot, Portia attempts to extricate marriage and the familial household at Belmont from Venetian homosocial networks of exchange. This concern over the infiltration of economic norms into sexual behavior and marital rules is also suggested in Bassanio's casket choice scene. As Bassanio observes while deliberating over the golden casket, gold "works a miracle in nature, / Making them lightest that wear most of it" (3.2.90–91). In his allusion to female sexual license (or "lightness"), Bassanio's comment further evokes representations of ethical lightness, a concern that in the late Elizabethan period was often associated with the contaminating circulation of Spanish gold.[44] Walter Raleigh, in his *Discoverie of Guiana*, complains that Spanish gold "creepeth into Counsels, and setteth bound loyalty at liberty," an anxiety concerning the number of English receiving stipends from Spain.[45] The dangers of foreign trade were thus perceived as reducing all values—even marital or national fidelity—to equivalences subject only to the rules of the marketplace.

Early modern English texts frequently associated the problem of what Marx terms "world money" with its supposed Spanish source.[46] In the process, Anglo-Spanish economic and national rivalries were figured in the languages of gender and sexuality, with the economic promiscuity of imperial Spain constructed as antithetical to the stability of the English domestic economy.[47] Donne sarcastically comments in "Elegy 11: The Bracelet" on his wish that his lost bracelet, a love token from his mistress, were, instead, "Spanish stamps, still travelling, / That are become as Catholic as their king."[48] Similar to Arragon's anxiety over the effacement of the "stamp of merit," the seal of the monarch conferring value on either coin or peer, the Spanish coins circulate regardless of national boundaries or affiliation. Donne depicts the universal acceptance of this "Catholic" currency as a contaminating force that ruins the countries in which it circulates: France, Scotland, and the Netherlands (ll. 39–42). The anxiety over the dominance of Spanish currency obscures how this economic hegemony provided a means to stabilize the chaos of early modern exchange: among the countries mentioned by Donne, 400 different currencies circulated in the Netherlands and 82 in France in the early seventeenth century.[49] Donne distracts attention away from England's subordinate position in the global market, as a marginal outpost whose own treasure of specie was drained overseas, and depicts Spain, the nation supposedly dominating the mercantile system, instead destroying itself and its neighbors through the economic monopoly and promiscuous circulation of its "world coin."[50]

Although an influx of specie was seen as essential to English commercial development, the economic effects of Spain's saturation with imported bullion were already evident in the late Elizabethan period; the influx of New World gold had caused massive inflation and a consumer economy in which consumption could not keep up with inflated prices and devalued specie.[51] In Bassanio's formulation, the prospect of gold is therefore rendered as a form of danger, "the guiled shore / To a most dangerous sea" (3.2.97–98). Many early modern texts interpreted Spain's economic and political decline as poetic justice, the necessary result of unfettered imperialist expansion.[52] Bassanio's reference to the prospect of quick profit as "The seeming truth which cunning times put on / To entrap the wisest" (3.2.100–01) is in keeping with arguments that attempted to distinguish England from its Spanish rival based upon differing economic as well as colonial practices. The representation of gold as "Hard food for Midas" (3.2.102) resembles one of Theodor de Bry's most striking images from *America* (1594), his virulently anti-Catholic travel anthology, that of Amerindians enacting a symbolic revenge on avaricious Spaniards by pouring molten gold down their throats (see figure 1.1).[53] John Lyly extends the association of Spanish imperialism with an "unquenchable thirst of gold" in *Midas* (1589), wherein the title character serves as an allegorical representation of King Phillip II. [54] Donne also applies the image of Midas to colonialism in "Elegy 20: Love's War," although in his formulation, the failure of English colonization in the Americas is depicted as a

Figure 1.1   "Hard food for Midas," from Theodor de Bry, *Americae pars quarta* (1594). Reproduced by permission of the Folger Shakespeare Library.

"Midas touch" that provides wealth but not the means for the colonies' survival: "And Midas' joys our Spanish journeys give, / We touch all gold, but find no food to live" (ll. 17–18).

Bassanio's likening of the pursuit of gold to Midas posits an alternative model for value production, one that counters the materialist conception of value characterizing early modern mercantilism and its most dominant participant, the colonial empire of Spain. In his analysis of early modern economics in the *Grundrisse*, Marx returns to the figure of Midas in order to contrast mercantilism's consistent efforts to embody wealth in the money-form to the immaterial and abstracted forms of value that enabled the formation of capital in the early modern period:

> Where wealth as such seems to appear in an entirely material, tangible form, its existence is only in my head, it is a pure fantasy. Midas. On the other side, as *material representative of general wealth*, it is realized only by being thrown back into circulation, to disappear in exchange for the singular, particular modes of wealth. It remains in circulation, as medium of circulation; but for the accumulating individual, it is lost, and this disappearance is the only possible way to secure it as wealth.[55]

For Marx, mercantilist economic thought constituted a "fantasy," a desire to reduce value only to its material embodiment in bullion and coin. Marx repeats the language of Sir Thomas Smith's critique of Tudor economic policy, which in the latter's view attempted to adjudicate value "after our own fantasies" of economic self-sufficiency and recuperated integrity. By contrast, the creation of wealth is realized only through entrance into what Smith termed "the universal market of the world," the realm of exchange and circulation that defies concerns of borders and sovereignty. Mercantilist thought mistook the function of money, rendering equivalent abstract forms of value with their material embodiment by equating reserves of coin and bullion (as "treasure") with national wealth. Mercantilism, for Marx, merely "grasped the semblance of things," perceiving wealth exclusively in terms of precious metal—what Bassanio would refer to as a focus on "ornament" (3.2.74), the outward signs of value—rather than analyzing the processes that enable value to be produced.[56] In the mercantilist system, specie functioned not only as measure of value but also as index of national power.[57] Yet the desire to increase national prestige by hoarding bullion, although an initial stage of capital accumulation, ultimately impoverished early modern Spain, the nation that had attempted to monopolize the extraction of bullion and circulation of specie.[58] Thus, for Marx, capital can accumulate only through a willingness to give it up, put it back into circulation, and allow its use by and for others.[59] In this context, the inscription of the lead casket—"Who chooseth me must give and hazard all he hath" (2.7.16)—reflects this emphasis on the creation of value through submission to a constant process of circulation that entails the possibility of loss.

In contrast to the Midas-like acquisitiveness of Spanish imperialism and the mercantilist embodiment of value repeated by Morocco and Arragon in the play, Bassanio's casket choice scene presents an advocacy of a velocity of circulation and "ideology of risk" quite similar to the arguments of Sir Thomas Mun, perhaps the first English economic thinker to conceptualize capital formation.[60] Mun, author of *A Discovrse of Trade* (1621) and *England's Treasure by Forraign Trade* (1623; published 1664), wrote his treatises in order to defend the English East India Company from critics who blamed it for draining currency overseas.[61] Although Mun's goal of restoring a favorable balance of trade for England on the international market connects him to early modern mercantilism, Mun theorizes capital by linking the restoration of a trade balance with an effort to extract surplus. Although this surplus takes the form of "treasure," an increase in the store of specie for the nation, Mun moves beyond the mercantilist embodiment of value in material form. For Mun, it is only the disembodied, limitless process of exchange that enables the production of capital.

The East India trade constituted one of the most profitable of early modern international markets, offering consistent profits of 100 percent (and a return of up to 300 percent with many of its early voyages) following the Company's incorporation in 1600.[62] Yet, like the ideology of risk inherent in Bassanio's choice of the lead casket, participation in the East Indies trade necessitated a key hazard for mercantilist thought, the potential drain of the nation's reserves of gold and silver. Asian traders were uninterested in European commodities such as heavy woolens, forcing English merchants to export huge stocks of specie to support commerce in the East Indies. Because strict regulations persisted in the early modern period prohibiting the export of coin,[63] and because England lacked direct access to mines in either America or Africa, the company was forced to locate another source for this necessary commodity and, as a result, imported silver from Spain. Ironically, English foreign trade in the Jacobean period was fueled by the same nation that only several years earlier had threatened to infiltrate the English economy and undermine national sovereignty. Through the means of this initial venture and expenditure, Mun envisages a replenishment of national treasure. By borrowing from the enemy, England would become economically independent.

In *A Discovrse of Trade*, Mun displaces the ideological ramifications of this necessary first stage in the circuit of exchange, and the ways that it placed the national economy in a subordinate role to its Spanish patron, with an emphasis on the ultimate profit of "treasure" for the kingdom. Although the company had to pay for Spanish silver in order even to engage in trade in Asia, Mun assures the Company's critics that "the brethren of the Company, shall yearely bring in as much siluer, as they send forth, which hath beene alwayes truly performed, with an ouerplus, to the increase of this Kingdomes treasure."[64] Mun, the consummate mercantilist, emphasizes a favorable balance of trade throughout his work. Yet his elaborate economic calculations ultimately attempt not to restore a preexisting balance but, rather, produce a surplus: "when the value of our commodyties exported doth ouer-ballance the worth of all those forraigne wares which are imported and consumed in this kingdome, then the remaynder of our stock which is sent forth, must of necessitie returne to vs in Treasure" (sig. d2). The language of balance and restoration is transformed into a calculation of "ouerplus" and "ouer-ballance."

Mun expresses his residual mercantilism by clinging to the representation of surplus in the form of "treasure," the material embodiment of value in coin and bullion. However, he also transforms treasure into capital by emphasizing its production through an ongoing process of circulation. Thus, the treasure returning to England is not hoarded in the Royal Mint but instead reenters circulation, providing the basis for further investment. The taint of importing Spanish gold is avoided through its use to accelerate the circulation of money and commodities. This form of exchange fits well with the English Protestant rejection of riches: the contaminating (i.e., imperialist, Spanish Catholic) money is expelled from the realm and instrumentally used in exchange; similarly, the imported Indian commodities (outside of "necessities") are reexported, so that the resulting profits may be seen to derive from industry and thrift.[65]

Mun displaces the association with Catholic Spain and specie depletion through an emphasis on the material embodiment of value in treasure, a necessary strategy given the fact that *A Discovrse of Trade* was written to defend the East India Company at a time when Parliamentary critics wanted to shut it down. Investors, too, had difficulty conceptualizing the Company's use of credit and inter-weaving trading routes. They also had little patience for delays in the return of their investment, which forced the Company to borrow further in order to pay them.[66] To appease Company critics, Mun consistently emphasizes the return of treasure into the kingdom. He thereby counters anxieties over the drain of specie that are metonymically linked in mercantilist language with a loss of national prestige and power. The reentry of the initial investment (along with incremental profits) transforms Mun's process of circulation to one that produces capital. In "The General Formula for Capital," Marx argues that the commodification of money depends upon "a reflux of money to its starting- point," a return home that "domesticates" circulation and capital formation by translating these emergent processes into residual economic categories.[67] This strategy obfuscates the precondition of the return of treasure, perhaps to assuage the doubts of investors and critics, namely, that the production of surplus depends upon "a renewal or repetition of the whole course of the movement" of circulation and exchange.[68]

Thus, these proto-capitalist modes of exchange and value production ultimately resisted and exceeded their incorporation into a nationalist rhetoric and economic program. Early modern texts, including *The Merchant of Venice*, consequently formulated and adapted tropes—"venturing," "the golden fleece," "hard food for Midas"—that attempted to create a national frame of reference for supranational economic phenomena. As a result, the commercial expansion of the English nation through international commerce was justified not in terms of the accumulation of value in the embodied form of treasure but, instead, in relation to the production of capital through an ongoing process of circulation. Yet, although this process offset the instabilities of devaluation and depletion associated with mercantilism, emergent forms of capital also created new dangers relating to the disappearance of material wealth and the abstraction of value. Mun's text, like *The Merchant of Venice*, minimizes the risks and hazards inherent in a process of capital formation by translating emergent forms of exchange into the residual mercantilist language of embodied material value. These efforts necessarily elide the preconditions of capital, effacing the processes of abstraction and limitless circulation upon which capitalist value production depends; instead, they conceptualize a manageable realm of exchange in which capital always returns home and thereby reinforces the stability of the domestic sphere.

✳✳✳

THE ROYAL EXCHANGE

Mun's networks of exchange exemplify the ways that English merchants increasingly prospered as commercial mediators and middle-
men, thereby assuming the economic role conventionally assigned to
scapegoated resident alien merchants. Jean-Christophe Agnew has
argued that market relations emerged, even as early as the classical
period, on the "threshold" of exchange: the marketplace was thus a
liminal space inhabited by "go-betweens."[69] The figures populating
the interstitial space of the market were associated not only with
mediation, in the form of exchange, for example, but also with an
ability to cross cultural and geographic borders. In the formation of
capital in the early modern period, money and commodities were likewise characterized by boundary transgression. As Marx comments,
"Gold and silver, like exchange itself originally, appear...not within
the sphere of a social community, but where it ends, on its boundary;
on the few points of its contact with alien communities."[70]

In early modern England, one of the key points of this contact was
at the site of international commerce in London, the Royal Exchange.
The Royal Exchange, first proposed by Sir Richard Gresham in 1537,
and completed by Sir Thomas Gresham in 1567, was opened by
Elizabeth in 1571.[71] This center for foreign trade in London was dominated by foreign financiers, especially from Italy, as well as domestic
organizations such as the Wool Staplers' and Merchant Adventurers'
companies. The Royal Exchange was associated with emergent practices
of exchange (credit, bills of exchange) as well as with foreign and resident alien merchant communities. In addition, the physical location of
the Royal Exchange evoked a history of cross-cultural economic relations, for it was situated on Lombard Street, the former center of
London's Jewish community before its expulsion by Richard I in 1290.
Representations of the economic practices at the Exchange, then, car-
ried the memory of London's expelled Jews. In his survey of the areas
around the Exchange, for example, John Stow repeatedly finds objects
that testify to the former presence of London's Jewish community.[72]

Although London's Exchanges arose from the site and practices of
the city's cosmopolitan population of international traders, they were
often represented as providing a centralized control over the money
market. In this section, I wish to delineate the process by which representations of the Royal Exchange and the New Exchange extricated
England's expanding networks of international commerce from an
economic context in which foreign merchants–as well as the domestic poor–played a crucial role in the production of value and capital.

For example, foreign merchants are absent from the Second Part of Thomas Heywood's *If You Know Not Me You Know Nobody* (ca. 1604–05), a play that represents Gresham's building of the Royal Exchange as inaugurating a centralized and ordered foundation for the national economy, a process correlated with the patronage of Elizabeth I.[73] By contrast, John Payne's *The Royall Exchange* (1597), which surveys the space of the Exchange and offers homiletic advice to the groups populating the bourse, not only acknowledges the presence of foreign merchants, whom he exhorts to remain loyal to their host nation, but also notes the destitute poor who congregate at the Exchange, advising, "they are not alone to be corrected and forced to labor / but to be pittied releved and helped / especially the syck lame and aged amonge that sort."[74]

In recent criticism, the Royal Exchange has frequently been discussed in reference to the emergence of proto-capitalist economic practices in early modern England. However, these critical accounts, like early modern representations of the Royal Exchange, tend to focus exclusively on the expanding and innovative effects of commodity circulation, overlooking the factors of labor and production that enabled the formation of capital. In this section, I wish to emphasize the role of social struggle in the early modern marketplace: in the first half of my discussion, I will consider how efforts to establish London's Exchanges as the sites of legitimate commerce attempted to blame foreign merchants and the poor for the Exchanges' history of discreditable economic practices, such as currency debasement and the extraction of profit through reminting coins. Nonetheless, currency manipulation remained prevalent throughout the early modern period, as a component of internal colonialism as well as a means by which England's laboring classes could maintain a degree of economic self-sufficiency through alternative currencies and economic practices. Because representations of London's Exchanges often defined these sites in reference to their counterparts on the Continent, particularly the Venetian Rialto, the second half of this section resumes discussion of *The Merchant of Venice* in order to examine the ways that Venice provided early modern England with a model for maintaining authority over both foreign merchants and the laboring classes.

According to William Camden's account of London's Exchanges, these trading centers emerged as early as the reign of Richard I and originated in efforts to extricate England's currency from the illicit economic practices of resident alien merchants. Camden describes how King Richard was forced to remint "Easterling money," coins noted for their purity, because they had been

> in a short time so corrupted and clipped by Jewes, Italian usurers called then *Corsini*, (who were the first Christians that brought in usury among us) and Flemings, that the King by proclamation was enforced to call in the old money, make a new stampe and to erect Exchanges where the weight of old money was exchanged for new.[75]

Camden significantly overlooks religious differences and links London's Jewish population with other groups (Lombards, Flemings) because of their shared economic practices of usury, counterfeiting, and the clipping of coins. Although Camden initially confines these fraudulent activities to England's resident alien communities, he later acknowledges how these marginal groups replicated the practices of the state. Remarking on the profit netted by the crown from reminting the nation's coins, Camden concedes that King Richard allowed only 13 pence for every pound brought in, "to the great damage of the people" (171). Rather than reestablishing the purity of the currency, the crown legitimated the commodification of the realm's coin. This complicity is reinforced by the description of the initially stable currency as "Easterling money," named after the Hanseatic League of German traders resident in London. Camden's account ultimately reveals how foreign merchants had established the integrity of the nation's currency, whereas the crown extracted a quick profit through manipulation of the proportion of silver content. The scapegoating of resident alien merchants therefore functioned to displace the uneasy similitude of margin and center, differentiating the strangers' criminal commodification of money from the crown's ostensible power to redeem money as a measure of value by restoring the English pound to its standard value.

Even though the discreditable practices of the Royal Exchange's past were transposed onto London's foreign traders, the office of the Royal Exchanger institutionally codified the use of currency as a manipulable commodity. The Royal Exchanger was responsible for manipulating the exchange rate of the English pound, often implementing practices used earlier by Sir Thomas Gresham and valuing the English pound at an inflated rate on foreign exchanges in order to bring in specie to England and thereby increase the importation of cheaper foreign goods. The arguments of Sir Thomas Mun, which placed emphasis on the nation's trade balance, were used against these institutionalized monetary manipulations, helping to put an end to the office of the Royal Exchanger in 1628.[76] In the process, the Royal Exchange was able to represent itself as the epitome of England's commercial "credibility," constituting itself as the center of legitimate commerce in contrast to the suspect practices of foreign traders, and also extend this sense of respectability to the practices of credit that became associated with the Exchange.

This transformation was marked by Sir Robert Cecil's construction of the New Exchange (or "Britains Burse") in the Strand, whose opening in April 1609 was accompanied with the performance of a recently discovered entertainment by Ben Jonson, *The Entertainment at Britain's Burse*.[77] Whereas Gresham's Royal Exchange coordinated functions of commerce and consumption, as reflected in its architectural features of a central, partly roofed courtyard for traders along with outer rings of shops, Cecil's New Exchange was intended exclusively for luxury shopping, particularly for exotic commodities drawn from distant markets such as China and India. The New Exchange was frequently alluded to in early modern plays, which associated the space with aspects of modernity made possible by the experience of urban shopping. As Karen Newman has noted, these representations often feminized both commodities and consumption, linking the New Exchange with the figure of an elite female consumer.[78] Through their emphasis on the pleasures of a consumer society, images of the New Exchange served to naturalize the role of foreign trade and commodities in the national economy. In contrast to the frequent denouncements concerning how the importation of foreign "trifles" disrupted the balance of trade, the New Exchange embodied a prospect of luxury consumption unlimited by constraints of trade balance, geographic distance, or even personal credit.

While the end of the office of the Royal Exchanger and the construction of the New Exchange signaled an alliance between elite consumerism and growing forms of capital, the economic resources available to the majority of England's population were much more sharply circumscribed. As Muldrew's groundbreaking research has shown, mechanisms of credit derived from necessity for these people, providing a way to acquire needed money in an economy marked by a frequent scarcity of coin.[79] Yet reliance on "credit" was not the only economic recourse available in early modern England: the clipping, melting, and counterfeiting of coins, which Camden had associated with England's foreign traders and the Royal Exchange's past, were ubiquitous tactics used throughout the period by groups who were otherwise excluded from networks of capital. Such practices demonstrate how—in a mercantilist economy that embodied value in the material form of money—the production of value was inextricably a site of social struggle between class groups. Whereas access to capital remained beyond the reach of the majority of the population, many subjects could nonetheless make use of unsanctioned and often illegal tactics in order to intervene in the process of circulation and construction of value.

Despite the concerted efforts of authorities to limit or eliminate these practices, most people seem to have regarded the counterfeiting and clipping of coins as harmless. The persistence of this illicit economy is remarkable, given the severe penalties for "coining": Elizabeth declared the clipping of coins as treasonous in 1563; in 1576, she extended this categorization to include any action that tampered with the circulation of coin.[80] In the late seventeenth century, as much as 10 percent of the realm's currency was removed from circulation, the silver content of coins either melted down or clipped. Yet the predominance of clipped coins did not affect trade as long as people still accepted them, evidence of a general confidence among the population in unsanctioned forms of commerce, whether informal credit arrangements or the circulation of clipped or counterfeit coins.[81] Clipped or debased coins could also be used to extract fraudulent profits from transactions; often, in fact, laborers were paid wages with coins of lesser value, allowing employers to further reduce labor costs.[82]

Because England's official currency was inherently unstable, consisting of coins of varying value from several different reigns, many of which could be further reduced in value through clipping, tradespeople and laborers often used an alternative economy of unsanctioned "base monies," copper coins or token forms of currency that enabled transactions in lieu of currency issued by the crown.[83] Similar to the context described in Camden's discussion of the Royal Exchange's past, these alternative economies blurred the boundaries between sanctioned and illegal commerce, between the counterfeiter and his counterpart at the Royal Mint.[84] Recognizing the dominant alternative economy of "farthing tokens," objects of base materials such as copper or tin used as a substitute currency among England's shopkeepers and laborers, James I even attempted to issue his own sanctioned farthing tokens in 1613. James's coinage featured the typical dimension of graft, with 50 percent of the profits accrued from minting to be reserved for the king, along with a sizable patent given to courtiers.[85] Contrary to the king's intentions, however, people refused to accept James's legitimate "fake" currency and continued to use their own base monies. Indeed, subsequent proclamations noted with alarm the fact that many people had discovered that the Jacobean base monies were easy to counterfeit, thus producing, in a sense, fake versions of official knock-offs of alternative monies! Such blurred distinctions prompted John Evelyn to remark later in the century that the counterfeiter of coins rendered the monarch "as great a Cheat and Imposter as himself."[86] Evelyn's comment acknowledges how the English state profited from its ability to manipulate currency long after Henry VIII's recurrent and disastrous debasements of the pound.

As noted earlier, Elizabeth's recoining of England's currency in 1560 is often heralded as an event that put an end to Tudor manipulations of the weight and value of the English pound. And, of course, this effort to restore the purity of the nation's currency was also successful in extracting an enormous profit for the crown. Yet, although discussions of this epochal event in the history of the English pound recognize the national impact of official efforts of currency regulation, these analyses generally overlook the ways that these economic policies were shaped and motivated by concerns relating to the position of England's laboring classes. In the proclamation announcing the recoinage, Elizabeth had justified the action based upon a desire to alleviate the condition of wage-laborers and hired servants, who were accurately perceived as having suffered the most from the circulation of debased coins. However, her recoinage actually further limited the supply of coin, reduced the buying power of wages, and attempted to put an end to the alternative economy of farthing tokens, thus exacerbating the eroded position of the laboring classes.[87]

These policies concerning currency regulation also served an instrumental role in relation to practices of internal colonialism affecting peripheral regions of the British Isles as well as England's poor. In 1601, Elizabeth debased the Irish pound, relegating Ireland to a subordinate economic position at the same time that her forces under Essex and Mountjoy succeeded in quelling alternative power sources among the Ulster chiefs.[88] However, Elizabeth's Irish recoinage failed completely, for the population generally refused to bring in older coins for reminting. Ironically, English soldiers and officials in Ireland suffered most directly from the debasement, while the profits expected for the state never materialized due to administrative expenses.[89] Despite its short-term failure, Elizabeth's Irish recoinage is noteworthy because of the precedent it established for an economic foundation to the English colonial system. The English state's assertion of dominance over its colonies through manipulation of currency would later be extended through its control of colonial trade, manufacture, and exports.

In their readings of *The Merchant of Venice*, Walter Cohen and Thomas Moison each caution against examining the play too strictly within the terms of what Moison describes as an "overly economic, overly Anglicized, perspective."[90] By contrast, I have attempted to situate the text in relation to debates in early modern England concerning the effects of capital formation on the production of value, a context that demonstrates the important role of domestic issues of class and labor in expanding networks of international commerce. However, Cohen's and Moison's own analyses helpfully point to the ways that texts interrogated social and economic change by comparing England to other commercial centers, particularly Venice. In a period that witnessed the construction of the Royal Exchange and the New Exchange, heralding the emergence of London as a center of commerce and consumption, comparisons with Venice, the archetypal mercantile entrepôt of the early modern period, offered a rubric for interpreting the changes affecting English culture.[91] The final portion of this chapter will therefore analyze the ways that Venice provided the English with a model for the regulation of labor in an expanding commercial environment.

In *Crudities* (1611), his popular European travelogue, Thomas Coryat observes the commercial center of Venice, the Rialto, through the lens of English commerce, terming the Rialto "the Exchange of Venice," although one he still finds "inferiour to our Exchange in London."[92] In his description of Venice's Piazza San Marco, Coryat remarks on the diversity of cultures and languages congregating in the area, so many that "a man may very properly call it rather Orbis then Urbis forum, that is, a market place of the world, not of the citie."[93] By placing this passage alongside the quotation from Sir Thomas Smith that began the chapter, one can see how Venice served as a model of commercial development.[94] The image of Venice was used to interrogate the effects of mercantile exchange on a nation, particularly in terms of the issues of citizenship and identity raised by a cosmopolitan population. Walter Cohen has argued that the setting of *The Merchant of Venice* helped allay anxieties about capital formation for an English audience who would have been familiar with Venice's reputation as a state wherein trade alleviated tensions between ethnic and class groups.[95] Yet few English texts depicted London's Royal Exchange in similar terms: in a 1647 letter that praised the Royal Exchange and placed it above its counterparts on the Continent, James Howell nonetheless noted that Venice's Rialto drew a "greater variety [of foreign merchants] than they are to be seen on our *Exchange*."[96] Similarly, in poetic descriptions of London's

Exchanges, including Joseph Hall's "A Satire on the Royal Exchange" (1599) and Francis Quarles's "The Walks of the Exchange" (1635), the cosmopolitan population of traders at the Exchange is associated with "Craft, Fraud, and Covetise" by Hall and likened to the "noise of Tongues begun at *Babel*" by Quarles.[97]

The difficulty of translating Venice's Rialto to the context of London's Royal Exchange demonstrates how Venice also provided a negative example for early modern England. Many English texts on Venice, such as Lewes Roberts's *The Marchants Mapp of Commerce* (1638), lamented the city's decline from the site of a mercantile empire to a center for moneychangers, a fate also anticipated for London.[98] Roberts reinscribes the opulence that so impressed Coryat and others as a symptom of Venice's decline; now no longer content to live within the means of their ever-declining trade, the Venetians have become the most ruthless imposers of customs taxes and fines.[99] Other texts emphasized the blurred distinctions between licensed trade and unlawful usury in Venice, evidenced, in particular, by the profits gained by the Venetian state from its subsidizing of Jewish usurers.[100]

The Merchant of Venice inherits the ambivalent representation of Venice found in early modern texts. When the bond becomes forfeit, Antonio remarks that Shylock's case cannot be dismissed because of the centrality of foreign merchants in the political economy of Venice:

> The Duke cannot deny the course of law;
> For the commodity that strangers have
> With us in Venice, if it be denied,
> Will much impeach the justice of the state,
> Since that the trade and profit of the city
> Consisteth of all nations. (3.3.26–31)

The inherent ability of commodities to circulate regardless of markers of nation or status necessitates the institutionalization of another "commodity," the trading privileges ensuring the rights of resident alien merchants.[101] But what does Shylock's commodity in Venice entail? Despite the "strange nature" of Shylock's stipulated surety for the forfeited bond, Portia initially admits that "Venetian law / Cannot impugn you as you do proceed" (4.1.178–79), and she therefore argues for property rights over immediate profit, declaring, "there is no power in Venice / Can alter a degree established" (4.1.218–19). Shylock occupies a problematic intermediate position as a result of his "commodity" in Venice: his commercially central role guarantees him protection by the law, yet this commercial identity also reflects on the commodification of social relations.

Perceiving that the Venetians have interfered in his commercial affairs and thereby infringed upon his rights over his property, Shylock demands that the Venetians free their own slaves and grant them the full rights of subjects: "Let them be free! Marry them to your heirs!" (4.1.94). This spectral reference to slaves within the commercial freedom of Venice has either confused or angered some literary critics, who point to the lack of slaves represented in the play and therefore view Shylock's statement as a rhetorical fiction that uses slavery merely as an analogy to prove a point.[102] Yet, as Shylock's own fate makes clear, Venetian prosperity is dependent upon a class excluded from citizenship (and from representation in the play, aside from the brief mention of the Moor impregnated by Launcelot [3.5.37–39]). Despite Shylock's own economically central position, as "the trade and profit of the city / Consisteth of all nations" (3.3.230–31), the judgment against him is based upon his status as non-Christian and non-Venetian. Thus, the confiscation of Shylock's goods stems from the threat of violence against a Christian—"if thou dost shed / One drop of Christian blood" (4.1.309–10)—while his death sentence results from the fact that he, as an alien, has sought the life of a citizen (4.1.348–53). Through the course of Act Four, Shylock's position is transformed from one of "commodity," as a member of a privileged trading class in Venice's cosmopolitan population, to that of a disenfranchised alien exempt from legal and commercial protection. Ironically, such a process of abjection confirms Shylock's characterization of Venice as a slave society, exposing the dependence of Venice upon a class excluded from positive rights.

More broadly, Shylock subversively exposes the unequal relations inherent in commercial exchange and capital formation. Although commodities may flow regardless of markers of nation, ethnicity, or status, the human subjects who participate in this economy—even if nominally protected by trading privileges—are always marked by differential power relations. In *A Treatise of Commerce* (1601), a text that defended the trading privileges of the Merchant Adventurers' Company, John Wheeler associated the proliferating outlets and forms of exchange with an emerging economy of slavery:

> for there is nothing in the world so ordinarie, and naturall vnto men, as to contract, truck, merchandise, and trafficque one with an other, so that it is almost vnpossible for three persons to converse together two houres, but they wil fall into talke of one bargaine or another, chopping, changing, or some other kinde of contract. . . . and in a woord, all the world choppeth and chaungeth, runneth and raveth after Martes,

Markettes, and Marchandising, so that all things come into Commerce, and passe into Trafficque (in a maner) in all times, and in all places: not onely that, which Nature bringeth foorth, as the fruites of the earth, the beastes, and living creatures with their spoiles, skinnes, and cases, the metalles, mineralles, & such like things, but further also, this man maketh merchandise of the workes of his owne handes, this man of another mans labour, one selleth woordes, another maketh trafficque of the skins, and blood of other men, yea there are some fou[n]d so subtill and cunning merchantes, that they perswade and induce men to suffer them selves to bee bought and solde, and we haue seene in our time enowe, and too manie, whiche haue made marchandise of mens soules[103]

While early modern capital formation depended upon an intermediate class of resident alien merchants, one whose commercial centrality necessitated special trading privileges and commercial protection, this economy additionally created other groups excluded from rights or profits. Wheeler's passage is frequently cited in studies of early modern trade as evidence of an unabashed celebration of the emergence of Smith's "universal market of the world" in the sixteenth century. However, all of these citations fail to comment on Wheeler's final allusion to slavery, overlooking how this reference complicates his more general pronouncements concerning the ubiquity of trade and exchange.[104] Although Wheeler presents economic exchange as an innate and natural activity, he equates two seemingly contradictory economic systems—wage-labor and the slave trade—in order to critique the potential abuses of a system of free trade wherein the rules of the market may be extended to all social relations. Wheeler uses the example of slavery in order to protect the controlled trade guaranteed by the long-standing privileges of the Merchant Adventurers' Company against competition from other unaffiliated groups. Thus, he envisages the nascent capitalist marketplace of competitive wage-labor as analogous to the emerging practices of chattel slavery in Europe's colonies.

Wheeler represents slavery as a demonic version of free trade unregulated by mercantilist state supervision and customary protections. However, his passage ultimately fails to differentiate acceptable market relations from their abuses. As a testament to the "intellectual confusion" so often ascribed to early modern mercantilist economic ideology, he is unable to conceive of a capitalist form of production; therefore, he represents the nascent capitalist forces that he opposes as both contrary to and contained within a natural economy of commerce. Wheeler equates the various manifestations of what Marx terms "appropriation," whether in the form of subsistence production, the appropriation of another's labor via wages, or the traffic in slaves: for Wheeler, each activity simply exemplifies trade and exchange.[105] The problem with this formulation lies in its inability to conceptualize the forms of coercion inherent in capitalist production; instead, even the slave owners merely "perswade and induce" men to allow themselves to be willingly enslaved.

If slavery represents the epitome of coerced labor, by equating slavery with wage-labor Wheeler's passage calls into question the terms upon which capitalist production establishes itself, revising the celebratory invocation of the "starting-point of capital" in the circulation of commodities. As Robert Brenner argues, the foundational presupposition for capital lies in conditions and corresponding class relations of "free" wage-labor.[106] While the effectiveness of the coercive instruments of the slave economy depends upon the visibility of their power, "free" wage-labor is constituted through an effacement of the exploitative mechanisms that enable this set of social relations: only after this process of abstraction can wage-labor be represented as being "freely" originating and "freely" disposed. Thus, the primitive accumulation of capital ultimately depends upon its absence from both representation and economic causality.

As Foucault asserts in *The Order of Things*, mercantilism, the dominant economic ideology of the early modern period, was unable to conceive of "production," and it therefore embodied value in terms of "wealth" (bullion, coin, commodities).[107] The predominant emphasis in recent criticism on international commerce and commodity circulation as the primary means of capital formation in the early modern period reinforces this "intellectual confusion" by mistakenly conflating mercantilism and capitalism. This critical approach overlooks the ways in which changing class relations, particularly the eroding social position of laborers, enabled the extraction of surplus that would later fuel England's expanding networks of international commerce. As Elizabeth Fox-Genovese and Eugene Genovese point out, "[c]hanges in the social relations of production, rather than in the sphere of circulation and exchange, determined the emergence of the capitalist mode of production" in the early modern period.[108] The equation of capitalism with commerce also serves to obscure the disjunctions inherent in capital formation, including its profound differences from the economic theories and conditions of mercantilism. The early modern theorization of capital, as found in Smith, Mun, and even Shakespeare, counters the mercantilist embodiment of value by casting it as "hard food for Midas"; instead, these texts offer an alternative model that acknowledges the immaterial forms of value that enabled capital formation, a position repeated in Marx's reference to representative forms of value that counter the "fantasy" of mercantilism. Nonetheless, this representation of capital depends upon an abstraction of labor.[109] As the money-form disappears in its conversion into capital, so too does the labor involved in its production, a process that converts labor into a generalized equivalence to be traded on the market. The effacement of the role of class and labor in the formation of capital is subsequently reproduced in analytical models that devote attention exclusively to topics of commodity circulation, commodity fetishism, and international commerce. These discussions, which also often confine their analysis to dramatic texts, ultimately ignore the abstracted forms of labor that enabled the early modern emergence of capital. By contrast, I wish to foreground how changing class relations—rather than expanding networks of commerce alone—served as the chief precondition of capitalism's transformation of forces of production.[110]

While "the myth of Venice" that circulated in early modern England conventionally represented Venice as an ideal of mercantile development, Venice also offered England a model for dealing with problems of labor in an expanding commercial economy. Gasparo Contarini's *The Commonwealth and Gouernment of Venice* (trans. 1599), perhaps the best-known account of Venetian social customs in early modern England, argued for the creation of subaltern classes excluded from representation and protection within the body politic:

> Now first I am to yeeld you a reckoning how and with what wisedome it was ordayned by our auncestors, that the common people should not be admitted into this company of citizens, in whose authority consisteth the whole power of the common wealth, then that this definiton of citizens was not with lesse wisedome measured, rather by the nobility of linage, then the greatnes of wealth, as in auncient commonwealthes it was wont, & as many old philosophers do prescribe: for though the citie is the company of citizens: yet all those men whose trauaile the Citie needeth, yea and that dwell within the walles thereof, are not generally to bee reckoned in the number, nor registered in the right of citizens: for euery citie standeth in neede of artificers, and many mercenarie people, and hired seruants, of which none can bee truely tearmed a citizen: for a citizen is a free man, but those are all seruile, eyther priuately or publikely: for mercenarie men & artificers, are all to be accounted as publique seruants: for it is to bee beleeued that a liuing creature is not otherwise made of nature, then it is needefull that the citie should bee of men: for as in a liuing creature are many

> partes that haue no life, yet the creature needeth them towardes the maintenance of life: so in a company of citizens, there is a necessary vse of many men, who neuerthelesse ought neither to bee, nor to be reputed or placed in the number of citizens (sigs. C4v–D1)

Contarini grounds his discussion of the polity of Venice in the language of economic exchange, offering the reader a "reckoning," or payment of debts, regarding the necessary exclusion of most class groups from political rule. By canceling the debt owed by the state to laborers and even wealthy merchants, Contarini attempts to associate political rule with "nobility" rather than "greatnes of wealth." Nonetheless, the state "standeth in neede" of laborers, servants, and even mercenaries, evidence of Venice's foundation as a commercial city. Contarini therefore reinscribes the body politic metaphor in relation to Venice, creating necessary or useful parts that have no life (and, therefore, political rights) of their own. As a result, he validates Shylock's characterization of Venice as a slave society. Jonathan Gil Harris has shown how the body politic metaphor was transformed in early modern England by defining the nation in contrast to the "foreign bodies" that threatened it.[111] This passage from Contarini demonstrates the ways that these terms of exclusion were also extended to class groups within the body politic, an important legacy of the Venetian model of commercial development on early modern English economic thought.

The tenor of Contarini's passage is repeated in one of the earliest and most influential descriptions of class relations in early modern England: Sir Thomas Smith's section, "Of the fourth sort of men which doe not rule," from *De Republica Anglorum* (ca. 1562–65, publ. 1583).[112] The comparison of Contarini with Smith reveals two important contradictions that link the early modern commercial centers of Venice and London. First, in each case the definition of the commonwealth was dependent upon a class excluded from the rights and protections of the state. Second, the increasing wealth and potential cosmopolitanism enabled through international trade occurred alongside—and even abetted—a reentrenchment of traditional class privileges and erosion of the customary rights of laborers. By situating Smith's comments from *De Republica Anglorum* in comparison to his praise of "the universal market of the world" from *A Discourse of the Commonweal of this Realm of England*, which began this chapter, one can see how concerns of international commerce in the early modern period were inflected by domestic factors of class, production, and social struggle.

Echoing Contarini, Sir Thomas Smith similarly disenfranchises laborers, distinguishing this "fourth sort of men" from the monarch, gentry, and yeomanry as a class—or "*proletarii*"—encompassing

> day labourers, poore husbandmen, yea marchantes or retailers which have no free lande, copiholders, all artificers, as Taylers, Shoomakers, Carpenters, Brickemakers, Bricklayers, Masons, &c. These have no voice nor authoritie in our common wealth, and no account is made of them but onelie to be ruled, not to rule other[113]

In Contarini's passage, the laboring poor are figured as the useful but lifeless limbs of the body politic, whose labor is necessary for the continued maintenance of the state yet who must be denied political representation. For Smith, however, such an arrangement fails to constitute a commonwealth, for laborers assume a merely instrumental role, one that he likens to mechanical tools or beasts of burden. Despite Smith's denial of voice and authority to the laboring classes, his formulation makes significant revisions to Contarini's model of the body politic, demonstrating an English adaptation of Venetian precedents. Smith argues for a degree of mobility inherent in a commonwealth, which must "turne and alter," allowing an adjustment of the constitution of classes, in order to prevent either oligarchical oppression or the revolt of frustrated subalterns.[114] He therefore concedes a degree of customary rights to laborers, who, although allowed "onelie to be ruled, not to rule other," may still hold lower and local offices such as churchwarden or constable.[115] Smith allocates a degree of social mobility to his English commonwealth, even as he codifies the social place of a nascent proletariat excluded from political representation and enfranchisement. These comments accurately reflect changes of status for subjects in the lower rungs of early modern England's social hierarchy: a small number of laborers were able to take advantage of expanding networks of capital and advance into the yeomanry, thereby serving as a buffer social group situated between the landless poor and their social superiors.[116] This process splintered potential alliances among lower-class groups, providing token exemptions whose social mobility could be used to minimize the effects of an overall structural erosion of the position of laborers. Thus, the stability of the social hierarchy was ensured by conceding a degree of mobility of status to a small number of subjects. In addition, this limited possibility of social mobility served to reinforce the impression of English "liberty," legitimating the tolerable abuses of domestic class hierarchies by distinguishing them from the comparably more severe conditions found in European cultures, including even the Venetian republic.

Cultural anxieties in early modern England consequently centered not on the possibility of mobility, which, like the use of mechanisms of credit and bills of exchange, had become a recognized necessity in the early modern period, but on the form that this mobility would take: the degree to which changes in status could be managed so as to ensure that vertical social movement produced subjects like Shakespeare's Antonio, who would give generously to maintain social hierarchies and feel indebted to the status quo for their social advancement. In contrast to the self-regulating mobility allotted to some of early modern England's merchants, chapter 2 will examine the anxieties produced by groups perceived to disrupt sanctioned avenues of mobility of class and status. In addition to the issues discussed in this chapter concerning the ways that economic innovation and commodity circulation increasingly undermined traditional structures of value in the early modern period, travel and commerce also created new opportunities for people to circulate despite barriers of nation and status. The representation of figures such as the pirate or the renegade demonstrates the repercussions stemming from the growing number of subjects traveling beyond the political and cultural borders of the English nation—and, as it was feared, beyond the reach of the state's power as well.

CHAPTER 2

A NATION OF PIRATES: PIRACY, CONVERSION, AND NATION SPACE

LAND-RATS AND WATER-RATS

Although Venice often served as a model of commercial development, representations of Venice were not always intended to stand in for England. In *The Merchant of Venice*, England is cast not as an analogous or even budding commercial empire but appears, instead, as a site of potential loss. While Antonio's multiple commercial ventures unite a network encompassing North Africa, the East Indies, Mexico, and England (1.3.18–21), only the latter entrepôt, seemingly the nearest and least perilous destination, is associated with the risks of international commerce. When Salerio reports the news of Antonio's losses at sea, he relates how one of Antonio's ships has "miscarried" in "the Narrow Seas" between England and France (2.8.28–29), a site he later specifies as "the Goodwins" (3.1.4), the channel of the Thames itself. Although the potential profits of commerce derive from exchange at distant ports, the sites of danger rest with domestic locations that would be familiar to the play's English audience.

Salerio earlier evokes the image of a particularly "English" threat, describing to Antonio how, if he were in the latter's position, he would suffer anxiety over the possible loss of an argosy like "my wealthy *Andrew*" (1.1.27). In granting this hypothetical argosy the name of a Spanish galleon captured by Drake in Cadiz in 1596, Salerio establishes a significant disjuncture between the perceptions of the Venetian characters and the play's English audience, making it clear that one person's (and nation's) loss is another's gain. The image of *The Andrew* disrupts the alignment of England with Venice within the play, placing English commercial interests and national aspirations in conflict with those of a royal merchant like Antonio as well as raising the possibility that the hazards associated with England result more directly from human agency and intent. Shylock more explicitly evokes the image of England as a "nation of pirates." As he considers the security of the loan to Bassanio and evaluates the degree of risk based upon the extent to which Antonio's "means are in supposition" (1.3.17), he specifies another factor potentially affecting Antonio's resources:

> But ships are but boards, sailors but men; there be land-rats and water-rats, water-thieves and land-thieves, I mean pirates, and then there is the peril of waters, winds, and rocks. (1.3.22–25)

Shylock relegates the dangers of the English coastline to secondary importance in comparison to the human predators who are metonymically linked with England. The true source of these anxieties derives from the threat of piracy; as Shylock obliquely suggests, "sailors are but men." Shylock's lines do not explain whether the acuteness of this peril stems from the number of "water-rats," and the fact that sailors are "but men" who cannot defend themselves from this onslaught, or from the implication that these fallible mariners themselves constitute the infiltrating body of pirates. This reference to the ubiquity of piracy points back to England as much as Salanio's references to commerce on the English Channel and the Thames's Goodwin Sands. As Paul Hentzner remarked while traveling in England late in Elizabeth's reign, the English make "good sailors, and better pirates."[1] Shylock's comment exposes two key points of ambiguity that will recur throughout this chapter's discussion of the Jacobean regulation of piracy: the inability to distinguish the identity of pirates from other mariners and the difficulties of differentiating a criminalized class from a state-sanctioned and valorized emblem of emergent national identity.

The play's concern over the precariousness of Venetian shipping further establishes a link to English piracy in the Mediterranean. Between 1592 and 1609, pirates captured an estimated 3,000 vessels in the region, a large percentage of which were Venetian.[2] The epidemic increase in Mediterranean piracy was caused by the arrival of Dutch and, especially, English mariners into the region.[3] Thus,

England's commercial ascendancy in the Mediterranean contributed to Venice's maritime and commercial decline. As attested to by the records of the Venetian ambassador in London, Nicolo Molin, a prime concern of Anglo-Venetian relations was the suppression of piracy,[4] and even Molin himself was a victim of English piracy, on a voyage to London in October of 1603.[5] One of James I's earliest proclamations attempting to stamp out piracy (September 30, 1603), in fact, resulted from Thomas Tompkins's plunder of a Venetian ship, the *Black Balbiano*. Tompkins defended himself by arguing that he possessed letters of reprisal from Queen Elizabeth that authorized him to attack Venetian shipping, an argument that was found unconvincing at Admiralty Court, where he was convicted on October 11, 1610.[6] The proclamation prompted by Tompkins was significant because it constituted the first royal statement addressing piracy since the reign of Henry VIII, and it served as the basis of future English law regarding piracy.[7]

Throughout much of the sixteenth century, England was able to use state-sanctioned piracy to gain commercial advantage over hostile nations, particularly Spain. King James brought this tradition to a halt with Tompkins's conviction, which provided the first opportunity to implement his proclamation of June 23, 1603 "concerning Warlike ships at sea," the statute that officially ended the Tudor sponsorship of privateering. Elizabeth's policies of privateering had provided private individuals either with letters of marque, which permitted merchants and their agents to intercept and capture foreign vessels at war with England, or commissions of reprisal, which allowed them to recuperate losses by seizing any ship from the nation responsible for the capture of their own vessels. The dual commercial and political objectives of such policies are clear in James's proclamation, which praises the "zeale and affection" that these merchants "bare to the good of their Countrey," while also lauding privateering's contribution to the "maintenance & employment of the Shipping and Mariners of England, otherwise through scant of Traffique at that time, not sufficiently set on worke."[8] Despite his efforts to end such practices, then, James was aware of the need to appease the ideological interests backing policies of privateering, realizing their economic as well as nationalist benefits.

James's efforts to suppress piracy, which had intended to extend his peace policies to the jurisdiction of maritime commercial activity, ended one of the few profitable enterprises for early modern English mariners. With the loss of licensed privateering missions, many of those engaged in these quasi-legal ventures turned to piracy.

Contemporaries were also aware of this turn of events. The pervasiveness of piracy, and its central place in the minds of early seventeenth-century readers, is evinced by the fact that John Smith includes a history of early modern piracy as the concluding chapter to his autobiographical *The True Travels, Adventures, and Observations of Captain John Smith* (1630). Under the heading "What occasioneth Pirats," Smith attributes the ubiquity of the problem to both James's policies and economic conditions:

> After the death of our most gracious Queene Elizabeth, of blessed memory, our Royall King James, who from his infancy had reigned in peace with all Nations; had no imployment for those men of warre, so that those that were rich rested with what they had; those that were poore and had nothing but from hand to mouth, turned Pirats; some, because they became sleighted of those for whom they had got much wealth; some, for that they could not get their due; some, that had lived bravely, would not abase themselves to poverty; some vainly, only to get a name; others for revenge, covetousnesse, or as ill; and as they found themselves more and more oppressed, their passions increasing with discontent, made them turne Pirats.[9]

In one of the period's rare applications of sympathy and economic causality to the topic, Smith accurately reveals how the transition from sanctioned Elizabethan privateering to outlawed Jacobean piracy had divergent effects on class groups. Surviving Elizabethan privateers, such as George Clifford, the third earl of Cumberland, could simply remain content with the profits they had gained during the war with Spain. Other former privateers, including Charles Howard, earl of Nottingham and Lord High Admiral under James I, could continue to profit from the recently outlawed piracy trade while using their offices to protect them from prosecution.[10] Common mariners, however, lacked access to the accumulation and retention of capital, having "nothing but from hand to mouth." Smith's observations had a basis in fact, for the wages of English mariners remained stagnant from 1585 through the Jacobean period.[11] Sir Walter Raleigh observed that sailors "went with as great a grudging to serve in his Majesty's ships as if it were to be slaves in the galleys," a comment echoed by Sir Henry Mainwaring, former pirate and Jacobean Admiralty official, who likened naval service to "a kind of slavery."[12] Employment in the Royal Navy proved such an undesirable vocation that James prohibited mariners from the more profitable service of foreign rulers in 1605, a proclamation he was forced to repeat in 1622.[13] Because of the continued lack of recruits, in 1623 James mandated punishments for sailors who evaded proscription and officials who dismissed conscripted recruits in exchange for bribes.[14] James's continued concern over staffing the Navy, as well as the failure of his earlier efforts, is demonstrated by a 1625 proclamation, which stipulated penalties both for mariners evading naval service and for any merchant who hired them, demanding the latter withhold their wages and, on pain of punishment, turn them over to the nearest constable.[15]

Sir Henry Mainwaring's treatise, "Of the Beginnings, Practices, and Suppression of Pirates" (ca. 1616–17), a text presented to James in 1618, exemplifies the ambivalence of Jacobean attitudes regarding the social place of piracy. In comments reminiscent of Smith's, Mainwaring estimated that the population of pirates had increased by ten-fold since Elizabeth's reign, and he accurately diagnosed the relation between underemployment and piracy, asking James "to devise some more universal employment than now we have, by which men of that spirit might not complain, as they now do, that they are forced for lack of convenient employment to enter into such unlawful courses" (2.41).[16] Despite his seeming endorsement of relief for poor mariners, though, Mainwaring is remarkably accommodating of the new tenor of Jacobean regulations, recommending that James use captured pirates as galley slaves, a policy that would allow the chance of reform "by giving them a long time of Repentance" (2.19) and yet still provide necessary manpower in case of war (2.18). Mainwaring pessimistically speculates "that the most part of them will never be reclaimed" (2.18); however, he does not find his punishment of perpetual service excessive since, for most mariners and pirates, "their whole life for the most part is spent but in a running Prison" (2.18). Mainwaring concedes the inevitable exclusion of pirates from the national imagined community, yet he also realizes the dependence of the state upon their labor. Ironically, Mainwaring himself was a pirate captain recently pardoned and knighted by James, a fact that does not dissuade him from advising James "never to grant any Pardon, and for those that are or may be taken, to put them all to death, or make slaves of them" (2.42).

Smith provides a more sympathetic alternative to Mainwaring, asking merchants "not to bee sparing of a competent pay, nor true payment; for neither Souldiers nor Sea-men can live without meanes, but necessity will force them to steale" (240). Lamenting that sailors and soldiers are now regarded as the "scumme of the world," he implores these groups to regain their reputations by engaging in colonial projects, "those faire plantations of our English Nation" (240–41).

Smith's gratuitous advertisement for Virginia colonization is fairly predictable, given his contributions to the promotional literature for English colonization of the Americas. Yet his comments also help explain the relation of his final chapter on piracy, what the editor of the recent *Complete Works* deems as "barely relevant," to the other sections of his *True Travels*.[17] The structure of Smith's text points to a transition from unauthorized forms of cultural exchange, such as his mercenary activities in Hungary and travels through Ottoman dominions, to hierarchically organized efforts at American colonization, as evinced by the supplements to his earlier *Generall Historie of Virginia* (1624), which update colonial projects in Virginia, New England, Bermuda, and Guiana. Smith attempts to establish the accession of colonization as the dominant form of cultural exchange, assuring his readers that despite the fact that plantation projects "in the beginning were scorned and contemned, yet now you see how many rich and gallant people come from thence, who went thither as poore as any Souldier or Sailor, and gets more in one yeare, than you by Piracie in seven" (241).

Although Smith ostensibly intends to demonstrate the progress of settlement in the Americas, he promotes colonization not by appealing to the reader's desire for land and prosperity in the Americas but by presenting the prospect of "rich and gallant people" who "*return from thence*" laden with wealth. This vision of colonization offers an ironic form of exchange: the realm is rid of the "scumme of the world" (240), the masterless and underemployed poor, who return to England transformed as "rich and gallant people" (241). The planters have not only earned much more than what is gained through piracy, Smith asserts, but have also enriched the kingdom, with "what custome they yearely pay to our most Royall King Charles" (241). In order to valorize colonization for his early Caroline audience, Smith must first counter the economic incentives of piracy, offering colonial projects as a way to reincorporate those class groups relegated to illegal practices after the Jacobean prohibition of privateering.

This chapter will look at the anxieties relating to class relations and cultural exchange articulated in the Jacobean era, a crucial period of transition from Elizabethan privateering to American colonization that exposes the central role of England's laboring classes in the consolidation of state power. Early modern commerce created unprecedented and potentially disruptive possibilities for the circulation of travelers, particularly among classes possessing limited mobility at home. The Jacobean efforts to suppress piracy in the Mediterranean and Levant served as a key component in a more general struggle to extend state control over subjects traveling abroad. My discussion will examine early modern travel and commerce as sites of class conflict through an analysis of a range of texts and practices, from the pamphlet literature on piracy and the ritualistic execution of pirates in the first section to my concluding section and its consideration of "apostasy sermons" marking the reconversion of renegades. These texts attempted to regulate travel by structuring the return of travelers from abroad, enabling either a formal reintegration of returning travelers or their expulsion from the body politic. Despite these state-sponsored rituals, the popular mythologization of Jacobean pirates, as well as the custom of maritime communities to shield returning travelers and apostates from the interventions of state and church authorities, attests to alternative expressions of community that ultimately served to disrupt the alignment of state with nation in early modern England. These points of opposition to official forms of nationhood expose the profoundly destabilizing effects of class conflict on the colonial and mercantile expansion of early modern England.

***

PIRACY AND STATUS: HEYWOOD'S
Fortune by Land and Sea

In Smith's text, the anxieties concerning the status of the subject who ventures outside the political body of the realm and beyond the boundaries of its jurisdiction are elided through the vision of a prosperous return voyage, one that brings both a reformed subject and a hoard of wealth for the realm's treasury. The prospect of the expulsion of England's poor and recuperation of national wealth also constitutes the dramatic structure of Thomas Heywood and William Rowley's *Fortune by Land and Sea* (1609). Forrest, the younger son of a decayed rural knight, is forced to flee England after having killed his brother's murderer in a duel. He is able to escape the country by becoming captain of a privateering vessel that targets Spanish vessels in the Mediterranean. After his capture of the pirates Purser and Clinton, historical figures executed in 1583, Forrest gains a pardon and knighthood from the queen along with a reward of £1,000 and "for the service of my country, / ... promise of employments of more weight" (5.2.2283–84).[18] Heywood and Rowley's play reflects the contradictions of Jacobean policies toward piracy and the maritime laboring classes. But rather than critiquing the economic causes underlying the problem, as Smith does, the text emphasizes the possibilities of social mobility enabled through trade and travel, presenting overseas commerce as the solution to domestic economic crises and tensions of status. The discrepancies of class—highlighted by the fact that the mobility of status accorded to the play's dual protagonists Forrest and Philip Harding is denied Purser and Clinton—are reinscribed onto a discrepancy of periodization. The play's Elizabethan setting blurs distinctions between sanctioned Elizabethan privateering and prohibited Jacobean piracy, calling into question the ability of changing state practices to reconstitute the status of subjects. Heywood and Rowley's play articulates anxieties particular to its early Jacobean composition, a period unable to address the problem of maritime labor; over time, however, the conditions that had been alleviated via privateering would ultimately be mitigated, as Smith proposes, through the incorporation of the poor into colonial projects.

The play attentively tries to distinguish Forrest from Purser and Clinton and establish an opposition between legally sanctioned privateering and outlawed piracy. For example, Forrest states his intentions as an "adventurer" to defend his "countries honour" and "the reputation / Of our own names" (4.2.1697, 1691–92). Forrest foregrounds the play's Elizabethan setting by stating his intentions to acquire only "lawful spoyl" (4.2.1716) by targeting "any Carract that do's trade for *Spain*" (4.2.1689). Despite the selection of two historical Elizabethan pirates, the play firmly places Purser and Clinton in the context of contemporary Jacobean efforts to suppress piracy, as when Purser renounces his status as an English subject, concluding, "since our country have proclaim'd us pyrats, / And cut us off from any claim in *England*, / We'l be no longer now call'd English men" (4.1.1618–20). Purser emphasizes the role of naming in the definition of the subject; as Fernand Braudel points out, the term "pirate" itself was of fairly recent coinage in the early seventeenth century, superseding the terms "privateer" or "corsair" and denoting the increasingly outlawed status of such maritime activities.[19] Purser also appropriately stresses that they have been *proclaimed* as pirates, a reference to James I's numerous Royal Proclamations concerning piracy. By contrast, the final Elizabethan proclamation that attempted to suppress piracy was drafted in 1580. Subsequent proclamations merely insured that privateers did not target allied shipping and that the state received a share of captured goods; in other words, Elizabeth acknowledged her participation in the economy of piracy in order to better regulate it.[20]

Due to the discrepancies between its Elizabethan setting and the Jacobean period's attitudes toward piracy, *Fortune by Land and Sea* exposes the failure and hypocrisy of state policy toward maritime labor. The Royal Proclamation declaring Purser and Clinton as pirates is delivered by the Clown, who announces it (in comically mangled form) on the order of a hoarse-voiced Pursuivant unable to perform the task himself (3.4.1529–74). The Pursuivant's strained voice accurately points to the repetitive qualities and ineffective results of official policies to suppress piracy; he, like the state, is debilitated by trying to shout down the problem. The Clown's double-voiced subversion of the proclamation's message, on the other hand, exposes the contradictions between the state's intentions to suppress piracy and its pervasive implication within the piratical economy. Significantly, when Heywood reworked this episode in *The True Relation, of the Lives and Deaths of the Two Most Famous English Pyrats, Purser, and Clinton* (1639), the Clown is described as "a Sayler, and thought to bee a favourite of that piraticall faction," an acknowledgment of the political intentions underlying this comic incident.[21]

The Jacobean reinscription of the social place of piracy depended upon the reconstitution of the Elizabethan privateer as international outlaw in order to justify an increasing centralization of authority over forms of cultural exchange. In this formulation, the illegal profits that had earlier benefited the body politic—whether Drake's estimated profit margin of 4,700 percent for investors or the symbolic capital afforded by the capture of *The Andrew*—were registered as a debilitating force to the national community.[22] *Fortune by Land and Sea* emphasizes the domestic costs of piracy; for example, after he is captured by Purser and Clinton, the character known only as the "Merchant," who had previously given Forrest command of a privateering ship, laments the losses that will be sustained by his creditors, including his benevolent sister Anne, Philip Harding's stepmother, who had earlier enabled Forrest's escape from arrest (4.1.1602–03, 1652–55). However, Heywood and Rowley's play also points to the fluidity of boundaries of license and transgression. For instance, the Merchant recognizes Clinton as one of his former officers and offers him future employment due to his skills; nonetheless, though, Clinton rejects the Merchant's promise of future patronage (4.1.1621–25), an action emphasizing that Clinton's position as a pirate had resulted from voluntary choice rather than economic necessity. Holinshed's *Chronicles* similarly presents Clinton Atkinson as "an example of degeneration" from a securely middling-sort background.[23]

This episode accurately points to the ease with which early modern mariners could begin to engage in piratical activities. In Admiralty Court records from the first four decades of the seventeenth century,

73 percent of pirates were listed as mariners by profession. Most of those arrested for piracy drifted frequently between piracy and legitimate employment such as the Newfoundland fishing industry or Newcastle coal shipping.[24] As Marcus Rediker has noted, piracy served as an attractive alternative to sanctioned forms of employment, one that offered better living conditions, a democratic structure of command, and a relatively egalitarian distribution of captured wealth.[25] Aware of the precariousness of his identity as a licensed privateer, Forrest promises that upon his promotion to Captain, he would "bear my self so even and upright / In this my charge" (4.2.1674–75). Part of Forrest's "upright" identity as a licensed privateer entails the appropriate distribution of profits. While Purser and Clinton declare that they will divide their spoil "[i]n equal shares" (4.1.1582), Forrest, after capturing the pirates and their goods, stipulates that the pirates' wealth be divided "in equal shares, / To very mans desart, estate, and place" (4.5.1851–52).[26] Early modern pirates continued to make use of the share system, the dominant means of payment used by ancient and medieval mariners. The early modern period saw this structure increasingly replaced with a wage system that enabled owners to retain exclusive control over capital.[27] Although Forrest appropriates the egalitarian language of the share system in stipulating the division of seized wealth "in equal shares," he maintains a hierarchical distribution of profits according to obedience, status, and position. Similar to Jacobean proclamations suppressing piracy, Forrest attempts to contain the egalitarian appeal of piracy within a commercial system that sustains a centralized ownership of capital.

Thirty years after his inclusion of Purser and Clinton in *Fortune by Land and Sea*, Heywood returned to these Elizabethan pirates in *The True Relation, of the Lives and Deaths of the Two Most Famous English Pyrats, Purser, and Clinton* (1639). Although the pamphlet begins with a ponderous discussion "Of the power of justice" and a history of piracy, Heywood includes an interesting biography of both figures, with new details missing from his earlier play regarding their background and initiation into piracy. At their first meeting, Clinton and Purser fall into a discussion of their economic straits,

> that in regard of their experience and skill in Navigation, what basenesse it was in them to bee no better than servants, who had both the Judgement, and the ability to command, and to bee onely Imployed to benefit and inrich others, whilst they in the Interim wanted themselves: They further reasoned that service was no heritage, and that in regard

they had eyther of them beene more than a prentiship to learne their
Art, it was now high time to be freemen of the Sea, and set up for
themselves.[28]

Echoing John Smith's earlier comments about the status of mariners
at the time of James's accession, the pirates are acutely aware of their
exclusion from mercantilism's network of circulating capital, "to bee
onely Imployed to benefit and inrich others, whilst they in the
Interim wanted themselves" (sig. A4v). One of the most threatening
aspects of piracy was that it enabled potential wage-laborers to
become economically independent, allowing them to seize the mechanisms and social rhetoric of merchant's capital. As Marcus Rediker
comments, early modern pirates "did not consider themselves wage
laborers but rather risk-sharing partners."[29] In Heywood and
Rowley's play, the pirates appropriate the language of early modern
commerce; for example, Clinton taunts the Merchant, his former
master, by inquiring whether he "wouldst not have us freely use our
trade?" (4.1.1609). Displaced from the customary economic protections of tenants or the economic freedom guaranteed apprentices in the
guild system, the pirates opt to "set up for themselves" and thereby
become "freemen of the Sea." This passage from Heywood's pamphlet makes use of one of the play's favorite comparisons, the application of property relations to piracy, as Purser and Clinton conclude
that "service was no heritage" (sig. A4v). In *Fortune by Land and Sea*,
the economic status of Philip Harding demonstrates a similar point as
he is disinherited and forced into domestic service to his own father
until he regains the fortune "by land" referred to in the play's title.
However, the conditions of piracy attest to the disruptive potential of
unsanctioned possibilities of social mobility, reflected in Purser's
depiction of himself and Clinton as "Lords, / Nay Kings at Sea,"
whose wealth is likened to the profits gained through domestic agricultural production: "the Ocean vvas our realm, / And the light bil-
lows in the which we sayl'd / Our hundreds, nay our shires, and
provinces, / That brought us annual profit" (5.1.2157–61).

Fortune by Land and Sea provides a model of social mobility, for
its two protagonists Philip Harding and Forrest move from analogous
marginal positions as disinherited son and fugitive to a mutual regain-
ing of fortunes and reincorporation into the social body. Each character's narrative of a loss of social position and eventual redemption
from service also implies a fluidity in status, suggesting that social
rank, like commodities or property, is acquirable and transferable. In
fact, a dialogue between the two characters' fathers reveals that the

families have exchanged social positions, with the Hardings rising from a status as the Forrests' tenant farmers to "Lord of all those Manors," while the fortunes of the Forrests have dwindled to the brink of poverty (3.2.1185–97). But the presence of the pirates belies the play's ameliorating emphasis on the ease and fluidity of status. Upon his seizure of the Merchant's ship, Clinton informs the Merchant that if he and his creditors are "undone" by their piracies, he should "impute it to thy fortune, / And not to any injury in us; / For he that's born to be a beggar know / How e'r he toyls and trafficks must dye so" (4.1.1610–14). Unlike the play's middling-sort characters, whose fortunes are lost and regained, Clinton emphasizes the rigidity of status for members of the underclass, whose ranks swelled in the Elizabethan and Jacobean eras, periods plagued by underemployment and recurring economic crises. When the Merchant questions whether "the providence of heaven / Would so have favoured men of base condition" (4.1.1595–96), he expresses his concern over the riches gained through piracy. Nonetheless, the spectacle of Purser and Clinton's apprehension and execution confirms Clinton's earlier statement that prosperity is denied to those of "base condition," a term that encompasses meanings related equally to moral nature and social status.

Jacobean texts on piracy elide its political ramifications and economic origins in favor of an emphasis on piracy as a personal drama. The recasting of the pirate in the narrative of the moral parable recurs in the anonymous text, *The Lives, Apprehensions, Arraignments, and Executions of the 19. Late Pyrates* (1610), which, as its title indicates, traces the lives of several pirates from their introduction to piracy to their executions on December 22, 1609. The text serves as an example of the genre of criminal biography, with the origin of its narratives often cast in doubt by repeated switches from the first to third person. The longest section, "The discourse of Captaine Harris under his owne hand," appropriately deals with the pirate of the highest social status. Under the tutelage of prominent Bristol merchants, Harris relates how he had gone to sea, although, as he concedes, less for commercial reasons than to "see the state and fashions of forraine countries, and to inrich my understanding with experience" (sig. A3).[30] In casting the fashionable traveler as potential pirate, the text points to the dangerous fluidity of identities opened up through cultural exchange. This ambiguity is also revealed by Harris's bond with the pirate Captain Bishop. After Harris is taken captive in Tunis, his redemption is accomplished by Bishop, rather than the English state. His subsequent decision to serve under Bishop therefore offers him a surrogate community in light of his home nation's failure to provide either economic survival at home or protection from captivity abroad. Yet, while travel and trade present ubiquitous dangers of a transformation of identities and social relations, the reconstitution of the subject as pirate is presented as an absolute and unalterable classification that will inevitably lead to final punishment, as suggested by the text's title.

If the lesson of Captain Harris's narrative speaks to the potential of sanctioned forms of social mobility to cross over into unlawful boundary transgression, the rest of the accounts in *Lives, Apprehensions* are firmly situated in the underclass. The next biography takes the form of a narrative supposedly dictated by its illiterate subject, Captain Jennings. The narrator consequently attributes the section's rough style to Jennings's "meane and low" social background (sig. C1v).[31] Similar to the Calvinist language evoked in *Fortune by Land and Sea*, Jennings's status is presented as predetermining his actions. Excluded from social mobility by his class status, Jennings lacks the prerequisite agency (as well as literacy) to render a dramatic presentation of his own narrative. Jennings's status thus denies him the ability to write his own life story, which can only be dictated—and told badly—leaving an absent narrator to represent Jennings. To be accurately described, Jennings must be deprived of authority over his narrative, allowing his story to be transformed into parable and legend, a process extended through its translation into a contemporary ballad, "Captayne Jenninges his songe, which he made in the Marshalsey and songe a little before his death."[32]

As the work of the economic historian Craig Muldrew has demonstrated, the status of subjects within early modern English communities was contingent upon their "credibility": their economic behavior, especially their repayment of loans, was held to reflect their underlying character. The description of the pirates in *Lives, Apprehensions* makes clear that their displacement from England and initiation into piracy resulted from improper economic behavior, superfluous expenditure that had ostracized them from their communities.[33] As the text moves on to discuss pirates of increasingly lower social status, William Minas, a Cornwall mariner, is condemned for "not [being] contented with that sufficient meanes that God and nature had provided for him" (sig. F1), while Captain Downes is associated with "superfluous expence" that "made him crack his credit amongst men of worth" and turn to piracy in order to escape his creditors (sig. F2v). In the cases of Minas and Downes, the desire for "superfluous" excess is cast as the initial temptation to transgress inherent limits dictated by class status and national allegiance.

The text emphasizes the moral implications of the pirates' lack of credibility, obscuring how piracy offered a means to recuperate credit in an economy defined by underemployment and scarcity of coin. An early seventeenth-century euphemism for piracy, of being "on the account," reveals how the gains of piracy could be used to restore one's "credibility" in terms of economic status as well as estimation of personal value, restoring one's position to the good books of a community's creditors.[34] While the wages of their counterparts in the Royal Navy remained abysmally low, Jacobean pirates were noted for their stunning accumulation of scarce coin: despite his characterization as "meane and low" in *Lives, Apprehensions*, John Jennings held a waistband containing more than £400 in Barbary gold and possessed more than £2,000 of merchandise upon his surrender, while Thomas Tompkins, arrested for his capture of the Venetian ship *Black Balbiano*, brought back to England £2,600 in silver. Conceding the economic gains of Jacobean pirates, James's general pardon of 1612 even allowed pirates to retain their treasure upon their surrender to authorities.[35]

The representation of the pirates' "base" character and economic status serves to displace the possibilities of social mobility enabled by piracy. The narrator of *Lives, Apprehensions* devotes the least attention to a person identified only as "Thomas," accused of having received stolen goods from the playwright-pirate Lording Barry.[36] The narrator concludes by stating that he deigns "[n]ot to lengthen out paper with this poor fellow, of more than appeared either by his confession, arraignment, or execution" (sig. F2). As the text descends the social ladder, it renders the pirates themselves, and not only their desires, increasingly superfluous, unworthy of the narrative time and textual space necessary for a biography, and therefore represented most accurately in terms of their status as juridical subjects produced from the actions of confession, indictment, and execution. As the interpersonal bonds of lending and credit typifying early modern communities gave way to economic scarcity and competitiveness, subjects deemed unproductive or wasteful were increasingly figured as superfluous, and even potentially dangerous, members of the body politic.

The example of "Thomas," executed merely for dealing in stolen goods, illustrates the extremities of the Jacobean prosecution of pirates. The *Lives, Apprehensions* text, in addition to Admiralty Court records, also attests to the commonplace practice of simultaneously arraigning and executing a large number of suspects, as in the case of 70 people arraigned in groups of seven or eight on September 1, 1608.[37] In light of such details, one can see what necessitated these texts' efforts to convert this deadly bureaucratic machine into a personal drama of conscience and atonement. Yet *Lives, Apprehensions* also elides an alternative narrative relating to its subjects, one that implicates the Jacobean state in the economy of piracy. The official chiefly responsible for suppressing piracy in the Jacobean period was the elderly Lord High Admiral and Armada hero, Charles Howard, the earl of Nottingham, who supplemented his income by selling offices under his command. In turn, these local officials, the vice-admirals of the coastline counties, accepted bribes and dealt in stolen goods acquired through piracy. The level of corruption in Nottingham's service finally prompted an investigation led by Henry Howard, the earl of Northampton, his cousin and long-time adversary. Northampton's main witnesses against the Admiralty office were the pirate captains Harris and Jennings: on December 8, 1609, James therefore ordered a temporary reprieve for the pair, "in hope of farther confessions from them."[38] Harris and Jennings implicated several of Nottingham's underlings, revealing that Sir Richard Hawkins, vice-admiral of Devon, and Hannibal and Francis Vivian, vice-admirals of Cornwall, received a portion of stolen goods trafficked through the West Country; that Hannibal Vivian had earlier accepted a £140 bribe to release Jennings from his custody; and that both pirates were protected by an official named Captain Williamson, who had been employed by the state to clear pirates from the Irish coast.

Northampton passed along his examination of Harris and Jennings to Secretary Lake and the Privy Council in December 1609, noting that he feared that the admiral would have the captains executed, "bycause they tell tales." As Northampton predicted, Nottingham saved himself from indictment by having Harris and Jennings executed within the month. Nottingham subsequently rid himself of some of his underlings, including Vice-Admiral Hawkins, who was dismissed from office, fined, and imprisoned. In all, 150 offenders were brought to London on charges of aiding pirates in the West Country. Yet the most elite figures escaped prosecution, including both state officials (Nottingham) and leading pirate captains (Harris's mentor, Captain Bishop); nonetheless, this fact did not escape notice. When John Stow records the execution of the 19 pirates in his *Annales* (1615), he alludes to unnamed figures "of note" who "hadde beene in consort with the forenamed pyrates"; yet, recognizing the power of those who had evaded punishment, Stow wisely leaves out their names.[39] By rendering the story of Harris, Jennings, and their fellow pirates as *The Lives, Apprehensions, Arraignments, and Executions of the 19. Late Pyrates*, the text creates a personal and moral parable rather than a political narrative, reducing the narrative to one that deals with 19 lower-class offenders—not 150, including state officials—and thereby redeeming the state from its complicity in the economy of piracy.[40]

The *Lives, Apprehensions* provides a context in which to analyze the significance of Purser and Clinton's scaffold speeches in Act Five of *Fortune by Land and Sea*. To an extent, Heywood and Rowley are drawing on a ballad tradition long applied to pirates and others facing execution, one exemplified by the ballads compiled as *Clinton, Purser, and Walton to their Countrymen Wheresoever* (ca. 1583).[41] The ballads differ from the play in their insistence on the pirates' continued obedience to queen and country: Purser pleads repeatedly that he "ever wisht my Queene and country well" (4), a point reinforced by Arnold's assurance that "lives he not that can in conscience say, / Purser or Arnold made one English praye" (11). Like the *Lives, Apprehensions*, the ballads enable state power to speak through the pirates, representing the captains as endorsing the position of the state that condemns them. Arnold, for example, acknowledges that the piracies he has committed against England's allies justify his punishment, stating a similar rationale to that provided by James in his 1603 proclamation ending privateering: "For if we live not under soveraigne awe, / but sencelesse seeke our own securitie, / the publike weale would perish presently" (11).

Whereas most Jacobean texts emphasize the expulsion of pirates from the representation of the body politic, Heywood's later pamphlet, *The True Relation, of...Purser, and Clinton*, associates piracy with a nostalgic expression of nationalism that is articulated most clearly through an emotional bond with Queen Elizabeth. Purser and Clinton's patriotism is demonstrated by their shouts of "Saint *George*, and amaine for the Queene of *England*" (sig. B3) as they board a Turkish man of war. The pamphlet also casts Elizabeth in a role of patronage, describing her as "ever a Royall incourager of all brave and resolute spirits" (sig. C6), who attempts "rather by her clemency to reclaime them, than by her Power utterly to subvert them" (sigs. C6-C6v) and promises Purser and Clinton "imployment in her owne Navy, so they would prove themselves true and Loyall Subiects" (sig. C6v). Nonetheless, just as Clinton declines the Merchant's offer of employment in *Fortune by Land and Sea* (4.1.1621–38), the pirates reject what they term as Elizabeth's "faire and sugred promises" (sig. C7v). Recognizing that the Admiralty Office might prosecute them despite Elizabeth's pardon, they choose rather "to hazard their fortunes bravely abroad, than by submitting themselves endanger their lives basely at home" (sig. C4). This passage exposes a key distinction between Elizabeth's promise of clemency and James's grants of pardons exclusively to pirates of higher status, aligning the image of Elizabeth with a populist celebration of the national community. But in order to justify Elizabeth's ultimate execution of figures who otherwise seem to celebrate her regime, Purser and Clinton must be represented as actively rejecting incorporation into the body politic.

Similar to their depiction in Heywood's pamphlet, Purser and Clinton's final speeches in *Fortune by Land and Sea* provide a sympathetic rendering of the pirates and their contributions to the English nation. These speeches cast the pirates in terms of a nostalgic narrative of Elizabethan heroism, as when Purser portrays himself and his fellow pirates as representatives of a past golden age:[42]

> how many gallant spirits,
> Equal with us in fame, shall this gulf swallow,
> And make this silver oare to blush in blood?
> How many Captains that have aw'd the seas
> Shall fal on this infortunate peece of land?
> Some that commanded Ilands, some to whom
> The Indian Mines pay'd Tribute, Turk vayl'd:
> But when we that have quak'd, nay troubled flouds,
> And made Armadoes fly before our stream,
> Shall founder thus, be split and lost,
> Then be it no impeachment to their fame,
> Since *Purser* and bold *Clinton* bide the same. (5.1.2200–11)

Purser commemorates Elizabethan victories, from the seizure of Spanish bullion (represented as "tribute") to Essex and Raleigh's 1597 raid on the Azores ("commanded Ilands") and the resonant memory of the defeat of the Armada. The vision of a lost prospect of Spanish gold, once possible through the Elizabethan privateers, served as a recurring Jacobean fantasy.[43] Purser's image of Spanish tribute demonstrates how the Jacobean nostalgia for Elizabethan mariners served to inflate their reputation, for despite 235 raids on Spanish America between 1585 and 1603, the English never once intercepted the Spanish *flota*, the yearly bullion fleet.[44] Purser's fanciful vision of an English humiliation of the dominant Ottoman Empire ("Turk vayl'd") is similarly ironic: in an Elizabethan context, Purser obscures how Elizabeth's regime actively sought alliances with the Kingdom of Morocco and the Ottoman empire; in a Jacobean context, Purser's reference deflects attention from the alternative alliances forged between English renegades and North African sultanates.[45]

In contrast to these foreign contexts, Purser depicts the unnamed commanders of privateering vessels as shipwrecked on "this infortunate peece of land" (5.1.2204), the execution site at Wapping, a location that stands in for the condition of mariners in Jacobean England. Despite Purser's elegy for the loss of a generation of English privateers, the Jacobean period also witnessed the continued recuperation and social advancement of some pirate captains, including several members of the Jacobean Admiralty Commission (Sir Henry Mainwaring, Richard Gifford, and Sir John Pennington).[46] Purser's lament that the "quick sand" of Wapping "shall swallow many a brave Marine souldier, / Of whose valour, experience, skil, and Naval discipline, / Being lost, I wish this land may never have need" (5.1.2237–40) offers both a yearning for the heyday of Elizabethan privateering and an ironic commentary on the complicity of Jacobean policy in the economy of piracy.

Heywood's play and pamphlet, like the anonymous *Lives, Apprehensions* text, culminate their narratives with an extensive focus on the execution of pirates. The centrality of this moment in these texts is appropriate given the ways these executions served to articulate the effects of the state's power on its subjects in the early modern period. The execution of pirates constituted a ritualistic process of expulsion. To serve as a visible reminder of the extension of state authority over its subjects abroad, pirates were returned to the metropolis in order to be punished for their crimes committed beyond the boundaries of the nation. Convicted pirates were taken to Wapping, a district on the north bank of the Thames, where they were hanged at low water. The site of execution was symbolically situated at the border of land and sea so that the corpses of the pirates would be drowned and consequently torn apart by the elements. Placed at the border of land and sea, pirates were expelled from the political body of the state while remaining at the boundary to the sea, thus serving as emblems of the dangers of leaving the geographic confines of the state and corollary allegiance to the nation. This procedure also served as a form of disavowal, for it was not the state but the sea, whose dangers and lack of order pirates were able to exploit, which ultimately destroyed the body of the prisoner. As Purser observes, "[w]e now are captives that made others thrall / Thus ebbs may flow, and highest tydes may fall" (4.5.1845–46). Clinton similarly internalizes this distinction, blaming fate (and not the state) for the nature of his death and rationalizing that it is at Wapping "[w]here now the fates have cast us on the shelf / To hang 'twixt air and water" (5.1.2193–94). Despite the efforts of antipiracy texts such as *Lives, Apprehensions* to depict the mass arraignments and executions of pirates as the culmination of personal dramas of voluntary transgression, Purser exposes the effects of this punitive bureaucratic machine by suggesting that these en masse executions will make the "silver oare," the badge of the civil court officer overseeing maritime affairs, "blush in blood" (5.1.2202).

In his final speech before his execution in *Fortune by Land and Sea*, Purser imagines the ultimate security of mercantile shipping, ensured through the punishment of the pirate:

> But now our Sun is all setting, night comes on,
> The watery wilderness ore which we raign'd,
> Proves in our ruins peaceful, Merchants trade
> Fearless abroad as in the rivers mouth,
> And free as in a harbor, then fair *Thames*,
> Queen of fresh water, famous through the world,
> And not the least through us, whose double tides
> Must o'rflow our bodies, and being dead,
> May thy clear waves our scandals wash away,
> But keep our valours living; now lead on
> *Clinton*, thus arm in arm lets march to death,
> And wheresoe'r our names are memoriz'd,
> The world report two valiant Pirats fell,
> Shot betwixt wind and water; so farewel. (5.1.2257–70)

The execution of the pirates provides the means to pacify the "watery wilderness" of maritime disorder and establish the peaceful conditions necessary for maritime exchange, so that the ocean may be likened to a safe harbor for merchant shipping. The Thames serves as a central symbol in Purser's speech: the main conduit and "mouth" of English commerce, the river spreads English fame and commodities through the world, analogous to "fresh water" reaching its tributaries. But the security of the Thames is obtained only by its course *through* the body of the pirate, "whose double tides / Must o'rflow our bodies" (5.1.2263–64). The doubling force of the Thames's tide both washes away the scandal of piracy (as it sails forth merchant ships) and keeps the pirates' "valours living." The metaphor implies that the pirates may be recuperated only through the destruction of their bodies; their "names are memoriz'd" (5.1.2268) only as a result of the destruction of their physical being by the elements: "Shot betwixt wind and water" (5.1.2270). The passage attests to the indebtedness of English commercial prosperity and nascent national identity to the figure of the pirate. While Purser casts maritime prosperity as economically dependent upon his and Clinton's execution, the nationalist sentiments that motivate the expansion of international commerce rely, instead, upon the preservation of their memory. The "double tide" associated with the Thames reflects this more pervasive doubleness of memory and forgetting in the representation of nation: the passage exposes how the economic indebtedness of the Jacobean state to the inroads made by Elizabethan privateers must be disavowed and forgotten, while at the same time these figures are memorialized as exemplars of national service and fortitude.[47]

In *Discipline and Punish*, Foucault casts the public execution as the archetypal manifestation of the early modern state's ability to reconstitute its threatened sovereignty through a spectacle of power. However, Foucault adds, the public execution functioned not only as the epitome of the successful reimposition of institutional authority over transgressing subjects; it also served as "a sort of battleground around the crime, its punishment and its memory," a process of contestation that he links to early modern practices of carnival.[48] Therefore, the state, its transgressing subjects, and those who observe and participate in the public execution all engage in a struggle of interpretation over the meaning of the ritual, a battle that extends beyond the actual performance of the execution. As Purser's final lines indicate, while the pirates' execution symbolically enacts state power on the bodies of its subjects, the interpretation of this ritual is subject to alternative meanings that accrue through its circulation in popular cultural memory. Thomas Laqueur argues that the carnivalesque environment of early modern executions served to undermine the representation of state power and instead place the crowd as the central actor of events. Borrowing from Stallybrass and White's *The Politics and Poetics of Transgression* (1986), Laqueur emphasizes how "carnival is part of the process through which social classification takes place.... Executions on this account are just such a classificatory and socially constitutive ritual, defining the boundaries between state and society, between the propertied and the propertyless, between high and low."[49] However, this reconstitution of cultural boundaries through ritual may bring about the subversion as well as reinforcement of social hierarchies. Heywood's texts similarly contain a carnivalesque dimension in the form of the Clown, who announces a garbled version of the queen's proclamation against Purser and Clinton.[50] Significantly, this moment of subversion is doubly displaced, occurring at the moment of proclamation rather than execution and set during Elizabeth's reign rather than James's, testifying to the efforts of state power to dispel a carnivalesque element from the ritualistic execution of pirates.

The execution of pirates nonetheless offered the opportunity to critique the inconsistencies and hypocrisy of state policies toward piracy and the maritime laboring classes. Yet, because lower-class mariners themselves were either deprived of narrative agency, as in *Lives, Apprehensions,* or elegized as necessary sacrifices to enable legitimate commercial expansion, as in Purser's scaffold speech in *Fortune by Land and Sea,* this critique had to come from elsewhere. Significantly, it was offered by the most prominent victim of the Jacobean suppression of piracy, Sir Walter Raleigh. Unlike Harris, Jennings, Purser, and Clinton, pirate captains who were characterized by their internalization of state power at their executions, Raleigh used his conviction as the opportunity to critique state policy. Raleigh, after his imprisonment on charges of pirating Spanish vessels, for which he was eventually executed in 1618, was reported to have said, "[h]e would have taken the Plate fleet if he could, and when told that it would be piracy, he said none were called pirates for milions, but only for small things, and he could have given 10,000 here and 20,000 there, and yet have 600,000 for the King."[51] Raleigh's transformation from heroic Elizabethan privateer to condemned Jacobean pirate demonstrates how changing state policies blurred the boundaries of subject and outlaw. Yet Raleigh's reconstituted role also placed him in a position from which to critique the Jacobean state, allowing him to expose the mercenary desires for profit that motivated the suppression of piracy. And, as Raleigh makes clear, this policy exclusively targeted the lower classes. Raleigh's own imprisonment would seem to belie this statement, of course, perhaps revealing how his critique might have been prompted by the resentment he felt from being treated as one of lower status, rather than being recognized as one who had-and could again-bring millions into the national treasury.

Raleigh's execution levels social distinctions, placing him alongside Purser, Clinton, Arnold, Harris, Jennings, and other commoners executed for piracy in the Elizabethan and Jacobean periods. Unlike George Clifford, earl of Cumberland, or Lord High Admiral Charles Howard, earl of Nottingham, Raleigh could not remain content with the profits gained from Elizabethan privateering. In this sense, he also resembles the pirate captains in his nostalgic desire to return to a previous era of heroic action and quasi-sanctioned profit. Following Raleigh's execution in 1618, many late Jacobean and early Caroline texts similarly expressed a nostalgia for the age of Raleigh and Drake. Narratives of Elizabethan-era voyages were often reprinted during the period, especially to capitalize on the revived anti-Spanish sentiment of the 1620s. Sir Francis Drake's nephew and namesake edited his uncle's West Indies journal, published as *Sir Francis Drake Reuiued: Calling vpon this Dull or Effeminate Age, to Folowe his Noble Steps for Golde & Siluer* (1626), while the notes of Francis Fletcher, Drake's chaplain, were printed as *The World Encompassed by Sir Francis Drake* (1626). In addition, Thomas Scott published two texts that evoked the memory of long-dead Elizabethan heroes: *Robert Earle of Essex* (1624), which presented Essex's admonitory advice to his nation from beyond the grave, and *Sir Walter Rawleighs Ghost, or, Englands Forewarner* (1626), in which Raleigh's ghost appeared in order to torment the Spanish ambassador Gondomar and reveal a Spanish conspiracy against England.[52] These texts resurrected images of an active English masculinity that could remain untouched from the foreign contamination associated with Jacobean negotiations with Spain. If Raleigh and Drake evoked populist ideas of national identity, this narrative, like the image of Elizabeth seen in other Jacobean texts on piracy, could exist only as a form of nostalgia, represented by dead privateers who could merely take on a spectral identity. The present Stuart state, on the other hand, was characterized by an effeminating affiliation with Spain.

The Jacobean efforts to suppress piracy are of crucial importance to histories of internal colonialism, class relations, and nationhood due to the central developments relating to national identification and class mobility that were furthered through this legislative program. The reconstitution of the Elizabethan privateer as outlawed pirate functioned to transpose a powerful populist articulation of nationhood, the popular sentiment for the heroism of the Elizabethan privateers, to a nostalgic invocation of lost national prestige and unity. The figures who had earlier served to rally national identification assumed, instead, a spectral form. Their continued presence served to haunt competing Jacobean efforts for national unity through legitimate commercial expansion, exposing the more fundamental absence of Jacobean aspirations for national unity.[53] The nostalgia for the Elizabethan era that resulted from the Jacobean suppression of piracy thus produced an unintended separation of national affiliation from state power, a populist form of nationhood able to articulate a critique of the effects of Jacobean state formation and commercial expansion on England's increasingly vulnerable underclass. Despite the popular sentiment evoked by Drake or Raleigh, this critique was revealed more strongly through the ambivalent depiction of less elite Elizabethan and Jacobean pirates such as Purser, Clinton, Harris, and Jennings. In the representation of these commoners, one witnesses how official efforts to suppress piracy were linked to anxieties relating to the forms of social mobility opened up through cultural exchange, the new possibilities for social and geographic movement made available to even the lowliest of subjects. It is therefore necessary to link the attempted Jacobean suppression of piracy to a more general effort to regulate the mobility and agency of subjects who had moved beyond the borders of the nation.

***

IRREGULAR TRAVELERS: APOSTASY SERMONS AND NATION SPACE

In Max Weber's classic formulation, the state achieves its authority through a successful monopolization of the legitimate uses of physical force, a correlation of state power and violence that has been further analyzed in the work of Anthony Giddens and Charles Tilly, among others.[54] In her study *Mercenaries, Pirates, and Sovereigns,* Janice E. Thomson expands Weber's analysis, exploring the ways that the early modern state's increasing centralization of power was effected not only through a monopolization of violence within the territory of the state but also as a result of a delegitimization of extraterritorial activities such as privateering, piracy, and mercenary service.[55] Thomson's thesis is most relevant to this study in terms of one aspect of this process: the state's efforts to maintain control over subjects who had passed outside its borders. As a complement to my earlier discussion of the symbolic expulsion of subjects from the body politic in the execution of pirates, the final portion of this chapter will examine how rituals of conversion and incorporation were used to reify cultural borders. In this section, I will examine the depiction of the "renegade" (convert to Islam) in the context of a more general debate relating to the agency of travelers and potential flexibility of cultural identity made possible by travel and cultural exchange.[56] The anxieties concerning the mobility of subjects often fixated on the traveler and potential apostate's ability to cross and even transgress the geographic and cultural boundaries of the nation; in addition, they also helped formulate the conditions under which travelers could return home and be reintegrated into their communities. This final section will analyze a key example of the concern for cultural boundaries, Archbishop Laud's ceremony for the reconversion of sailors who had converted to Islam while held captive in North Africa, and will also discuss sermons attesting to the implementation of this ritual. The apostasy sermons demonstrate the employment of spatialized rituals to offset fears regarding the potential of travel and exchange to subvert cultural borders.

The Jacobean state instituted a number of legislative efforts to regulate the movement of subjects passing beyond the boundaries of the nation. In 1607, James had prohibited travel outside England without the prior authorization of the monarch and members of the Privy Council, exempting only previously licensed merchants and the sailors and factors in their employ.[57] A proclamation in the following year further required that oaths of allegiance be given to returning travelers, with the exception of those "being knowen Merchants or men of some qualitie."[58] The Jacobean regulation of travel focused primarily on the lower classes, suspect groups whose allegiance was maintained through licensing and surveillance. Merchants and factors, on the other hand, were seen as self-regulating subjects whose obligations to capital and property would ensure their loyalty to state and commerce. Nonetheless, the Jacobean state also concurrently recognized the limitations of such centralized control over travel; a 1606 proclamation delegated the responsibility of conferring passports to the commissioners of English ports, thereby conceding that the sheer number of travelers prevented the implementation of direct surveillance over travel.[59]

The legislative efforts (and failures) to regulate cultural exchange necessitated, therefore, an alternative means to structure the experience of travel, producing a large number of "directions for travelers," texts that offered advice and guidance on travel.[60] For the most part, these texts were intended for an elite audience of readers engaged in ambassadorial embassies and other forms of state service, international commerce, and fashionable travel. The title of Thomas Palmer's travel advice text, *An Essay of the Meanes how to Make our Trauailes, into Forraine Countries, the More Profitable and Honourable* (1606), reveals the increasing symbolic capital allotted to foreign travel, which was seen as contributing both to the English economy and national prestige. Palmer's text includes several charts presenting a detailed classification of types of travelers (see figure 2.1). Central to this taxonomy of persons engaged in exchange, however, is the category of "irregular" travelers. Despite their marginal position in the chart illustrating classes of travelers, Palmer exposes their central place in his narrative by stating in his prefatory comments to the reader that his text is intended to "encounter the imputation to our Countrie" as

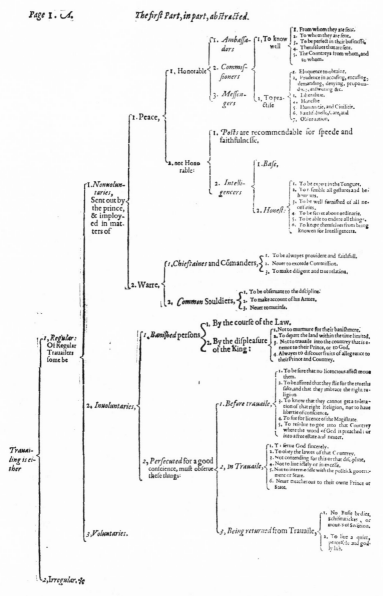

Figure 2.1 A taxonomy of travelers, including "Irregular travelers," from Thomas Palmer, *An essay of the Meanes how to make our Trauailes into forraine Countries, the more profitable and honourable* (1606). Reproduced by permission of the Folger Shakespeare Library.

a supplier of outlaws, fugitives, and pirates:

> seeing not only we here in *England* may, as all other Nations in the
> world doe, account it a shame that there should be so many and such
> fugitives (vnworthie of the honourable name of Trauailers) as this Land
> hath affourded hertofore, who haue not afterwards made conscience of
> their owne wayes nor of others, but like the most pernitious haue com-
> municated with all euill and mischiefe in their trauailes, to subject their
> own Countrie, Princes, State, Parents, friends and all that is held deare
> in this life; let me discouer so much of my secretest affection vnto thee
> (discreet Reader) that the preuenting hereof, was one of the first
> motiues to undertake this worke.[61]

Palmer links pirates with other "fugitives," subjects whose travel
serves to disguise their lack of national affiliation, groups including
foreign spies, Catholic seminarians, and even renegades. Palmer
counters the reputation of England as a nation of pirates and fugitives
by generalizing the problem, asserting that such figures are not specific or endemic to England and that England shares other nations'
condemnation of such practices. For Palmer, Englishmen who leave
the geographic confines of the realm run the risk of degenerating
from "the honourable name of Trauailers": the possibilities of travel
loosen the constraints imposed by local and national authorities,
allowing travelers to be exposed to forms of "euill and mischiefe" that
may by extension contaminate their families and home nation.
Expressing concerns that would later be shared by Archbishop Laud,
Palmer locates the dangers of piracy and conversion not merely in
their ubiquity, or how they opportunistically profit from sanctioned
forms of cultural exchange, but particularly in their invisibility. After
their return to England, travelers may easily hide their pasts, their
former identities as pirates or apostates, from their communities
and even their own consciences. Palmer casts as his own "secretest
affection" to the reader the desire to expose these secret identities to
public scrutiny, which he presents as his primary motive in writing the
text. Thus, although Palmer casts these "irregular travelers" as an
exception to the rule of travel, a marginal and sterile branch in his
family tree of travelers, and dissevers pirates and renegades from the
English body politic, he ultimately reveals the symbolic centrality of
the possibility of these subjects' transgressiveness to his entire effort
to codify and regulate travel.

The Elizabethan pirates analyzed in the previous section—in both
their historical and fictional forms—were depicted as embodying an
expression of Englishness that endured despite their travels and even

their ultimate punishment by the state. In the Jacobean period, by contrast, the figure of the renegade was associated with a dangerously permeable subject position, one that testified to the ways in which travel and cultural exchange could potentially destabilize national identification. Jacobean texts consequently gave greater visibility to these "irregular travelers," thereby revealing the large number of early modern English pirates, mariners, travelers, and captives who had actively rejected English culture and national identity, whether by targeting English shipping, assimilating within their host cultures (most often in North Africa), or converting to Islam.[62] For Jacobean commentators, conversion to Islam presented a disturbing vision of the potential forms of social mobility opened up to travelers and mariners, for it offered these subjects the prospect of advancement in Muslim society: renegades became Ottoman grand viziers, North African administrators (*qaids*), and corsair admirals (*raïs*), while the Janissaries, the military officers of the Ottoman Empire, swelled their ranks with Europeans.[63] As the former captive Francis Knight commented, "in the great *Turkes Soray*, who are his *Courtiers*? who his *Councellors*? who his *Vissiers*? who his Bashawes? who his greatest Instruments, but these denyers, the sonnes of Christians."[64] Although Sir Thomas Sherley condemns renegades as being "for the most parte roagues, & the skumme of people," he nonetheless acknowledges the economic causes of their conversion, for those "vnable to liue in Christendomme, are fledde to the Turke for succoure & releyffe."[65]

Similar to the Jacobean regulation of travel, texts concerned with the number of English converts to Islam often fixated on the lower classes. Singling out the dangers of conversion that threaten young merchants and mariners, who are not "of rype aage & mature vnder-standinge," Sir Thomas Sherley implies a direct relationship between location, customs, and character in his warning how "that place [Constantinople] & conuersation with infidelles doeth mutch cor-rupte,...in euerye 3 yeere that they staye in Turkye they loose one article of theyre faythe."[66] A comment in Richard Hakluyt's "Discourse of Western Planning" (1584) reveals the class-based repercussions stemming from the conversion of mariners, as Hakluyt notes "howe divers have bene undon by their servauntes wch have become Renegadoes, of whome by the custome of the Contrie their M^{rs} can have no manner of recoverye, neither call them into Justice."[67] Whereas the character of the Merchant in *Fortune by Land and Sea* bewails the property losses incurred by piracy, Hakluyt casts apostasy as a loss of human property in the form of the servants who have become renegades and placed themselves under the protection of foreign leaders, thereby exempting themselves from legal punishment in England.

The work of Nabil I. Matar has examined the variety of cultural exchanges between England and Islamic areas in the early modern period, emphasizing how the networks of affiliation established by travelers, converts, and other figures attest to a more immediate and complicated relationship between East and West in the early modern period than has previously been recognized.[68] Matar's paradigm alters significantly the model of Orientalism formulated initially by Edward Said, wherein Orientalist discourse is associated with "commemorative *absence*."[69] In Said's argument, the Orientalist scholar studies the archives of a temporally distant Oriental past, asserting the East's present as a form of degeneration; more generally, the Orient circulates as an imaginary landscape spatially removed from the metropolitan site of Orientalist textual production. Yet this sense of geographic and imaginative distance between Western Europe and the Islamic world fully emerged only as a result of the imposition of a colonial, "executive" authority in the nineteenth century.[70] The early modern period demonstrates a form of Orientalism that defines the East not in terms of distance and absence but as an encroaching and threatening presence. This was particularly the case in early seventeenth-century England, where pirate ships from Ottoman-controlled North Africa had begun to make repeated incursions on the English coast. Corsairs from the Barbary Coast had entered the Thames channel in 1616 and 1617, while raids on West Country and Irish coastline settlements occurred in 1625, 1631, and 1640, resulting in the abduction of several hundred English people.[71] Including those taken at sea, an estimated 3,228 English people and 184 ships were captured between 1616 and 1642.[72] Although most captives remained in Ottoman territories for the rest of their lives, extensive redemption efforts led to the repatriation of many prisoners. As a result of these efforts, authorities became concerned over this population of returning captives and whether any had converted to Islam and become renegades or "apostates" (a term that refers more specifically to religious conversion) during their travels and captivity.

The final portion of this chapter will examine the cultural anxieties that centered on the figure of the returning captive. The texts that I will discuss include the elaborate three-week public ritual for the reconversion of apostates established by William Laud, archbishop of Canterbury, two sermons given to accompany these reconversions— William Gouge's *A Recovery from Apostacy* (1639) and Edward Kellet

and Henry Byam's *A Retvrne from Argier* (1628)—and a text
written to encourage redemption efforts, Charles Fitzgeffrey's
Compassion Towards Captives (1637). In contrast to the forms of
distance and commemorative absence that define so many of the post-
Enlightenment examples of Orientalist discourse analyzed by Said,
these texts emphasize the spatial immediacy and fluidity of the
encounter of East and West, Islam and Anglicanism, in the Caroline
period, a liminality best represented by the figure of the returning
captive and apostate. In my analysis of this figure, I wish to highlight
the ways that the demand for a coherent and unified Anglican identity in the Laudian period was fixated with the uncertain status of
boundaries and margins, the ability of subjects to pass beyond spatial
and subjective ties to the community. The apostasy sermons attempt
to reincorporate their suspect subjects through a reenactment of the
performative identities of apostates, making use of the spatial immediacy of the encounter with Islam in order to contain discontented
social groups marked by subordinate class position and economic
disenfranchisement.

A large number of redeemed captives returned from North Africa
in 1637, presenting Anglican authorities with the dual problem of
determining the identity of returning apostates and ensuring a coun-
terbalancing conversion that could legitimate their return to the
Church of England. After consulting with the bishops of London,
Ely, and Norwich, William Laud, the archbishop of Canterbury,
devised an elaborate ceremony for the reconversion of apostates.
Laud's directive attempted to devise an appropriate "penitential
form" to denote reconversion, an emphasis on producing a countervailing performance of penance to negate the act of apostasy. The ritual addressed, in Laud's words, how former captives and converts
"having renounced their Savior, and become Turks, might be read-
mitted into the Church of Christ, and under what penitential
form."[73] Laud stipulated that the apostate should first face a hearing
before the Bishop's court, "his detection or confession" (372), after
which the official decree of his excommunication would be
announced in his home parish. After he has had several conferences
with his minister, a notice of his penance was to be announced in the
parish church. The penitent then began a three-week public ritual.
Significantly, his reintegration to church and community was represented in spatial terms, a process that began with the apostate standing in the church porch (or outside the church door), where he
requested the forgiveness of parishioners while dressed "in a penitent
fashion in a white sheet, and with a white wand in his hand" (372).

On the second Sunday, the apostate entered the structure of the church following the *Te Deum* and kneeled during the service, after which he delivered a public submission (the text of which Laud includes in his directive) and returned to the church porch. On the third Sunday, the apostate was seated near the minister's pew, and he delivered another rather lengthy text, asking for the pardon of the entire congregation, a request then repeated by the parish priest; following another text delivered by the apostate (this time while bowing his head to the floor), the priest absolved his sin, laying the Book of Common Prayer on his head, and removed his penitential robe, allowing him to receive the Eucharist.[74]

Laud's concerns were shared by a number of Anglican divines, some of whom delivered sermons that accompanied the reconversion of renegades. William Gouge's sermon, *A Recovery from Apostacy* (1639), was given on the occasion of the reconversion of a cook's apprentice named Vincent Jukes. The fact that the ceremony warranted much attention is revealed by Gouge early in his sermon: the vicar of Jukes's parish of Stepney, near the east London docks, had conferred with Laud and arranged to bring in Gouge as a "star speaker" to mark the event. As noted by Margo Todd, the symbolic importance of Jukes's reconversion ceremony is evident due to its ability to unite the disparate theological and political interests of adversaries like Laud and Gouge.[75] Gouge begins with the selection of his sermon's text, Luke 15:31 ("He was lost, and is found"), and quickly places the spotlight on Jukes, as he directs the congregation's attention to the penitent, names him, and supplies a brief biography.[76] First apprenticed to a cook on a voyage to Newfoundland, Jukes was taken captive on a subsequent voyage to Genoa and sold at Algiers, where he was exchanged several times, from the vice-regent, to the leader's brother, to a Moor, whose daily beatings forced Jukes to convert to Islam. Jukes continued to be passed down the Algerian social ladder, and he was ultimately sold to a Greek renegade and placed in service aboard his pirate ship. Aided by two English captives and another renegade, the captives mutinied, killing some of their captors and selling the remaining Turks as slaves in Spain. Having divided the profits from the ship's goods between themselves, Jukes's partners converted to Catholicism and remained in Spain, while Jukes chose to return to England (sigs. B1v-B3).

After this initial biography, Gouge quickly transforms Jukes's story into "a *Parabolicall History*, or Historicall Parable" in his sermon: "The *Place* whereon it was represented, is the *Church*. For out of the Church did the Prodigall depart: Into the Church did he returne: And most of the memorable matters therein related, are related as performed in the Church" (sig. B4).[77] Gouge positions Jukes's case as an exegetical rendering of Luke's parable of the Prodigal Son (sigs. B4v-C1), establishing a correlation between Jukes's departure from the Church, or "his Father's house," and his progress to apostasy (sig. C1). Gouge theatricalizes the process of Jukes's reconversion, creating a list of characters seemingly drawn from medieval allegorical drama: God, penitent apostate, lewd tempters, covetous worldling, hard-hearted neighbors, obedient servants, and sympathizing friends (sigs. B4-B4v). In "DissemiNation," Homi Bhabha analyzes how the representation of a national community is split between the "pedagogical," the invocation of historical tradition through narratives of the past, and the "performative," the speech acts that attempt to make the past manifest and create a community through the signification or "performance" of a present identity. Bhabha argues that this cultural identity creates fissures at multiple levels: in part, between the past and its present invocations, but, more fundamentally, between the attempted monological signification of community and the alternative narratives that it effaces.[78] By insistently generalizing from Jukes's story, and reinscribing his narrative on a parabolic and allegorical level, Gouge attempts to link the pedagogical matrix of his sermon with its performative task, producing a countervailing penance and reconversion to reincorporate Jukes within the community. The parabolic space of the church and the scriptural traditions from which Gouge draws his sermon also become linked to the performative place of the pulpit, the site of his and Jukes's performance of spatial and imaginative reintegration with the congregation. Yet this process effaces Jukes's personal history of economic displacement and diaspora, an often involuntary journey that took him from England to Newfoundland, Genoa, Algiers, and Spain. By recentering Jukes's narrative in the Church, Gouge reconstructs the parish—and thus England—as "home."

Near the conclusion of his sermon, Gouge reveals more candidly the cultural stakes implicit in Jukes's reconversion, directly addressing Jukes and requesting his assistance in encouraging other renegades to return to the Church (sig. N1). Gouge had earlier alluded to the potential presence of other apostates among the population of returning captives, and even among his auditors, stating "I feare, I feare, that there are some even now here present...that have played *Renegadoes*" (sig. C4v) and yet not appealed to the Church like Jukes. Although the anxiety expressed by Gouge concerning the number of apostates who had returned undetected to their communities would seem to be an exaggeration, Gouge's fears were validated in at least one instance: a mariner named Thomas Norton had been captured by pirates and taken captive in Algiers in 1620, where he converted to Islam and engaged in piracy until he was able to ransom himself and return to Dartmouth. Norton, who did not seek redress from Anglican authorities, lived inconspicuously as a carpenter until he was ultimately discovered in 1637 by fellow released captives who had known him in North Africa.[79]

Ten years earlier, during his tenure as bishop of Bath and Wells, William Laud had initiated the reconversion ceremony for an anonymous sailor in the West Country maritime community of Minehead in Somerset.[80] The sermons preached separately on that occasion by Edward Kellet and Henry Byam were later published as *A Retvrne from Argier* (1628).[81] Together with Gouge's sermon, they provide the only examples of extant apostasy sermons. Like Gouge's sermon, Kellet's concludes with a request that anyone in the congregation with "like offences, which yet lye hid" should make "publike acknowledgement of their sinnes" (sig. G3). Gouge and Kellet attempt to institute a theater of conscience among their parishioners, an attempt to make visible the hidden motives and secret allegiances of their auditors in order for them to give consent and declare themselves as conforming members of the congregation and, by extension, a unified national community.

The texts of both Laud and Gouge had attempted to protect the apostate during his vulnerable transition to reintegration into the community. Laud's directive, for instance, stipulated that the penitent should not be taunted by boys while standing outside the church door, while Gouge counseled the Stepney parishioners not to upbraid or shun Jukes but allow him to reenter the social and commercial traffic of the community.[82] Kellet, on the other hand, recognizes a greater need to enforce conformity in his maritime congregation. Kellet finds the parishioners too willing to unconditionally forgive a penitent "out of a Compassion vncharitably-charitable," which, for him, raises the question of whether "Diuerse present, haue runne the same course, with the delinquent (though it cannot be proued as yet)" (sig. F4v). The invisible threat of apostates returning inconspicuously to their communities and resuming their identities as Englishmen is rendered, instead, as a form of collective guilt in which the parishioners themselves are transformed into renegades.

Kellet casts doubt on the stories of those who converted under duress, like Jukes and the unnamed sailor whose reconversion is commemorated in his sermon, because of the rarity of forced conversions in Islamic cultures: "we haue heard and read, that the Turkes compell none to their Religion" (sig. E4). For Kellet, the mariner's conversion was motivated by a desire for social advancement, not prompted by coercion. The message of his sermon, which derives its text from Galatians 5.2 ("If yee be circumcized, Christ shall profit you nothing" [sig. B1]), attempts to counter the possibilities of social and economic mobility enabled by conversion to Islam. In his text, Gouge had also emphasized the unprofitable exchange that conversion exacts upon the body of the apostate, speculating that even if in his audience "there are some that have played Renegadoes," the evidence of conversion revealed on their bodies would inevitably expose that fact and preclude the possibility of disguising their past allegiance (sig. C4v). The loss of mariners and factors to captivity and conversion provides a loss of human capital for both the church and national economy, one from which Kellet suspects apostates economically benefit, for these men, "being intrusted with much goods of their master, turne Turkes, to be masters of those goods; destroying their soules to cozen the honest-braue Merchants-Aduenturers" (sig. F2). In Kellet's formulation, apostasy is not merely theft but also a form of class warfare that allows a subaltern class to become the masters over commodities and capital, enabling them to control the terms of international commerce.

But if apostasy is likened to theft, allowing a subaltern class to escape the jurisdiction of their masters, Kellet reinscribes apostasy as a loss exacted on the body of the apostate. Kellet designates the donning of the Turban as a "capital" crime that signifies a complete reconstitution of allegiances: "Thy deforming of thy head, thy *Crimen crinium*, I will call, naturally, morally, in a double sense *Capitale*" (sig. G1). Satiric images of the renegade in dramatic texts frequently allude to Kellet's point, punning on *caput* (head) to refer to circumcision and even castration: in Massinger's *The Renegado* (1624), Vitelli's comic servant Gazet initially denies he will turn Turk due to a fear of circumcision ("Nor dare I barter that commoditie" [1.1.41]), only to later embrace the possibility of castration as a worthy exchange for acquiring the privileges bestowed upon a court eunuch (3.4.50–56).[83]

The emphasis on apostasy as a status-based crime against property, and one that leaves an indelible physical taint on the culprit's own "capital," counterbalances anxieties over the inability of authorities to detect conversion. Kellet demonizes the improvisational abilities of apostates, calling them "*Amphibia*" who "can liue, both on Land and Water, . . . Chamelions which will change colour with euery ayre, and their beliefe, for matters of small moment" (sig. F2). In *The Arte of*

English Poesie (1589), George Puttenham uses the term "amphibology" to refer to the ambiguous uses of language capable of leading
people into rebellion.[84] As Steven Mullaney has shown, the rhetorical
figure of amphibology was associated with a variety of treasonous
acts, from domestic uprisings such as Kett's Rebellion (1549) to the
interrogation of Father Garnet following the Gunpowder Plot.[85] For
Kellet, this rhetorical figure reveals the conjunction of apostasy and
political subversion; in addition, though, it also describes a more
troubling form of social unrest, the ability of a subordinate class to
achieve a mobility of social allegiance and geographic position without
having the signs of this disruption registered and interpreted.

Kellet's anxiety over the ease of conversion and reconversion
focuses on the donning of Turkish clothing, especially the turban,
what Henry Byam in the second sermon calls "that Embleme of
Apostacie, and witnesse of your wofull fall" (sig. L2). For Kellet, the
wearing of Turkish clothing attests to the voluntary nature of the
apostate's conversion: "your yeelding to their allurements, rather
than to their violence" (sig. E4). More threateningly, the turban
signifies a role that may be donned and doffed, reflecting a more
general subversion of boundaries of identity. In this sense, community
affiliation is merely contingent upon one's temporary residence; during
travel, it is thus changed along with one's clothes. As Byam comments, "many hundreds, are Musselmans in Turkie, and Christians at
home; doffing their religion, as they doe their clothes, and keeping a
conscience for euery Harbor wheere they shall put in" (sig. L1v).
Even more dangerous, these "Apostates and circumcised Renegadoes"
often remain undetected: "they can Returne, and (the fact vnknowne)
make profession of their first faith" (sig. L1v). Further demonstrating
the link between costume and custom, some renegade Englishmen
later in the century emblematically suggested their return to their
native country's laws and religion by publicly trampling on their
Turkish turbans and sashes.[86]

The apostasy sermons correlate disruptions in class and national
identity with analogous transformations of clothing. As the recent
work of Valerie Forman has demonstrated, the term "investment"
expanded in meaning in the early seventeenth century, changing from
a definition related to the donning of clothing or conferral of office
to a more modern sense of the term as "capital," money employed to
accumulate interest or additional income through "investment" in
commercial ventures.[87] The earlier senses of investment, as clothing
or sign of office, manifest themselves materially and visibly: the Lord
Mayor's investiture, for example, is represented by his chain of office.

By contrast, capital investments involve abstraction and disappearance, as the material amount of money is converted into the disembodied form of capital, a process that disrupts the mercantilist embodiment of value in coin and bullion. Appropriately, the *OED* locates the first examples defining investment as capital in the early correspondence of the East India Company, speculating that this definition had its roots in the Levant trade that preceded the founding of the Company in 1600.[88] While the term "investment" signals the commercial possibilities opened up through trade in the Levant, these emergent commercial networks also render obsolete the embodiment of value in the visible indices of class status such as clothing or signs of office. Therefore, the anxieties stemming from English travelers' donning of Turkish clothing testify to a social struggle for control of the nascent mechanisms that enabled an unprecedented production of value and wealth. Partly, the fixation on clothing as a sign of class transgression reflects the residual influence of an earlier sense of investment, thereby demonstrating an inability to think of value production or class status except in terms of its visible and material markers. In addition, the comments cited earlier by Kellet reveal a more profound anxiety regarding the power of a subaltern class "to be masters of those goods" (sig. F2), in other words, to control the flow—and thus profits—of emergent forms of capital.

The abstracted and disembodied forms of value produced through capital formation and "investment" share the characteristics of invisibility and inscrutability associated with the renegade. Both capital and laborers must consequently be rendered visible and faithful. Therefore, unlike the degree of cultural autonomy and improvisational license allowed to merchants and elite travelers, mariners and laborers marked by subordinate class position must be made subject to visible demonstrations of allegiance to national and local communities. As mentioned earlier, Jacobean and Caroline regulation of travel manifested a need to institute forms of surveillance and control over laborers traveling beyond the borders of the nation. Mariners returning from captivity were also subjected to examinations by local authorities, procedures used not only to determine possible cases of apostasy but also to gather intelligence on the political and military condition of the Barbary Coast states.[89]

As maritime communities, the Minehead and Stepney congregations who witnessed these apostasy sermons served an integral role in English national and commercial expansion in the early modern period. Singling out those in his audience who "goe downe to the sea in shippes, and occupie your businesse in great waters,"

Byam acknowledges the centrality of the parishioners' labor, admitting that "the state of the world cannot stand without buying and selling, traffique and transportation" (sigs. L2v-L3). In *A Recovery from Apostacy*, Gouge contrasts the labor of mariners and merchants, who are by necessity placed in danger of being taken captive by "the mortall enemies of Christians" (sig. I1), from the unnecessary and voluntary hazards of travel taken on by elite fashionable travelers, those "who goe to sea for pleasure, to be sea-sick, or to see strange countries" (sig. I2). The apostasy sermons must therefore concede the increasingly precarious material life of maritime communities and imagine these communities based upon their economic displacement and geographic dispersal. The sermons reconstitute the parish as a community in flux, emphasizing what John Wall describes as the "processional" arrangement of the Anglican liturgy, a social ritual that embodies social change and disruption in order to reinstate communal forms of continuity and integration.[90]

Whereas Byam's and Gouge's apostasy sermons attempt to manage social change, Charles Fitzgeffrey's *Compassion Towards Captives* (1637), a sermon given to encourage efforts to redeem English captives in North Africa, offers a critique of the destabilizing social effects of capital formation on the laboring classes. Fitzgeffrey expands the threat of conversion exemplified by the figure of the renegade to a national level, warning that North Africa's historical decline from the birthplace of church fathers to the site of "dens of theeves" can be replicated through the emergence of a competitive society in England: "O that *England* may be warned by these sad examples. God can turne great *Britaine* into *Barbary*."[91] Fitzgeffrey represents Islamic culture as a demonic version of mercantilism, where "they make marchandize of *men. Horse-fayres* are not more frequent here then *Men-markets* are there" (sig. B2). Echoing Shylock's reference to "land-rats and water-rats," Fitzgeffrey establishes an analogy between the prospect of captivity and more familiar domestic forms of servitude, warning his audience that even if one avoids captivity merely by staying on land "thou maist fall fowle with *Turkes* at home, *Land-pyrats, Vsurers, Oppressours*, or into some other misery" (sig. F3).[92]

The spatial immediacy of the cultural encounter between Anglicanism and Islam provided the opportunity to examine the importance of domestic tensions of class and status to early modern cultural exchange. Fitzgeffrey even speculates that the recent raids of Barbary corsairs on the English coastline were led by English renegades, who used their cultural knowledge to exact revenge on their former nation:

> And art thou sure if thou adventurest not thy selfe on Sea to be safe on
> land? Though thou com'st not neare the *Turkes* may not they come too
> neare thee?....What threates have they sent us of late that ere long
> they will make some of us see *Algier*? And who were these but some of
> our owne nation turned *Turkes*, threatning to bring us unto their owne
> condition because wee would not free them in season? Can we forget
> that *Tragicall transportation* of our brethren from *Baltamore* into that
> *Babilon*, *Barbary*? All of them *English*, most of them *Cornish* (sig. F3v).

Fitzgeffrey's statement would have evoked very tangible fears for his
Plymouth audience. Pirate ships had begun to make regular incursions on the English coast in the second quarter of the seventeenth
century, particularly in the West Country and Wales.[93] In 1625, a
fleet of 30 Barbary corsairs seized 27 ships and 200 prisoners within
a space of ten days, while in 1640, 60 people were kidnapped from
Penzance.[94] The most notorious raid by North African pirates
occurred with the abduction of 237 people from Baltimore, County
Cork in 1631, to which Fitzgeffrey refers.[95] Ironically, the pirates targeted a fledgling English colony, whose inhabitants had only recently
been transplanted to Ireland. The leader of the raid, as Fitzgeffrey
suggests, had indeed been a renegade, the Dutchman Jan Jansen,
who later changed his name to Morat Rais. It is doubtful, though,
that his conversion resulted from the failure of his government to
redeem him from captivity.[96] The presence of North African pirates in
British waters was often attributed to renegades' motives of revenge:
a popular early modern urban legend accused John Ward and Simon
Danseker, the subjects of Richard Daborne's play, *A Christian
Turn'd Turke* (1612), of having taught North African pirates to sail
past the Straits of Gibraltar, thus enabling them to attack England.[97]
   The raid on the English settlement at Baltimore exemplified
the vulnerability of English cultural identity to Turkish "invasion"
not only due to the scope of the raid but also because the event exemplified a reverse colonialism within British dominions, with a recently
settled plantation in Ireland overrun by foreign invaders. The
Baltimore raid exposed the instability and porousness of the margins
of the British empire. Subsequent efforts to control piracy, therefore,
fixated on the unstable character of the nation's geographic and cultural boundaries. In addition to forbidding ships from coming within
12 miles of the Irish coast, Sir Henry Mainwaring recommended the
commission of a regular naval patrol to guard the English coastline.[98]

Even more unrealistically, Henry Robinson called for a naval blockade of Constantinople, cutting off the pirates at their supposed source.[99] Many commentators turned to the Navy to counter the threat that the presence of pirate ships offered to the integrity of English national borders. In a text reporting the escape of a group of Barbary prisoners, Anthony Munday referred to the Navy as "a second wall (besides that girdle of the Sea that encompasseth her body) to defend our Iland."[100] But the failure of English naval action against Algiers in 1620 and Salé in 1637 demonstrates the irrelevance of the Royal Navy in attempts to suppress piracy, especially since these efforts were linked to subsequent rises in piratical activity.[101] At other times, the presence of Turkish or North African pirate ships off the coast seems to have become commonplace and generally accepted. In a 1618 letter to Sir Thomas Roe, Sir George Carew notes that the numerous ships have not harmed anyone, "although it was in their power," an acknowledgment that counters the image of predatory pirate ships taking advantage of the vulnerable defenses of the English coastline. Carew instead reverses positions of pirate and victim, mentioning how locals had sold fish to the Turkish pirates at exorbitantly high prices.[102]

Perhaps justified by the actions of cunning West Country fishmongers willing to defraud even Turkish pirates, the suspicions of authorities were often directed toward those at home, including maritime communities thought to harbor pirates and trade in stolen goods.[103] Mainwaring's recommendation for naval convoys to guard the English coastline could have been intended as much to block this illicit trade and the alliances it forged between English maritime communities and ostensible national enemies as to protect those communities from raids and abductions. Pirates had long used the Cork coast as a refuge from authorities and market for stolen goods. The raid on the English colony at Baltimore, in fact, may have resulted from the suppression of some of these markets. In his treatise on piracy, Mainwaring called Ireland "the Nursery and Storehouse of Pirates," appropriately so, since Cork harbors had served as his base, as they had for the Jacobean pirate captains Harris and Jennings, until his pardon and more gainful employment by the Royal Navy.[104]

The piratical economy of south Ireland served as a locus of exchange where legal and illicit economies and figures intersected, a space in which the identity of legitimate commerce and its participants was irreducibly blurred. Cork was also the site of one of the most bizarre measures taken to suppress piracy in the early modern period. Sir William Monson, while he served as admiral of the Royal Navy, had sailed to Broad Haven in Cork in order to impersonate Sir Henry Mainwaring, who was still at that time a pirate captain and often traded with Irish coastal settlements. While in disguise, Monson was entertained by the residents of a town known to traffic with pirates. At the height of their festivities, he revealed his identity, informing the villagers that their lives were forfeit for dealing in stolen goods. Witnessing the mass hysteria that ensued, Monson issued a general pardon on the condition that the villagers promised "never to connive again at pirates."[105] Monson's impersonation of the pirate captain Mainwaring demonstrates an effort to reveal and thereby regulate the illegal economies of the lower classes by entering into their systems of exchange. But as with the apostasy sermons, this improvisational power further destabilizes divisions between legitimate and outlawed social roles, casting the positions of admiral and priest as analogous performative categories to those of pirate and apostate.

Monson's impersonation exemplifies an exceptionally successful performance of power in the archive of early modern cultural traffic with the Orient, one that was not replicated with Laud's directive and the apostasy sermons of Gouge, Laud, and Byam. Aside from these texts, no extant records attest to the official reintegration of mariners who had converted to Islam. Despite Kellet's statement that "learned" theologians may be "vpright Iudges of others," and his offer of aid and counsel to his "fellow-Ministers" as well as "the halfe-learned, and the vnlearned" (sig. G2v), it is unlikely that parish priests ever felt compelled to call in leading orators to chastise their parishioners. As Kellet suspected, they seem to have accepted returning members of their maritime congregations from captivity and travel with few questions. Aside from these apostasy sermons, there is no evidence that the elaborate theatrical details of Laud's reconversion ceremony were ever implemented.[106]

The lives of the members of the Stepney, Minehead, and Plymouth congregations addressed in these sermons were inextricably tied to the exigencies of early modern cultural exchange, and a large number had the misfortune to become captives in North Africa.[107] The majority of these captives were never redeemed; despite the efforts of charitable organizations such as Trinity House, or portions reserved from customs and taxes to help redemption efforts, few ever saw England again.[108] Outside of lists of redeemed captives, such as those included in the anonymous *A Relation of the Whole Proceedings Concerning the Redemption of the Captives of Argier and Tunis* (1647) providing the captives' names and prices, few records exist to identify these people. Although a number converted to Islam, most captives spent their lives in domestic service or confined in North African *bagnios* (slave ghettoes), never rising up the Barbary social ladder or becoming renegade corsairs so as to attack European commerce. Although much of this discussion has focused on well-known pirate captains, including some who apostatized, several who were pardoned and held official posts, and others who met their ends at Wapping, not much is known or recorded about the members of their crews: their former occupations, what necessitated their turn to piracy and departure from England, or even their eventual fates. In his discussion of the early modern renegade, Matar has noted how conversion to Islam and assimilation to North African culture was reflected by a disappearance of the apostate from the English state archive.[109] But it was precisely the invisibility of common mariners and apostates, their power to remain undetected, that ultimately thwarted official efforts to suppress, conscript, detect, or reform them. It was this invisibility that ensured their survival.

CHAPTER 3

VENTING TRINCULOS:
The Tempest AND DISCOURSES
OF COLONIAL LABOR

LABOR AND COLONIAL PROMOTIONAL
TEXTS, 1580–1607

A conventional motive ascribed to European colonialism is that it gave states the opportunity to expel their cultural undesirables beyond the borders of the nation. Certainly, early modern England's own use of practices of colonial transportation constitutes a long and varied history, one that traverses three centuries and includes, among many examples, the deportation of Scots and Irish to the American colonies beginning as early as the Jacobean period as well as the settlement of Australia with convict labor in the late eighteenth century. Nonetheless, despite the implicit recognition of England's long history of colonial transportation, scant critical attention has been paid to this topic.[1] This chapter attempts to remedy the remarkable critical silence on this issue and explore the contexts in which policies of what I will term colonial "venting" first began to be formulated.

One of the earliest literary references to the venting of the poor to the colonies is found in *The Tempest*'s "mooncalf" scene (2.2). As the drunken butler Stephano pulls the "lesser legs" of the four-legged, double-voiced "mooncalf" out from under its gabardine, only to find his "good friend Trinculo," Stephano demands to know: "How cam'st thou to be the siege of this mooncalf? Can he vent Trinculos?" (2.2.105–07). Through the metaphor of "venting Trinculos," the image of the jester Trinculo shat out and expelled from a monstrous body, *The Tempest* refers to one of the most dominant ideas expressed in the colonial promotional literature of the early modern period: the use of colonialism as a means to rid England of its poor, masterless, unproductive, and potentially mutinous laboring classes.

For a Jacobean audience, the term "vent" possessed a wide range of associations, including Stephano's sense of the term, the bodily discharge of waste (OED, sb.^{2}, II.9.b and v.^{2}, I.2.b), as well as meanings relating to an escape from a small or confining space (sb.^{2}, I.2.a and v.^{2}, II.11.a), the expression of emotion (sb.^{2}, I.5.a, v.^{2}, I.1.b, and v.^{2}, I.4.a), the circulation of coin (sb.^{2}, I.4.b and v.^{2}, I.8.b), the spread of news and opinion (v.^{2}, I.5.a), and, finally, what the *Oxford English Dictionary* terms as the "obsolete" sense of "to rid (a kingdom) of people" (v.^{2}, I.8.a). At its base, venting is an economic term that refers to trade and exchange (OED, sb.^{3}, 1 and v.^{3}, 1), an idea linked with the mercantilist preoccupation with "vending" and commerce. Its recurring appearance in promotional literature testifies to what Carole Shammas has called "the commercializing of colonization."[2] But in calling attention to the economic foundations of early modern English colonialism, I also wish to deconstruct the pervasive economic concerns that are often held to characterize the English "trading empire." Rather than beginning with an assumed commercial basis for English colonial enterprises, this chapter traces a genealogy of the term venting in order to illustrate, to use the words of Joyce Appleby, how a "conception of a commercial economy took shape."[3] And I wish to emphasize the ways that commercial models of English colonialism emerged in response to perceptible crises regarding the social position of early modern England's laboring classes.

My discussion also intends to chronicle some of the more ephemeral voices and narratives provided by the vented classes themselves, looking for points of critique and opposition to the emergence of commercially based English colonial discourses. As demonstrated by the definitions from the *Oxford English Dictionary*, the multiple valences of "vent" testify to the nuances and ambivalences embedded in this keyword. Thus, while venting illustrates the increasing commodification of labor, as people are vended like goods, and demonstrates the declining status of laborers through a likening of the nation's poor to waste expelled from the body politic, the term also possesses contrary implications, meanings that hint at the potentially liberating aspects of colonial migration—the escape from a confining space, the ability to express previously suppressed opinions or emotions. Thus, the term vent suggests not only the increasingly draconian codification of colonial labor but also a powerful countercurrent in the possibility of colonial liberty, implicitly recognizing the forms of resistance and agency wielded by the same laboring, serving, and masterless classes whose eroded status in early modern England rendered them subject to emergent practices of colonial transportation.

The formulation of colonial labor must be situated in the context of the unprecedented upheavals that affected the position of laborers and the poor in early modern England. The labor crisis of the sixteenth century is often attributed to demographic factors: the most reliable estimates regarding population growth indicate that the population of England grew by 35 percent, or 1.3 million people, in the last six decades of the century.[4] Yet the focus on overpopulation, in early modern promotional texts as well as by later economic historians, obfuscates the foundational role of changing class relations and conditions of production in the reconstitution of labor in the early modern period.[5] Transformations in landholding produced a more fundamental disruption of labor relations, a process that relegated 20 percent of laborers to a permanent surplus pool, with seasonal fluctuations of unemployment reaching up to 50 percent.[6] Alongside agricultural laborers, domestic servants constituted approximately 10–15 percent of the population in England and comprised part of one-quarter to one-third of households in England.[7] At the same time, real wages of laborers and servants declined by half from 1500–1650, with the lowest point coming around 1620.[8] Historians such as Eric Hobsbawm, Immanuel Wallerstein, and Barry Supple have appropriately characterized the sixteenth and seventeenth centuries as an era of economic crisis.[9] During this time, particularly in the half century between the 1570s and 1620s, the period of early modern England's initial formulation of colonial practices and entrance into a colonial economy, the poor suffered the most directly from economic change and, consequently, found themselves rendered as the objects of both the aspirations and anxieties of colonial development.

Contemporary observers, including advocates of colonial efforts, were quite aware of the social and economic crises motivating colonial expansion. In his sermon, *Virginia* (1609), William Symonds lists the abject condition of the poor as the primary of the "Causes to seeke abroad" (sig. D2). What first strikes his attention is overpopulation: "The people . . . doe swarme in the land, as yong bees in a hiue in *Iune*" (sig. D2). However, Symonds extends his metaphor to note how England's economic crises result from more direct social causes, for "[t]he mightier like old strong bees thrust the weaker, and younger, out of their hiues" (sigs. D2-D2v). The insistent references in early modern texts to problems of overpopulation serve to mask the ways that early modern class conflicts resulted not merely from a scarcity of resources but, more fundamentally, from a battle over the control of surplus production.[10] Symonds is extraordinarily direct in his accusations against the improving practices of capitalist landlords, noting how their enclosure of land has necessitated the eviction of their tenants, who, as a result, are "now in many places turned labourer, and can hardly scape the statute of rogues and vagrants" (sig. D2v). He also castigates the urban rich, including shopkeepers who take advantage of the debts of displaced laborers (sigs. D2v-D3). This critique is surprising, considering the fact that many members of his audience, which included the Council of the Virginia Company and various investors and future colonists, were representatives of the rural gentry and urban plutocracy against whom he spoke so strongly.[11] Instead, he unites the disparate Company members as "adventurers," traders who through their overseas colonial and commercial ventures are able to support a population that would otherwise "finde an extreame famine" (sig. D2v).

For Symonds, foreign trade (or "venturing") offers a remedy for domestic crises of labor and poverty. In the early modern period, in fact, international traders were termed "adventurers" so as to distinguish them from domestic merchants, a group whose interests were often opposed to the new trading companies. Symonds thus creates an alliance between the "venturing" classes, an urban bourgeoisie and capitalist gentry, and the "vented" classes, an emergent proletariat of displaced laborers and superfluous apprentices. Writing in the wake of the granting of the Virginia Company's second charter in 1609, Symonds collapses distinctions between investors and laborers, between those who venture their capital and those who venture their own bodies and labor power in the new colony. Other advocates of the project similarly failed to distinguish between investors remaining in England and colonists leaving for Virginia.[12] In a recent article, Andrew Fitzmaurice has reexamined Virginia promotional texts and Company policy in the context of the civic discourses of humanism.[13] This rhetoric attempted to reinforce the mutual obligations of class groups, asserting interdependent social relations as the foundation upon which to construct a national economy. Fitzmaurice's argument reveals a significant utopian aspect of early colonial texts: the desire to use colonial trade and migration as the means to transform displaced and seemingly idle English laborers into a productive force within the domestic economy.

Early promotional literature had emphasized the interdependence of investors and laborers as "adventurers" in the project of colonialism. But by 1611, and the first performance of Shakespeare's *The Tempest*, important distinctions had emerged between investors and laborers in the Virginia enterprise, a reconstitution of class alliances that further abetted a centralized control of capital and helped transform the colony's laborers into a dependent, indentured class.[14] This emerging split between capital and labor in the Virginia colony will be among the concerns of the second and third sections of this chapter. These sections will analyze *The Tempest* alongside one of its key sources, William Strachey's *A True Reportorie of the Wrack, and Redemption of Sir Thomas Gates, Knight* (ca. 1610), as well as in comparison to other contemporary Virginia Company documents that influenced both Shakespeare and Strachey in their representation of the uneasy place of labor in England's American colonies.[15] But in order to establish the context for these texts' consideration of labor, it is first necessary to trace the development of policies of colonial transportation. Therefore, I will begin with a discussion of colonial promotional texts of the 1570s and 1580s, texts that proposed colonial venting as a way to introject the laboring poor into the national economy and thereby reform their previously underproductive status. Through an examination of contemporary anti-vagrant legislation in the period 1576–97, I will explain how the failure of the workhouse economy established by these statutes created a perception of the laboring poor as a commodity unable to be converted into a system of exchange. As a result, colonial venting increasingly became part of a project in both England and Virginia that legitimated stricter forms of social control through an expulsion of subjects from the body politic and entrance into an emerging colonial economy of servitude.

***

Robert Hitchcock's *A Pollitique Platt* (1580) was one of the earliest texts to propose making use of expanding commercial and colonial networks as a means to reform the social position of England's poor and laboring classes.[16] Hitchcock, a Buckinghamshire gentleman and former soldier, elaborates a "plot" to expand the English economy through a national, subsidized fishing industry. Hitchcock's text is noteworthy for its ability to conceive of the English economy in national terms: his plans entail levying money from throughout the country, establishing chief officers in eight principal ports, soliciting payments from major corporate towns, and distributing profits to maintain a permanent stock in 225 decayed towns that will further contribute to poor relief (sigs. bi., di.). The increase in English exports of fish to the Continent will also provide England with a major item to use in exchange for foreign goods, a trade that will increase imports as well as provide a way to pay for them, thus limiting the drain of the country's bullion supply (sig. a.ii.v).

Hitchcock's text reflects a key component of mercantilist economic ideology: the establishment of a national economic policy so as to create conditions for full employment.[17] The main portion of Hitchcock's argument deals with using the fishing industry to employ the poor. Hitchcock proposes that the capital raised by contributions be used to finance the construction of 400 fishing vessels, each to be staffed by a small crew of unemployed mariners along with 12 "of the strong lustie Beggers, or poore men: taken vp through this Lande" (sig. a.ii.). Whereas Hitchcock's view of the role of his fishing enterprise in an intra-European trading context otherwise shows a mercantilist outlook, intent on correcting a trade imbalance and drain of specie by encouraging a nascent national fishing industry, his view of the poor as a productive resource demonstrates the forms of capital underlying his project. In conceptualizing a national economy, Hitchcock transforms the laboring classes into a latent resource, thereby creating a sense of general or abstracted labor contained in the nation's population.

The prefatory poem to the text, written by Hitchcock's brother Frances, emphasizes the common benefits accruing to all social classes through the fishing project: "To profite all"; "excepting none"; "To people of eche degree" (sig. *iiii). Despite this endorsement of the model of the commonwealth, the opening of Hitchcock's text addresses the fundamental ways that the presence of the poor complicates this imagined community. Hitchcock chronicles how the attempts of poor relief and anti-vagrant statutes dating back to the reign of Edward III have not only failed to eliminate idleness and induce productivity through "sharpe and seuere punishement" but may have even exacerbated these problems (sig. a.i.). Recognizing the failures of increasingly draconian Tudor antipoverty measures, Hitchcock proposes an alternative way to reform the poor so that "they will proue good and profitable subiects" (sig. e.i). Significantly, Hitchcock substitutes the punitive disciplinary measures of Tudor England with more positive and productive forms of power that will allow the state to win the consent of the poor, providing them with a livelihood through the state so that they will feel an obligation to support and defend it. Acknowledging the intractable poverty in which a majority of the population lived, Hitchcock concedes that England's poor expect relief and would even support rebellion or invasion so as to alleviate their condition. Hitchcock envisages a scenario in which England's underclass would serve as willing guides to an invading army, domestic and foreign enemies united as the lower classes direct foreign troops in looting the wealth of the rich (sig. e.i.v). But by extending the benefits of the national fishing industry to the poor, granting £20 salaries to conscripted unemployed mariners (sig. c.iii.), the poor are invested into the national economy, associating their own economic self-interest with that of the nation (sig. e.i).[18] In contrast to the previous intransigence of the masterless poor, who seem "past all remedie to be brought to work," Hitchcock's reformed lower classes are incorporated into the system, even internalizing its values, for example, a desire for conspicuous consumption, "to liue in estimacion emongst men" (sig. e.i.v).

In its stance on domestic poverty, Hitchcock's text can be seen as an extension of the commonwealth tradition, a sixteenth-century civic-minded version of humanism that emphasized the integrity of the domestic economy and, in particular, the role of reform and a "moral economy" in ensuring that the benefits of the commonwealth became common to all its subjects.[19] However, later in his text, as Hitchcock responds to a number of potential objections to his project in the form of hypothetical questions and answers, he begs the question of whether his counsel would even be heeded.[20] Perhaps to compensate for these underlying doubts, Hitchcock cites the approval of several members of Parliament who had read his proposal. But as he gives voice to the consent of the MPs, he allows a different rationale to be expressed, namely, that the investment of the state will be repaid not through the reform but through the expulsion of its poor subjects:

> other some saied, it were good to giue a subsidie for this purpose, to shippe these kinde of people in this sorte, for if they should neuer retourne, and so auoided: the land were happie, for it is but riddaunce of a number of idle and euill disposed people. (sig. f.iiii)

Although this argument enters Hitchcock's text as an aside on its penultimate page, this statement marks a decided shift in English attitudes toward the poor—progressively, they were classified not as a latent resource to be reformed and channeled into productive use on a national scale but as a superfluous and potentially dangerous group who should be expelled beyond the boundaries of the commonwealth.

Hitchcock's plot for a nationalized fishing economy demonstrates how recommendations for American colonization emerged from a domestic context of efforts to reform the declining position of England's laborers. His text also reveals how England's economy was already tied to commercial networks that expanded beyond the nation, including a prosperous triangular trade linking England with Newfoundland and Europe. Several other promotional texts from this period derived their arguments from this commercial context, including Sir Humphrey Gilbert's *A Discourse of a Discoverie for a New Passage to Cataia* (1576), Sir George Peckham's *A True Report of the Late Discoveries, and Possession ... of the New-found Landes* (1583), and Richard Hakluyt's "Discourse of Western Planting" (1584). Gilbert and Peckham, early explorers and proponents of the Newfoundland colony, endorsed the project in terms of its domestic economic benefits. Alongside the employment of mariners, Gilbert even envisaged that the colony could create a cottage industry for the poor, who would produce the trinkets necessary to conduct trade with the indigenous population of Newfoundland.[21] Hakluyt's "Discourse of Western Planting" extended Gilbert's suggestion, adding that whereas the poor "now are chardgeable to the Realme at home, by this voyadge [they] shalbe made profitable members by employinge them in England in makinge of a thousande triflinge thinges, wch will be very goodd marchandize for those Contries where wee shall have moste ample vente thereof."[22] The poor are not themselves "vented" to the colonies; rather, they are converted into "profitable" bodies through their incorporation into a cycle of trade, producing the trinkets that may be exchanged at a profitable advantage for more valuable and necessary goods that will be imported back to England. Demonstrating the interconnected interests of colonial trade and domestic manufactures, Hakluyt even forecasts that this trade in trifles may expand into a long-term industry that could potentially profit the nation as a whole.[23]

Of central concern to these early promotional texts of the 1580s was the use of colonial expansion as a means to improve the domestic economy. Using the terminology of D.B. Quinn, these texts placed foremost importance on the "supplementary economy" produced through mercantile expansion, the increase in goods already produced by the English, as with Hitchcock's fishing industry.[24] Advocates of the Newfoundland enterprise also speculated on the creation of new trades, including the cottage industry in trinkets. These efforts attempted to create a second component of the early modern English colonial economy, what Quinn terms a "complementary economy" constituted through the importation of foreign goods, whether the continental goods that Hitchcock hoped would be traded for English fish or the American goods exchanged at profit for English trinkets in the texts of Gilbert, Peckham, and Hakluyt.[25] Nonetheless, early promotional texts relegated both of these economies to a subordinate and instrumental role; thus, colonial expansion was advocated solely to reinforce the threatened integrity of the national economy.

While emigration constitutes the final component of the English colonial economy in Quinn's formulation, I wish to emphasize the ways that colonial migration potentially destabilized the subordinate position of colonial production in the national economy. The root of the idea of venting England's superfluous population derived from mercantilist economic ideology and its emphasis on the flow of a nation's superfluous goods into new markets.[26] Yet the application of this idea to England's laboring poor provided a tacit recognition of the inability of the national economy to maintain its own subjects, thereby conceding the dependence of the realm not upon the reformation but the elimination of its excess laborers. As I will discuss later in the chapter, the ultimate failure of reformist efforts to create employment and induce productivity through colonial trade transformed venting from a term denoting the incorporation of the poor in commercial projects to a sense of expulsion from the body politic. The changing significations of venting signal an important reconstitution of the position of labor in the domestic economy. The application of venting to refer to the poor reflects a crucial stage in the commodification of labor, not only in terms of how labor becomes a commodity and enters into a system of market relations but, more significantly, how mercantile commodity exchange—rather than customary rights—becomes the standard frame of reference through which to conceptualize the place of labor and the laboring classes.

In the same year that his more famous cousin and namesake composed his first treatise, the "Discourse of Western Planting," the elder Richard Hakluyt wrote a "Pamphlet for the Virginia Enterprise" (1584), which first applied the idea of venting to an exporting of England's laboring population.[27] Hakluyt, like Hitchcock before him, places the condition of English labor in an intra-European mercantile context, and he attributes the decline in English trades, particularly the cloth trade, to the destabilizing policies of Spain, whose colonial production had glutted the market with woolens, thereby reducing prices and upsetting the balance in trade. He therefore recommends that England join Spain in the colonial economy, although not in order to find supplementary bases of production in the colonies or induce the importation of complementary goods; rather, the new colonies will create a unidirectional market "for vente of our Idle people" (343). Hakluyt's ultimate intentions for the poor are left disturbingly ambiguous. By contrast, Hitchcock and the promoters of the Newfoundland colony had not thought in terms of permanent colonial settlements, hoping, instead, to employ the poor in domestic cottage industries or conscript them into seasonal fishing. For these writers, the creation of a market, rather than settlement, was of primary importance. Hakluyt is the first to conceive of venting in terms of emigration.[28] In marked contrast to Hitchcock, who hoped that laborers, once regularly employed, could return as productive members to their communities, Hakluyt does not envisage such a return voyage. Hakluyt implies that the stability of the English body politic relies upon a colonial solution for England's labor problems; as he ominously concludes, "otherwyse in shourte tyme many mischeifs maye ensue."[29]

It is with Hakluyt that we arrive at the sense of venting found in *The Tempest*'s mooncalf scene, of emitting or discharging the poor from the body politic. Shakespeare uses this application of venting to refer to an expulsion of the lower classes in other instances as well. In *Twelfth Night* (ca. 1601–02), Sebastian advises Feste, "I prithee vent thy folly somewhere else" (4.1.10), a command that prompts Feste to reply, "Vent my folly! He has heard that word of some great man, and now applies it to a fool" (4.1.12–13). Feste's comment has puzzled editors of the text, who find it strange that Feste should deem a term as common as vent to be affected.[30] Yet Feste's passage is rendered intelligible when placed in the context of early promotional texts, wherein the term vent was indeed a novel concept debated among "some great m[e]n." In addition, Feste's mock trepidation that such a term could be applied to a lowly clown like himself appropriately alludes to the class groups affected most directly by policies of venting. In Shakespeare's *Coriolanus* (ca. 1607–08), the title character similarly links the term to an expulsion of the lower classes from the body politic, embracing news of an imminent war with the Volscians because "then we shall ha' means to vent / Our musty superfluity" (1.1.225–26).[31] Like promotional texts, Coriolanus conceptualizes the laboring classes as an excess and superfluous population, one best "vented," in lieu of colonial projects, through a potential massacre in battle.

By the first years of the seventeenth century, the idea of forced emigration, of venting the poor, had become a rhetorical common-place in promotional literature.[32] In part, this focus resulted from the fact that permanent colonies had become a possibility in the years following Raleigh's patent and initial settlement at Roanoke.[33] But the involuntary nature of this proposed emigration diverged sharply from the early practices of English colonial ventures. As Edmund Morgan has observed, the initial plans for English colonialism "did not include slavery or forced labor of any kind."[34] So, if the idea of venting the poor was actually at odds with English colonial practice, what gave rise to this notion, and how can we account for its currency in the early years of the seventeenth century?

I wish to argue that the impetus for policies of colonial transportation derived from the context of domestic social relations and the problems attending early modern England's growing masterless and landless population. The notion of forced emigration emerged from precedents established in anti-vagrancy legislation of the late Elizabethan period. The first institutional advocacy of venting the poor is found in "An Acte for Punyshment of Rogues, Vagabondes and Sturdy Beggars" (39 Elizabeth, c. 4), 1597.[35] This statute, along with a companion act "for the Reliefe of the Poore" from the same year (39 Elizabeth, c. 3), established the primary model of poor relief that would remain in place for the next 200 years.[36] The former piece of legislation, which repealed all previous anti-vagrant Acts (354), reconstituted the poor as a criminal class, subjecting to its authority "all wandering persons and common Labourers" able to work (355). As this description implies, the statute attempted to limit the mobility of the unemployed poor and eliminate their idleness through enforced employment. The link between dangerous mobility and idleness is evident in the punishments stipulated for apprehended vagrants: to be stripped to the waist and whipped until bloody, then whipped back to their parish of birth, or the parish where they most recently resided, "there to put him or her selfe to labour as a true Subject ought to do" (356). In lieu of being able to reverse the cycle of mobility by returning vagrants to their "home," vagrants are simply whipped and returned to their most recent domicile, where they may be placed in a house of correction (356).

A final penalty is added so as to deal with a dangerous class who refused to be reformed either through a return to one's home parish or commitment to the workhouse. Those who "shall appeare to be dangerous to the inferior sorte of People where they shalbe taken, or otherwyse be such as will not be reformed of their rogish kinde of lyfe by the former Provisions of this Acte" (357) will be transported from the country:

> and then such of the same Rogues...shall and may lawfully by the same Justices or the most part of them be banyshed out of this Realme and all other the Domynions thereof, and at the Charges of that Country shall be conveied unto such partes beyond the Seas as shalbe at any tyme hereafter for that purpose assigned by the Privie Counsell unto her Majesty her Heires or Successors[37]

Transportation to the colonies, in this context, is cast as the final option for subjects unamenable to the workhouse economy. This course of action startlingly reverses the stated intentions of the statute. Whereas the Act earlier attempts to eliminate mobility by returning vagrants to their birthplace or previous domicile, this final clause banishes the poor beyond the boundaries of the nation. And while both practices seem similarly motivated by the desire of authorities simply to rid their own jurisdiction of the poor and have them become someone else's problem, the final destination of the poor, as with the elder Hakluyt, is left disturbingly open-ended: any colonial space to be determined by the Privy Council. It was not until the first year of James's reign that the Privy Council finally specified and implemented this clause, ordering that vagrants be exiled to the colonies or placed in military service on the Continent.[38]

The proposal for the forced transportation of the vagrant poor also contradicts the intention of the 1597 statutes to oversee the employment of the poor. Rather than serving as a means to reincorporate the poor as productive members of the body politic, the local workhouse constituted the final stop for vagrants before a potential transportation to the colonies. The 1597 statutes followed the 1576 "Acte for setting the Poore on Worke, and for the avoyding of Ydleness" (18 Elizabeth, c. 3) in stipulating a peculiar form of labor to occupy workhouse inmates, calling for authorities in cities and corporate towns to acquire a stock of "Woole Hempe Flaxe Iron or other Stufe" that civic officials, often the appointed collector or Governor of the Poor, could distribute to the poor so as to set them to work (332). The workhouse economy was structured around a cycle of threshing wood-based raw materials. As a contemporary ballad describes it, "to the hempe blocke packe yee: / Thumpe, and thumpe, and thump apace, / for feare the whipper take yee."[39] The collector would sell the wrought form of these commodities, using the profits to reinvest in more material. Significantly, this economy did not attempt to end poverty or ameliorate conditions for the poor but simply keep them within a cycle of work. Indeed, the statute seems most concerned with whether this new labor market might drive down the price of these finished goods (333).

As Foucault notes in his discussion of "the great confinement" in seventeenth-century workhouses and hospitals, the use of incarceration in the early modern period was intended to increase production while masking the social effects of poverty. The deliberate segregation of the workhouse population replaced temporary measures of punishment with a permanent classification of exclusion: according to Foucault, the early modern state "acquired an ethical power of segregation, which permitted it to eject, as into another world, all forms of social uselessness."[40] Although Foucault largely discusses late seventeenth-century France, early modern England had its own great confinement in the late sixteenth and early seventeenth centuries: provincial England contained approximately 70 workhouses by 1630, with dozens more in larger cities and towns.[41] In the Bridewell economy, labor was transformed into a form of punishment rather than serving as a means to reform subjects, who were increasingly classified as both dangerous and unprofitable. The 1576 statute, for example, stipulated that subjects who refused to work be sent to a House of Correction, "there to be straightlye kepte, as well in Diet as in Worke, and also punisshed from tyme to tyme," according to the discretion of the keeper (333).

An often-overlooked component of Foucault's discussion of early modern disciplinary technologies is the connection between forms of social control and economic production.[42] The workhouse economy created new modes of discipline after earlier reforms had failed to create greater productivity among subjects. Proposals for the forced transportation of the laboring poor developed in the wake of a perceived failure of civic efforts of reform. In the forty years following Hitchcock, Peckham, and the Hakluyts, there was a progressive marginalization of proposals aiming to create or resuscitate commercial and manufacturing networks that could offer productive outlets for labor. According to A.L. Beier, the periods of economic crisis in the mid-1590s and 1620s marked the intensification of the enforcement of Elizabethan poor laws.[43] In the ensuing culture of the workhouse, the sense of the poor as a productive resource to be employed and rehabilitated in the national economy was replaced by a view of the poor as a commodity whose profitability was contingent upon stricter forms of social control. This changing view of labor transformed a residual moral economy into what Hilary McD. Beckles has described as a "market system of brutal servitude."[44] Labor regulations emphasizing mutual obligation were thus increasingly superseded by a system of property relations in which labor became an alienable commodity to be exploited for maximum profit.[45] I wish to locate Beckles's subject, the growth of colonial indentured servitude, within an earlier domestic context of labor regulations and failed efforts of reform. The view of the lower classes as unamenable to reform and potentially dangerous to the nation provided the justification of a system of indentured servitude that began to be broadly implemented in the English colonies by the 1620s.

The historian Eric Williams first established the link between the growth of colonial indentured labor and a nascent slave trade, an argument that has been extended in the work of Edmund S. Morgan, Hilary McD. Beckles, and Theodore W. Allen.[46] For Allen, England's American colonies depended not only upon a large supply of labor but also a degree of social control necessary to exploit that labor and expand capital.[47] Demonstrating the intersection of social control and capital expansion, the application of the term venting to forms of expulsion and forced transportation reflects the declining influence of earlier ideologies of civic reform and productive labor. The subsequent economy of the workhouse marked a shift from an attempted recuperation of the position of laborers in the national economy to an extraction of greater productivity through a segregation of the workforce and concentrated forms of social control.

In early modern England, the idea of slavery was strongly associated with the labor regulations of anti-vagrant and poor relief statutes. A 1547 Act, the harshest of Tudor statutes, had, in fact, created the category of "slave" as a means to punish the recalcitrant, idle poor.[48] As a sign of the residual importance of the customary rights of laborers, this statute was soon repealed; in fact, there is little evidence that it was ever enforced. Early modern commentators on the English class system made a concerted effort to remove the imputation of slavery from labor relations. In his *Description of England* (1577), William Harrison praised his nation due to the fact that "[a]s for slaves and bondmen, we have none," adding that the privilege of English liberty even ensured that foreign slaves would become enfranchised upon their arrival in England. Despite this denial, Harrison concedes that England's servants "are profitable to none" and may indeed prove "enemies to their masters."[49] Showing the influence of the 1547 anti-vagrant statute long after its repeal, Harrison even proposes that convicted thieves be enslaved by those whom they have robbed.[50] Harrison expresses an important ambivalence toward labor: permanent or hereditary servitude is seen as antithetical to the English social system, while at the same time servants' rights further degenerate nearly to the point of slavery. The slippage between servitude and its harsher incarnations becomes even more pronounced with the emergence of the workhouse system in early modern England.

Although colonialist readings of *The Tempest* have traditionally emphasized the American contexts of the text (and, increasingly, the Mediterranean influences on the play as well), I wish to emphasize how these colonial contexts themselves emerged from and were interconnected to a labor environment in early modern England that was at an important stage of transition in the early seventeenth century.[51] The fact that Caliban's initial labor would have resonated with a Jacobean audience familiar with work regulations for the poor is evidenced by Jonson's description of Caliban in *Bartholomew Fair* (1614) as a "*Seruant-monster*" (Induction ll. 127–28), the name frequently given to him by Stephano and Trinculo as well (3.2.3 ff.). Jonson's play also alludes to Caliban's first scene with the pair, assigning the name "Mooncalf" to Ursula's servant. In *The Tempest*, Prospero's first description of Caliban further connotes the status of English servants, as "he ... / Whom now I keep in service" (1.2.285–866).[52] However, throughout the remainder of the play, Prospero refers to Caliban not as a servant, whose labor would be contractually protected, but as a "slave." Prospero's description of Caliban is linked to the category of slavery in English anti-vagrant legislation due to the fact that Caliban's status is not hereditary; rather, it results both from a transgression (particularly the attempted rape of Miranda) as well as a continued resistance to the work regime instituted by Prospero. Thus, Prospero may claim of his island, like Harrison had of England: "[a]s for slaves and bondmen, we have none."

The Tempest inherits the ambivalence toward labor and the poor expressed in Harrison's *Description of England*, which described the serving classes as elevated above slavery and yet potentially dangerous as well as "profitable to none." Thus, although Prospero initially lists one of Caliban's chief tasks, the gathering of wood, among his "offices / That profit us" (1.2.312–13), even conceding his dependence on Caliban ("But as 'tis, / We cannot miss him [1.2.310–11]), the threat posed by Caliban increasingly outweighs the profitability of his labor. The relations of labor between Prospero and Caliban parallel events in early modern England, where initial efforts to transform displaced laborers and the poor into productive bodies had ultimately failed to achieve their aims, consequently prompting new efforts to induce productivity through intensified forms of discipline and social control. Caliban's status has been reconstituted in a similar manner: as Prospero describes him, "Thou most lying slave, / Whom stripes may move, not kindness" (1.2.344–45). The strategies used to exact obedience in the workhouse and on Prospero's island depend upon the deliberate use of physical violence. Each context shows an emphasis on the confinement of recalcitrant laborers, seen in Prospero's threats to Ariel to "peg thee" in an oak (1.2.295) or Caliban's complaint of being styed "In this hard rock, whiles you do keep from me / The rest o' th' island" (1.2.343–44). In *The Tempest*, like in Bridewell ballads, the laboring subject is regulated and corrected through "straightening" physical punishment, witnessed by Prospero's various threats to Caliban: "Thou shalt be pinch'd" (1.2.328); "I'll rack thee with old cramps" (1.2.369). These punishments culminate in Prospero's literalization of the straightening of the bodies of disobedient laborers: he promises to punish Caliban and his fellow conspirators by grinding their joints, cramping their sinews, and marking their bodies with sores (4.1.258–61). Even Caliban's primary labor, the collection and bearing of wood (1.2.312; 2.2.1 SD), recalls the labor stipulated by the 1576 anti-vagrant act. And, just as the statute had created a form of labor that produced unnecessary goods and functioned merely to keep the poor within a cycle of work, Caliban responds to Prospero's initial call for more wood by grumbling "There's wood enough within" (1.2.314); his labor is similarly divorced from questions of utility or survival.

The failure of the Bridewell system to ensure consent and effect productivity necessitated a further recategorization of laborers. Rather than ascribing failure to either the economic system or the mechanisms of reform, anti-vagrant statutes placed blame on the subjectivity of laborers. In *The Tempest*, this reconstitution of the laboring poor as irredeemably dangerous bodies is seen in the description of Caliban's "vile race" as having "that in't which good natures / Could not abide to be with" (1.2.358–60).[53] Caliban's identity, specifically the identification of his difference, is attributed to an internal deficiency, the quality of his "race" that disallows acculturation and incorporation. Similar to descriptions of the "dangerous" nature of workhouse inmates, this formulation intends to account for subjects unable to be integrated into the labor and social system: those who are not to be "abided" may be detained and, ultimately, vented. The segregation of idle laborers in the workhouse, which, in the early modern imagination, constituted an "other world," as Foucault noted earlier, provided a frame of reference that enabled a more thorough process of expulsion through practices of colonial transplantation.

This reconceptualization of labor was further necessitated due to the recurring threat of social unrest and lower-class rebellion. In 1607, the same year as the first instance of laborers forcibly transplanted to the colonies, the House of Lords endorsed proposals to "vent" England's surplus population. In the wake of the Midlands Rising, a protest against enclosure and food hoarding that erupted in several counties, the Lords agreed that the poor should be sent elsewhere, or else "there must break out yearly tumours and impostures as did of late."[54] The Virginia Company text, *A True and Sincere Declaration of the Purpose of the Plantation Begun in Virginia* (1610), published by the council shortly after the shipwreck of Governor Thomas Gates, used this disaster to argue for the prevention of a larger catastrophe that might ensue from overpopulation; consequently, it endorsed

> trans-planting the rancknesse and multitude of increase in our people; of which there is left no vent, but age; and euident danger that the number and infinitenesse of them, will out-grow the matter, whereon to worke for their life, and sustentation, and shall one infest and become a burthen to another.[55]

Significantly, this passage advocates the creation of a colonial economy as the only outlet for the poor. Unlike earlier texts, which advocated the reintroduction of the poor into a prosperous economy, transportation is equated with the only previous "vent" of the poor, aging and natural death. The Virginia Company's rhetoric calls to mind Coriolanus's invocation of war as an outlet to "vent / Our musty superfluity" (1.1.225–26), and it addresses more candidly the ultimate destination of laborers, unlike the indeterminate fate elaborated earlier by the elder Hakluyt and others. Appropriately, both Shakespeare's *Coriolanus* and responses to the Midlands food riots, an event that influenced the play's opening scene, make use of the term "vent," demonstrating the shaping role played by class insurrection in the development of policies of colonial transportation.[56]

The depiction of the contagious bodies of laborers was intended to contain the threat of collective action and rebellion. The 1597 Act "for Punyshment of Rogues, Vagabondes, and Sturdy Beggars," the first codification of transportation, had introduced the notion of venting laborers out of fear that they will be "dangerous to the inferior sorte of People" who had been placed with them in the workhouse (357). A perceived threat of masterless men—that they actively recruit others to their ranks and may potentially form an idle counter-society—is illustrated in *The Tempest* through the affiliation of Caliban with Stephano and Trinculo. Caliban's terms of indenture with the masterless pair conform to anti-vagrant texts' representation of the ways that England's underclass flaunts its secession from the norms of dominant culture by mimicking and appropriating many of its rituals, including labor regulations.[57] Caliban's new alliance also demonstrates his inability to conceptualize alternative labor relations; he remains tragically ingrained in the language of servitude and deference, casting Stephano alternately as his god, ruler, and master (2.2.149, 152, 185). Caliban's declaration of his "freedom" is undercut by the fact that this liberty is obtained only by entering into new terms of servitude—"Has a new master" (185). Caliban, then, is never truly masterless, for he becomes subject to the imperious rule of his fellow social inferiors.

Caliban's final appearance in the play is rendered more intelligible when situated in the context of early modern labor regulations. Caliban is separated from Stephano and Trinculo, each of whom is returned to his proper "owner." Few readings of this scene recognize the important parallelism of Prospero's statement to Alonso—"Two of these fellows you / Must know and own"—with his own acknowledgment of "this thing of darkness," Caliban (5.1.274–76). These lines place the Caliban-Prospero relationship in the context of labor relations between master and servant, a context reaffirmed by Prospero's final command that Caliban resume his menial duties and clean the chamber (5.1.292–94). But what exactly does it mean for Prospero to have "acknowledged" Caliban? A conciliatory reading of this line is possible, of course, with Prospero assuming ethical responsibility for Caliban and offering him forgiveness, as, in a manner of speaking, he had done earlier to Alonso, Antonio, and Sebastian. But the tenor of his acknowledgment, paralleled as it is with the assertion of Alonso's property rights over Stephano and Trinculo, qualifies this interpretation.

This exchange is rendered much less opaque when contextualized alongside the stipulations of the Statute of Artificers (1563). Under early modern labor regulations, laborers could neither refuse apprenticeships nor leave their masters without completing their terms of service. The Statute of Artificers also placed important constraints on the power of masters, limiting their ability to dismiss apprentices and laborers.[58] Contemporary labor conditions thus provide an explanation of Prospero's acknowledgment of Caliban as well as his demand that Caliban reenter his service. If Caliban had refused to do so,

Prospero himself would be at fault under the terms of the Statute of Artificers. This context additionally provides insight into the anxious negotiations surrounding Ariel's length of service. Prospero, who had agreed to "bate" Ariel's term by one year for good behavior (1.2.249–50), threatens to rescind that offer and even punish Ariel, if he "more murmur'st" (1.2.294). Despite the statute's emphasis on reciprocal obligations, the stipulated punishments for masters or servants breaking the terms of their contract were highly unequal: servants who left their masters' service were subject to imprisonment, whereas masters who dismissed a servant without previous notice received a 40-shilling fine (341). The Statute of Artificers, intended to defend customary labor practices, exemplifies the moral economy underlying the efforts of English state policy to forestall the destabilizing effects of capital formation. However, the statute helped construct more efficient workhouse conditions for laborers and has therefore been characterized as "the most powerful instrument devised for degrading and impoverishing the English labourer."[59] In *The Tempest*, despite the fact that he exits with Stephano and Trinculo, Caliban's final statement—that he will be "wise hereafter, / And seek for grace" (5.1.295–96)—makes clear that he has fully internalized the rules of Prospero's power. A key part of that consent lies in a rejection of collective action: Caliban blames himself for following the false rule of Stephano (5.1.296–98), implying that he has finally complied with the terms of his labor. The play thus ultimately offers the prospect of laborers reduced to the exploitative, paternalistic terms of the Statute of Artificers, a restoration of an equilibrium in social relations upset by domestic capital accumulation and colonial development.[60]

In keeping with the nostalgic tone of Shakespeare's Romances, the final act of *The Tempest* moves away from the labor context so important to its conflicts and character development.[61] However, contemporary to the play's initial performance in 1611, the social position of labor was undergoing an important redefinition. The idea of compulsory transportation to the colonies, first recommended in Hakluyt's "Pamphlet for the Virginia Enterprise" (1584) and initially codified in Elizabeth's 1597 anti-vagrant statute, established precedents that were increasingly implemented during the early years of James's reign.[62] The years surrounding the first performance of *The Tempest* witnessed the emergence of an economy in vented laborers, evidenced by the 300 youths involuntarily shipped from London to the colony from 1619–22.[63] In this sense, we can view *The Tempest* as a text actively involved in a process that reconstituted the role of colonial labor, a point of transition from the civic arguments of early promotional texts to the emergent forms of colonial servitude that became codified by the early 1620s.[64] In this new context, Prospero's "acknowledgment" of Caliban gains new meaning, no longer as the resumption of paternalistic authority mandated by the Statute of Artificers but as a claim of absolute rights of ownership: "this thing of darkness I / Acknowledge *mine*." As John Pory commented, marking the ascendancy of an economy of "vented" laborers: "Our principall wealth (I should have said) consisteth in servants."[65]

***

COLONIAL LABOR/COLONIAL LIBERTY: THE VIRGINIA COMPANY, 1606–25

While the first section of this chapter delineated important transformations in the position of laborers and the poor in the decades prior to the first performance of *The Tempest*, this second section will analyze the immediate context of the play in order to examine its ambivalent representation of the place of labor in England's new American colonies. The play's inability to give adequate representation to the role of laborers is replicated in many colonialist readings of *The Tempest*. Even the most significant discussion of issues of class and labor, Greenblatt's essay, "Martial Law in the Land of Cockaigne," still elides many details of laboring-class insurrection chronicled in Shakespeare's key source, William Strachey's *True Report*.[66] Therefore, I will give due attention to contemporary anxieties relating to the possible rebellion of colonial laborers, using the historical presence of lower-class revolt as a means to reconsider Stephano and Trinculo's "conspiracy" with Caliban in Shakespeare's play. These figures evoke the perceived dangers of the "liberties" obtainable in the colonies, marking a transition from earlier Virginia Company policy, which attempted to recruit laborers precisely through a guarantee of traditional liberties and economic advancement. I will use this ambivalence—of laborers' dangerous "liberty" and the "liberties" that must be ensured them—to chart a reconstitution of class alliances in which Virginia Company adventurers attempted to align their interests only with those artisanal laborers perceived as necessary to the colonial economy. This policy recast both armigerous gentlemen and unskilled laborers as idle, irredeemable classes and thereby justified the latter group's venting abroad and entrance into an emerging economy of colonial servitude.

The Virginia Company's second charter, granted in May 1609, was issued to accompany the new governor, Sir Thomas Gates, to the Virginia colony, which was on the verge of collapse only two years after its initial settlement. The shipwreck that Gates's fleet experienced in July 1609 prompted William Strachey, the Virginia Company secretary, to compose his prose narrative. The second charter that commissioned Gates contributed to a significant reconstitution of the position of labor in England's colonies. The new charter repeatedly critiqued the perceived communalism and egalitarianism of the first Company charter of 1606, characteristics that came to be associated with a general environment of excessive liberty in the colonies. Nonetheless, the second charter similarly offered investors the promise of "liberties," the maintenance of English legal freedoms, as well as the possibility of "liberty," in terms of economic freedom and potential social mobility. It even retained some aspects of the egalitarianism of the first charter, granting equivalence between capital and labor so that a share of Company stock could either be purchased by an investor (adventurer) for £12.10s or gained through an indenture of seven years' labor.[67] The charter also featured residual aspects of the Statute of Artificers that had intended to protect laborers; for instance, the time of servitude was limited, in sharp contrast to the terms that quickly developed in the colony. In addition, the contractual period of service, like apprenticeship, guaranteed the laborer's "freedom" in the traditional sense, a "liberty" gained through entrance into the community as a freeman practicing a trade. Laborers were thus allowed to retain ownership over production and remain exempt from further forms of servitude. But unlike the rights ensured through the guild system, and unlike adventurers who had put forward money, indentured laborers for the Virginia Company were not entitled to share Company profits, a key point of departure from the first charter.[68] Whereas promotional texts and Company documents had elsewhere blurred the distinctions between those who venture their capital and those who adventure their persons, as seen in Symonds's sermon, Company policy ensured that the ultimate authority over capital remained within Company jurisdiction in England.

Even though the charter facilitated an increased and centralized control over the production and flow of capital, the document was nonetheless dependent upon a rhetoric of liberty. In this way, the second charter can be situated within the framework of Marx's discussion of "free colonies."[69] For his model of colonial development, Marx discusses "free colonies," settlements based upon an availability of land for independent production (934). The Virginia colony would initially seem to subvert a monopolistic accumulation of capital because laborers were allowed to become independent through the institution of private property and their ownership of the means of their subsistence. In early modern Virginia, the flow of capital was increased, instead, through what Marx describes as "a relative surplus population of wage-labourers in proportion to the accumulation of capital" (935). In this sense, the colony's economy depended upon superfluous laborers, the same groups recommended for venting from the domestic economy. The charter's generous terms were intended to recruit an artisanal class able to purchase a share and thereby serve as a "middling sort" in the colonies, a buffer social group hierarchically situated above its fellow laborers. The Company's stipulations for land ownership otherwise ensured that property would remain out of reach for other laborers, forcing them to enter the labor market as wage-laborers or servants. The example of a prosperous artisanal class served to motivate other laborers to become similarly independent through land ownership. In order to do so, though, they had to enter into agreements of indenture and thus remain in the serving class (938). In this context, the surplus labor contributed in return for wages, or the labor power purchased in exchange for transportation, produced the capital necessary to propel the colonial economy. In turn, this capital could be reinvested into the recruitment of more laborers (939), a cycle that ensured a centralized control of profits while maintaining a class structure dependent upon a promise of a social mobility ultimately unobtainable for the majority of colonists.

The measures put in place under the second charter by Sir Thomas Smythe, treasurer of the Virginia Company, demonstrated both the need to attract capital as well as the use of surplus labor to propel its further accumulation. Smythe's promise of 50 acres per share verifies Marx's correlation of colonial emigration with a desire for land acquisition: whereas only 31 individuals had invested in the Company prior to the new charter in 1609, 802 invested that year.[70] But the rate of capital investment further increased the need for laborers, a demand exacerbated by the fact that few of the nearly 1,000 adventurers who invested in the Company would themselves venture to the colony. In addition, many of those who did migrate could not contribute to the needed labor pool: the proportion of gentlemen in Virginia, who were by definition excluded from labor, exceeded that of England by six times.[71]

The drive for investment under the second charter thus produced a disjuncture between the two forms of capital it had intended to attract: the financial capital of investors and the human capital of laborers. In this process, social relations were reorganized, reimposing distinctions between adventurer and planter, owner and laborer. The unexpected proportion of gentlemen among the investors who migrated to Virginia placed them in a category of idleness alongside their lowest social inferiors. On the other hand, large merchant investors, including Company officials, allied themselves with the skilled artisans who they hoped would fill their indentured labor pool. In *The Tempest*, this realignment of class groups is demonstrated by the play's linking of its dangerous and idle classes—both noblemen (Antonio and Sebastian) and servants (Stephano and Trinculo)—whereas Ferdinand, in his role as colonial "husband" and laborer, is depicted in positive terms, despite the fact that his labor seems to transgress his social position.

The descriptions assigned to Stephano and Trinculo in the First Folio's dramatis personae list help contextualize their social status and gauge how Jacobean audiences might have perceived them. Stephano, "a drunken butler," and Trinculo, "a jester," are situated as domestic servants and retainers, groups often represented as part of England's population of masterless men. Critics often seem to have difficulty interpreting the social roles of Stephano and Trinculo.[72] Prospero lacks such confusion, pejoratively calling them "varlots" [i.e., varlets], a term that referred specifically to servants and domestic menials (4.1.170 and note). The text adds several incidents that further reinforce the association of Stephano and Trinculo with England's comic, if potentially dangerous, masterless classes. In this sense, Trinculo, in his informed knowledge about what induces a "holiday fool" in England to part with his money (2.2.29), seems to be speaking from experience, perhaps as a counterfeit "lame beggar" who was unable to receive "a doit" while begging (2.2.31–33). Trinculo is also prepared to prove his valor by seeking "to justle a constable" (3.2.26), the civic officer responsible for controlling the movement of vagrants within a parish.

One of the few results of Stephano and Trinculo's conspiracy with Caliban is the attempted theft of clothing conveniently left hanging outside, a practice that Shakespeare had earlier associated with England's masterless population in his depiction of Autolycus in *The Winter's Tale* (4.3.23). Prospero himself sees the clothes, or "trumpery" (4.1.186), merely as bait with which to trap them, a "stale [i.e., decoy] to catch these thieves" (4.1.187). Stephano and Trinculo's attraction to the "glistering apparel" (4.1.193 SD) that Caliban recognizes as "but trash" (4.1.224) associates the clothing with the flamboyant costumes described as the staple of gypsies and other vagrants.[73] In asserting that he knows "what belongs to a frippery" (4.1.225–26), or a secondhand clothing store, Trinculo is also claiming possession of a new wardrobe, an act of significant cultural capital for one whose assigned clothing (livery) provided a badge of his subordinate status as a servant. As Ann Rosalind Jones and Peter Stallybrass point out, livery began to be perceived as a sign of excessive subordination by the seventeenth century.[74] And, although the Jacobean period saw a repeal of sumptuary laws in 1604, clothing still reflected the disturbing social transformations enabled by class mobility. In a letter from Jamestown, John Pory focused on dress as a marker of how the prosperity of planters had led to a blurring of class lines in the colony; for example, he describes one colonist, a collier's wife in England, who now "weares her rough bever hatt with a faire perle hatband, and a silken suite thereto correspondent."[75] Stephano and Trinculo's livery also provides a visible conferral of ownership, a fact that illuminates Prospero's statement to Alonso: "Two of these fellows you / Must *know* and own" (5.1.274–75, emphasis added). As Jones and Stallybrass note, "livery acted as the medium through which the social system marked bodies so as to associate them with particular institutions. The power to give that marking to subordinates affirmed social hierarchy."[76]

Stephano and Trinculo's class status is a relevant question due to the ways that the pair's actions and self-perception challenge and attempt to transform social distinctions. Much of the comedy of their scenes stems from how the two fail to perceive themselves as retainers or masterless men, often assuming what they misconstrue to be the language and behavior of their social betters. With his "servant-monster" bearing his bottle before him, Stephano takes on aristocratic airs upon realizing the power vacuum that has resulted from Alonso's absence and likely death (2.2.174–75). Despite the predominance of gentlemen among Virginia colonists, *The Tempest* associates the problems of a group exempt from labor and social control not with the colony's idle leisure class but in relation to the mutinous and masterless poor. Contemporary accounts of colonial life were far more direct in their accusations against the aristocratic ethos of Virginia, especially under the first charter of 1606–09. John Rolfe found that the initial form of government ruled "aristocratically": "all would be *keisars*, none inferior to other."[77] The writings of John Smith frequently castigated his gentrified colleagues on the original Virginia Council, whom he characterized as both idle and desiring "dissolute liberty."[78] Smith's reference to the colony's "Tuftaffaty humorists" (1.212), gentlemen who conspire against the colony rather than work to ensure its survival, describes these groups by highlighting their gaudily fashionable clothing, terms reminiscent of the "trumpery" (4.1.186) that Prospero places to lure Stephano and Trinculo. Significantly, the accusations against Virginia's superfluous gentlemen lodged by Smith and others are transposed in *The Tempest* to the comic figures of the serving class.

Following the Virginia Company's second charter of 1609, promotional texts attempted to distance the present state of the colony from its fitful start of 1606–09. Texts assigned blame chiefly to the egalitarian social relations in the colony, which, according to Robert Johnson, was "now augmented with such numbers of irregular persons, that it soone became as so many members without a head."[79] The representation of popular rule as a "many-headed monster," an early modern commonplace, was frequently evoked in promotional literature as one of the primary evils arising from the loosening of social restraints in the colonies.[80] Stephano and Trinculo are described in similar terms: their many-headed conspiracy is depicted as inherently empty-headed; when, for example, they realize that they and Caliban constitute a majority of the island's inhabitants, Trinculo comments appropriately, "if th' other two be brain'd like us, the state totters" (3.2.6–7). The pseudo-democratic character of their rebellion culminates in Stephano's garbled version of social levelling: "Every man shift for all the rest, and let no man take care for himself" (5.1.256–57). Virginia Company documents written after 1609 also mocked the first charter for having forced colonists to "shift for all the rest" at the expense of individual productivity and profit. Because the communitarian charter had eliminated private land ownership, requiring colonists to give their crops to the common store, colonists were thought to have labored at a more leisurely pace, so that, in Ralph Hamor's estimate, the labor of 30 men produced as much as what "three men [would] haue done for themselues."[81]

The rebelliousness and social pretenses of Stephano and Trinculo are particularly relevant to a colonial context in which the liberties guaranteed by the Virginia Company to induce investment were feared to have weakened traditional social hierarchies.[82] While Company documents promised social advancement to necessary artisanal groups, this mobility became a destabilizing force, disturbing the social hierarchies that had been in place in England and raising the threat of social relations in the colonies distinct from those of the home nation. The problem left for promotional texts was thus to reaffirm the promise of "liberties," the guarantee of traditional economic rights associated with tradesmen, while curtailing the possibility of laborers using these rights so as to effectively achieve a greater "liberty" in terms of unchecked social mobility and a differential creole identity.[83]

Despite the disparate interests of Company members, Virginia Company texts repeatedly emphasized a rhetoric of liberty. In her book-length study of *The Tempest*, Donna B. Hamilton has noted the important connections between the Virginia Company under its second charter and constitutionalist views of power.[84] Likewise, Robert Brenner has established the numerous links between early investors and antimonarchical thought.[85] One of the political arguments advocated by Company leaders—that of sovereign bodies limited on a contractual and constitutional basis—found a parallel in the Company's efforts to codify labor under the second charter. In order to reduce the possibility of absolutist and arbitrary forms of power, the Company proposed to ensure customary rights and liberties. Johnson's *New Life of Virginea* (1612), for instance, advises the Virginia council to let colonists "live as free English men, under the government of just and equall lawes, and not as slaves after the will and lust of any superiour."[86] Even though Johnson's evocation of the natural liberties of Englishmen resembles the rhetoric of later radicals of the English Revolution, the liberties admitted by Company officials were severely circumscribed.[87] As Andrew Fitzmaurice has noted, the radical implications of arguments for liberty at home did not necessarily entail an advocacy of egalitarian social relations in the Company-run colony.[88] Thus, the accusations of domestic "slavery" put forward by Company texts dissociated forms of monarchical political absolutism from the Company's own economic monopoly in the colonies. By contrasting colonial liberty with English slavery, these texts supported the contractual rights of owners over goods and property, claims that were often asserted at the expense of the customary rights of laborers. Ironically, the opposition to domestic forms of absolutism abetted the increasingly diminished rights of laborers in the colonies, thereby accelerating the deteriorating conditions of colonial servitude.[89]

Despite the Virginia Company's co-optation of the language of colonial liberty in the service of free trade and bourgeois authority, *The Tempest* offers competing articulations of this rhetoric, particularly as expressed by the figure of the Boatswain in the play's opening scene. The representation of the shipwreck of Gates's fleet related in Strachey's *True Report* is altered in its dramatic portrayal in *The Tempest*. As Stephen Greenblatt has shown, the opening scene of

The Tempest is significantly distinct from Strachey's account of the storm, wherein Gates's presence as a laborer alongside his men incites the crew—commoners and aristocrats alike—to unite in their labor and save the ship.[90] By contrast, in the play it is the Boatswain who assumes authority, calling on his men (1.1.5) and even challenging Sebastian to join in rather than criticize their efforts: "Work you then" (1.1.42). The Boatswain defines a hierarchy of labor that effectively exempts the noble characters, defining status based upon the value of one's labor—"What cares these roarers for the name of king?" (1.1.16–17). As demonstrated by the Boatswain, the verbal rebelliousness of laborers serves to reflect a more general intransigence and unamenablity to forms of social control, a threat that intensifies due to the crucial position they occupy in the colony.

Testifying to the importance of these class groups, the Virginia Company published a series of broadsides that intended primarily to help recruit necessary artisans and laborers. These documents, in fact, consisted largely of lists of the skilled laborers needed in Virginia, a narrative focus that exposes the central role served by laborers in the fledgling colony.[91] Unlike many documents, the first of the Company broadsides did not attribute the colony's failures solely to its lower-class members. The "idle crue" that it describes as having accompanied Gates on his voyage consists not only of "bad servants" or vagrants conscripted to the voyage but also "lascivious sonnes" and "ill husbands" whom elite families had hoped to vent to the colonies.[92] The broadside reveals the roots of the antiaristocratic critique found in the opening scene of *The Tempest*. The "idle crue" that the broadside describes as serving "to clogge the businesse" very much resembles Alonso's party, to whom the Boatswain complains: "You mar our labour" (1.1.13). In contrast to Strachey's account, in which they lead the rescue efforts, the aristocrats merely obstruct labor in the play's opening scene and thereby "do assist the storm" (1.1.14). *The Tempest* and the Company broadside both use the storm that shipwrecked Gates's fleet as a symbol of the breakdown of authority and social control, what Strachey also refers to as "the tempest of Dissention" that followed the actual hurricane (67). Rather than cast blame on the usual target, the colony's vented laborers and servants, these texts point to how the colony's problems result from the broader failures of the ruling class. In the opening scene of *The Tempest*, the aristocrats Antonio and Sebastian are the ones associated with idleness, unable to contribute needed labor due to their status, and are additionally linked to the traditionally rebellious laboring classes through their power of cursing (or, in their case, complaining). Hearing their cries from below deck, the Boatswain exclaims, "A plague upon this howling! they are louder than the weather, or our office" (1.1.36–37). The complaints of the aristocrats drown out both the storm and the noise of the mariners' labor, pointing to the threat that elite colonists posed even from their seemingly marginal, idle position.

Despite the predominance of gentlemen among early colonists, Virginia Company documents and promotional texts were remarkably silent on the problems caused by a large and disgruntled leisure class in the colony. The only writers who even commented on this issue were John Rolfe, Captain John Smith, and William Strachey. As noted earlier, Rolfe's critique was limited to a reference to the failures of the colony's "aristocratic" council. In the final section of this chapter, I will discuss how Strachey's *True Report* often censured its own class-based critique, incorporating official Company accounts so as to minimize the damage of its report. But John Smith's numerous texts provided the most direct and comprehensive attack on the colony's initial leaders, attributing the colony's early failures not to the poor quality or idleness of its laborers but, instead, to the feuding, desire for quick profit, and lack of foresight of its leaders. All of these accounts may have been perceived as scandalous, explaining their omission from the canon of published Company documents.[93] Nonetheless, my discussion of Smith will situate his works in the context of a more general effort to construct a new identity for England's colonial leaders. The progressive acceptance of Smith's model of colonial labor attests to a subsuming of Smith's critique within the ideology of the Virginia Company.

Smith's *A Map of Virginia* (1612), like many promotional texts, concludes with a rebuttal of false reports of Virginia. Smith singles out the reports circulated by elite adventurers, "[b]eing for most part of such tender educations and small experience in martiall accidents," who have returned to England due to their inability to survive in a colonial environment:

> because they found not English cities, nor such faire houses, nor at their owne wishes any of their accustomed dainties, with feather beds and downe pillowes, Tavernes and alehouses in every breathing place, neither such plenty of gold and silver and dissolute liberty as they expected[94]

The privations of the colonial experience, Smith argues, require an ability to adapt to a new environment, to improvise according to a new cultural script.[95] Elite adventurers had, by contrast, sought "their accustomed dainties," luxury items associated with aristocratic idleness (soft pillows and expensive beds) and the intemperance of the ale-house. Smith establishes an implicit contrast between metropolis and colony on the basis of codes of gender and status, opposing the effeminating and enervating luxuries of England, suitable for those of "tender educations," to a masculinized and disciplined identity in the colony.[96] Instead of offering dreams of gold and silver, likened to the fancies of intoxicated minds, Smith proposes a type of transformative labor in the colony. In contrast to the forms of "dissolute liberty" expected by elite adventurers, Smith intends to reconstitute the identities of colonists, transforming idle gentlemen into laborers for the colony.

The Tempest, similar to Smith's *Map of Virginia* and Strachey's *True Report*, attempts to reconstitute and transform the definition of labor in the struggling colony. Faced with an excessive leisure class, these texts construct the identity of a gentrified laborer, a role exemplified by Ferdinand in Shakespeare's play. This strategy attempts to forge an alliance between the colony's elite leaders and its necessary laborers by levelling the forms of labor associated with each group. One can see this process at work in *The Tempest*, wherein Ferdinand's courtship of Miranda necessitates the assumption of a form of labor debasing to his status. His entrance in 3.1, "bearing a log" (1 SD), replicates the labor associated earlier with Caliban (2.2.1 SD) and even calls to mind the punitive forms of labor normally confined to the English workhouse. Yet Ferdinand differentiates his own "mean task" (3.1.4) based on its voluntary nature as well as the hope of profit it promises:

> There be some sports are painful, and their labour
> Delight in them sets off; some kinds of baseness
> Are nobly undergone; and most poor matters
> Point to rich ends (3.1.1–4)

In contrast to the illusion of gold, which, for Smith, inebriates the minds of dissolute adventurers, Ferdinand's "delight" in his task is able to "set off," like a foil setting for a gem, the base form of labor he has assumed. This statement reinscribes the identity of the elite colonist in terms of his desire and ability to redefine his own status. Although seemingly placed in a degrading situation, these "poor matters" will lead the way to ultimate profit, an argument suitable for the deprivations and lack of riches characterizing the colonial experience in Virginia. Whereas Adrian's earlier search for promise in the new

landscape ("Though this island seem to be desert" [2.1.35])
prompted Antonio's deprecatory comment regarding its promise of
everything "save means to live" (2.1.51), Ferdinand presents a realiz-
able alternative to the utopian fantasies of Adrian and Gonzalo.
Strachey's *True Report* reaffirms this model of colonial labor: "Adam
himselfe might not live in Paradice without dressing the Garden"
(68). In this sense, it is the debasing labor itself that augurs the possibility of profit and enables a reconstitution of identity in the colony.

Ferdinand's new role as colonial laborer can be seen in the context
of more general efforts by promotional texts to redefine the Virginia
colony's superabundant gentlemen, and even colonial leaders, in the
terms associated with the colony's underrepresented skilled artisans
and laborers. In a passage reminiscent of Ferdinand's statement, John
Smith describes how he had recruited gentlemen in Jamestown to
help fell trees for timber. Smith is aware of the radical implications
of this conscription, but he cautions his reader to acknowledge the
benefits of his policy:

> By this, let no man think that the President, or these gentlemen spent
> their times as common wood-hackers at felling of trees, or such like
> other labours, or that they were pressed to any thing as hirelings or
> common slaves, for what they did (being but once a little inured) it
> seemed, and they conceited it only as a pleasure and a recreation.[97]

Smith makes a concerted effort to elevate the status of the gentlemen's labor, emphasizing that it did not reduce them to equivalence
with the colony's vented laborers or even the inmates of the domestic workhouse, either of whom could be described as "common
wood-hackers." Rather, the labor is merely "a pleasure and a recre-
ation," a sign of *noblesse oblige* similar to Ferdinand's casting of his
labor as a "sport." Even in this scene of social "levelling," class distinctions are preserved through Smith's emphasis on the gentlemen's
superior acumen for labor; as a marginal note declares, "One gentleman better than 20 lubbers" (239).

The model of colonial labor functioned to consolidate greater
forms of social control in Virginia and justify the erosion of the customary rights of laborers in the colony. This effect is made clear in
Strachey's *True Report* with its description of the efforts made by
gentlemen and colonial leaders to bail water from the ship during the
storm at sea. Whereas these men "lower" themselves and engage in
labor, the laborers themselves are rhetorically transformed into slaves:
"The common sort stripped naked, as men in Gallies" (9–10).

Smith's passage likewise evokes the image of "common slaves" so as to differentiate the value of the gentlemen's labor, a tactic that may then be used to justify stricter terms for subordinates: if the members of the colony's elite are forced to labor manually, giving up their customary rights, then so too can laborers relinquish their own liberties and traditional protections.

As Winthrop Jordan has pointed out, early modern definitions of slavery encompassed perpetual servitude as well as class status or "baseness."[98] Slaves, in this sense, were categorized not only by exemption from legal protection but also by the forms of labor specific to their class position. However, when Ferdinand asserts, "some kinds of baseness / Are nobly undergone" (3.1.2–3), he is divorcing the labor one voluntarily engages in from the labor inherently prescribed by one's status. The role of colonial labor thus offers a possibility of mobility for its gentlemanly practitioners: they debase themselves by engaging in labor merely in order to achieve "rich ends"; by doing so, they need not fear permanently lowering their own status. This position offers a contrast to that of the other aristocrats in *The Tempest*, particularly Antonio and Sebastian, "Ebbing men" who are defined instead by "Hereditary sloth" (2.1.226, 223). The depiction of colonial labor also changes the definition of "baseness" in relation to the servitude of the laboring classes. In the early colonial context, Karen Kupperman argues, "slavery" became defined as a form of servitude that "would have occurred because the base person was naturally expected to serve his betters."[99] And, in the context of the Virginia colony, Company officials were able to justify the deterioration of the condition of colonial servitude due to the analogous downward mobility of colonial leaders, forced by the exigencies of colonization to give up the traditional privileges associated with their class status.

In his *True Report*, Strachey reveals how the erosion of customary liberties is masked through the ability of the colonial government to effect forms of hegemony, winning the consent of subordinates through an emphasis on the shared project of colonial labor. When Gates asks his men to fell trees upon their arrival in Bermuda, Strachey describes "how contentedly doe such as labour with us, goe forth, when men of ranke and quality, assist, and set on their labours" (48–49). Strachey even cites the words of "the inferioor people," expressing how they are inspired "to doe their best...when such worthy, and Noble Gentlemen goe in and out before them" (49). By gaining the consent of the subaltern classes, natural hierarchies are restored in the colony as laborers reaffirm their faith in their superiors. Showing the link between social control and production, the laborers even pledge to work harder when led by example, a policy that, Strachey adds, "made our people at length more diligent" (28). This passage provides a relevant context for Prospero's ultimate hegemony in *The Tempest*, confirmed by Caliban's final lines that he will "be wise hereafter, / And seek for grace" (5.1.295–96).

In order to disguise the forms of social control necessary to effect the transformation of laborers, the rhetoric of colonial labor must displace its prerequisite violence onto the colonial landscape. In his discussion of what he calls "Shakespeare's Virginian Masque," John Gillies examines how *The Tempest* constructs a moralized landscape associated with the land's temperate climate and fruitful soil as well as the characteristics needed of its inhabitants, "a new and more realistic mood of forbearance in inevitable hardship."[100] What Gillies does not fully address in his analysis of the "masque of Ceres" in 4.1, however, is how this moralized landscape is less temperate than austere. The landscape described by Iris is not only a tended landscape, reflecting a preference for husbandry to natural "foison," but also a space that features practices of enclosure, with Ceres's livestock contained within "natural" enclosures of "flat meads thatch'd with stover" (4.1.63). By contrast, Gonzalo's utopian plantation envisages a landscape with "Bourn, bound of land, tilth, vineyard, none" (2.1.153). The reference to "bourn," a word that is not found in Florio's translation of Montaigne's "Of Cannibals," alludes to a specific early modern practice, the demarcation of property lines between fields.[101] The description of Ceres's tended landscape conjures images of the devastation resulting from agrarian capitalism found earlier in William Symonds's sermon. The presence of the displaced is further communicated through the solitary figures that populate the landscape, from the rejected suitor ("dismissed bachelor") seeking comfort in Ceres's groves (4.1.67) to Ceres's own retreat on her "sea-marge, sterile and rocky-hard" (4.1.69).

Ceres's landscape must be characterized by barrenness and austerity in order to serve as a counterpoint to her blessing of "Earth's increase, foison plenty, / Barns and garners never empty" (4.1.110–11). Jeffrey Knapp argues that the masque of Ceres advocates an expansionism that does not extend English power through colonialism so much as emphasize a colonial form of husbandry, representing practices of inhabiting and cultivating the land as a form of marriage to the colonial space.[102] The fact that the landscape of enclosure and austerity is associated with Ceres's realm, rather than Prospero's island, also serves to displace the threat of sterility and failure away from the colonial site of that "marriage," perhaps even associating England—rather than Virginia—with "Scarcity and want" (4.1.116). As a consequence, this displacement creates forms of difference between metropolis and colony, constructing an identity based upon colonial husbandry that is defined by its distance and distinctiveness from the home nation.

The conceptual separation of nation and colony is reflected by the inability of texts to employ holistic models of a body politic, demonstrating a movement away from the civic assumptions that had motivated earlier promoters of colonization. In their advocacy of colonial transplantation, these later texts not only depict laborers as incapable of reform and rehabilitation; they also extend this condemnation to the national economy. As Paul Slack has commented, "there was the increasing use of the paradigm of the body politic, not to bind together a varied social whole, but to show the damage which untreated disease, disorder or decay in any one member might do to the rest: the diseased members should be cut off."[103] In *A Plain Pathway to Plantations* (1624), Richard Eburne speculates that without the necessary "venting" of superfluous apprentices and servants, their idleness "else viperlike will in time root out and destroy the land itself wherein it is bred."[104] While Eburne repeats the fear of contamination seen earlier in depictions of recalcitrant workhouse inmates, he extends the contaminating effects of the poor from other destitute laborers to the land itself.

Even though the majority of promotional texts endorsed the venting of laborers to the colonies, none fully dissevered the poor from the national economy and body politic—even when these groups were described in the harshest terms as idle, useless, and dangerous. Promotional literature contained ubiquitous references to the crises of labor in England, the economic factors of underemployment and overpopulation that motivated colonial expansion. Nonetheless, very few of these texts were able to address these concerns as economic processes that required domestic redress and reform rather than a venting of excess labor. To acknowledge that the underlying problem derived from the domestic economy and social relations would disrupt the representation of the nation space as a unified body politic and thus subvert the depiction of England as "home." William Symonds's sermon *Virginia* (1609), whose candid critique of capital accumulation began this chapter, is one of the few examples to address the structural economic problems underlying domestic social relations, describing England as a sterile landscape unable to support its inhabitants. Robert Gray's *A Good Speed to Virginia* (1609) also concludes that the English body politic "hath not milke sufficient in the breast thereof to nourish all those children which it hath brought forth" (sig. B4), while John Smith's *A Description of New England* (1616) praises the abundance of the colony in contrast to England's "scarcity and want," declaring "Heer nature and liberty affords us that freely, which in England we want, or it costeth us dearely."[105] One would expect that colonial promotional literature would have endorsed emigration based on the prospect of a better life in the colony. Yet, in a survey of promotional texts published between 1576 and 1625 (along with many manuscript sources), I could locate only these three examples that even approximated an endorsement of colony over the English nation.[106]

What factors can explain why promotional texts restricted themselves in their key objective of promoting colonial emigration? One cause might stem from the perception that emigration and an increasingly distinct form of life in the colonies could potentially undermine definitions of a stable, integral national economy. As discussed in my survey of the earliest promotional texts, the first advocates of colonialism—Hitchcock, Gilbert, Peckham, the Hakluyts—were concerned primarily with the benefits that colonial expansion might bring to the domestic economy, whether in terms of a supplementary market for English goods or a means to import complementary foreign wares. These texts placed emphasis on the domestic market, not on colonial settlement. Yet this strategy nonetheless implied that only colonial expansion would enable the national economy to maintain itself, an assertion that ultimately decentered England, placing it in a dependent relation to its own colonies. Promotional texts following the Virginia Company's second charter reworked the body politic metaphor so as to recontain the colonies within the domestic economy. Robert Johnson's *Nova Britannia* (1609), for example, likens colonial emigration to the grafting of branches from a larger tree, a practice that serves to preserve the host body through "a disburdening...of those superfluous twigs, that sucke away their nourishment."[107] But while Johnson's metaphor is immersed in the ideology of venting excess labor, a later text, John White's *The Planters Plea* (1630), revises the horticultural analogy so as to recenter the domestic economy. Emigrants, in White's account, are not superfluous twigs but extended roots of the body politic, which are dispersed, not severed, "drawing nourishment to the maine body, and the tree is not weakened but strengthened the more they spread."[108]

Jonathan Gil Harris's study of early modern applications of the model of the body politic emphasizes the emergent uses of this metaphor to register forms of social pathology. In Harris's argument, the body politic metaphor was increasingly used to represent boundaries as sites of contamination, a strategy that transposed concerns over fissures in domestic forms of social control to fears over the infiltration of foreign bodies.[109] In this sense, the rhetoric of venting labor reinscribed domestic crises of labor into metaphors of spatial boundaries, expelling the dangerous bodies of excess laborers beyond the borders of the nation so as to retain a sense of the integrity of the national economy. Both Johnson and White make use of the trope of colonial husbandry as a means to convert venting from an expulsion of excess into a productive cycle that returns surplus. One of the most important examples of this process is found in John Donne's endorsement of colonial emigration in "A Sermon Preached to the Honourable Company of the Virginia Plantation" (1622):

> It shall sweep your streets, and wash your dores, from idle persons, and the children of idle persons, and imploy them: and truely, if the whole Countrey were but such a *Bridewell*, to force idle persons to work, it had a good use. But it is already, not onely a *Spleene*, to draine the ill humors of the body, but a *Liver*, to breed good bloud; already the imployment breeds Marriners; already the place gives essayes, nay Fraytes of Marchantable commodities[110]

In contrast to the image of an engrafted garden found in Johnson and White, Donne envisages a landscape denuded of laborers, with the streets figuratively swept clean of vagrants. The vented laborers are replaced by the prospect of the commodities they may create as productive bodies in the colonies. Mercantile exchange thus stands in for the reformation of the subject, signaling the incorporation of "idle" labor into a cycle of work and production of surplus. Donne thus describes the reinvigorated national economy as a large-scale Bridewell, indicating the enduring impact of the workhouse economy and ideas of vented labor. But Donne transforms this image from that of the spleen, connected to expulsion and draining, to that of the liver, which is able to "breed good bloud" (272). In *A Good Speed to Virginia* (1609), Robert Gray had similarly used the metaphor of the body's blood to depict the role of labor in the national economy, concluding that "euen as blood though it be the best humour in the body, yet if it abound in greater quantitie then the state of the body will beare, both indanger the bodie, & oftentimes destroyes it."[111] While acknowledging the central and instrumental role of labor in the national economy, Gray depicts an excess of labor as a debilitating and even destructive force. By contrast, Donne, like Johnson and White, reinscribes excess as a precondition for the production of surplus-value, thus incorporating colonial venting as a key ingredient in the expansion of domestic capital.

In the formulation of a national community as a "social body," the lower classes served a crucial role. But as Mary Poovey has argued in relation to nineteenth-century England, the abstraction that creates the sense of a national community as an aggregate of individuals also establishes an important exception for the lower-class members of this social body, groups who must additionally be subject to special forms of social control so as to ensure their compliance.[112] Promotional texts, such as those by Donne, Johnson, and White, similar to the civic-minded arguments of earlier texts, posited colonial labor as a redemptive process that would enable superfluous groups to be reincorporated into the national economy, even if forced to reside in a colonial outpost. However, unlike the earlier recommendations of Hitchcock or Hakluyt, the entrance of laborers into a system of exchange was predicated upon a reconstitution of their identities, a process dependent upon more coercive forms of social control and enforced productivity. A good example of this strategy is found in Crashaw's *A Sermon Preached in London Before the Right Honorable the Lord Lawarre* (1610). In his advocacy of an economy of vented laborers, Crashaw places emphasis not on the quality of the colonist, or the conditions under which he is conscripted, but the forms of discipline that enable a transformation of his identity:

> we much care not what the generalitie is of them that goe in person; considering we finde that the most disordered men that can bee raked vp out of the *superfluitie*, or if you will, the very *excrements*, of a full and swelling State, if they be remoued out of the fat and feeding ground of their *natiue countrey*, and from the licentiousnesse and too much libertie of the States where they haue liued, into a more bare and barren soile, as euery countrie is at the first, and to a harder course of life, wanting pleasures, and subiect to some pinching miseries, and to a strict forme of gouernement, and seuere discipline, doe often become new men, euen as it were cast in a new mould, and proue good and worthie instruments and members of a Common-wealth[113]

Crashaw reverses the language of Smith and others, which represented England's austerity as a cause prompting colonial emigration. Instead, England is characterized as a "full and swelling State," a body politic requiring the evacuation of its social "excrements." The colonial space, depicted as "a more bare and barren soile," offers the possibility to reform the superfluous and "disordered men" vented from England.[114] Greater forms of social control and discipline, transposed onto the austere landscape, provide the preconditions for a reform in subjectivity, allowing laborers to be "cast in a new mold" and thereby reintroduced into the body politic as "good and worthie instruments and members." Laborers are depicted ambivalently both as crucial members of the body politic and as its superfluous excrements, necessary bodies who can become part of the commonwealth only when subjected to extraordinary forms of social control and regulation. Yet some texts, especially Strachey's *True Report* and Shakespeare's *The Tempest*, express skepticism as to whether vented laborers would even subscribe to this ideology of colonial husbandry. These texts therefore consider the extent to which the colony's liberties could produce a colonial identity, one that, rather than serving a complementary role to the home nation, would enable colonists to rebel against the imposed authority of Company and nation.

WILLIAM STRACHEY'S *TRUE REPORT* AND THE BERMUDA MUTINIES

In the large body of promotional materials relating to the Virginia Company, Strachey's *True Report* deals most candidly with the dangers associated with laborers in the colonial environment. It may seem surprising that Strachey's text was not published until 15 years after its composition—when it was included in Samuel Purchas's compilation *Hakluytus Posthumus, or, Purchas his Pilgrimes* (1625)—especially since Strachey's account of Gates's shipwreck on Bermuda and eventual arrival in Jamestown is one of the most detailed and evocative accounts of the early years of the Virginia colony. Yet the text is also often ambivalent in its description of the colonial experience in Bermuda and Virginia, which might explain why Company officials chose not to have it published after its arrival in England in September 1610; instead, it was allowed to circulate privately, when, it is believed, Shakespeare most likely read it.[115] The volume of Company textual production, especially during the period 1609–12, illustrates the surprising omission of Strachey's text from print.[116]

Strachey's *True Report* is a central text in the corpus of colonial promotional literature, and it provides significant insight into the reconstitution of labor relations in England and its colonies. Past literary studies analyzing Strachey's *True Report* alongside *The Tempest* have tended to relegate Strachey's text and other promotional literature to a secondary status as contextual material considered solely in relation to *The Tempest*, a play that may in turn serve as a template for the early history of English colonialism.[117] Stephen Greenblatt's essay, "Martial Law in the Land of Cockaigne," exemplifies this problem: despite the fact that he highlights the sections of Strachey's text dealing with labor relations and lower-class rebellion, Greenblatt analyzes this context solely in order to expose similar dynamics within the literary text; consequently, he disregards the larger histories of class and labor to which Shakespeare's and Strachey's texts both contribute.[118] In its exclusive focus on issues of power and sovereignty, Greenblatt's approach also replicates the forms of power it attempts to critique, reimposing a hierarchical, unidirectional model of the circulation of power.[119] Greenblatt's essay, therefore, ultimately tells the story of authority—Prospero, Governor Thomas Gates—at the expense of those who are subject to this power. By contrast, I wish to analyze further Strachey's account of the period spent by Gates and his men on Bermuda, devoting greater attention to the three mutinies that were organized during this period, events that articulate crucial fissures relating to the role of labor and class relations in the first wave of English colonialism.

The first mutiny began among the mariners in Gates's fleet, a revealing detail given the fact that *The Tempest* allows the Boatswain to voice a critique otherwise elided in the text. Likewise, it is significant that the mariners must remain asleep, "clapp'd under hatches," during the course of the play (1.2.230, 5.1.231), a choice that separates this group from the comic conspiracy on the island. In contrast to Shakespeare's representation of Stephano and Trinculo's alliance with Caliban, Strachey depicts all three mutinies as having an explicit ideological foundation: while the first rebellion was led by a nonconformist named John Watt, the second was organized by the minister's clerk, Stephen Hopkins, who argued from both a scriptural and legal basis to assert that Gates's authority was limited to the Virginia colony and was therefore null and void in Bermuda (31). The final group extended this argument, questioning whether Gates consequently had the authority to punish anyone, including the mutineers (32). The second group of mutineers additionally justified its rebellion based upon a perception of the circumscribed social conditions in Virginia: "when in Virginia . . . they might well feare to be detained in that Countrie by the authority of the Commander thereof, and their whole life to serve the turnes of the Adventurers, with their travailes and labours" (31). This statement reveals the accuracy of the mutineers' knowledge of colonial labor conditions. Despite the fact that they were nominally protected under the Company's second charter, they impose a distinction between their own "travailes" and the motives of "Adventurers," investors who might institute exploitative conditions in order to extract additional profits. The mutineers also feared the prospect of being "detained" in the colony, aware of how they were no longer protected by customary rights but by a contractual relation that Company adventurers might be willing to alter.[120] By referring to the extension of their service to the term of "their whole life," they further articulate a concern that their rights could effectively be eroded to the condition of perpetual servitude.

Strachey's transcription of the mutineers' grievances exposes how the circulation of power in the fledgling colony operated in a highly visible and contestable manner. This degree of open resistance counters the clichéd New Historicist model of "subversion-containment" most directly due to the transparent failure of authorities to impose dominant models of hierarchy and obedience on social relations in the colony.[121] As Theodore Allen concludes in his discussion of the growth of forms of servitude and enslavement in the Virginia colony, "some knew it was wrong."[122] Among many contemporary examples, a laborer named Thomas Best decried, "My Master Atkins hath sold me for a £150 sterling like a damnd slave," while John Rolfe commented that the emergence of an economy of indentured servants and vented laborers, "buying and selling men and boies...was held in *England* a thing most intolerable."[123] Rolfe's statement reveals the discrepancy between domestic and colonial conditions of labor. Yet the erosion of the customary rights of laborers in early modern England had made possible the conditions of labor that developed in the colonies, a process that had begun even before the earliest waves of colonial migration in the first decade of the seventeenth century. In addition, however, underlying Best's and Rolfe's critique of colonial "slavery" is an implicit differentiation of indentured servitude from a racialized slave trade; in other words, a laborer like Best can decry being treated like a slave due to the presence of African slaves in the colony, a group whose position at the bottom of the social hierarchy enables him to recuperate his own status.

The rhetoric of colonial liberty codified in the second charter had taken advantage of the declining status of laborers in England in order to recruit necessary artisanal groups. Yet, instead of becoming a constituency of colonial "husbands," this class organized the mutinies among Gates's company on Bermuda. The first mutiny offered a particular threat once its instigators had recruited the fleet's chief smith as well as a carpenter named Nicholas Bennett to join the conspiracy (29). In Strachey's text, necessary skilled laborers—not poor vagrants or idle gentlemen—offered the most direct challenge to the colonial project. The final mutiny, in fact, collapsed only after one of its more elite members, the abusive gentleman Henry Paine, had assaulted the guard (33). Despite the centrality of their labor to the Virginia colony, these artisans also advocated staying on Bermuda (28). After the first group of conspirators had been apprehended, Gates even agreed to their demands and banished them to "an Iland farre by it selfe" (30). The leaders of the third mutiny, Christopher Carter and Robert Waters, were similarly left behind when the fleet sailed to Virginia (37–38).

Strachey's account emphasizes the failure of the mutinies, as each group ultimately expresses "sorrow and repentance" and commitment "to the common cause" of the Virginia colony, enabling Gates to "reacknowledge them againe" (30). Greenblatt's analysis, like Strachey, marks the containment of the subversive energies of the mutinies by emphasizing Gates's ultimate, Prospero-like pardon, an action that reflects a reinforcement of official power and general social reintegration among the Company.[124] However, the closure attempted by these accounts is dependent upon an elision of the presence of those mutineers left behind on Bermuda. Whereas the workhouse inmates unamenable to reform and discipline were reconstituted as a racialized group subject to colonial transportation, the mutineers who remain on Bermuda were expelled from the workings of power as well as the text itself. Despite Strachey's attempt to omit these recalcitrant mutineers from his subsequent narrative of the colony, one of the leaders, Robert Waters, later returned to England.[125] These mutineers reflect a return of the repressed narrative of labor in the archive of early modern colonization. The leader of the second mutiny, Stephen Hopkins, who also returned to England, later led an insurrection while traveling on the Mayflower to the Plymouth colony, an action that led to the formation of the Mayflower Compact.[126] Hopkins's role on the Mayflower testifies to the lasting contributions of the Bermuda mutineers to traditions of colonial liberty. In addition, the status of these figures attests to transatlantic networks of migration and diaspora that possessed a significant element of social radicalism, an alternative history that has begun to be explored in the work of Peter Linebaugh and Marcus Rediker.[127]

Strachey's *True Report* limits the radical implications of the Bermuda mutinies through its frequent citation of official Company documents within its narrative. For example, much of Strachey's account of Gates's arrival in Jamestown, sections 3 and 4 of his text, reworks an earlier document, "Letter of the Governor and Council of Virginia to the Virginia Company of London" (July 7, 1610), which Strachey, in his institutional role as Gates's secretary, would have helped compose.[128] In the section of his text describing Gates's arrival at Jamestown, Strachey even informs the reader that he will omit a narrative of the colony's notorious early history, "all these disasters, and afflictions descended upon our people" (46); instead, he refers the reader "to the Booke, which the Adventurers have sent hither intitled, Advertisements unto the Colony in Virginia" (46).[129] Many other passages in Strachey's text are borrowed from the "official" Virginia Company version of events, *A True Declaration of the Estate of the Colonie in Virginia* (1610).[130] Strachey even cites this text, deferring his own often-critical stance toward the colony to the "pub-like testimonie" of the corporate text (67). Strachey thus attempts to legitimate his own narrative by stressing his shared advocacy of the program of colonial labor.

Significantly, *The Tempest* borrows most heavily from those incidents and passages in Strachey that are derived from Company documents, illustrating how Shakespeare's play similarly advocates a model of colonial labor that depends upon an elision of the narratives of the Bermuda mutineers.[131] These efforts to efface concerns of labor and social control exemplify what Paul Brown describes as "euphemiza-tion," a process wherein power relations are reinscribed on a metaphorical or transcendent level.[132] One key moment of euphemi-zation occurs at the conclusion of the Masque of Ceres, when Iris calls upon "temperate nymphs" (4.1.132), figures representing the land, to join laborers, or "sunburn'd sicklemen" (134), in a country dance. It is this entrance, of "certain Reapers" (4.1.138 SD), that triggers Prospero's memory of Caliban's "foul conspiracy" with Stephano and Trinculo (4.1.139), causing him to put an end to the performance. Although critical accounts have noted the incongruity of Prospero's anger, and its indication of a point of weakness in his power, the source of Prospero's response has generally been over-looked.[133] Yet the appearance of the reapers links Caliban's conspir-acy with Stephano and Trinculo to contemporary debates on the role of laborers in England's new colonies.

Strachey's text exercises its own forms of euphemization through its deference to corporate texts such as *A True Declaration* and Gates's letter to the Virginia Company. However, I wish to fore-ground the potentially antagonistic nature of this intertextual rela-tionship. The rhetoric of colonial labor operated not as a uniform or monolithic discursive strategy but as a tactic used to achieve certain effects; specifically, it served to create a consensus and win consent for a colonial program that could assert itself only by defining and demonizing its antithesis. Therefore, one can locate the points of ideological anxiety in Strachey's text by noting when he chooses to defer to a Company publication rather than provide his own account. In an example of how the rhetoric of colonial husbandry attempted to redefine and control labor, Strachey defines the antithesis of Virginia's "temperate climate," in a passage taken verbatim from Gates's letter, as the "distempered bodies" of the colony's laborers.[134] Implicit in this formulation is an opposition, rather than a conjunction, between the temperate land and its colonial husbands. If, following Knapp's reading of the play, the masque of Ceres attempts to wed the colonial inhabitants to the land, it must also produce a divorce, not only from the indigenous population but also from the colony's idle and mutinous laborers.[135]

Prospero's "our revels now are ended" speech offers a poetic displacement of the concerns of labor evoked moments earlier by the appearance of the reapers in the wedding masque. However, the metaphorical content of this passage, particularly its architectonic language, nonetheless reveals the foundational role of colonial labor. Prospero's metatheatrical speech conjures images of masque designs and the public theater—"The cloud-capp'd tow'rs, the gorgeous palaces, / The solemn temples, the great globe itself" (4.1.152–53)— all depicted as a "baseless fabric" to a vision (151), a structure both dreamlike and without a foundation. This gesture toward transcendence ensures its "insubstantial" character (155) through a movement away from its base, from the forces that enable the structure's construction, in other words, from labor. In his *True Report*, Strachey similarly concedes, in language reminiscent of Prospero, that he must "truely acknowledge" the continued presence of laborers, "men of such distempered bodies, and infected mindes" that nonetheless "must be the Carpenters, and workemen in this so glorious a building."[136] Strachey's ire seems to encompass both elite and lower-class colonists, both the Antonios and the Stephanos among Gates's fleet. Yet, unlike most accounts of laborers in promotional texts, Strachey makes a striking "acknowledgment" of their crucial role in the construction of the colony.

At the end of the first section of this chapter, I had addressed the possible meanings evoked by Prospero's "acknowledgment" of Caliban. In conclusion, I would like to return to this passage in order to consider the links between these two passages in Shakespeare and

Strachey and gauge, in each case, what it means to "acknowledge" labor and laborers. Far from conceding similitude and mutual dependence, I wish to argue that these lines in *The Tempest* and Strachey's *True Report* attest to a codification of class as a category of difference, a classification that buttressed a centralization of capital and erosion of laborers' customary rights. A relevant description of this acknowledgment of labor is provided by Max Weber in his discussion of what he terms "appropriation."[137] In the early modern period, notions of liberty did not represent positive, inalienable rights; rather, they were based upon the power to exclude another from one's own property.[138] For Weber, appropriation defines this type of "closed relationship," the ability of those controlling capital to extend power over the rights and bodies of laborers. In this sense, Prospero's statement to Alonso establishes a claim of their parallel ownership over their rebellious subordinates: "Two of these fellows you / Must know and own; this thing of darkness I / Acknowledge mine" (5.1.274–76). Prospero's comment serves as a form of appropriation, enabling him to speak for Caliban, Stephano, and Trinculo and deprive them of their powers to curse, mock authority, and even conspire. He is thereby able to relegate them in their silence solely to a relational identity, a closed relationship founded upon ownership rather than mutual obligation. This moment of appropriation, not Prospero's pardon, as Greenblatt would have it, represents the apotheosis of Prospero's power. These lines serve to displace Prospero's earlier acknowledgment of the centrality of Caliban's labor—"We cannot miss him" (1.2.311)—just as Strachey had done to the Bermuda mutineers through his reference to the laborers' "distempered bodies, and infected mindes." The mutinies among Gates's company, like Caliban's conspiracy with Stephano and Trinculo, offer the pretext for the assumption of full control over the rights and agency of servants and laborers.

This appropriation of labor culminated a process of capital formation that had successfully eroded the customary rights of laborers in England, one that replaced models of the commonwealth and body politic with the enforced production of the workhouse. The failure of these domestic forms of social control gave rise to an advocacy of practices of venting labor to the colonies, policies that effectively drew attention away from the crises embedded in domestic class relations following an early period of capitalist accumulation. Shakespeare's *The Tempest*, Strachey's *True Report*, and the variety of promotional materials written for the Virginia colony illustrate how the unresolved crises of labor endemic to early modern England shaped the conditions of the early colonial experience. And, even as the liberties associated with the "brave new world" of the American colonies provided important examples of agency and resistance, the Virginia Company utilized this environment of colonial liberty to create new labor conditions that "freed" the colony from the protective constraints of customary labor relations in England. As a result, the Virginia Company was able to centralize capital and increase forms of social control, thereby producing an environment for laborers far more restrictive than what would have been conceivable in England. However, even in this labor context, the forms of social mobility and creolization made possible by colonial migration created a social landscape that profoundly transformed definitions of class and nation, ultimately enabling the vented classes to reclaim the social role and forms of agency appropriated from them.

CHAPTER 4

"COUNTERFEIT EGYPTIANS" AND IMAGINED BORDERS: JONSON'S *The Gypsies Metamorphosed* AND THE UNION OF THE REALMS

COUNTERFEIT EGYPTIANS

Upon his initial entrance in Jonson's *The Gypsies Metamorphosed* (1621), the figure of the Patrico (or "hedge-priest") calls the audience's attention to himself, "that am bringer / Of bound to the border" (134–35).[1] The concern for control of borders was an appropriate one in Jacobean England. At the local level, vagrant groups, including gypsies, defied anti-vagrant legislation that attempted to limit their geographic mobility and keep them within their home parish.[2] But the neighboring counties of England and Scotland known as the Borders were particularly notorious in the Jacobean period as a haven for gypsies and vagrants, groups who could evade prosecution in an area already populated by cattle raiders (or "reivers") noted for a similar disregard of the Anglo-Scottish border.[3] The border counties presented a threat to civil order and ideas of cultural unity because of the ease with which the cultures of gypsies, vagrants, and reivers could interact and mix together, even forming the possibility of an alternative community. The Borders region was therefore defined by the fluid character of its boundaries, the lack of distinct barriers between regions and constituent cultures. And while the Patrico characterizes the Borders as an area specifically beyond social control, he casts his role, like that of James VI and I during his joint rule of Scotland and England, as one that is able to define as well as control that border.

Jonson's *The Gypsies Metamorphosed* replicates the evasive character of gypsy cultural difference through its own remarkable lack of aesthetic boundaries. The masque frequently blurs traditional distinctions between masque and antimasque, most exceptionally by giving many of its main speaking roles to courtiers rather than professional actors, who instead direct the performance in their gypsy roles as the Patrico and the Jackman (or "educated beggar"). In addition to casting the king's favorite, George Villiers, the marquis of Buckingham, as Captain of the Gypsies, members of Buckingham's family and circle impersonated the remaining gypsies.[4] *The Gypsies Metamorphosed* was Jonson's most popular masque, a work performed on an unprecedented three occasions: at Buckingham's new estate at Burley-on-the-Hill on August 3, 1621; at Belvoir, the estate of Buckingham's father-in-law, the earl of Rutland, two nights later; finally, a month later at court in Windsor.

The most substantial analysis of the masque, Dale B.J. Randall's *Jonson's Gypsies Unmasked*, argues that the lack of differentiation between masque, antimasque, and court audience produced by the gypsy disguise enabled Jonson to express more safely the potentially subversive comparison of the king's favorite and his followers to a band of gypsies.[5] Randall's analysis, which emphasizes the subversiveness of the masque's portrayal of Buckingham, nonetheless does not fully explain either its popularity or the generous compensation subsequently awarded to Jonson.[6] Martin Butler qualifies Randall's discussion, arguing that the masque makes public the compromised ethical position of Buckingham and his circle so that they may be tested and ultimately "royally vindicated."[7] Yet Butler's impressive analysis of the masque in the context of court politics does not concern itself with the status of gypsies or with possible reasons for Jonson's choice of this group for the masque; nor does Butler, in his appraisal of the importance of Buckingham's patronage of Jonson, fully account for the masque's incomplete closure. As I will argue, the ultimate lack of metamorphosis in the masque's conclusion results more immediately from the nature of the central gypsy metaphor itself—and the protean, "counterfeit" performativity of gypsy identity— than from the tenuous, unresolved relationships of members of the court. Therefore, rather than center the gypsies in the court like Butler, or relegate them to the margins like Randall, my own discussion places gypsies in a liminal position analogous to the contested status of the Borders in Jacobean culture. This chapter therefore emphasizes the importance of Scottish contexts for both the gypsies and James VI and I: gypsies were often linked with Scotland, a pejorative association that James himself often faced as England's Scottish king. In addition, James's ambivalent policies toward gypsies during his tenure in Scotland help explain their subsequent, unique status in Jacobean England.

Past discussions of Jonson's masque have overlooked how the presence of gypsies may relate to James VI and I's concerted persecution of nomadic cultures and practices of internal colonialism toward peripheral regions. The figure of the "counterfeit Egyptian" often served to represent a general lack of social control and national unity. Harrison's *Description of England* (1577) estimated these vagrant groups as numbering 10,000, depicting gypsies as an alternative community that threatened to add to its ranks with the displaced poor.[8] The image of vagrant groups was similarly evoked during debate on James's attempted Union of the Realms of England and Scotland; Union opponents, in fact, frequently attributed a Scottish origin to account for both vagrancy and support for the Union. By using the figure of gypsies, Jonson's *The Gypsies Metamorphosed* questions a key component of Union rhetoric: the emphasis on James's power as a "British" monarch to reconcile cultural differences among his subjects. As Jonathan Goldberg has observed, we see in this masque Jonson's "art of turning the king's self-perception against himself."[9] Jonson's masque reinscribes the imagined redrawing of borders attempted by James I's proposed Union of the Realms as an analogous performance to the "counterfeit" identities and lack of geographic location of vagrants and gypsies. By foregrounding the performativity of both gypsy and British identities, *The Gypsies Metamorphosed* exposes how the rhetoric of national unity ironically mimics the protean character of these vagrant groups. But the ultimate lack of metamorphosis with which the masque concludes points to the comparable inability of the Jacobean Union to effect a transformative reconstitution of national borders and identities.[10]

***

THE ANGLO-SCOTTISH BORDERS AND THE UNION OF THE REALMS

Recent studies of the history of nationalism have emphasized the performative character of national affiliation.[11] In *Imagined Communities,* his seminal work on the historical origins of nationalism, Benedict Anderson discusses the imaginative construction of national identification.[12] Anderson contrasts how modern nations define their borders, as "finite, if elastic," with the "older imagining" of the pre-modern dynastic realm, in which "states were defined by centres, borders were porous and indistinct, and sovereignties faded imperceptibly into one another."[13] Yet James VI and I's joint rule of Scotland and England from 1603–25 is a case that evades such rigid categorization: the sovereignties in Jacobean Britain were configured in the same person, complicating the definition of a center when the two thrones were jointly occupied by one monarch. Critics of the Union of the Realms responded to this conceptual impasse by arguing that James could be king either of England or Scotland, not of both.[14] The recognizably nationalist sentiments that the Union project provoked from its English and Scottish opponents demonstrate the nascent development of a modern imagining of borders, the association of national sovereignty with the integrity of "finite, if elastic" borders.[15] Yet the failure of James's Union of the Realms may be attributed more directly to the lack of a consensus regarding an imagined British community, perhaps resulting from the ways that James's Britain constituted neither a dynastic realm nor a modern nation. Jacobean Britain exemplified what J.H. Elliot terms "a composite monarchy," wherein the personal rule of the monarch functioned to unite disparate populations and noncontiguous territories.[16] Given the common presence of such political arrangements in early modern Europe, the Union of the Realms represented a startling failure, for debate on the Jacobean Union was unable to resolve how specific cultural institutions could be reconstituted, thus accentuating the differences between English and Scottish parliaments, legal institutions, and procedures of naturalization.[17]

The status of the Borders and their gypsy inhabitants produced a fundamental crisis of social control due to the symbolic importance of the region's geographically central location. James's initial proposal of the Union of the Realms, his "Proclamation for the uniting of England and Scotland" (1603), was, in fact, concerned exclusively with control of the Borders. Realizing that his constitution of empire necessarily entailed a redefinition of cultural borders, James renamed the adjoining counties on both sides of the Anglo-Scottish border "the Middle Shires." But the praise James lavished on the Borders, calling them "the very heart of the country" and "the best parts of the whole Ile," was tempered by his admission that his efforts to make the Borders "no more the extremeties, but the middle" were ultimately based upon a desire to wield more effective control over the area, with "the Inhabitants thereof reduced to perfect obedience."[18] Appropriately, James's proclamation followed an order from two days earlier that had demanded the voluntary surrender of groups who continued to practice raids on either side of the Anglo-Scottish border.[19]

Perceiving a lack of general support for his proposed Union of the Realms following his initial declaration, James, like the Patrico in Jonson's masque, fashioned himself as the force to set "bound" to the boundaries within his realm. In a speech delivered to the English Parliament on March 1, 1603/04, James emphasized his power to erase and redraw borders, his ability to make boundaries "so indivisible, as almost those that were Borderers themselves on the late Borders, cannot distinguish, nor know, or discerne their owne limits."[20] James, like other supporters of the Union project, stressed the lack of natural and geographic boundaries between England and Scotland; as James asked of the English Parliament, "who can set downe the limits of the borders, but as a mathematicall line or idæa?"[21] One of James's chief proponents of the Union, Francis Bacon, had similarly asserted that England and Scotland "have no true but an imaginary separation," a lack of boundaries he describes as "badges and memorials of borders."[22] Union supporters disregarded representations of difference between England and Scotland as memories of former conflicts that belie both geographic and political realities: "in our mind and apprehension," Bacon declared, "they are all one and the same nation."[23] Yet the persistence of such "memorials of borders" is attested to by the fact that Bacon notes in one of his Union texts the need to create "some further device for the utter and perpetual confounding of those imaginary bounds, (as your Majesty termeth them)," including a uniform legal code to rule over the entire region.[24] Significantly, Bacon's efforts to offset anti-Union prejudice—and its reliance on "imaginary" borders—requires "some further device," the construction of an equally imaginary Union.

But to imaginatively construct "Great Britain" as a distinct community called into question the relation of monarchical power to areas characterized by a lack of centralized authority, for it became unclear how the rhetoric of empire was able to either ensure social control in these regions or cancel out residual forms of cultural difference. The inhabitants of the Borders were now "British" subjects; however, rather than being pacified, critics of the Union project complained that the Borderers themselves consequently failed to recognize "their owne limits," to rephrase James's earlier declaration.

In James's reformulation of British boundaries, the margins were moved to the center. In a speech to Parliament, James depicted the Borders, once "confining places," as transformed through the imperial reconstitution of boundaries into "the navell or umbilicke of both kingdomes," both the center and the lifeline of the body politic.[25] In order to cancel out forms of cultural difference, James and Union supporters had to establish the foundation of the United Kingdom on the principle of difference itself. The general disregard of components of the Union, such as official efforts to rename Scots and English as "North Britons" and "South Britons,"might have resulted from the ways that this formulation defined both cultures as margins within a more abstracted entity; the center of "Britain," on the other hand, remained undefined, "an empire nowhere." This reconstitution of boundaries thus subverted any integral foundation of national identity among its component parts; according to Bacon, post-Union England and Scotland would merely be considered parts of Britain, "and consequently neither of these are to be considered as things entire of themselves, but in the proportion that they bear to the whole."[26]

Gypsies, with their supposedly protean ability to change appearance and allegiance, thus served as an appropriate metonym for the desired reimagining of cultural identities in the Jacobean Union project. The figure of the gypsy had similarly been employed in a masque that Thomas Campion composed to be performed for James I during the monarch's only return visit to Scotland in 1617.[27] When Anglo-Scottish tensions increased following James's Northern Progress, tensions further exacerbated by James's promotion of the unpopular Buckingham to the Privy Council of Scotland during the trip, Campion's masque incorporated in its antimasque figures of gypsies and rustics, emblems of the region's disorder, to celebrate the pacifying influence of the royal presence.[28] The emphasis on the Borders' pacification is appropriate, as will be discussed later, given the fact that the masque's host, the earl of Cumberland, amassed considerable wealth from the wide-scale land confiscations that accompanied the Jacobean suppression of reiver clans.[29] Jonson's masque, often seen as influenced by Campion's earlier entertainment, similarly functioned to assuage Anglo-Scottish tensions.[30]

James's 1617 Northern Progress had revitalized English interest in Scotland, evidenced by Jonson's own extended visit from the summer of 1618 to January 1619. Jonson even proposed writing a pastoral drama set in the Loch Lomond district that he had visited, and he composed a travel narrative of his Scottish journey, "including some account of Scottish institutions, legends and antiquities," which is believed to have been destroyed in a fire in his lodgings in 1629.[31] Nonetheless, Jonson's Scottish visit did produce one major extant text, his *Conversations* with his Scottish host, William Drummond of Hawthornden. In addition to writing a poem commemorating James's Progress, "Forth Feasting," Drummond supplied Jonson with antiquarian information on Scotland following the visit, including a map of Loch Lomond sent in a letter of July 1, 1619, a demonstration of Jonson's continuing interest in Scottish history and geography.[32] Thus, Jonson's attention to Scotland helps explain his inclusion of Anglo-Scottish issues in *The Gypsies Metamorphosed*, even though active debate concerning the Union had ended by 1621.[33]

Despite the efforts of the Jacobean Union of the Realms to subsume cultural difference within the representational framework of British identity, James's policies more often attempted to legislate and enforce conformity. In lieu of a successfully imagined British community, James VI and I constructed his British empire through a process of internal colonialism. Certainly, many Union opponents found the colonial metaphor relevant: as the Scottish pamphleteer John Russell demanded, "Sall ane frie kingdome, possessing sua ancient liberteis, become ane slave?"[34] This chapter is most concerned with the status and definition of borders in this process. Far from being "porous and indistinct," as in Benedict Anderson's formulation, cultural borders were contentious sites of struggle in Jacobean England and Scotland. As Richard Marienstras has argued, questions regarding the king's authority over "wild spaces" is closely linked to debate concerning "the power of the king over conquered lands and kingdoms."[35] Some areas within the borders of James's "Great Britain" constituted equally both "wild spaces" and "conquered lands," areas nominally under state control that nonetheless continued to exist as semiautonomous regions, areas that included not only the Anglo-Scottish Borders but also the Scottish Highlands and Hebridean Islands.[36]

During his tenure in Scotland, James VI had begun to institute political commissions and missionary programs that attempted to establish more effective control over peripheral regions such as the Hebrides, continuing these efforts even after his accession to the English throne. James's commission for "the Improvement of the Isles" possessed several goals: to facilitate religious conformity in the region, improve revenue collection for the crown, and offset the reputation of Scotland's incivility and backwardness.[37] In *Basilikon Doron* (1599), James had differentiated the Highlands from the Hebrides; while the former region's population demonstrated "some shewe of ciuilitie," and could abide by the laws of their clans, James, by contrast, characterized the Hebrideans as completely barbarous. He therefore found the Islands suitable for colonization by lowland Scottish settlers, and he recommended "planting Colonies among them of answerable In-lands subiects, that within short time may reforme and ciuilize the best inclined among them; rooting out or transporting the barbarous and stubborne sort, and planting ciuilitie in their roomes."[38] James's policies toward the Islands are of central importance because they constituted James's first effort to organize a colony and, therefore, witness the ways that James's earlier tenure in Scotland provided a framework for later colonial projects in Virginia and Ulster. However, the continued resistance of the Hebrideans to centralized authority, demonstrated by the ultimate failure to plant a permanent colony in the region, testifies to how this initial Jacobean colonial effort provided a negative lesson for the prospects of later "British" colonies. State policies toward the Hebrides may even exemplify an alternative to colonization, although this legacy is overlooked in criticism that focuses exclusively on the colonies that emerged later in James's joint reign of England and Scotland.

A power vacuum among Hebridean leaders in the 1590s prompted the Scottish government to attempt to extend its authority into the region. Making use of a type of legal maneuvering that would later characterize Sir John Davies's tenure as attorney general of Ireland, the Island of Lewis was forfeited to the crown in 1598. Three successive missions to conquer Lewis and settle the island with lowland Scottish colonists failed in 1595–1602, 1605–06, and 1609. Despite his stated intentions to the contrary in *Basilikon Doron*, James opted ultimately for a negotiated settlement, the Statutes of Icolmkill (or Iona), passed in August 1609. Under the terms of this agreement, in exchange for recognition of the monarch's chief authority, the region was left to its own devices.[39] In reward for his service, James appointed his chief agent in the Iona compromise, Andrew Knox, bishop of the Isles, as bishop of Raphoe in Donegal (Ulster). Nonetheless, the Highlands and Hebrides remained exempt from the policies of land confiscation and transplantation of populations that would characterize both the Jacobean colonization of Ulster and the pacification of the Borders.[40] The exemption of this area of the "Celtic fringe" allowed the region to persist in a noncolonial, semiautonomous environment. In the following century, this region of future Jacobites would ironically also serve as one of the last bastions of support for the House of Stuart and a crucial internal enemy of the British state.

In contrast to the Highlands and Hebrides, James's efforts to extend centralized authority took on a particular urgency in the Borders region because of its strategic location and symbolic place in the rhetoric of Union. In *Basilikon Doron*, James had predicted that an eventual Union of the Realms would put an end to the problems of social control associated with the Borders.[41] By 1605, however, James was forced to take more direct action, and he appointed a Border Commission, composed of five officials from each nation and headed by his leading Scottish counselor, James Home, the earl of Dunbar, to look into and resolve disputes in the border counties. Rather than facilitating a peaceful unification of cultures, the Commission was noted for its severity, producing an exceptionally large number of convictions and summary executions.[42] Despite its own Anglo-Scottish composition, the Commission failed to offset fears of cultural mixing and infiltration on either side of the border. Although the Commission successfully revoked March Treasons, which prohibited unlicensed marriages, tribute, or economic exchanges between individuals of either nation, James ultimately rejected Bacon's proposal for a mixed Anglo-Scottish law code to govern the area.[43] While these policies were initially successful in pacifying the region, the Borders remained autonomous and noted for their disorder after Dunbar's death in 1611.[44] The status of the Borders, to quote Brian Levack, "stood as a reminder not only that the King's Peace was not being maintained in all his shires, but that English and Scots were still at war with each other."[45]

James's efforts to efface differences between English and Scottish cultures in the creation of Great Britain produced an uneasy status for the vagrants and gypsies who populated the border counties of Scotland and the North Country. The anxieties evoked by vagrant groups were particularly acute because of their location in the geographic heart of the empire. Attempts to control the Borders and their gypsy inhabitants during the Jacobean period consequently exposed the inherent contradictions in the status of subjects in the largely imaginary British empire. Robert Pont's Union treatise listed the inhabitants of the Anglo-Scottish border among the main opponents of the Union of the Realms, for a unified legal jurisdiction over the area would suppress an economy based upon raids and pillaging, effectively tying the Borderers to the land.[46] Another Union text hoped that "extinguishing the memorie and name of Bordours" would additionally remove the threat of cultural difference and "deface and burie all memorie of our former divisions."[47]

James's reconstitution of the Borders as the Middle Shires necessitated a disavowal of the region's past history as a lawless region dominated by generally autonomous reiver families. In 1609, the Lord Chancellor of Scotland, the earl of Dunfermline, described the Borders as a landscape denuded of its inhabitants, as "clean," "purged," and "free and open."[48] The representation of a pacified region wherein the Borders and their inhabitants were erased provided the ideological palliative for a brutal campaign of mass execution and transplantation of the Borders population during the first decade of James's joint reign. Edward Said has noted the racialized valences of the trope of "cleaning the land" in his discussion of nineteenth-century colonial discourse.[49] The creation of a cleared land is predicated upon a disavowal of the process of its creation, an effacement of the human subjects whose disappearance is prerequisite for the "clean" landscape. Its appearance in reference to the Jacobean Borders witnesses how these practices of internal colonialism served as an interpretive framework and precedent for later overseas colonial practices.

The Jacobean regulation of the Borders consequently witnesses a separation of the intentions of the monarchical state from the violence of its agents. One of the most notorious of Jacobean Borders officials was Sir William Cranstoun, commander of the Scottish horse garrisons and therefore the agent chiefly responsible for the capture and punishment of offenders north of the Anglo-Scottish border. Cranstoun's ruthlessness even prompted the entire town of Dumfries to conspire to attempt his assassination. In this bizarre incident, the townspeople lured Cranstoun and his officers into town under the pretense of a May Play, using the performance as a chance to ambush the officials.[50] The practices of officials such as Cranstoun prompted a disapproving letter from James, who found the commissioners' practices "savouring altogidder of barbarisme."[51] Despite this critique, James granted a blanket pardon to Cranstoun only months later, justifying his officer's actions based upon the fact that he served in a region that "mycht not alwyse permit those prolixe formes accustumed in the civile pairtis of the kingdome to be used at all tymes."[52] Despite James's rhetoric of an erasure of borders and assimilation of the region, the pacification of the region was dependent upon an acknowledgment of the Borders' difference: as a region that did not operate according to the civil laws of the rest of the kingdom, it could, therefore, be pacified by any means necessary. In reward for his efforts, Cranstoun was elevated to the peerage in 1610.[53]

The "cleaning" of the Borders was accomplished not only through summary executions but also through the implementation of practices of transplantation, of venting populations abroad. Significantly, the forced transportation of a prominent Borders clan, the Grahams, served as the first example of the use of such policies in the history of the "British empire." James's first proclamation "for the uniting of England and Scotland" (May 19, 1603) concerned itself exclusively with the regulation of the Borders and, in particular, the control of the Grahams.[54] James's proclamation reveals the ideological importance of the continued autonomy of a group situated not only in the heart of the kingdom but also on potentially profitable land. A subsequent proclamation, "for transplantation of the Greames" (December 4, 1603), authorized the earl of Cumberland to begin rounding up members of the clan for transportation. The Graham lands were surveyed within two months of the latter proclamation, enabling Cumberland to seize a large portion of the territory for himself. It is therefore appropriate that the entertainment given by the earl of Cumberland to mark James's 1617 Northern Progress emphasized the pacification of the Borders, a policy from which the family had made a fortune.

The process of internal colonialism in the Borders region entailed not only an erasure of the violence through which cultural unity was achieved but also an elision of the presence of the Borders' displaced population. James's latter proclamation even offers the testimony of the Grahams themselves, who request their voluntary removal from the Borders:

> and doe all (but specially the Greames) confesse themselves to bee no meete persons to live in those Countreys, And therefore have humbly besought us that they might bee removed to some other Parts, where with our gracious favour, they hope to live to become new men, and deserve our Mercy.[55]

Similar to representations of the execution of pirates, the supposed voices of the accused are transcribed, allowing state power to speak through them and render their punishment as a voluntary act. The Grahams are expelled from the region as well as the conceptualization of the body politic and deemed as unfit to inhabit their home counties. And, as with the rhetoric of venting found in colonial promotional materials, their forced transplantation promises a transformation of their subjectivity into "new men," a process that will enable their eventual reincorporation into the body politic.

The forced venting of the Grahams did not begin until the summer of 1605, by which time the earl of Cumberland had already seized most of their land. A group of 150 Graham men was conscripted into military service in the Low Countries. Testifying to the involuntary nature of this removal, many of these men illegally returned to Scotland by the end of the year. As a result of the continued presence of Grahams in the Borders, the remnants of the clan were transplanted in 1606 to the harsh and unfertile environment of western Ireland and Sir Ralph Sidley's plantation in Connaught. Again, many Grahams returned to Scotland before the end of the year, leaving only a half dozen families in Ireland by 1608.[56] The unexpected return of most Grahams from abroad prompted a subsequent proclamation in 1614 stipulating the punishment of any returnees from Ireland or the Low Countries.[57] Yet the continuing inability to control these groups is witnessed by a 1617 proclamation that redirected the transplantation of Borderers to Virginia, where "they may no more infect the places where they abide within this our Realme."[58] The same goal was hoped for in the suppression of gypsies: yet a group of Scottish gypsies convicted in 1624 of being "Egyptians" technically complied with James's sentence of banishment simply by crossing the border into England.[59] Thus, while James's power was defined by his ability, like the Patrico, to bring "bound to the border," the populations of reivers, vagrants, and gypsies who populated the Anglo-Scottish Borders were noted for a literal ability to subvert boundaries and, by extension, preserve forms of cultural difference that thwarted the terms of the Jacobean Union of the Realms.

***

GYPSIES AND MASTERLESS MEN

Along with their ability to disregard borders, gypsies subverted categorization as either a domestic or alien group because they were situated both within and outside English culture. In sixteenth-century Scotland and England, gypsies were recognized and protected as a distinct culture. In 1540, James V had acknowledged John Faw as "lord and erle of Litill Egipt," conferring on him all authority and legal jurisdiction over gypsy groups.[60] In addition to this acceptance of gypsy local autonomy, James even subordinated Scottish authority to gypsy command, granting Faw the power to command Scottish officers to assist him in carrying out "the laws of Egypt" among his subjects.[61] Whereas Scottish policy acknowledged the distinctiveness of gypsy communities, English law attempted to assimilate the gypsies; yet each strategy resulted in a similar failure to regulate gypsy culture by legal means. In early modern England, gypsies were also technically English citizens.[62] The 1562 Act "for further Punishment of Vagabonds, calling themselves Egyptians" confirmed the status of native-born gypsies as English subjects, thereby assuring their immunity from subsequent anti-gypsy legislation that attempted to deport them. The statute instead singled out for punishment "counterfeit Egyptians," masterless men who disguised themselves as gypsies, stipulating penalties ranging from loss of goods to death.[63]

In their uneasy status as naturalized aliens, the gypsies possessed their own separate traditions, including their own monarchs. Jonson's *The Gypsies Metamorphosed* foregrounds the monarchical social structure of the gypsies, a representational strategy that lends a sense of legitimacy to gypsy culture. Gypsies often cast themselves in these terms, emphasizing their status as displaced nobility, as a way to evade anti-vagrant legislation.[64] As the Jackman informs the audience, "though we seem a tattered nation," the gypsy band nonetheless possesses a hierarchy and geographic home, for they "yearly keep our musters" at "the famous Peak of Derby / And the Devil's Arse there hard by" (112, 107–09). The Jackman's opening explanation of the gypsies' origin borrows from Samuel Rid's *Martin Markall* (1610), which describes how Giles Hatcher organized vagrants in the area around the Peak Cavern in Castleton, Derbyshire, where he "ruled almost two-and-twenty years."[65] Despite Rid's depiction of the gypsies as a domestic group, other texts emphasized their foreign origin. After having elected Higgen as "King of *Beggars*" (2.1.7), the vagrants in Fletcher and Massinger's *Beggars' Bush* (1622) declare their intention to transplant their "tatterd Colony" to England, thus linking them to the recently arrived gypsies (5.2.219–21).[66] Even though Higgen's gypsy band is depicted as diasporic and geographically displaced, its departure for England is ironically represented as a colonizing venture, an inversion of the power relations between gypsies and authorities.[67]

The association of gypsies with the king is appropriate, considering the itinerant identity of the court on Progress. In Jonson's masque, the Porter's prologue extends the analogy between the court and its vagrant subjects, noting James's "good grace" in allowing the gypsies to follow the court during its own peregrinations (37–38). The Porter might be alluding to the large number of vagrants who had followed James on his 1617 Progress through the North Country and Scotland.[68] Vagrants were noted for their efforts to associate themselves with the court, a fact that prompted proclamations expelling vagrants from the court in 1618 and 1619.[69] By foregrounding the court's "vagrant" status while on Progress, the analogy reinscribes monarchical power as a mobile, labile force, one that enables the court to encompass and better control its margins, although only by replicating the suspect nomadic qualities of vagrants.[70] The status of outlawed groups resembles that of the monarch, as Richard Marienstras has pointed out, because both exempt themselves from legal jurisdiction.[71] In Jonson's masque, the gypsies compare their status to that of wild game preserved in royal parks, "the king's game" (90): they remain similarly under the king's protection from outside threat (and civic jurisdiction), while also becoming fair game for the king himself to hunt down.

The status of gypsies, culturally different yet legally naturalized, further complicates definitions of subject and stranger. Although gypsies were often categorized as an alien group, a classification that allotted them protected status, their continued presence created doubts regarding their foreign origin, especially as the boundaries between foreign gypsies and domestic vagrants became increasingly more indeterminate. Upon the gypsies' initial entrance in *The Gypsies Metamorphosed*, the Jackman presents the gypsy children in his entourage as "the five princes of Egypt," whom he describes as "begotten upon several Cleopatras in their several counties" (52–56). Though connecting these figures with their "Egyptian" origin as "the offspring of Ptolemy," and calling attention to their intrinsic exoticism, the character of the Jackman also domesticates this group, identifying them with the English *county* where they reside. Thomas Dekker, in his anti-vagrant text, *Lantern and Candlelight* (1608), likewise emphasizes the gypsies' domestic origin and status:

> If they be Egyptians, sure I am they never descended from the tribes of any of those people that came out of the land of Egypt. Ptolemy king of the Egyptians, I warrant, never called them his subjects; no, nor Pharaoh before him.[72]

Like many pieces of anti-gypsy legislation, such as the "Act anent the Egyptians" (1609), Dekker conflates "gypsy" and "Egyptian," a correlation used to give a false genealogy to gypsy culture. Jacobean legal documents extended this connection, referring to gypsies as "Egyptians" on the basis of their supposed geographic origin.[73] Increasingly, though, "Egyptian" came to refer exclusively to "counterfeit" gypsies, displaced laborers who disguised themselves as gypsies in order to evade anti-vagrant statutes. In *The Interpreter* (1607), John Cowell defines "Egyptians" as

> a counterfeit kinde of roagues, that being English or Welch people, accompany themselues together, disguising themselues in straunge

roabes, blacking their faces and bodies, and framing to themselues an vnknowne language, wander vp and down, and...abuse the ignorant common people[74]

Despite their frequent domestic origin, the association of gypsies with "foreignness" is appropriate, due to the fact that the status of gypsies in Jacobean England paralleled that of strangers, whom Bacon viewed as potential enemies only temporarily subject to and protected by the Common Law.[75] The contingency of gypsies' protected status is important to note: whereas their distinctive cultural traits and monarchical structure legitimate this status, their lack of cultural origin and geographic location necessitates a reclassification that will place them under the jurisdiction of the law. But this juridical categorization is defined by its flexibility: in other words, the law mimics the protean nature of gypsy identity, adapting itself to changing circumstances. In this context, gypsies may be punished as subjects, because of their domestic origin, or denied privileges as strangers, because of their alien status.

The Jackman's discussion of the origin of one of the gypsy children in his entourage points to the ease with which gypsies subvert distinctions of nation and subject. This episode correlates the geographic vagrancy of the gypsy nation with a threat that they may add to their ranks. The gypsy child is born in Flintshire, Wales, to the daughter of Justice Jug, the local official who, as Justice of the Peace, would have been in charge of controlling vagrants within his district.[76] After his daughter runs off with the gypsy band of her child's father, the Justice unsuccessfully pursues them through the Marches of Wales, the semi-autonomous counties along Wales's border with England. When the Justice finally confronts his daughter at Chester, their reconciliation is commemorated and "ever since preserved in picture upon the stone jugs of the kingdom" (64–65). The gypsies' progress continues along the "dark corners" on the nation's margins, from the Marches of Wales to the North Country. In the early modern period, both Wales and Chester remained under nominal local control, as represented by the Council of the Marches and the County Palatine and Earldom of Chester.[77] The reunion of family and cultures also mimics the proliferation of Union insignia in the punning reference to (re)union Jugs. But during Union negotiations, even plans for an Anglo-Scottish flag were left unfinished, for no one could achieve an acceptable balance between the crosses of St. George and St. Andrew.[78] The success of the Jacobean Union, like the reconciliation of the Jug family, is thus called into question. In the latter case, gypsy cultural difference remains unchallenged; after all, Justice Jug's grandchild still remains among the gypsies.

The Porter evokes the court's Scottish ties earlier in the masque as well, welcoming James and the court with the sign of St. Andrew: "As many blessings as there be bones, / In Ptolemy's fingers, and all at once / Held up in an Andrew's cross for the nonce" (29–31). The Scots are linked with the gypsies not only in the alien origin of their customs, as St. Andrew is likened to Ptolemy, repeating the frequent equation of gypsies with Egyptians, but also in their inherent disorder, as the blessing consists of a confused jumble of fingers held up "all at once." The problems of social control raised by vagrants and gypsies became associated with Scotland in the early modern period: one early Jacobean statute in Scotland, "Act against transporting beggarly Scots into England" (1607), was prompted by a desire to counter "the grite reproche and sclander of this natioun" as the source of vagrants issuing into England.[79] In a letter to the Scottish Privy Council, James similarly noted that the association of Scots with vagrancy, although justified due to "the multitude of idle people" traveling to England, nonetheless "hath bene no small disgrace to our said kingdome in other nations."[80] As further evidence of the connections made between vagrants (including gypsies) and Scotland, the character of Springlove takes on a northern Scottish dialect upon resuming his role as an itinerant beggar in Brome's *A Jovial Crew* (1641).[81] A number of early modern ballads, such as "The Cunning Northern Beggar" and "The Begger Boy of the North," associate gypsies and vagrants with a general northern origin, testifying to the southward pattern of migration for vagrants in the period: as the "begger boy" of the latter ballad explains, "In the North Countrey I first had my birth; / From whence I came naked unto London City."[82]

Anti-Scottish pamphlets written both during and following debate on the Union of the Realms often equated Scots with vagrant groups, depicting the influx of courtiers into England from James's Scottish court as an analogous incursion of beggars. Francis Osborne's satire of the Jacobean court, written following James's 1617 Northern Progress, had described the "beggarly rable, attending his majesty," which had first entered England with James's accession and continued to stream across the border throughout his reign. "Such a beggarly addition," Osborne commented, "must needs be destructive," for Scots offer little aside from what they may steal or what "may be found under our hedges"; the Scots, who "turne pedlers," ultimately "ruine all about them."[83] The anxiety that Scots would transform the

English into beggars prompted one pro-Union text to borrow a false etymology of Briton as "pirate" in order to joke that Union opponents must somehow believe that by becoming British they will become thieves.[84] Significantly, contemporaries equated the subversion of cultural borders brought on by the proposed Union of the Realms with the continued ability of vagrant groups to evade the law.[85] Sir Edward Coke, responding to James's earlier plans to naturalize the Scots, had cast these efforts to reconstitute borders and national identities as a political infiltration, fearing that "strangers might fortify themselves in the heart of the realm."[86] Although James had intended to establish the integrity of cultural and geographic borders concomitantly with his imagined constitution of empire, neither the Union project nor the attempt to control vagrant groups was able to achieve these objectives.

The early modern English had cause to associate gypsies with Scotland. The earliest extant records of a gypsy presence in the British Isles document their arrival in Scotland in the early sixteenth century, a migration most likely caused by their expulsion from France in 1504.[87] Scotland was noteworthy for its fairly lenient treatment of gypsies: only three statutes were proposed against vagrants in the sixty years between the gypsies' arrival and James's accession. By contrast, James VI and I actively prosecuted vagrant groups, writing 23 pieces of legislation that targeted them from 1567–1621.[88] Many of James's early statutes followed precedents in England, where anti-vagrant bills had emerged following the influx of gypsies in the late 1520s. Gypsies fleeing Scotland's anti-vagrant statute of 1540 only exacerbated England's own vagrancy problems, which reached a crisis point in the 1540s when unprecedented crop failures and inflation further increased England's masterless population.[89] The harshest Tudor legislation soon followed, such as the statute (1 Edward VI, c. 3 [1547]) ordering that vagrants be branded with a "V" and that a two-year sentence of slave labor be given to these "unprofitable membres or rather ennemyes of the Comen wealthe."[90] Although this law was rarely enforced and in fact repealed in 1549, "Egyptians" were later classified together with other categories of "idle and strong beggars and vagabonds" in England (1562) and Scotland (1574). The fact that the Scottish law was revised several times from 1597–1617 testifies both to the permanence of anxieties concerning vagrants and the ineffectiveness of legislative attempts to control them.[91]

Yet, despite his aggressive legislation against these groups, James VI also continued the sixteenth-century Scottish court's tradition of patronage and protection of the gypsies. The earliest records attesting to the presence of gypsies in the British Isles derive from theatrical performances at the Scottish court. In 1505, the Lord High Treasurer of Scotland gave £7 to a gypsy band on the command of James IV, while James V paid gypsies to dance at Holyrood House in 1529.[92] Scottish officials and rural gentry were also noted for their patronage of gypsy performers. Sir William Sinclair, Lord Justice General under Queen Mary, kept under his protection a group of gypsy players, who were "accustomed to gather in the stanks [marshes] of Roslin every year, where they acted severall plays dureing the moneth of May and June."[93] In Jonson's masque, the Third Gypsy alludes to the long association of the court with gypsy performers:

> And ever at your solemn feasts and calls
> We have been ready with th' Egyptian brawls,
> To set Kit Callet forth in prose or rhyme,
> Or who was Cleopatra for the time (245–48)

The carnivalesque tradition of annual plays at Roslin castle endured from 1559 to 1628. The plays seem to have centered on versions of the Robin Hood story, a popular theme for May-tide entertainments.[94] It is therefore appropriate that the townspeople of Dumfries had used a May Day performance to camouflage their attempted assassination of Sir William Cranstoun and his Borders officers. The Robin Hood subject matter of the gypsy plays further links these performances with the illicit, for plays dealing with this topic were prohibited by a 1555 Act of the Scottish Parliament. However, this statute, like many of those aimed against the gypsies, was rarely enforced.[95] The rustic clowns in Jonson's masque further evoke the connection between gypsies and Robin Hood legends, noting their surprise upon their initial encounter with the gypsies to find that "there is no Maid Marian nor friar amongst them" (696–97). *The Gypsies Metamorphosed* correlates the rustics with the gypsies because of their mutual association with rural pastimes and festive traditions: the clowns comment, for example, that the gypsies "should be morris-dancers by their jingle" (693).[96] But the gypsies ultimately disrupt this idyllic pastoral setting, stealing the clowns' purses during their "country dance" (738) and even purloining the "jet ring" that the country maid Prudence owned "to draw Jack Straw hither a holidays" (854).

The eventual conflict between the gypsies and their rural host culture is appropriate considering the changing status of gypsies in Jacobean England. Demonstrating James's increasingly draconian legislation in both Scotland and England against gypsies and other masterless men, the final suppression of the gypsies of Roslin closely followed the performances of Jonson's masque. The Privy Council of Scotland finally induced Sinclair's son William, in his capacity as sheriff of Roslin, to enforce the realm's anti-vagrant laws against the gypsies in 1623.[97] The fact that performances continued for five years after Sinclair's commission demonstrates the ineffectiveness of attempts to control gypsy bands as well as Sinclair's own possible lack of enthusiasm for his task. Although James ultimately pardoned the gypsies apprehended by Sinclair, he intervened only after eight of their leaders had been executed. In 1616, James had similarly withdrawn the death sentence against four gypsies on condition of their perpetual banishment, demonstrating a continued tradition of personal leniency even in an environment of increasingly punitive legislation.[98]

The status of gypsies was therefore unique in early modern England: a group at the center of both exceptional care and persecution. And because of their position as vagrants paradoxically under royal or aristocratic protection, the status of gypsies also paralleled that of early modern players.[99] One of the rustics in Jonson's masque appropriately implies that the gypsies (like players) are the king's servants: "The king has his noise of gypsies as well as of bear wards and other minstrels" (937–39). The history of anti-gypsy legislation intersected with early modern attempts to regulate both vagrants and theatrical performers. For example, Edward VI associated these groups with other politically subversive elements in a 1549 journal entry that remarked how "there was a privy search made through Sussex for all vagabonds, gipsies, conspirators, prophesiers, all players, and such like."[100] Yet James, even when actively prosecuting gypsies and vagrants while on the Scottish throne, was known for his patronage of actors. Leah Marcus describes an early instance of "the politics of mirth," James's defense of festive and theatrical customs, in his protection of traveling English players. When their public performances in Edinburgh provoked the opposition of the Scottish Kirk in 1599, James personally intervened on their behalf. And, of course, James's licensing of the Lord Chamberlain's Men as his own players following his accession provides further evidence of his patronage, or, in Marcus's words, of how James "enclosed theatrical license within the structure of royal power."[101]

The inconsistencies in James VI and I's policies toward gypsies result in part from the changing status of gypsies, who were increasingly differentiated from the two groups with whom they were often associated: vagrants and actors. An idea of the subtle distinctions drawn between gypsies, vagrants, and actors can be inferred from Elizabeth I's "An Acte for Punyshment of Rogues, Vagabondes and Sturdy Beggars" [39 Elizabeth, c. 4] (1597).[102] This statute potentially affected each of these three groups, targeting "all idle persons going about in the Cuntry eyther begging or using any subtile Crafte or unlawfull Games and Playes" (2.355). The groups were categorized together not only because of their lack of geographic place ("going about in the Cuntry") and their poverty but also due to the suspect content ("subtile Crafte") of their theatrical activities, or "unlawfull Games and Playes" (2.355). The statute conflated a large array of the "undeserving" poor, including beggars unable to practice their profession (scholars and sailors), itinerant salesmen (peddlers, tinkers, and petty chapmen), entertainers (fencers and bear wardens), destitute former felons, and, most especially, "common Labourers" (2.355).

Significantly, the 1597 Act includes able-bodied laborers traveling to find work in its list of suspect vagrant groups, revealing how the statute's jurisdiction encompassed a potentially vast number of subjects. Nonetheless, the statute, in its effort to classify the varied forms of the undeserving poor, attempts to preserve the integrity of each category. The definition of laborer undermines the statute's taxonomy not only because of its scope but also because labor is intrinsically and obviously distinct from idleness. The inclusion of laborers thus concedes the economic causes underlying the poverty and vagrant status of these subjects, who, displaced from customary rights and residences, must travel in order to survive. The category of "laborer" potentially encompasses all the other categories of vagrancy enumerated by the 1597 Act, ultimately undermining the classificatory principle that drives the statute. The character of Christopher Sly in Shakespeare's *The Taming of the Shrew* (ca. 1593–94) reveals how vagrant identities were often constituted by temporary occupations assumed out of necessity. Sly, described as "a tinker and beggar" in the dramatis personae list, defines his own identity based upon the fluctuating forms of his labor: "What, would you make me mad? Am not I Christopher Sly, old Sly's son of Burton-heath, by birth a pedlar, by education a card-maker, by transmutation a bear-herd, and now by present profession a tinker?" (Ind. 2.17–21). Far from exemplifying idleness, Sly's varied labors attest to his ability to adapt to economic necessity and find precarious employment. Patricia Fumerton has remarked how fluctuations in occupation produced a kind of "vagrant subjectivity" among itinerant laborers.[103] In this sense, Sly foregrounds his own occupational migrancy as a way to explain and rationalize why he has been "transformed" into a landed squire.[104]

The 1572 and 1597 anti-vagrant acts are most often noted due to their classification of actors as a vagrant category, albeit one that is excluded from the statutes' jurisdiction based upon playing companies' networks of patronage; consequently, the 1597 statute exempts "Players of Enterlude belonging to any Baron of this Realme, or any other honorable personage of greater Degree."[105] Despite its concerted omission of professional actors, the statute otherwise associates vagrant groups with forms of theatricality, for it singles out for prosecution "all such persons not being Fellons wandering and pretending themselves to be Egipcyans, or wandering in the Habbite Forme or Attyre of counterfayte Egipcians."[106] The association of gypsies with theatricality goes beyond the simple link between gypsies and actors. In the minds of authorities, gypsies constitute a performative social category, for vagrants counterfeit cultural difference in order to evade anti-vagrant legislation. Because gypsies were legally accepted as a distinct culture, they could not be prosecuted as vagrants. A vagrant could become a gypsy and thereby be placed beyond the law's reach. In addition, gypsies themselves were classified as "counterfeit Egyptians" because they lacked origin and occupation: even gypsies were therefore not "real" Egyptians. But if there were no real gypsies, how could authorities differentiate English vagrants pretending to be gypsies from gypsies pretending to be Egyptians?

The targeting of "counterfeit Egyptians" who are specifically *not* felons reveals that this identity was not perceived as a threat because it allowed criminal offenders to conceal themselves from arrest; rather, it was the act of disguising itself that was subversive. As with the categories of "counterfeit cranks" (vagrants who feigned physical illness to justify begging) or "sturdy beggars" (vagrants who feigned an inability to work), gypsies were characterized by their lack of an integral identity. But unlike other vagrants, gypsies were no longer associated with "dissimulation," with assuming a false identity; rather, as differences were elided between categories of gypsy, vagrant, stranger, and player, the indeterminacy of the identity of "counterfeit Egyptians" called into question the basis of any distinction between categories of identity and difference. To paraphrase Baudrillard's differentiation of dissimulation and simulation, whereas dissimulation implies a real presence beneath the disguise, simulation undermines the boundaries between a real and imaginary identity.[107] Baudrillard categorizes the dominant early modern law of value as the scheme of the "counterfeit": the image of the counterfeit testifies to an irrevocable disruption of signs of class privilege; yet, for these signs to retain coherence, they reinscribe the threat of their unintelligibility onto the groups inhabiting the cultural margins (gypsies, vagrants, players, laborers), equating the dangers of class mobility with forms of theatricality.[108]

The reinvention of vagrant groups as possessing simulated, counterfeit identities was a recent development in early modern England: prior to Elizabeth's Act "for the Punishement of Vacabondes" [14 Elizabeth, c. 5] (1572), whose language is repeated in the 1597 statute, anti-vagrant legislation did not differentiate among the poor based upon the authenticity of their need.[109] One reason for this change can be attributed to the influx of gypsies from Scotland to England during the sixteenth century. The legislation against "counterfeit Egyptians" was further necessitated due to the perceived threat that gypsies added to their ranks with masterless men. The blurring of distinctions between the masquer gypsies and the antimasquer clowns in *The Gypsies Metamorphosed* points to the unstable and interchangeable social positions of each group. Despite Puppy's declared initial hatred of "rogue gypsies" (710), and his efforts to differentiate himself from a group he places among his social inferiors, the country bumpkin changes his view in response to the Patrico's promise that the gypsies will fulfill his wishes, declaring that "this is better than canting by t'one half" (761–62). Puppy's comments reveal how his own poverty already scarcely distinguishes his social position from that of the gypsies; the promise of freedom from economic deprivation thus provokes "a terrible grudging now upon me to be one of your company" (1054–55). Recognizing the immunity of most gypsies from anti-vagrant prosecution—"a wise gypsy...is as politic a piece of flesh as most justices in the county where he stalks" (767–69)—Puppy inquires, "will your captain take a prentice, sir?" (1055). In his satire of the apprenticeship regulations mandated by the Statute of Artificers, Puppy foregrounds the incentives for domestic vagrants to shield themselves among the seemingly exotic and more autonomous gypsies: "we'll be all his followers," Cockerel declares (1068). The Patrico intimates that some of his followers, such as the gypsy child born to the gypsy Captain's kinsman and Justice Jug's daughter, are domestic vagrants who have become naturalized in gypsy culture. When the Patrico later commands his gypsy followers to flee in different directions so as to evade the "beck-harman" (constable), he justifies his order on the basis of their differing cultural backgrounds: "We are not all brothers" (823).[110]

Distinctions between gypsies and domestic vagrants are further blurred in the Jackman's song describing Cock Lorel's feast for the Devil, an episode in Jonson's masque that borrows heavily from anti-vagrant texts, particularly Samuel Rid's *Martin Markall* (1610). In a section of his text entitled "The Runagates' Race, or the Original of the Regiment of Rogues," Rid traces a genealogy of vagrant groups in England. Rid's narrative revises a standard chronology that locates the origins of vagrancy in developing practices of enclosure and agrarian capitalism in sixteenth-century England, tracing the vagrancy problem, instead, to an earlier displacement caused by England's fifteenth-century wars in France and the Wars of the Roses.[111] Rid constructs a lineage of social unrest that blends historical rebels such as Jack Cade and Perkin Warbeck with fictional personages ("Jenkin Cowdiddle" and "Puffing Dick"), a succession that concludes with the figure of Cock Lorel. Rid only later introduces gypsies into his chronology, describing the subsequent appearance "in the northern parts [of] another sort of vagabonds" who organize at the Devil's Arse in Derbyshire under the leadership of Giles Hatcher and Kit Callot, taking on "the name of Egyptians." It is at this point that the previously separate communities of vagrants and gypsies merge as Cock Lorel joins forces with the king and queen of gypsies.[112]

Jonson's masque frequently alludes to Rid's description, from the Jackman's relation of how the gypsies retain the annual "musters" at Devil's Arse begun by Giles Hatcher (107–10) to the Third Gypsy's promise to "set Kit Callet forth in prose or rhyme" (247). Jonson also subversively inserts Buckingham into the gypsies' genealogy, for it is his command as Captain of the Gypsies that has ensured that they have "kept our station, / As we preserved ourselves a royal nation" (235–36). Yet, previous to Jonson's depiction of his feast for the devil, Cock Lorel was described in anti-vagrant literature not as a gypsy by birth but as a vagrant who had assimilated into gypsy culture.[113] The Patrico suggests the type of genealogy outlined by Rid when, in response to the clowns' desire to join the gypsies, he explains, "Ye aim at a mystery / Worthy a history" (1081–82). But he also cautions them that "There's much to be done" (1083) before they can join the community: "'Tis not so soon / Acquired as desired" (1086–87). In tracing the origins of a vagrant "race" and gypsy "nation," Rid's text reveals the linked formation of definitions of race, nation, and class in the early modern period; all of these terms intersect in the representation of vagrants and gypsies as an alternative community separated from dominant English culture.

To a certain extent, the ability of gypsy culture to assimilate and naturalize new members would seem to constitute it as a model of the type of integrated imagined community desired by proponents of the Union of the Realms. Instead, the Patrico's comments demonstrate how exclusiveness and bigotry permeate gypsy culture as well, a parallel closer to the anti-Scottish stereotypes provoked by efforts to naturalize the Scots.

Puppy's desire to join the Patrico's gypsy band illustrates the attractiveness of the idea of gypsy "liberty" to an early modern audience. Jonson later draws on this idea in *The New Inn* (1629), wherein Lord Frampul joins the gypsies for a number of years in order to "study" their culture and, subsequently, continues to hide his identity as Goodstock the Host (5.5.91–102). In Brome's *A Jovial Crew* (1641), the character of Springlove leaves his position as Oldrents's steward each spring in order to roam the countryside with vagrants, a fanciful idealization of the fluidity and recuperation of vagrant identities, which, as with Jonson's Lord Frampul, allows characters to enjoy the supposed freedom of a vagrant's life and return freely to the settled life of work and family. An early modern ballad, "The braue English Iipsie" (1626), represents gypsies as an archetype of native English "liberty," depicting their lives as an ideal alternative for the country people who attempt to emulate them.[114] Whereas the ballad elevates the status of English gypsies above that of their counterparts on the Continent, in Middleton's *The Spanish Gypsy* (1623), English gypsies are derogated as thieves and contrasted with the nobility of Spanish gypsies (all of whom in the play are aristocrats in disguise).[115] Unlike Springlove and Frampul, Middleton's aristocrats merely use their gypsy disguise as a means to an end, not as an alternative identity they may assume for periods of time.

"The braue English Iipsie" is significant because it offers a rare example of a text reflecting popular, rather than official, sentiment toward gypsies. Popular images of gypsies attest to the use of the gypsy figure to represent an idealistic escape from social realities, an alternative space in which economic deprivation could be reinscribed as a release from social constraints. The allusion to gypsy "liberty" makes use of a term associated with the customary economic rights of tenants and laborers, thus demonstrating how the idealization of gypsy liberty additionally served as a frame of reference that could be used to critique contemporary social conditions. It is significant, though, that the ballad emphasizes the gypsies' *Englishness*, a strategy that links gypsies to a primeval national identity, a striking contrast not only to the transcultural relations between English and Scottish gypsies but also to those between gypsies and other vagrant groups, social relations that exceeded and defied national affiliation.

Although most early modern vagrants were isolated and displaced migrant laborers, their ubiquitous presence prompted anxieties regarding their ability to organize themselves into a larger community or become assimilated with other groups, including gypsies.[116] Jacobean anti-gypsy laws, such as the Scottish "Act Anent the Egiptians" (1609), consequently reinforced categories of identity in an attempt to offset the ability of gypsies and vagrants to band together for their mutual protection from legal prosecution. The 1609 Act levied penalties on vagrants who associated with gypsies for a period of one month. Through the imposition of a time limit, this statute replaced questions of conversion, which would force officials to determine whether or not a vagrant had become a gypsy, with absolute guilt by association. Similarly, the law also stipulated penalties for gypsies, including banishment, forfeiture of goods, and execution, based not upon any proven crime but simply because of their identification *as* gypsies: "that they are called, knawn, reput, and halden Egiptians."[117] As the wording of the act intimates, gypsies could be convicted even on the basis of circumstantial proof.

Whereas gypsies had been categorized and protected as a separate culture abiding by its own laws and customs in sixteenth-century Scotland, the threat of potential alliances with other vagrant groups—and with laborers and the rural poor in general—necessitated harsher legislation in order to set the interests of these groups against one another. A 1619 statute in Scotland had targeted "the preposterous pitie of the countrey people" toward gypsies, stipulating fines and penalties for the granting of alms to unlicensed beggars.[118] The Scottish Privy Council's decision to execute a group of gypsies in 1624, so as "to gif a terrour to the whole companyis," was justified on the basis of the supposed harm the gypsies had inflicted to "poore labouraris."[119] Nonetheless, in the same year, an Edinburgh mob freed one gypsy prisoner en route to his execution, and nearly gained the release of the entire group of prisoners, evidence of the continued popular support for gypsies.[120] Laborers and the rural poor could perhaps recognize how they were often equated with gypsies and vagrants in the eyes of the law. Elizabeth I's "An Acte for Punyshment of Rogues, Vagabondes and Sturdy Beggars" (1597) had, after all, listed "common Labourers" alongside gypsies, vagrants, actors, and other groups subject to punishment. J.A. Sharpe therefore concludes from his analysis of county legal records that the position of the poor in general was hardly distinguishable from that of vagrants, an equivalence based upon each group's similar lack of legal protection and susceptibility to economic displacement.[121]

Jacobean policies of internal colonialism extended with particular force to the poor of England and Scotland. One 1607 proclamation in Scotland ordered the forceful capture of any coal miner who had left his employment, and it additionally licensed sheriffs to apprehend vagrants and force them to work in the mines.[122] This conflation of miners and gypsies is evoked in *The Coleorton Masque* (1618), which was performed to accompany a wedding at the Beaumont family estate in Leicestershire. Because the family had acquired their wealth through mining interests, Thomas Beaumont's miners are consequently referred to in the masque as "Tom's Egyptians."[123] The miners are both exoticized, likened to the gypsies and represented as a distinct ethnic group as a result of their labor's "blackening" effects, and commodified, rendered as the property and possession of the gentry capitalist Beaumont.

Despite the efforts of James VI and his Scottish Privy Council to enforce anti-vagrant laws regulating the movement and cultural practices of gypsies and other vagrants, gypsies were still often protected by members of the Scottish gentry, who continued the sixteenth-century Scottish tradition of patronage of gypsies and respect for their autonomy. As noted earlier, the gypsy performances at Roslin castle continued throughout the reign of James VI and I, as the Sinclair family, who served as both lairds and sheriffs, refused to arrest their resident gypsies despite repeated orders from the Privy Council. The harboring of gypsies was first outlawed in a statute of October 1579.[124] Due to the continued protection of gypsies by the rural gentry, the "Act Anent the Egiptians" (1609) even stipulated that those found to "reset, receaue, supplie or intertein" gypsies could have the entirety of their estates confiscated.[125] Subsequent statutes reflected a greater concern for enforcing the laws against the gentry than the gypsies: the residual patronage of the gentry was used to explain the continued presence of gypsies as well as the ineffectiveness of the numerous statutes aimed against them. By 1616, the Scottish Privy Council began to equate the two groups, representing the landowning class, who only "outwardlie pretendis to be famous and unspotted gentilmen" while secretly harboring gypsies, in the same terminology of secret customs and counterfeit identities typically applied to gypsies; as a consequence, the Privy Council concluded, the gentry "salbe persewit and punist for the same [offenses] with all rigour."[126]

The status of gypsies, particularly following the "Act Anent the Egiptians," thus served to exemplify alternative social alliances that were perceived as inimical to the increasingly centralized authority of the state. Gypsies disrupted forms of social control because their protean identities and affiliations created alternative networks of alliance and patronage, allowing them to unite their interests with laborers and the rural gentry. The unique position still held by gypsies in Jacobean England and Scotland is illustrated by the case of a Scottish gypsy named Moses Faw. Following the Scottish "Act Anent the Egiptians," Faw petitioned the Scottish Privy Council, asking to be exempted from the statute due to the fact that he had dissociated himself and his family from the "infamous society" of "Egyptians." Emphasizing his current status as an "honnest, lauchfull and trew" subject, Faw offered a caution (bail) of £1,000, promising to forebear from harboring or associating with gypsies in order to remain in Scotland. The Privy Council granted Faw's request, and his bail was posted by two lords, David Lindsay of Quarrelhill and David, earl of Crawford.[127]

By April 1611, however, Faw had rejoined the gypsies once more. In June, Faw and his band retreated to the Border town of Selkirk, where, to the Privy Council's dismay, local authorities refused to arrest them. To complicate matters further, the gentlemen who had stood as surety for Faw were also declared outlaws after having failed to pay his bond. A commission specially authorized by the Privy Council finally arrested Faw and his accomplices in July 1611.[128] Despite the fact that his offenses warranted a death sentence, Faw remarkably managed to evade punishment, as evidenced by a later notice of his arrest along with other gypsies in September 1637. On this last occasion, Faw once again appealed to the Privy Council, although he accepted exile and overseas military service in exchange for clemency.[129] No further records refer to Faw, a clue that his venting abroad may have finally put an end to his long-standing ability to thwart authorities. Nonetheless, the example of Moses Faw illustrates the alternative social alliances that persisted in Jacobean Scotland, networks that served to unite disparate groups in their resistance to centralized political authority. Faw's career also attests to the relatively porous distinctions that differentiated subject from outlaw, demonstrating the ability of gypsies to negotiate between competing alliances and obligations and thereby survive—and even prosper–in a social environment increasingly hostile to them.

Particularly in Scotland, gypsies came to be associated with bonds of alliance and hospitality that were perceived as a threat to the centralized authority of the state. The contemporary Scottish legislation targeting the "resetters" of gypsies provides a context in which to reexamine *The Gypsies Metamorphosed*'s ambivalent representation of James's relationship with Buckingham. If, as Randall suggests, the masque provides a veiled critique of the monarch, the gypsy frame itself serves to do so, since early modern anti-gypsy laws increasingly targeted the patrons of gypsies more than gypsies themselves. In this sense, the subversive comparison in the masque is not of Buckingham and his family to a band of gypsies but of James to a harborer and resetter of outlaws. As Buckingham declares to the king in his role as Captain of the Gypsies, "Myself a gypsy here do shine, / Yet are you maker, sir, of mine" (329–30). Buckingham's social advancement is thus attributed to the protection of the monarch, casting James in an analogous role to the Scottish lairds who harbor gypsies; Buckingham, as the Porter described him earlier, is James's "creature" (16).

Yet the masque tempers this potential analogy by dissociating itself from a Scottish context. Because the masque's second performance, hosted by the earl of Rutland at Belvoir, fell on the anniversary of the Gowrie conspiracy, the Patrico playfully distinguishes between the roles of host and attempted assassin: "This is no Gowrie / Hath drawn James hither, / But the good man of Bever" (1183–85). In this sense, the masque distances itself from the treasonous hospitality of Scottish lairds, who, as in Shakespeare's *Macbeth*, receive their king in order to attempt his murder. Ironically, the masque confirms a stereotype of the violent political climate of early modern Scotland, an image repeated by opponents of the Jacobean Union such as the English MP Christopher Piggot, who had described Scots as "rogues" who "have not suffered above two kings to die in their beds these 200 years."[130] The masque evokes a Scottish parallel in order to elide it, insisting that the Villiers are *not* Gowries, and it emphasizes, instead, the extent to which their estate—and even their status itself—results from the king's patronage. Welcoming the monarch, the Porter notes, "The house your bounty'ath built, . . . / . . . / . . . / The master is your creature, as the place" (13, 16). The analogy thus domesticates Buckingham's band of gypsies, who are rendered as settled and politically docile. In contrast to a Scottish context, in which a powerful gentry mediates the state's control of its vagrant population, the masque displaces the comparison of James to Scottish resetters by presenting a fantasy in which the gypsies directly owe their preservation to an all-powerful monarch.

While gypsy social practices were held to resist the mandates of the state, their sexual customs were often depicted in anti-vagrant texts as openly defying conventions of marriage and kinship.[131] These texts therefore link residual social networks of patronage and protection with forms of sexual union that undermine boundaries of class and the patriarchal family. In Brome's *A Jovial Crew* (1641), for example, Oliver, the son of the vagrant-hating Justice Clack, looks for a quick sexual encounter with vagrant women but restrains himself out of fear of committing incest, an acknowledgment of the pervasive and illicit sexual links between women of the underclass and gentlemen, including even the Justices of the Peace commissioned to punish vagrants (3.1.350). Oliver's anxiety is actually validated later in the play, as Springlove is revealed to be the son of the squire Oldrents and the Patrico's sister, the result of a union that Oldrents seems to have long forgotten. The perception of gypsy sexuality, simultaneously alluring and threatening, points to a more fundamental ambivalence regarding gypsy culture, an awareness of consanguinity that accompanies efforts to marginalize and suppress gypsies. The continued persistence of gypsy culture is therefore depicted as having sexual causes. In Shakespeare's *Antony and Cleopatra* (1606), Philo uses images of cultural infiltration through sexual means in his opening description of Cleopatra's effect on Antony: "his captain's heart, / . . . / . . . reneges all temper / And is become the bellows and the fan / To cool a gipsy's lust" (1.1.6–10).[132] By contrast, in Middleton's *The Spanish Gypsy* (1623), the character of John, a nobleman disguised as a gypsy, deflects the advances of the hostess Cardochia by emphasizing the endogamous sexual customs of gypsies: "For marriage, 'tis a law amongst us gipsies / We match in our own tribes" (4.1.180–81). Despite its hyperbolic denunciation of gypsy sexual customs, Thomas Harman's *A Caveat for Common Cursitors* (1566) exposes the economic forces underlying the sexual exploitation of vagrant women both by vagrant men, who are supposedly able to live off their labor, and householding men, who manipulate the isolated social position of these women in order to attempt to coerce sex from them.[133]

The Gypsies Metamorphosed also employs the association of gypsies with unsanctioned or immoderate sexual desire. It is on this issue that Jonson's use of the gypsy analogy most carefully balances sanctioned and subversive meanings. James's enthusiastic response to the masque may have resulted from its use of the gypsy disguise to offer a coded representation of his relationship with Buckingham. As Randall points out, the masque's first performance occurred on Friday, August 3, 1621, the seventh anniversary of their first meeting.[134] The masque therefore affords Buckingham the opportunity to present an anniversary gift to his patron and lover. James must have been delighted when Buckingham, in his role as Captain of the Gypsies, used his skills at palmistry to conclude, "You are no great wencher, I see by your

table [hand], / Although your *mons Veneris* says you are able"
(279–80). Unlike the debilitating "gypsy's lust" affecting Antony,
James's passion for Buckingham is depicted as an active, energizing
force (James's love line, after all, hints at his "ability"). Earlier in the
masque, noting how James's bounty has "built" Buckingham's reno-
vated estate of Burley, the Porter confers ownership on James—"the
master is your creature, as the place" (16)—and requests suggestively
that James choose to enter *both*: "for please you enter / Him, and his
house, and search them to the center" (24–25). The entrance into
Burley, and into the gypsy frame of the performance, ties the margin
to the center: the gypsy disguise, an integration of social margins,
allows the opportunity to represent the court's most private moments.

Whereas the masque's gypsy disguise enables a coded representation of James's relationship with Buckingham, some anti-Jacobean
texts drew on the open secret of James's queerness to formulate
opposition to the monarch's political policies. A pamphlet illegally
printed in the year following Jonson's masque, *Tom Tell-Troath*
(1622), had similarly emphasized the protected secrecy of James's
sexual relations with his favorites: "Hee may solace himselfe as
securely in his bed-chamber as the Grand Signor in his serglio…
There may he kisse his minions without shame, and make his grooms
his companions without danger."[135] The pamphlet not only links
James's same-sex desires to arbitrary and absolutist forms of power,
comparing James to the Turkish sultan, but also casts these desires as
the cause of the Union project's failure: although "a desire, worthy
your selfe, to unite the people as well as the countryes of England and
Scotland…It is not to be done by choosing the minion alternatively
out of each nation" (436–37). The pamphlet rejects proposals of a
mixed aristocracy, naturalization, and Anglo-Scottish political marriages as "too weake and counterfeite ingredients to compound a love-
potion," encouraging James to cement Anglo-Scottish ties, instead,
through the masculine enterprise of joint military adventurism (437).

Similar to the nostalgic invocation of the age of Drake and Raleigh
found in the texts from the 1620s discussed in chapter 2, the perceived lack of an integral, masculine English identity stands in for a
more pervasive failure of national identification. Yet, whereas texts
such as *Sir Walter Rawleighs Ghost* (1626) replaced the monarch with
a spectral figure of a past generation, *Tom Tell-Troath* links the counterfeit imperial identity of Jacobean England with the queer desires,
and thus "counterfeit" sexual identity, of its monarch. James himself
had linked together sodomy and counterfeiting in *Basilikon Doron*,
wherein he listed the two among the offenses that a prince could

not pardon.[136] The reference to the Union as "counterfeit" in *Tom Tell-Troath* may also derive from the class differences between James and his favorites Buckingham and Robert Carr. Alan Bray has noted how male friendships that crossed class boundaries were often marked as sodomitical in early modern England and perceived as motivated by economic desires for social mobility.[137]

In order to displace the sodomitical associations evoked by both the Union's Anglo-Scottish "love potion" and Buckingham's social mobility, the Jackman's ballad of Cock Lorel's feast for the Devil counters the penetrating intimacy of the court's entry with a process that expels cultural undesirables. Whereas the masque links together high- and low-class groups through the association of courtiers and gypsies, the Devil's feast consists exclusively of the middling sort: lawyers, usurers, yeomen, sheriffs, mayors, and citizens (981–1030). This list of ingredients places the groups who threaten gypsies along- side the social forces inimical to the court, including civic officials ("aldermen lobsters" [1029]) and nonconformists ("a Puritan poached" [981]). Similarly, the songs that the Patrico later offers in praise of James's physical senses target such unappealing figures as Puritan women ("the loud pure wives of Banbury" [1258]) as well as foundries and other nascent urban industries ("the candlesticks of Lothbury" [1257]).[138] By mocking the court's enemies, the masque displaces any overt criticism of the court intimated by the possible comparison of Buckingham's entertainment for James to Cock Lorel's feast for the Devil, especially with the notably anal figuration of the "Devil's Arse" story. Such a critical reference to the nature of James and Buckingham's relationship would have been unwise for Jonson. Sir Henry Yelverton had been imprisoned after making inflammatory comparisons between Buckingham and Edward II's favorite Hugh Spenser in a speech before the House of Lords on April 30, 1621. Such comments were punishable under James's December 24, 1620 proclamation against "excess of Lavish and Licentious Speech of Matters of State": as Randall concluded, Jonson's masque was therefore "playing with fire."[139]

***

A Counterfeit Empire

The persecution of gypsies occurred partly because their distinctive- ness as a community belied efforts to impose a greater uniformity of cultural identification throughout England and Scotland. Yet the persistence of gypsy cultural autonomy posed a greater challenge to aspirations of national unity because of the nature of its difference. Although gypsy culture evinced similar practices of voluntary naturalization as those intended by proponents of the Union of the Realms, gypsies ultimately threatened ideas of national identity. This challenge was based less upon an explicit opposition to civil authority than an alternative cultural affiliation that seemed to disregard the imagined national community and its values. As David MacRitchie comments, early modern anti-gypsy legislation targeted this community not "*as a race*" but because of its voluntarily vagrant status.[140] In this sense, gypsy identity was viewed suspiciously not because of its innate, "racial" character but because it was constituted by a set of customs and conventions that were consciously adopted, produced, and performed. The performativity of gypsy culture thus denaturalized the racialized grounding of communal identity, thereby reflecting on the comparably imagined foundations of James's British empire.

Gypsies' recalcitrant cultural difference was therefore associated with a particular form of performance and counterfeiting of identity, the use of blackface to create the illusion of physical difference. Thomas Dekker comments in *Lantern and Candlelight* (1608) that although one would think "that they were tawny Moors' bastards" as a result of their "filthy complexion," gypsies are not "born so"; rather, they have voluntarily painted their faces and become "counterfeit Egyptians."[141] For Dekker, gypsies merely assume signs of difference, willfully appropriating signifiers of blackness. Sir Thomas Browne's *Pseudodoxia Epidemica* (1646) therefore terms gypsies "counterfeit Moors," "unsettled nations" of vagrants who have inexplicably "out-lasted others of fixed habitations."[142] Browne's comments reveal how gypsies served as an interpretive framework in the encounter with foreign cultures both at home and abroad. Relating how he came upon a "great multitude" of "rouguish Egyptians" in France in his travel narrative *Crudities* (1611), Thomas Coryat emphasizes that they "disguise their faces, as our counterfet western Egyptians in England."[143] Similarly, in the description of his travels in 1583 through the Euphrates valley, John Eldred compares the Arab merchants he met to English gypsies: "Their haire, apparell, and colour are altogether like to those vagabond Egyptians, which heretofore have gone about in England."[144]

Because gypsies blur distinctions of domestic and foreign, early modern texts associated them with other forms of hybridity and boundary subversion. George Abbot highlights gypsies' polyglot identities and seeming lack of allegiance to any nation, calling them "runnagates" and "the refuse or rascality of many Nations," thus linking them to renegades as well as populations transplanted to the colonies.[145] Ultimately, the association of both domestic gypsies and foreign cultures with ideas of festive performance and counterfeiting, including the intentional blackening of one's face, serves to counter the threat of cultural difference. A festive culture is one that lacks its own forms of order; because these groups are out of control, state officials can therefore justify the imposition of authority. To define a culture through performance implies that its characteristics are nothing more than a role that can be assumed or abandoned. A performance-based culture is thus not an authentic culture—such a culture, like that of the gypsies ("counterfeit Egyptians," "counterfeit cranks," and "sturdy beggars"), not only lacks identity; it insistently performs the illusion that it has one.

The anticlimactic conclusion to Jonson's *The Gypsies Metamorphosed* suggests a similar undercutting of the autonomy of both gypsy and court cultures. In an epilogue spoken by the now-metamorphosed Buckingham in the Windsor performance, Jonson explains why the intended climax of the masque, the promised transformation of the gypsies to courtiers, occurred not as a spectacle depicted onstage but as an unrepresented event whose process is implied but not seen: "Good Ben slept there, or else forgot to show it" (1384), the epilogue concedes. In lieu of a metamorphosis, Buckingham breaks the remaining vestiges of theatrical illusion by foregrounding the role played by "Master Wolf" (Johann Wolfgang Rumler), the king's apothecary, who concocted the blackface that created the courtiers' gypsy disguise, a mixture "without spells" that "was fetched off with water and a ball [of soap]" (1389, 1391): "to our transformation this is all" (1392).

> For to a gypsy's metamorphosis
> Who doth disguise his habit and his face,
> And takes on a false person by his place,
> The power of poetry can never fail her,
> Assisted by a barber and a tailor (1394–98)

But despite Jonson's insistence on his complicity, his protestation that the power of his poetry will never fail to refashion and redeem even the most discredited of courtiers, the lack of a performed transformation subverts the metamorphosis that the masque promises. As for the transformation of the courtiers, "this is all"—it is nothing more than the blatant stage devices that attempt to enact illusion and thereby counterfeit identity. But the gypsies' identity is counterfeit in a more fundamental sense, for it is based upon the assumption of "a false person" (1396), an inherent simulation of one's "place" that is only "assisted" by blackface and spectacle. Distinctions are thus blurred between Buckingham's counterfeiting of gypsy identity and the performativity of that identity itself: each is, in this sense, a "false person."

The masque's central metaphor of metamorphosed gypsies takes on special meaning in the context of transcultural relations within Jacobean Britain. David Lindley notes how Jonson's *Irish Masque at Court* (1613) similarly undermines its concluding transformation: in the end, the Irish masquers are revealed to have been Anglicized gentlemen all along.[146] The masque dodges the issue of cultural difference by refusing to acknowledge its residual presence among James's subjects. In *The Gypsies Metamorphosed*, the emphasis on the counterfeit cultural identity of gypsies ultimately reflects back on the incapacity to constitute a Jacobean imperial identity founded on an Anglo-Scottish imagined community. As Homi Bhabha comments, the imagined unity of the nation "fills the void left in the uprooting of communities and kin, and turns that loss into the language of metaphor."[147] In this process, the sites of loss, the figures and forces that resist incorporation and unity, serve as the loci of the imagined community: in the Union project, the Borders become the Middle Shires; in anti-vagrant texts, the counterfeit disguises of vagrants and gypsies are interpreted and revealed; in the increasingly draconian anti-gypsy legislation of the Jacobean era, social categorization becomes absolute and punitive; in Jonson's masque, courtiers are transformed to gypsies, then metamorphosed back into courtiers. However, each of these examples attempts but ultimately fails to translate and subsume residual forms of cultural difference within the rhetoric of imperial unity. Cultural difference thus signals the limits of enforced national uniformity: as Bhabha remarks, "the threat of cultural difference is no longer a problem of 'other' people. It becomes a question of otherness of the people-as-one."[148] This sense of otherness infiltrates the signification of nation, which takes on the protean, performative traits associated with gypsy and vagrant groups. The recalcitrant cultural difference of gypsies and vagrants constitutes a liminal space, like that of the Borders region, which testifies to how the unassimilated presence of the heterogeneous cultures upon which the nation attempts to establish itself reconstitutes the performativity of national identity as a site of contestation.

In the anthropologist Victor Turner's definition of liminality, the liminal represents a position "betwixt and between all fixed points of classification."[149] Turner emphasizes that liminality is defined as an identity in process, a distinction that illuminates the underlying conceptual links between the analogously counterfeit identities of gypsies and the Anglo-Scottish Union in the Jacobean period. Both cases demonstrate identities in process: the example of the Union of the Realms testifies to the uncertainties that accompany an attempt to redefine national cultures and boundaries; early modern gypsies embody the reconstitution of subject positions and affiliations envisaged by the Union of the Realms, an ability manifested by their connections and alliances with other groups, including vagrants, reivers, laborers, actors, the gentry, and royal favorites. The representation of the "counterfeit" subject, like that of the "imagined" border, attempts to reinscribe the disruptions and discontinuities that mark the transitional reconstitution of cultural identities as forms of absence and illusion. As Mary Douglas comments, "[d]anger lies in transitional states, simply because transition is neither one state or the next, it is undefinable."[150] Gypsies challenged definitions of cultural boundaries in Jacobean Britain because they resisted taxonomic hierarchies; they exemplified a subject position that lay on the border between communities as well as between interpretive systems. The status of gypsies epitomized the various forms of "pollution" described by Douglas—an infiltration from external boundaries, a transgression of internal hierarchies, a danger along a community's margins, and a threat derived from internal contradiction, whether systematic or conceptual.[151] The position of gypsies thus served to pollute the efforts to preserve social order and cultural purity exemplified by Jacobean anti-vagrant legislation. And through their model of a performative communal identity, gypsies reflected on the analogously counterfeit foundation of the Jacobean Union of the Realms.

The efforts to create an imperial identity during debate on the Union of the Realms demonstrated an imperative need, using Bhabha's words, to "fill the void" inherent in an act of imperial naming—the creation of "Great Britain"—that merely rang hollow. In a draft of a text that announced James's new choice of title as British emperor, Francis Bacon felt compelled to defend James's creation from charges that it was little more than a rhetorical fiction:

> especially considering the name of Britany was no coined or new-devised or affected name at our pleasure, but the true and ancient name which God and time hath imposed, extant and received in histories, in cards [maps], and in ordinary speech and writing, where the whole island is meant to be denominate; so as it is not accompanied with so much as any strangeness in common speech.[152]

Bacon emphasizes that the title of Great Britain is neither an invented tradition nor an arbitrary designation, citing precedents in histories, maps, and "ordinary speech and writing" (238). In his insistent rejection of the imputation that the newly imagined British identity is only "coined," "new-devised," or "affected"—in other words, *counterfeit*—Bacon seems aware that his audience is either unwilling to accept or unable to comprehend the premise that national identity is nothing more than a performed act of affiliation. Bacon's own reluctance to acknowledge the intangible foundations of empire is reflected in his urgent search for any sort of precedent for British identity. Bacon's overcompensatory efforts constitute a vagrant search for meaning, one that ranges from obscure antiquarian myths of origin to the tempting illusion of practical, "ordinary" language. Ultimately, the performed speech act declaring an empire with redrawn—and erased—cultural borders takes on a very gypsy-like form: lacking geographic placement, the empire becomes a counterfeit performance "affected...at our pleasure" (238). Therefore, despite James's best efforts to expel, eliminate, or assimilate gypsies and other vagrants in early modern England and Scotland, their cultural difference did more than simply persist and subvert any attempted incorporation. Gypsy identity, in both its performativity and its practices of naturalization, provided a model of the reconstitution of borders and political affiliations necessary for an imagined Anglo-Scottish national community. Ultimately, the representation of "counterfeit Egyptians" served to mirror the failure to construct a British form of nationhood in the Jacobean period.

CHAPTER 5

FORGETTING THE ULSTER PLANTATION: JOHN SPEED'S *The Theatre of the Empire of Great Britain* (1611) AND THE COLONIAL ARCHIVE

"MORE ADO WITH IRELAND": THE STATE PAPER OFFICE

In a document entitled "Generall heads of things in the Office of the Papers. July 29, 1618," Sir Thomas Wilson, the Keeper of Records under James I, catalogued the archival records and diplomatic correspondence he had been organizing at Whitehall since 1612 as the State Paper Office. Among 12 geographically arranged sections, he noted that the largest set of holdings was to be found among the "Hibernia" papers: 120 books of documents that included 30 books of letters from deputies and officials in Ireland dated from 1560–1612, 24 papers on trade, six packets of private letters and petitions, as well as "some discourses about the gouerment thereof."[1] Wilson's efforts to organize the State Papers soon gained the attention of the highest officials at Whitehall, even prompting an official visit to the office by King James himself. In a letter to James I dated

March 10, 1619, Wilson reminded his monarch of this earlier visit, recollecting the king's reaction of wonder at the size and scope of the archival collection, including James's exclamation, "wee had more a dooe, wth Ireland than wth all ye world besides."[2]

The State Paper Office, founded in 1578 as a library for the Privy Council and Secretary of State, was reorganized under James I, who advanced Wilson to a permanent position as Keeper of Records, promising that he would help him "make it the rarest office of that quality in christendom."[3] As James I toured the State Paper Office, the archive represented an innovative intersection of writing and power. But the power of the archive was predicated upon the relative anonymity of its contributors and, ultimately, the invisibility of its workings. Even though Wilson's archive shared the space of Whitehall Palace with other key administrative offices, the State Papers assumed a necessarily marginal existence. Unlike other record depositories, the holdings of the State Paper Office were considered state secrets and remained generally inaccessible. Thus, while contemporary guides directed readers on how to search for documents among Chancery, Exchequer, or Tower records, the State Papers remained closed to access and, by extension, cultural memory.[4] The centrality of its documents, and the necessary practices of secrecy surrounding their accumulation and dissemination, made the office inconspicuous enough for King James to forget its existence, only to be startled upon realizing the labyrinthine size and complexity of the state apparatus operating within his own palace. Despite James's intentions, and perhaps because of its necessary secrecy, Wilson's frequent petitions attest to the neglect his office received. After Wilson's death, the State Papers remained in a state of disarray until the formation of the Public Record Office began in 1838.[5]

The archive, in its incongruous blend of meticulous documentation alongside a necessary disappearance from memory, provided a key technology in the textual production and institutional maintenance of the project that concerned the majority of its records—the expropriation of more than three million acres and displacement of a population of six counties that was known, and then forgotten, as the Ulster plantation.[6] Despite the pervasive and visceral currency of several key events in seventeenth-century Ulster—the Flight of the Earls (1607), the Ulster Rising (1641), the Cromwellian massacre at Drogheda (1649), the Siege of Derry (1689)—the Ulster plantation resists mythologization.[7] In part, this resistance to narrative may result from the nature of the state-sponsored construction and administration of the plantation, which, unlike other colonies, consequently lacks myths of origin, initial settlement, and survival.[8] J.P.A. Pocock has noted the connection between English state formation and the centralization of archives in London, corollary processes that enabled a monopolization of narrative and representational power.[9] Unlike the other major plantation effort in early modern Ireland, the Munster plantation, Ulster also lacked a resident poet like Edmund Spenser to both commemorate it and urge its reform.[10] This lack of a canon of literary texts associated with the Ulster plantation helps explain why literary studies of English colonialism—even those dealing with Ireland—have generally omitted any consideration of Ulster.[11] Yet this omission is appropriate, since early seventeenth-century commentators on the Ulster project themselves made a concerted effort to emphasize the nonliterary character of the plantation: Sir Francis Bacon, for example, contrasted the efficiency of a proposed London council on the Ulster plantation with its precedent in the Virginia Company, "an enterprise in my opinion differing as much from this, as Amadis de Gaul differs from Caesar's Commentaries."[12]

The Ulster plantation was textually located, instead, in a documentary form of writing, an accumulation of records within the archive. The forms of writing that emerged out of the Ulster plantation testify to important transformations in the role of historical memory in the production of knowledge. Sixteenth-century historians, writing in the first wave of English colonialism, had turned to historical narrative to establish a foundation for cultural continuity. William Camden, for example, had declared his intention at the opening of his massive *Britannia* (1586; revised 1607) to "restore antiquity to Britaine, and Britain to his antiquity."[13] Despite the mythologizing tone of this passage, Camden's antiquarianism is noted for its skepticism, a concerted opposition to myths of cultural origin.[14] Camden's efforts to "renew ancientrie" are instead accomplished through a method that attempts to "cleare doubts, and recall home Veritie by way of recovery," a recuperative history constituted by an accumulation of artifacts: documents, inscriptions on monuments and graves, coins, alphabets, and etymologies of place names.[15] Camden, whose empiricism has led to his frequent characterization as the first "modern" historian in England, exemplifies a historiography that, as Foucault describes in *The Archaeology of Knowledge*, "undertook to 'memorize' the *monuments* of the past, transform them into *documents*, and lend speech to those traces."[16]

Camden's "monumental" history is dependent upon the reconstruction of memory: as a historical method, Camden's work collects the material documents of the past; as a form of cultural memory, his

project memorializes the past in order to establish historical continuity and legitimacy. Even though Camden was a near contemporary of
Thomas Wilson and the formation of the State Paper Office, Wilson's
archive and the early colonial era represent an alternative tradition, an
emergent history of documents, record-keeping, and the forms of
knowledge and forgetting specific to its institutional operations. The
document, as Foucault has argued, "is not the fortunate tool of a history that is primarily and fundamentally *memory*."[17] Rather than serving as an inert repository of the past, the mass of documentation
accumulating in the archive serves the administrative, bureaucratic
needs of the present moment; these documents embody the constructedness of the writing of history and demonstrate a discontinu-
ous relation to the past. The archive, in its situation as both a site of
state authority and a practice of writing, depends upon a necessary
erasure: as Michel de Certeau comments in *The Writing of History*,
"what is *perishable* is its data."[18] The archive does not merely accumulate documents and produce knowledge; it also exercises forms of
selection and erasure.[19] While the archive seems predicated upon the
desire to preserve the past through its material documents, the writing of history, de Certeau argues, reiterates forms of loss and break-
age from the past; however, it is out of this struggle against loss that
it constructs positions of historical distance and historiographical
objectivity. The documentary form of writing allows the process of
plantation to be transformed into an inert repository of documents,
as power relations are effaced and restructured into an ordered
"quarry of facts."[20] The Ulster plantation thus produces a system
of knowledge dependent upon a disjunctive relation to historical
objects, a knowledge based upon loss and forgetting that finds its
articulation through the technologies of history writing and cartography and its accumulation and disappearance within the contentious
site of the archive and the conflicts waged over its accessibility and
control.

* * *

JOHN SPEED'S MAP OF ULSTER, 1610

This chapter examines several indices of the necessary gaps in
knowledge and historical memory that converge with the discursive
formation and forgetting of the Ulster plantation. Much of my discussion will consider a key text in the documentation and displacement of the Ulster plantation, John Speed's *The Theatre of the Empire*

of Great Britain (1611).[21] Speed's *Theatre*, along with its companion volume, *The Historie of Great Britaine* (1611), borrowed much of its historical material from Camden's *Britannia*.[22] Speed's cartographical atlas was innovative, though, because it presented the first completed set of county maps for regions of England, Wales, Scotland, and Ireland.[23] While the majority of the 67 illustrations in Speed's *Theatre* consisted of county maps of England and Wales, the inclusion of Scotland and Ireland constituted Speed's text as the visual representation of James I's multinational empire of Great Britain. On his general map of the "British Isles," Speed's *Theatre* opens with a banner designating the title of James's consolidated kingdom "of Great Britain and Ireland." This foundational act of imperial naming offers an appropriate starting-point for the empire's first cartographical atlas, demonstrating the mutually reinforcing discourses of sovereignty and territorial possession.[24] In his proclamation declaring his new title as "King of Great Britaine," James had, in fact, justified his imperial title on the basis of the previous use of the term "Britain" in both maps and diplomatic correspondence. While acknowledging cartography and archival documentation as two primary sites where national identity is constructed and performed, James nonetheless emphasized the antiquity of his new title,

> the true and ancient Name,... received in Histories, in all Mappes and Cartes, wherein this Isle is described, and in ordinary Letters to Our selfe from divers Forraine Princes, warranted also by Authenticall Charters, Exemplifications under Seales, and other Records of great Antiquitie, giving Us president for our doing.[25]

Speed, like James I and other Union supporters, is confronted with a dilemma in representing James's "new" empire: while these texts attempt to celebrate the novel achievements of the Union (Anglo-Scottish unity, the conquest of Ulster, the future promise of empire), they also reflect an inability to conceive of the present moment as profoundly "new," as a disjuncture from the past; therefore, rather than emphasizing the modernity of James's United Kingdom, Speed constructs myths of its antiquity.

In an engraving that forms part of the front matter to Speed's text, Jodocus Hondius's illustration of James I's imperial coat of arms (see figure 5.1), the shield of the kings of Ireland is included among the arms "of the Severall kings that have aunciently raigned within his nowe [new] Dominions."[26] Speed distinguishes the past ("auncient") reign of the Irish from James's newly constituted and recently

Figure 5.1 Jodocus Hondius, James I's imperial coat of arms, from John Speed, *The Theatre of the Empire of Great Britain* (1611). Reproduced by permission of the American Geographical Society Library, University of Wisconsin-Milwaukee.

consolidated dominion over his territories. Hondius's engraving features a sequential arrangement of crests, depicting a process of state-building that begins with the conquest of Britain by the Romans (whose arms are featured in the upper left-hand corner) and proceeds to the bottom and right with the new territories and cultures that have been assimilated and subsumed within the empire (Saxons, Angles, Danes, Normans). By beginning British history with the Roman conquest, the design institutes a narrative of a civilizing process that culminates with the conquest of Ireland, the final stage in an inevitable consolidation of titles and corresponding territories. Speed follows other early modern historiographers in justifying the conquest of Ireland by analogy with the Roman conquest of Britain:[27] for William Strachey, "[h]ad not this violence, and this Iniury, bene offred vnto vs by the Romanes," Britons would have remained cannibalistic "overgrowne Satyrs."[28] As William Camden concluded, "a blessed and happy turne had it beene for Ireland, if it had at any time been under [Roman] subjection."[29]

Speed, like Strachey and Camden, posits conquest as the precondition of modernity; without the Roman conquest, the British empire would not have entered its linear historical narrative. And in James's new dominions, the erasure of Ireland ensures that it too will enter history. James's new empire necessarily entails a selection, to quote de Certeau, of "what must be *forgotten* in order to obtain the representation of a present intelligibility."[30] The imperial crests foreground these past cultures, calling to memory what must ultimately be forgotten for the present political body to become intelligible.[31] Hondius's depiction of James's empire demonstrates a version of what Bhabha terms a sense of "double-time" employed in the signification of nationhood: on one hand, an atavistic national past is conjured, predating the nation to a mythic past and tracing its descent from that originary moment; yet, on the other hand, the narrativization of nation is only comprehensible from the contemporary location of the enunciation of that sign.[32] In Hondius's illustration, the empire can only be represented in the present, specifically, the moment when the cherubs pull the curtain back to reveal James's *new* dominions *now*.

The titular basis of James's dynastic realm, as opposed to a more culturally homogeneous identity, allows Jacobean Britain to possess a temporal and spatial synchronicity. This emphasis on state-building through an absorption and subsuming of other cultures minimizes the role of conquest in the constitution of empire, a strategic choice given the position of Wales and Scotland in Hondius's design, both of which flank the crest of Ireland. The conquest of Ireland is thus rendered comparable to these earlier territorial acquisitions nominally acquired through peaceful "incorporation" and hereditary succession. At one level, the depiction of James's "auncient" Scottish throne foregrounds the antiquity and, therefore, legitimacy of his claim to his new imperial title.[33] Yet Hondius's engraving evokes another sense of "auncient"—that of a defunct, past culture—a definition made explicit through the juxtaposition of Wales, Scotland, and, finally, Ireland.[34] In order to enable a forgetting of the contentious recent history of Ulster, James's imperial title must first forget its Scottish origins, rendering its Scottish crown among the "auncient" (and thus defunct) kingdoms whose political and cultural disappearance is prerequisite for their entrance into the historical narrative of British identity. But read in this manner, what is the cultural identity of the British empire? James's empire becomes, in Jeffrey Knapp's terms, "an empire nowhere," one whose component cultures must fade into the past in order for the empire to acquire coherence.[35] The one cultural entity omitted from Hondius's design, though, is England. This absence lends a form of historical and territorial presence to England that the set of crests denies to the empire's other constituent cultures. To offset the perception that James's empire is merely England writ large, Hondius foregrounds the polymorphous nature of James's Britain, casting the empire's identity in a manner that resists either historical or territorial location.[36]

This dislocated representation of James's British empire results from specific ways that this image attempts, but ultimately fails, to rewrite historical and geographical divisions. The placement of the Scottish title in the past demonstrates an inability to coordinate James's English and Scottish crowns within the framework of a unified British identity. The language of a British empire itself was already charged with significance, having first been formulated as a way to express English sovereignty over Scotland in the 1540s.[37] The Ulster plantation, which attempted to subsume the identities of English and Scottish undertakers within a general classification as British, ironically locates its origin in a history of Anglo-Scottish conflict.[38] The earlier colonialist uses of the term "British" would seem to contradict, if not empty of significance, the gesture of imperial foundation offered by James I's new title; however, this reinscription of meaning is an integral part of the constitution of imperial identity. As Ernest Renan points out, "to forget and . . . to get one's history wrong, are essential factors in the making of a nation."[39] In the construction of James's Great Britain, the Ulster plantation provides the necessary means to efface a history of Anglo-Scottish relations by collapsing national distinctions within the joint project of the conquest of Ulster.[40] The construction of Britishness thus conforms to Eric Hobsbawm's notion of national identities as "invented traditions."[41] The Ulster context in which this identity developed also illustrates the violence inherent in its signification, which not only invents cultural traditions but, as Ernest Gellner adds, "often obliterates pre-existing cultures."[42] The effacement of Scottish cultural difference and historical traditions thus creates a precedent for a similar erasure of the contemporary presence of the non-British inhabitants of Ulster. The only space allotted for Scotland or Ireland in James's Britain lies under the rubric of the empire and dynastic realm. And, as Michael Hechter has argued, a primary characteristic of internal colonialism entails the denial of political sovereignty to peripheral and regional cultures.[43]

Unlike earlier sets of county maps, Speed's *Theatre* culminates with the inclusion of a general map of Ireland along with maps of each of the four counties, a literal incorporation of Ireland into the theatrical panorama of James's new British empire that serves to commemorate the recent pacification of Ulster in 1603. Yet, in Speed's map of Ulster (see figure 5.2), the historical space allotted for Ireland in Hondius's engraving, in an imprecise yet past moment of British antiquity, finds a cartographical parallel in Speed's inability to fix Ulster in any precise spatial or temporal location. The most puzzling aspect of Speed's map of Ulster lies in the fact that, although engraved in 1610, its details do not reflect any awareness of the Jacobean Ulster plantation. Instead, Speed anachronistically attributes much of Ulster to regional Irish chiefs, demarcating the land along the lines of sixteenth-century divisions that reflect Ulster's earlier status as a region largely resistant to English colonial infiltration. There were empirical reasons for Speed's inability to map contemporary Ulster, including the fact that there was no authoritative map that he could use as a model.[44] In earlier published images of Ulster, such as the maps of Ireland by Gerard Mercator (1564) and Baptista Boazio (1599), Ulster was given few details, especially in the interior of central Ulster, leaving the province as an empty territory that resembled early depictions of the interior of North America.[45] In addition, two Elizabethan cartographers, Richard Bartlett and John Browne, were killed as they attempted to survey Ulster.[46] As John Davies noted, the Gaelic Irish of Ulster "would not have their country discovered."[47]

The landscape of Ulster had changed substantially in the fifteen years prior to Speed's map, particularly as a result of Ulster's role as

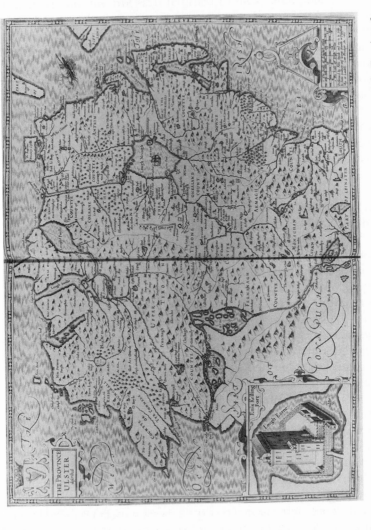

Figure 5.2 John Speed, "The Province Ulster described," from *The Theatre of the Empire of Great Britain* (1611). Reproduced by permission of the American Geographical Society Library, University of Wisconsin-Milwaukee.

the site of Gaelic Irish resistance to English rule in the Nine Years' War of 1594–1603, when Irish forces were led by Hugh O'Neill, the earl of Tyrone, and Hugh Roe O'Donnell.[48] At the war's end, the Ulster lords had surrendered their lands and were reinvested with title and tenure by the English state. O'Donnell's brother Rory, for example, was created earl of Tyrconnell by James in September 1603. Speed's map reflects its early Jacobean construction and attests to the detente achieved following the reinvestment of Ulster leaders with English titles. This emphasis on Ulster's stability resembles other early Jacobean panegyrics that praised James's role as a peacemaker. Even the bardic poet Eochaidh Ó hEodhasa marvelled at how James's power had enabled an erasure of Ulster's recent past: "More remarkable than that is the fact that we, the troubled people of Ireland, . . . [have] forgotten the tribulation of all anxieties."[49] Ó hEodhasa benefited more directly from his ability to forget the past, receiving 300 acres in County Fermanagh as a "deserving native."[50] Appropriately, Speed's map also emphasizes the accommodation of the old Gaelic order in James's Britain, attributing land not only to former rebels such as Tyrone and Tyrconnell but also to several Irish lords who had secured their titles by assisting England in the Nine Years' War, including Sir Cahir O'Doherty on the far-northern peninsula of Inishowen and Donal O'Cahan in County Coleraine.

Unlike earlier maps of Ulster, Speed's map bears traces of the recent Nine Years' War, with an English presence noted primarily through the identification of fortifications and passes built by Lord Deputy Mountjoy in his pacification of the Ulster chiefs. Large star-shaped marks indicate sixteen of these sites, including Mount Norris in Armagh, Fort Mountjoy in Tyrone, and the fortifications at Derry in the north.[51] In his maps of the other three Irish provinces, Speed provides detailed cartouches containing panoramic views of major Irish cities such as Dublin, Galway, Limerick, and Cork. The map of Ulster features, by contrast, a prominent inset of Enniskillen Fort (see figure 5.3), a key stronghold besieged and captured by English forces in 1594. While testifying to a lack of corporate towns in Ulster and the continued dominance of Irish systems of land tenure, the depiction of Enniskillen also points to its strategic role in the conquest of Ulster and subsequent English defenses of their gains. The depiction of Enniskillen might additionally be intended to emphasize the long history of cooperation between regional Irish lords and the English crown. Hugh O'Neill had assisted Sir Henry Bagenal and English forces in the campaign against Hugh Maguire, chief of Fermanagh, which culminated with the siege. Yet, as evidence of the

Figure 5.3   Enniskillen Fort, detail from Speed's map of Ulster, *The Theatre of the Empire of Great Britain* (1611). Reproduced by permission of the American Geographical Society Library, University of Wisconsin-Milwaukee.

fluctuating nature of these alliances, O'Neill had secretly negotiated with Maguire and used the campaign to secure his own position. Thus, while the memory of the battle may be intended to emphasize Irish cooperation in the pacification of Ulster, it testifies as well to the complexity of Ulster politics and the underlying degree of resistance to English rule.[52]

Speed's cartouche is even more directly related to the siege of Enniskillen due to the fact that Speed derived his illustration from a sketch of the siege made by John Thomas, an English foot-soldier (see figure 5.4).[53] One of the few contemporary details in Speed's map thus derives from sketches used for military intelligence and reporting. Speed's borrowings demonstrate the interconnections

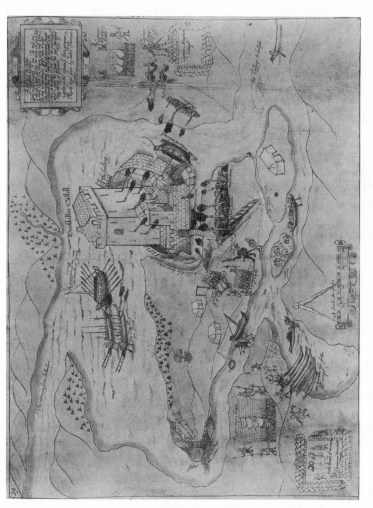

Figure 5.4 John Thomas, sketch of siege of Enniskillen Fort (1594). Reproduced by permission of the British Library.

between the disciplines of geography and military strategy, practices that equally, in Foucault's terms, "come to inscribe themselves both on a material soil and within forms of discourse."[54] But a comparison of the two illustrations reveals the strategies Speed employs to efface this debt. Thomas's bird's-eye-view sketch depicts major events in the siege, specifying the location of encampments, strategies of land- and water-based assault, and forms of English military technology.[55] It also prominently displays the heads of rebels placed within the English camp in the lower left-hand corner of the drawing. Speed's illustration limits the frame of the sketch, transposing the central figure of the fort onto an empty landscape. Speed retains the boats that Thomas had depicted laying siege to the fort; however, this image is transformed to that of a single boat being rowed toward the open gates of the now-pacified fortification. Speed's revision of the military sketch provides a way to memorialize the Ulster conquest while effacing the means through which this victory was accomplished, producing a bloodless conquest in which impaled heads are transposed to an empty perspectival landscape.

The circulation of Thomas's sketch also testifies to the conflict over documentary material among cartographers, antiquarians, and civil servants such as Sir Thomas Wilson. Thomas's sketch is now located in the "Augustus Collection" of the British Library's Cotton Manuscripts. This collection was compiled by the antiquarian Sir Robert Cotton and drawn from materials he had permanently borrowed from the State Paper Office.[56] As Keeper of Records, Wilson had repeatedly written for assistance in barring the kleptomaniacal Cotton from his office.[57] Wilson had reason for concern; unlike the keepers of other depositories, such as the Chancery or Treasury offices, he was obliged by oath to recover lost records.[58] Cotton, on the other hand, was one of Speed's chief patrons; a fellow member of the Jacobean Society of Antiquaries, Cotton provided Speed with documents otherwise unavailable to him.[59] In his "summary Conclusion" to the *Historie of Great Britaine* (1611), Speed describes Cotton as "another *Philadelphus* in preseruing old Monuments and ancient Records: whose Cabinets were vnlocked, & Library co[n]tinually set open to my free accesse."[60] Yet despite Cotton's successful efforts to create an alternative state archive, borrowing an estimated one-third of the holdings from Wilson's Office of Papers, most of the maps and surveys of Ulster remained inaccessible even to him.[61]

Speed's map of Ulster is thus profoundly ambivalent: it commemorates the unsettled status of the region, marking the necessity of fortifications and military rule in the province, while also emphasizing its pacification, eliding signs of the recent conquest, as in its revision of the Thomas sketch. Despite this emphasis on Ulster's pacification, the inclusion of the cartouche of Enniskillen Fort emphasizes the need for continued vigilance against future attack, a characteristic not found in the other Irish provincial maps. Nonetheless, Speed's map divides the Ulster landscape primarily along the lines of regional Gaelic Irish lordships, memorializing a social hierarchy that had effectively been displaced from Ulster by 1610. The earls of Tyrone, Tyrconnell, and Maguire, who are attributed to control much of western and central Ulster, had fled to the Continent in 1607, opening up the majority of the region for confiscation and redistribution. They had left Ulster not to escape imminent military conquest but to avoid the more subtle forms of domination that the English colonial government had devised to eliminate remaining sources of Gaelic Irish authority, particularly through manipulation of the parliamentary franchise, the justice system, and land tenure.

Lord Deputy Sir Arthur Chichester and Attorney General Sir John Davies subsequently found the means to entrap, prosecute, and dispose of their former Irish allies in Ulster and gain the remainder of the six escheated counties through quasi-legal maneuvering. Resurveying the Ulster counties depicted by Speed, the attribution of the northern peninsula of Inishowen as the possession of the Gaelic Irish leader Sir Cahir O'Doherty is surprisingly incongruous, considering the fact that O'Doherty had been killed in 1608 while defending himself in Derry. Because he had died while fighting against English authorities, O'Doherty was posthumously convicted of treason, his lands attainted and seized for Chichester's personal use.[62] In Coleraine, Sir Donal O'Cahan, who was never granted the lands the English had guaranteed him for his aid against Tyrone, was captured as he arrived to claim his land title in Dublin and sent to the Tower of London for the remaining twenty years of his life. O'Cahan was joined in the Tower by many leading figures of the Ulster aristocracy, including Tyrconnell's cousin, who was also the heir to his title, as well as both the brother and son of the earl of Tyrone.[63] In 1608, O'Cahan's lands had been granted to the City of London, forming much of the territory of the Londonderry plantation.[64]

As Speed prepared his map of Ulster for publication in 1610, the six escheated counties had been surveyed, redistributed, and already settled by Protestant English and Scottish undertakers. Not only had the Irish landowners noted by Speed been killed, banished, imprisoned, or deprived of their estates, but, in addition, some of the counties and territorial boundaries no longer even existed in

1610: Tyrconnell had become Donegal; Coleraine (along with portions of Tyrone), the plantation of Londonderry; Inishowen, the personal property of the English lord deputy; much of Armagh and Tyrconnell, granted to one of the plantation's largest landowners, Trinity College, Dublin. Although not officially part of the Ulster plantation, the remaining three counties of Ulster had similarly been escheated and settled: the northeastern counties of Down and Antrim became the regions of Ulster most extensively settled by English and Scottish undertakers by the early 1620s, while Monaghan had been confiscated in 1591 following the execution of Hugh Roe Macmahon, lord of Monaghan, and leased to six members of the Macmahon family.[65] When the reorganization of land in Ulster was completed in 1610, the same year that Speed's map was engraved, Irish landowners of all ranks—Gaelic Irish and Catholic Anglo-Irish alike—held only 20 percent of the land in Ulster.[66]

Speed's map of Ulster defies an analysis of early modern cartography that locates mapping as a technology ensuring a more efficient political control over a region through the detailed surveying of the land.[67] In his omission of the Ulster plantation from visual representation, Speed's map attests to how early modern maps constituted power not only through their technical claims to accuracy and "scientific" objectivity.[68] Maps also possessed power through the forms of knowledge they produced, and, it should be added, through the types of knowledge that were not produced due to a map's silences and gaps.[69] Some of these cartographical silences resulted from deliberate policy and reflect how maps and surveys were important components in often-contentious networks of power. But the shocking absence of the Ulster plantation from Speed's map raises a more profound question regarding the limits of a map's knowledge: in other words, how could Speed or any contemporary surveyor have mapped or visually depicted the expropriation of land and displacement of human subjects that constituted the Ulster plantation, a massive confiscation of land that in the previous three years had amounted to 3,798,000 acres?[70] Speed's representation of the stasis of Gaelic Ulster might then be less a result of the motivated suppression of information than a key example of what Foucault defines as an *episteme*, the "conditions of possibility" that "in a given period, delimits...the totality of experience of a field of knowledge."[71]

I want to argue, though, that the epistemic limits expressed by Speed's map of Ulster also point to the important role played by the Ulster plantation in a process of capital formation in early modern Britain. The withholding of cartographical information regarding the Ulster plantation reveals the important commercial advantages sought by both state officials and private investors. J.B. Harley speculates that the practices of secrecy endemic to the history of cartography bear a parallel with the activities of monopoly capitalism, the ensuring of commercial advantage through exclusive rights to cartographical knowledge.[72] But the process of capital formation is itself predicated upon an absence from representation, whether the erasure of human subjects as their labor is abstracted or the disappearance of the money-form as it is converted into capital.[73] Gilles Deleuze and Félix Guattari extend this comparison: a process of capital formation, like that found in the Ulster plantation, "that divides the earth as an object and subjects men to the new imperial inscription, to the new full body, to the new socius" is best seen as "a movement of deterritorialization."[74] Cartography thus functions as a technology that reflects a primitive logic of capital, a process of accumulation that necessarily effaces and forgets the human toll of its workings. The mapping of Ulster, therefore, does not operate as a strategy instrumental to forms of centralization, territorialization, and accumulation but as a technology complicit in forms of displacement, deterritorialization, and dispersal. Speed's map of Ulster testifies to how the "new socius" of New English authority in Ulster under Chichester and Davies is, in a sense, unrepresentable: its power operates through an absence from representation and effacement of the process of its domination.

The technologies that document Ulster not only abet the political displacement central to the plantation project; they also help produce the forms of knowledge necessary to ensure the plantation's maintenance. To offset the deterritorialization upon which the Ulster plantation was predicated, the project was made analogous with a process that accumulated knowledge and documents. Cartography thus functioned as what Anthony Giddens terms an "authoritative resource," a mechanism intended for "the retention and control of information or knowledge" that constitutes itself through practices of notation and documentation.[75] Equally important to the dissemination of meticulous records and "knowledge" of Ulster, though, was control over the accessibility and interpretation of this information. It was Sir Thomas Wilson, in his role as Keeper of Records of the State Paper Office, who was instrumental in preserving the institutional secrecy of the Ulster plantation. When Wilson assumed the position of Keeper of Records in 1612, his oath of office stipulated:

> you shall carefullie and faithfullie keepe secret and conceale from ye knowlege of others eyther by writting or relacon all such things therein

> contayned as shalbe fitt eyther for reason of state or otherwise for his Maties seruice to be concealed and keepe secrett[76]

Wilson's official duties illustrate the ways that cartography and history writing were employed to help ensure monarchical state authority, demonstrating how these technologies were among the state secrets to be concealed from all but authorized officials.[77] Similar to Richard Rambuss's analysis of the importance of Spenser's "secret career" as a colonial official in Ireland, Wilson's role as secretary entailed an authority over institutional secrecy through his bureaucratic identity as the official in control of the access to "secret" documents.[78] As an example of how cartographical information often constituted the secret knowledge bequeathed to a secretary, Robert Beale (1541–1601), a clerk to the Privy Council, noted in his "A Treatise of the Office of a Councellor and Principall Secretarie to her Ma[jes]tie":

> A Secretarie must likewise have the booke of Ortelius['s] Mapps, a booke of the Mappes of England,... and a good descripc[i]on of the Realm of Irelande, a note of the Noblemen and surnames English or Irish of their Septs, Enraghes, Galloglasses, Kerns and followers, and if anie other plotts or mapps come to his handes, let them be kept safelie.[79]

As Beale states, although a secretary should possess particular knowledge concerning the cartography and military situation of Ireland, he must also preserve the secrecy of this information. Appropriately, Wilson was recommended to his post as Keeper of Records after having previously served as chief secretary to Sir Robert Cecil, the earl of Salisbury, the primary architect of the Ulster plantation.[80] It would have been Wilson, then, who had earlier directed correspondence between Salisbury and his commissioners in Ireland during the crucial years of 1608–10. Reinforcing the importance of Wilson's task to collect and organize documents, Salisbury commanded that his correspondence with officials either be returned to him or destroyed. Many of these returned letters were incorporated into Wilson's State Paper Office, while the number of destroyed documents attests to a necessary concomitant erasure.[81]

Wilson had entered Salisbury's service between 1605 and 1606 and was appointed as Keeper of the State Papers shortly after Salisbury's death in 1612. One of his first duties entailed transferring Salisbury's papers to the State Paper Office. Perhaps because these papers outnumbered the documents previously held in the Office of Papers, Wilson seems to have regarded his tenure as Salisbury's secretary and Keeper of Records as a continuous period of service. In a 1615 letter to James I, for example, Wilson complained of having spent "more than 10 painful years" working to "have reduced them into that due order and form, that your majesty and most of the Lords have seen and approved."[82] Wilson had a more literal investment in the success of the Ulster plantation during this period, having petitioned along with his brother for a grant of 2,000 acres in 1618; this potential income was most likely what prompted him to write a treatise proposing military rule in Ireland that same year.[83] Wilson had earlier written two important texts dealing with Ireland: "On the state of England A.D. 1600, with a description of this country and of Ireland" [ca. 1601] helped him secure the patronage of Cecil and James I, while his "Booke on the State of Ireland" [ca. 1599] contains a pastoral dialogue between "Peregryn" and "Silvyn," figures named after Edmund Spenser's sons, Peregrine and Sylvanus. Wilson had also intended to write a chronicle history of Ireland that updated Holinshed and covered the years 1584–1619, a project he never accomplished.[84]

The oath of office given to Sir Thomas Wilson indicates how practices of note-taking and documentation were located in a network of contending social forces, demonstrating the mixed investments of subjects engaged in a battle over the archive's accessibility and control, including antiquarians, cartographers, civil servants, and colonial investors. The Ulster plantation points out larger social fissures as well: the competing objectives of the monarch, his chief ministers (such as Salisbury), and colonial administrators (including Davies and Chichester), each of whose fluctuating policies affected differently the various communities located in Ulster.[85] In addition, one must recognize the conflicts as well as coalitions formed between earlier communities in Ulster—including Gaelic Irish, Catholic Anglo-Irish (or "Old English"), and Ulster (or Highland) Scots—and the Protestant New English arrivals: lowland Scottish Presbyterians, English tenant farmers, decommissioned English soldiers (or "servitors"), London merchants, and colonial officials. Perhaps another reason for the Ulster plantation's resistance to narrative and myth results from the complexity of early modern Ulster politics, a social hybridization that counters the Manichaean community politics often conjured in present-day Northern Ireland.

As Wilson's oath of office demonstrates, the power of documents— whether histories, maps, or surveys—results not from their accuracy of detail but from their legally mandated ability to control what may enter and disappear from the level of discourse and documentation. Similarly, Speed's map of Ulster demonstrates how early modern cartography was concerned less with questions of detail or accuracy than with the forms of knowledge produced, and sometimes elided, from the invention of imperial self-representation.[86] However, in his table of contents to *The Theatre of the Empire of Great Britain*, Speed protests that his collection depicts the literal "contents" of the British empire, what it "hath now in actual possession" (sig. A2). Among the dedicatory poems, Sir John Davies combines his roles as poet and colonial official, commending Speed for his "anatomizing" of Ireland:

> In euery *Member, Artire, Nerue*, and *Veine*,
> Thou by thine *Arte* dost so Anatomize,
> That all may see each parcell without paine. (sig. ¶2)

Actually, though, Speed's maps had already been superseded by official surveys in each of the previous two years: the first, in 1608, was used to measure the extent of James's new holdings in Ulster; the survey of the escheated counties conducted by Sir Josias Bodley the following year facilitated land redistribution in the region.[87] As attorney general of Ireland, Sir John Davies had a central role in the quasi-legal maneuvering that helped ensure the escheating of Ulster, including the surveys of 1608 and 1609.[88] These surveys formed the basis of John Norden's detailed map of the new property holdings of Protestant undertakers in Ulster, also completed in 1610. But like most plantation-era maps and surveys of Ulster, Norden's was unpublished, its manuscript circulation sharply curtailed. The circulation of the maps resulting from Bodley's initial 1609 survey, which were presented to Salisbury and later deposited in Wilson's Office of Papers, was so tightly controlled that they were not located and identified until 1860.[89]

Why then does Davies praise Speed's obviously inaccurate, if not anachronistic, "anatomizing" of Ireland? The desire to limit—and even prohibit—the visual representation of the Ulster plantation might have resulted from the need to promote investment in the project while curtailing the power and autonomy of prospective undertakers and their financial backers. As Davies's poem indicates, Speed's map was intended for the domestic consumption of an elite English audience who would "see each parcell without paine"; in other words, they would survey the lands of Ulster, and perhaps gain interest in colonial investment, but do so without having to endure the risks of personal travel.[90] Speed's map thus conforms to the image of Ulster found in promotional texts such as Thomas Blenerhassett's *A Direction for the Plantation of Ulster* (1610), wherein Ulster is depicted as a depopulated and unclaimed territory requiring English intervention and investment.[91] The popularity of Speed's maps among an elite English audience is evidenced by the fact that George Carew, president of Munster from 1600 to 1602 and an avid collector of Irish maps and manuscripts, was known to have decorated the walls of his study with Speed's maps of the Irish provinces.[92] As an indication of their symbolic capital, the display of these objects is used to advertise an Englishman's knowledge of "state secrets," even though these maps reflect few details of the process of plantation. Other texts emphasized how Speed's maps had political as well as ornamental uses: in a text reporting on the state of the Irish economy, *Advertisements for Ireland* (ca. 1622–23), Richard Hadsor, an Old English lawyer residing in London, explained that in order to "lay open unto your Lordships the present visage and face of the now [new] state of Ireland," he would first turn to Speed's maps of Ireland, "the new map of that island that is so well known to your Lordships and most statists here" [i.e., in England].[93] Hadsor does not register any unease concerning whether Speed's "new" map accurately depicts the present territorial divisions of Ireland, emphasizing, instead, how Speed's maps served as a common reference point for colonial landowners in Ireland as well as state officials back in England.

The circulation and reception of Speed's Irish maps also reveal the political struggle engaged in by those competing for position in the Ulster plantation. In his prefatory poem to Speed's *Theatre*, for example, Davies still recognizes the importance of official control over the dissemination of geographical knowledge. Davies therefore praises Speed, even though he himself had access to the survey maps that helped him redistribute land as a member of the Ulster plantation committee.[94] The English colonial government, in fact, used the inaccuracy of earlier surveys—including those conducted under its own authority—as a justification to invalidate, and thereby claim as its own, titles held by Irish landowners.[95] Officials even used this practice, the discovery of "concealed lands," as a way to periodically adjust the landholdings of Protestant New English undertakers. William Farmer, a supporter of Chichester's administration, complained that surveys had underestimated the size of escheated properties, allowing for uncontrolled social mobility among undertakers who thereby seized larger tracts of land; he therefore recommended that James invalidate these tenures and confiscate the land recently planted by English settlers.[96] The absence of a standard survey of property in Ulster also allowed Davies to alter the parliamentary franchise, which helped ensure the first Protestant majority in the Irish Parliament of 1613.[97] In addition, without an official survey of Ulster, the regional English government could adjust taxation at will.[98] In all of these examples, the mechanisms of colonial authority operated not only through their invisibility and absence from representation but also from a general lack of referentiality.

This recognition may help us understand why Davies may then praise Speed's "anatomizing" of Ireland despite—or perhaps because of—its lack of recognition of the Ulster plantation. This omission had little to do with the recent date of the Ulster plantation in 1610. When Speed subsequently revised his collection in 1627, he retained his Irish maps. Speed's original Irish maps were also reproduced in posthumous editions of Speed's *Theatre*,[99] and they formed the model for later seventeenth-century continental engravers such as Jansson (1636) and Blaeu (1654), among others, each of whom printed ornate maps of Ulster.[100] Even as late as 1673, the English map-maker Richard Blome based his Irish maps on Speed's for the collection *Britannia*, while other publishers retained Speed's maps throughout the eighteenth century.[101] I want to emphasize the exceptional incongruity of this trend; it is significant that Blome chose Speed's maps as his model, for example, rather than the Down Survey conducted by William Petty during the Cromwellian invasion. Petty's mapping of Ireland, a five-year effort completed in 1657 that mobilized 1,000 workers, 40 clerks, and numerous surveyors, was not even published until 1685.[102] Thus, the Ulster plantation remained unrepresented in published cartographical atlases during the first seventy-five years of its existence; on the map, the Ulster plantation did not exist.

***

SURVEYING CAPITAL: RICHARD NORWOOD AND JOSIAS BODLEY

Among English colonial holdings in the seventeenth century, the Ulster plantation's status was exceptional as a space whose identity was produced out of its resistance to—and absence from—cartographical representation and knowledge. In contrast to his map of Ulster, Speed copied and included Richard Norwood's recent survey of the Bermuda colony ("the Somers Islands") in *A Prospect of the Most*

Famous Parts of the World (1627), a collection that constituted the
first general world atlas published in England (see figure 5.5).[103]
Norwood completed his survey of Bermuda in 1617, making his map
a contemporary of the Ulster plantation surveys. His detailed survey
enabled the company to settle every plot of the island with 1,500
inhabitants by 1622.[104] Norwood's map emphasizes how the success
of the Bermuda colony was achieved through a standardized division
of the land: the island, "exactlie surveyed," is marked by consistently
organized plots of land, depicted visually as a series of uniform and
numbered lines marking the landscape and demarcating property.
The verticality of Bermuda colonial culture was based upon the division of land and people into "tribes." Although the equivalent of
parishes, these units were named after leading figures in the Bermuda
Company. To further emphasize the foundational role played by the
company's investors, the bottom margin of the map lists the investors
in each "tribe" along with the number of shares owned by each person. The map reproduces a construction of land as property through
absolute and hierarchal demarcations of ownership, strategies that
separate possession from other forms of affiliation, whether habitation
or labor. After all, neither the tribal company leaders nor the listed
investors actually lived in Bermuda or worked the land. The tenant
farmers, indentured servants, and African slaves who formed colonial
society in Bermuda, on the other hand, are absent from representation.[105] The map testifies to a separation of capitalist production from
labor and human agency: as J.B. Harley comments, "for map makers,
their patrons, and their readers, the underclass did not exist and
had no geography."[106]

While the Norwood/Speed map of Bermuda commemorates the
ascendancy of capital, it differentiates this success from colonial failure in Ireland. The designation of "tribes"—a term often applied
pejoratively to regional Irish septs—rewrites Irish social institutions in
the language and logic of capital. Ireland appears on the map in other
ways as well: the uninhabited island in the far northeastern corner of
Bermuda, whose inaccessibility makes it undesirable for plantation, is
significantly named "Ireland." By contrast, Speed's map otherwise
celebrates the Bermuda colony's commercial prestige and strategic
geographic location, evidenced by the text of the map's central cartouche as well as the images of the shorelines of Virginia, New
England, and Hispaniola located within convenient proximity to the
colony. The organizational capabilities of the Bermuda Company are
also emphasized in a small note that appears to the left of the scale of
miles, which records how five people had left Bermuda for Ireland

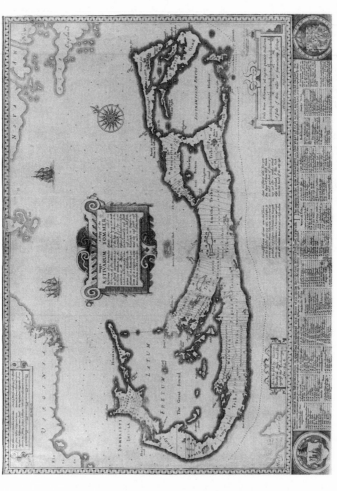

Figure 5.5 John Speed, "A Mapp of the Sommer Ilands" (Bermuda), from *A Prospect of the Most Famous Parts of the World* (1627); based on survey and map by Richard Norwood. Reproduced by permission of the American Geographical Society Library, University of Wisconsin-Milwaukee.

in a small boat in 1616: the event is recorded as a feat "ye like hath scarce bene heard of in any age." This comment serves as a smug testimony to the fortitude and skill of Bermuda's successful colonists, who have moved on to greater challenges in Ireland. But the note also exposes the forms of dispossession inherent in the intersection of capital formation and colonial practices. After all, it fails to specify why the colonists opted to leave the prosperity of Bermuda, nor does it explain why they chose such a dangerous form of travel. In addition, while their successful arrival in Ireland is recorded as an unprecedented marvel, their journey effects a disappearance from both the map and historical memory. But rather than testify to the disruptive potential of capital and colonialism, the note can only register this violence as a form of self-inflicted loss and disappearance, although one displaced onto that embarrassment of English colonialism, Ireland.

Unlike the successful control over space and divisibility of property and populations demonstrated by the Bermuda colony, the Ulster plantation was seen to resist cartographical knowledge and control. This inability to master the Irish landscape produced a textual recognition of the limits of colonial practices—a proliferation of images of mourning and loss that exposed the effects of dispersal and dispossession on geographic spaces and the human subjects who only marginally inhabited them. In contrast to the successful efforts of accumulation accomplished by his older brother, Sir Thomas Bodley, whose book collection at Oxford still bears his name as the Bodleian Library, Sir Josias Bodley's survey of Ulster (1613) testifies to the disruptive material effects of colonialism in Ireland. An engineer by training who held the offices of Superintendent of Castles and Director General of Fortifications in Chichester and Davies's colonial administration, Bodley had served as the main surveyor in the first full attempt to calculate the size of the confiscated territories of Ulster in 1609.[107] Following unfavorable reports about the state of the Ulster plantation, Bodley was commissioned to survey the settlement once more, producing a list and description of 195 plots in five of the escheated counties completed between February and April of 1613.[108] Commissioned to report on the progress of plantation, Bodley instead chronicles its effects; despite his training as a builder of fortifications, Bodley serves as a witness to the devastating impact of a primitive accumulation of capital on the human and natural landscape of Ulster.

As he proceeds through new holdings in County Cavan, Bodley notes the extent to which land remains in the de facto possession of

Irish tenants; repeatedly his survey remarks on "Irish inhabitants continuing yet on ye same as in former times" (sig. X1). Despite their continued presence, the Irish of Ulster were being converted from itinerant herders and retainers in the households of Ulster lords to tenant farmers and wage-laborers. The Orders and Commissions for the Ulster plantation, in fact, stipulated that native Irish could inhabit only one-quarter of any estate, usually the bogs and waste areas; also, except in rare cases to reward past service, such as military aid against O'Neill and his allies, Irish tenants could not own land. These stipulations regarding the separation of English from Gaelic Irish populations were subsequently disregarded by most landowners, largely because Irish tenants would out of necessity pay exorbitantly high rents so as to be allowed to reside and work in their communities.[109] Noting the dependence of English undertakers upon the continued presence of Irish laborers, Bodley comments how an undertaker in Loghtee, County Cavan named John Taylor still waits for tenants; in the meantime, "diuer of ye Irishe are yet remaining both on this proportion & others, without whose assistance for a which they pretend impossibly of procuring in theyr undertakings" (sig. C1).

Despite his ideological commitment to military rule in Ulster, Bodley describes the plantation as unfortified, uninhabited, and impoverished. He attributes the plantation's waste to the profit motives of the colonists, who have not "planted the country as the very name of plantation itselfe enioyneth them, . . . as if nothing els hade beene intended by it but to make them gainers."[110] Bodley also notes the absence of English and lowland Scottish landowners, such as John Archdale, who "only came ouer, viewed his proportion, tooke possession and returned into England, leauing neither Englishe nor Irishe vpon his land" (sig. H1). He reports how prospective English tenants have deserted their holdings as well, including those engaged to work Bernard Lindsay's holdings in Tyrone, "who at ye first view of ye barrennes thereof, made their instant retrait," leaving the land "wholy waste" (sig. T1). Despite its critique of the immediate effects produced by capital formation in Ulster, Bodley's survey has difficulty attributing causes for the devastation he witnesses in the colony. On one hand, an absentee landlord such as Archdale creates waste spaces, leaving the land barren as he travels to Ireland merely to ensure his land claim with little regard to what is subsequently done with that investment. On the other hand, industrious English tenants refuse to settle on the already barren escheated holdings, which remain uninhabited as they return to England.

Bodley's inability to locate a point of origin for the Ulster problem finds a parallel in Marx's discussion of primitive accumulation. As he revises a history of capitalist production found in Adam Smith and other political economists, Marx rejects a search for a self-originating moment in the history of capital, so as to then be able to chart its "growth," "development," and "progress"; rather, he focuses on a process, moments when "great masses" of human subjects are "forcibly torn from their means of subsistence, and hurled as free and 'unattached' proletarians on the labour-market."[111] Marx's language emphasizes the violence of expropriation and displacement not as a point of origin for capital but as its necessary precondition. Primitive accumulation, in this sense, constitutes the limits of intelligibility of economic causes, the process of dispossession that must be forgotten for the imperial economy to gain coherence and, ultimately, be able to write its history of ascendancy.

Bodley's survey constitutes an important counternarrative that contests histories of the success and inevitability of both the capitalist basis of English colonialism in Ireland and its concomitant Protestant ascendancy. In reward for his candor, Bodley was ultimately deprived of his position and pension. After his 1613 survey, he was commissioned in June 1614 to conduct another survey, completed in September of that year, of which only the section on Londonderry is extant. Bodley's report of the poor conditions of the Londonderry plantation prompted King James to threaten to revoke undertakers' leases, and the king gave undertakers a deadline of August 31, 1616 to accomplish necessary improvements. Bodley was then commissioned to resurvey holdings in November 1616; this, his final survey, prompted an investigation into the failures of plantation efforts. Yet, perhaps in retaliation for the candor of his earlier surveys, he was not a member of that commission. Bodley died in 1618, before he could appeal for restitution.[112] Unlike many officials, he was also denied the customary gift of property in Ulster to compensate for the otherwise poor conditions of colonial service.[113] Bodley's survey ultimately came to rest as a dead letter among Attorney General Davies's papers.[114]

* * *

COUNTER-MEMORY IN THE ARCHIVE

I conclude with Josias Bodley's survey precisely because his sentiments of disgust and mourning in reaction to the nexus of capitalism and colonialism in early seventeenth-century Ulster demonstrate the boundaries of what can be said within the archive of English colonialism, a recognition of discursive and institutional limits reinforced by his text's subsequent dispersal and neglect. While the accumulation of materials in the archive of Wilson's State Paper Office reflects its instrumental role in the functioning of state power, the forgetting of Bodley's survey demonstrates how this process of formation necessarily entailed a forced erasure of institutional and cultural memory. The Ulster plantation's disappearance from the map and archival record reveals the violence upon which colonial practices and capitalist production were built. But the insistent need to erase Ulster from cartographical location and historical narrative ultimately shows that this violence is not an action located in the past; on the contrary, it is a set of forces renewed and reactivated in the present. The subsequent elision of the Ulster plantation from the narrativized memories of communities illustrates how the violence of colonialism has been rearticulated by mutually contradictory mythologies of the besieged community and its others.[115]

One intention of this chapter has been to explain how forms of knowledge production—history writing, documentation, cartography—were instrumental to early modern colonial practices in Ireland. This intersection is demonstrated by the surprising number of archival collections formed out of the Ulster plantation, including the product of Wilson's State Paper Office, the Public Record Office, as well as several collections composed of the papers of officials involved in the Ulster project: Sir John Davies (the Huntington Library's Hastings Papers and the Carte Collection at the Bodleian Library); Sir Arthur Chichester (the Carte Collection, the Philadelphia Papers at the PRO, and the Clarke Collection at Trinity College, Dublin); Sir George Carew (the Carew Papers at Lambeth Palace and the British Library's Harleian Manuscripts); Sir Robert Cecil, earl of Salisbury (the Salisbury Manuscripts at Hatfield House); and Sir Robert Cotton (the British Library's Cotton Manuscripts), among others.[116] Yet the "archive," to use Foucault's sense of the term from *The Archaeology of Knowledge*, consists of more than a repository of documents or the institutions devoted to their preservation. Rather, for Foucault, the archive constitutes "the law of what can be said, the system that governs the appearance of statements as unique events."[117] The material archive of documents is thus produced by the epistemic archive that defines acceptable methods and types of evidence, the rules and criteria necessary to validate historiography's objective processes and totalizing conclusions.

The archive, in Foucault's definition, additionally constitutes the site of this power's limits, the necessary blind spots of historical memory. As Foucault comments, "it is not possible for us to describe our own archive, since it is from within these rules that we speak."[118] Foucault's statement reveals how the archive may also positively establish the discursive parameters of historical inquiry. Any search for unities and origins is thwarted through the archive's own contradictory tactics of accumulation and disappearance. And it is through this failure that a space is opened up for new possibilities of inquiry. The archive, Foucault argues, "deprives us of our continuities; it dissipates that temporal identity in which we are pleased to look at ourselves when we wish to exorcise the discontinuities of history."[119] Through its memorial of the historical discontinuities of the Ulster plantation, the archive provides a shared colonial history of displacement and exploitation for present-day communities, a counter-memory that offsets both a memory of loss and mourning—the Flight of the Earls—and a narrative of violence and ascendancy—the victory of the Orangemen.[120] In this project, as Paul Ricoeur once commented, "this exercise of memory is here an exercise in *telling otherwise*"; the archive, the site of these narratives' construction, can thus provide "a space for the confrontation between opposing testimonies."[121] Remembering how the Ulster plantation was forgotten not only enables a critique of colonial discourse and the production of knowledge in the archive. This critical practice functions as well to intervene in the present ways that communities know of themselves and act politically.

Conclusion

The Unmaking of the English Working Class

The title of this final section makes a conscious reference, of course, to E.P. Thompson's seminal work on class relations in England, *The Making of the English Working Class*.[1] Thompson's model of history from below has been an important influence on this study, and his exploration of the significant agency of the lower classes establishes a precedent that I have attempted to follow in this book. Emphasizing the extent to which social relations, class hierarchies, and networks of power were in a process of formation and change in the early modern period, I have tried to demonstrate how there were also crucial alternatives to dominant discourses and classes. My title alters that of Thompson's study, though, in order to foreground the significant ways that contemporary criticism has effected an "unmaking" of the English working classes. To an extent, Thompson himself provides merely an abbreviated history of class relations in early modern England by beginning his analysis with the industrial revolution of the late-eighteenth and early-nineteenth centuries in England. Although Thompson examines the eighteenth century in other works, his classic survey, *The Making of the English Working Class*, does not include sustained discussion of the sixteenth and seventeenth centuries.[2]

In this final section, therefore, I wish to extend the scope of Thompson's research back to this earlier period in order to explore the histories that are elided within a chronology that aligns the creation of the working classes with nascent forms of industrialization. In an important passage in his work, Thompson clarifies that "The making of the working class...was not the spontaneous generation of the factory-system. Nor should we think of an external force—the 'industrial revolution'—working upon some nondescript undifferentiated raw material of humanity."[3] Thompson emphasizes the role of historical memory for the nineteenth-century industrial proletariat, who retained and wielded the memory of customary rights and protections as historical support for political action: "The working class," Thompson concludes, "made itself as much as it was made."[4] Elsewhere in his work, Thompson stresses the conservatism and forms of nostalgia inherent in populist national sentiment, expressions articulated through actions of protest and riot that attempted to reassert a residual "moral economy."[5] However, by extending the implications of Thompson's passage, I wish to emphasize the extent to which defenses of customary rights could also offer a critical stance to centralized forms of authority, potentially creating alliances and alternative communities that challenged or ignored official expressions of nationhood. In drawing attention to the interconnections of class and nation in the early modern period, I have attempted not only to foreground a longer history of class struggle; I have also intended to recuperate the significant agency of those class groups who constituted early modern England's internal colonies.

While critical studies frequently align histories of class and industrialism, two other topics central to this study are often given a similar chronology: internal colonialism and nationalism. Although Michael Hechter's *Internal Colonialism* has been a shaping influence on this book, the structure of Hechter's project is based upon an imposed division between pre-industrial and industrial eras. Even though Hechter acknowledges the extensive links between core and peripheral cultures in a pre-industrial context, his own study devotes only cursory attention to the period before 1850. As a result, the early modern period functions merely to introduce and provide a context for the industrial era, which Hechter locates in the mid-nineteenth century, an even later date than Thompson. By correlating the creation of the working classes exclusively with the beginnings of industrialization, other social historians, like Hechter, efface the operations of class as an effect of relations of production in the early modern period. In *The World We Have Lost*, Peter Laslett characterizes industrialism as the force that, in a sense, created England's class system. In Laslett's nostalgic formulation, pre-industrial England was a harmonious "one-class society" dominated by the household and workshop, paternalistic sites of labor that he contrasts with the competitive and individualistic social relations produced by industrialization and the factory system.[6] However, as Nancy Armstrong and Leonard Tennenhouse have argued in their critique of Laslett, this model presents an atomistic view of culture as structured around immediate and affective familial ties.[7] By focusing on the "domestic" in its most literal and localized sense, Laslett is unable to conceptualize the relation of these familial units to either an emergent national body or more general economic processes. His analysis also disregards the ways that national identification is often constructed precisely by tapping into the rhetoric of "home" and "family" in order to effect a national form of belonging that is ultimately not based upon face-to-face contact.[8]

The critical failure to conceptualize the workings of class in the early modern period is linked, in many ways, with an inability to narrativize the nation. Studies of the genealogy of nationalism, such as Eric Hobsbawm's *Nations and Nationalism Since 1780*, use a chronological framework nearly identical to the correlation of class with industrialization found in Thompson, Hechter, and Laslett. Is the development of class and nation part of the same process of construction? Moreover, is this process necessarily and exclusively linked with a late eighteenth- and early nineteenth-century history of industrialization? If so, how then should critics refer to class and nation when analyzing the sixteenth and seventeenth centuries? As Hobsbawm suggests, it is necessary to distinguish nationalism from nationhood: whereas the former term is linked to the emergence of the modern industrial state, nationhood, by contrast, implies an identity-in-formation and need not cohere exclusively to a territorial body.[9] In addition, I would add, nationhood is partly constituted through the affective bonds it enables; it thus relates not only to the legitimacy of imposed authority but also to the affective power generated among those subject to the nation's power. While national sentiment may at times be produced or manipulated by state officials, often so as to garner popular support for a regime, nations are also derived from a populist base that may articulate ideas of nationhood in spite of—and potentially against—the state's efforts to monopolize national rhetoric and ideology.[10]

Despite an influential body of criticism that has considered the topic of early modern English nationhood, these studies have not fully addressed the populist foundations of national identification and the interrelationship of nation and class. For example, while Richard Helgerson's *Forms of Nationhood* and Claire McEachern's *The Poetics of English Nationhood* present nationhood as a field of contestation between competing social forces, they generally limit the number of participants in this social struggle. In their respective chapters on chorography, for instance, Helgerson and McEachern both devote attention to the uses of this genre by monarchical agents as well as proto-bourgeois forces, particularly the rural gentry, who were potentially hostile to the court.[11] This "Whiggist" critical model thus analyzes how "nationhood" (the dynastic realm) is superceded by "nationalism" (the bureaucratic state as administered by bourgeois and professional wealth). England's laboring classes, including its sizable underclass, are omitted from consideration. This approach to nationhood thus limits its attention to the official narratives of nation pronounced by dominant or ascendant social groups. However, as I have argued in this study, the idea of nation in the early modern period also offered models of social community—"the commonwealth," "the body politic"—that could potentially critique the dominance of either the monarchical state or a potentially antagonistic proto-capitalist bourgeoisie.[12] This study has explored a range of alternative forms of nationhood associated with the laboring classes, expressions of community that were often conveyed through acts of agency and oppositional social practices: the use of alternative currencies; the memorialization of executed pirates; the protection of returning apostates; the discourses of colonial liberty; the petitions of shipwrecked laborers; the alliances of gypsies and masterless men; and the resistance to English colonialism in Ulster.

As a final example in this study, I wish to examine the status and position of a growing class of "cottagers" in early modern England, small communities of squatters who, displaced by enclosure, resettled on common lands or outlying waste areas of estates.[13] Communities of cottagers also formed near manufacturing centers for the cloth trade, coal mining, iron smelting, and other industries. This class therefore emerged alongside nascent industries and forms of manufacture in a period prior to wide-scale industrialization. Cottagers constituted a sizable class in early modern England, a group that comprised one-fourth of rural laborers (or approximately 18 percent of England's total population).[14] The status, if not the existence, of early modern cottagers belies critical efforts to align the formation of class, capital, and nation with the industrial proletariat "created" in the nineteenth century. In fact, the term "laborer" itself has a longer history; in the early modern period, it denoted an agricultural worker who was either landless or possessed merely a cottage and small plot.[15] Cottagers occupied an uncertain, transitional social position in early modern England; they were the tenants uprooted from the land in a primitive accumulation of capital as well as the "free" and unattached laborers subsumed within nascent industries.[16] Yet, despite their numbers, England's population of cottagers was relatively absent from representation in the variety of texts that commented on the social and economic changes of the early modern period.[17] Also, unlike the popular image of London's "underworld," an ostensible criminal class of vagrants, the figure of the cottager did not appear in literary and dramatic texts. (This absence from representation is only further reproduced in critical models that focus exclusively on literary materials.) However, in the 1690s, the economic writer and statistician Gregory King estimated the number of cottager households, a category comprising laborers, paupers, and out-servants, as 764,000; by contrast, he calculated the size of England's seemingly ubiquitous population of vagrants as numbering 30,000.[18]

Cottagers perhaps assume a marginal position in critical and historical consciousness because of the particular social and geographic space they occupied in early modern England, located far from the urban environment of London that dominated the attention of anti-vagrant texts and early modern drama. The lack of critical attention to rural communities such as cottagers reflects the more general failure of historicist criticism to fully address the agrarian foundations of early modern English capitalism, a consequence of an overdetermined attention to the urban setting of nascent market economies. In addition, the non-vagrant status of cottagers defies the association made between England's underclass and a spatial disruption of class boundaries and social order. Richard Halpern has argued that vagrants represented a demonic version of modernity, offering a potent symbol of the forms of displacement attendant to increasing urbanization and capital formation.[19] Yet cottagers, as the largest group of early modern England's laboring poor, formed a class that was neither vagrant nor idle.[20] The size and ubiquity of this group testify to a less visibly disruptive aspect of emergent class relations. The ease with which the position of tenant farmers and laborers could decline to poverty demonstrates the underside to the fluidity of status often held to characterize early modern England. Moreover, the absence of cottagers from representation attests to the ways that definitions of an English national community increasingly depended upon the exclusion of its most economically abject members.

One of the few texts to comment on the presence of cottagers was John Norden's *The Svrveiors Dialogve* (1607). In a section headed "Cottages, and Folk far from Church," Norden makes a brief reference to the social place of cottager communities:

> But it is obserued in some parts where I haue trauelled, where great and spacious wastes, Mountaines, Woods, Forests, and Heaths are, that

many such Cotages are set vp, the people giuen to little or no kinde of labour, liuing very hardly with Oaten bread, sowre whay, and Goates milke, dwelling farre from any Church or Chappell, and are as ignorant of God, or of any ciuil course of life, as the very Sauages amongst the Infidels, in a manner, which is lamentable, and fit to be reformed by the Lord of the Mannor.[21]

Far from representing the poor as an embodiment of modernity, Norden associates cottagers with a residual primitivism that he locates in peripheral and economically underdeveloped sections of the country. Similar to poor laws and anti-vagrancy statutes, Norden attributes poverty to idleness and lack of productivity, reinscribing the structural disjunctions of the national economy as a personal and subjective failure on the part of the poor. However, the few extant records of cottagers' economic activity testify to their remarkable ability to persevere even in catastrophic economic conditions. Many of these families survived, in particular, as a result of the work of cottager women and girls, who earned additional wages through piece-work employment as weavers.[22] And despite Norden's association of cottagers with a backward agrarian economy, they also resided near the manufacturing centers where they were increasingly employed. In his depiction of the cottagers as "savages," Norden employs the colonialist analogy of the poor as "Indians at home" discussed in the introduction. Yet if the cottagers represent internal colonies, this status is one that they themselves assume due to economic necessity, demonstrating how forms of internal colonialism could often take place not only through the efforts of local authorities and the state but also with the participation of those subject to their power.

Even though displaced tenant farmers and laborers could resettle as cottagers in order to survive at a subsistence level, this form of life nonetheless reconstituted them as a class that was distinct and separated from English society. Because they dwelled "farre from any Church or Chappell," cottagers were situated outside the parish, the primary stratum of social organization in early modern England. The parish served as the social unit most directly responsible for poor relief in this period. In addition, it constituted one's residence, so that anti-vagrant legislation often intended to minimize the problems of poverty and vagrancy simply by returning vagrants to their home parish. By lying outside the jurisdiction of the parish, cottagers were excluded from religious as well as socioeconomic forms of community and figured as far from both God and civil society. The racialization of class difference seen in Norden's depiction of cottagers as savages is economically buttressed through their exclusion from the unit of the parish. Their marginal geographic location, in underdeveloped waste lands and heaths, might have offered them protection from local Justices of the Peace in their administration of anti-vagrant statutes. Yet, in their newly constituted status as "free" laborers, their social position outside the parish also exempted cottagers from the administration of poor relief and other material benefits of community. Despite images such as Norden's that attempted to relegate poverty to the nation's most peripheral spaces, cottagers were a ubiquitous presence throughout the realm, demonstrating how underdevelopment pervaded early modern English culture.

Although the social position of cottagers testifies to a dissolution of feudal ties between tenants and landlords guaranteeing service and customary rights, Norden still clings to the residual social relations typifying traditional feudal agriculture. In his view, cottagers do not represent an emergent social formation, a class of free and unattached wage-laborers displanted from agricultural production; rather, cottagers retain a status as tenants tied to the land and their traditional social superiors and are therefore "fit to be reformed by the Lord of the Mannor." In his view of cottagers' labor as a latent resource to be channeled into productive use, Norden's argument is situated in a civic-minded tradition of humanism. Like many other figures discussed in this study—Charles Fitzgeffrey, William Symonds, Robert Hitchcock, and others—Norden retains a belief in the possibility of social reform, a moral economy that supports a conservative effort to reinforce bonds and obligations between class groups in order to retain the laboring poor as viable members of the body politic. Yet, by positing the lord of the manor as the agent to enable reform, Norden grounds his definition of the commonwealth upon an increasingly antiquated feudal model, one that was essentially powerless to respond to the changes effected by agrarian capitalism. One key reason for this failure derived from the fact that many landlords had themselves instituted capitalist forms of agriculture and lease-holding on their properties. Similar to early modern labor regulations—the Statute of Artificers, anti-vagrancy legislation, poor relief laws—Norden can enact reform only through an effort to minimize social change and keep the laboring poor temporally and spatially suspended in a quasi-feudal status as tenants, despite their large-scale displacement from the land and an older model of social relations. Ultimately, Norden's proposal for reform is inadequate to address a situation in which the mutual bonds of class groups have dissolved. In this context, capitalist improving landlords desired not the dependence but the absence of their tenants, while cottagers took up residence in homesteads on commons or near manufacturing sites outside the jurisdiction of manor and parish, thus further constituting themselves as groups exempt from traditional forms of community.

In his representation of England's cottagers, Norden relegates this class to the margins of the realm, depicting cottagers as an aberration of stable social relations rather than a potent symbol of the ubiquity of poverty and dissolution of social bonds attendant to capital formation. Norden's description of cottagers is also profoundly nostalgic, situating this class in a residual and increasingly archaic feudal environment. In the following centuries, particularly in the period of large-scale industrialization of the late eighteenth and early nineteenth centuries, a number of texts—including homiletic Christian works, "fireside" songs and stories, and musical entertainments—extended Norden's nostalgia, using the figure of the cottager to represent a bucolic country existence that was depicted as having disappeared as a result of industrial development and urbanization.[23] Each period responded to social change by hearkening back to a seemingly more stable past, a nostalgia that consistently effaced the place of cottagers in the historical present. The association of cottagers with a nostalgic invocation of the past demonstrates a profound inability to represent the modernity of emergent class relations. Thus, while the construction of the English nation in many ways relied upon the modernizing economic changes of industrialization, the concomitant development of the national economy effected an unmaking of the role of England's working classes in representations of the national community.

While this alignment of nation and economic development allowed a representational space for England's laboring classes only within a nostalgic image of the past, the place occupied by early modern England's working poor within the national body politic was further transformed through the possibilities of colonial migration. In his colonial promotional text, *A Plain Pathway to Plantations* (1624), the West Country clergyman Richard Eburne lists cottagers as one of the primary groups of potential colonists. Eburne envisages colonial migration as effecting a disappearance of the human subjects whom he figures as pestilent sores ("dangerous aposthumes") on the body politic.[24] And, just as local Justices of the Peace often destroyed the physical structures of any cottages built on commons, Eburne offers colonialism as the means to complete this process by also eliminating these communities' human subjects from the landscape, so that they "might be quite taken down and utterly razed forever" (92).[25]

In contrast to the nostalgia of Norden and others, a last gasp of the reformist agenda of civic humanism, Eburne embraces a version of modernity predicated upon the violent erasure of those groups unable to contribute to the nation's economic development. Disregarding residual models of community, Eburne comments that the laboring poor "have little reason to be so in love with that country that is so much out of love with them" (121):

> Be not too much in love with that country wherein you were born, that country which, bearing you, yet cannot breed you, but seemeth and is indeed weary of you. She accounts you a burden to her and encumbrance of her. You keep her down, you hurt her and make her poor and bare; and, together with your own, you work and cause, by tarrying within her, her misery and decay, her ruin and undoing. Take and reckon that for your country where you may best live and thrive. Strain not no more to leave that country wherein you cannot prove and prosper than you do to leave your fathers' houses and the parish wherein you were born and bred up for fitter places and habitations.
>
> And if you will needs live in England, imagine all that to be England where Englishmen, where English people, you with them, and they with you, do dwell. (And it be the people that makes the land English, not the land the people). (11–12)

In this remarkable passage, Eburne disjoins membership in a national community from intrinsic criteria of birth and birthright, a significant gesture given the use of the rhetoric of "freeborn Englishmen" to assert the rights of the propertyless classes during the English Revolution.[26] Instead, any sense of belonging to the nation is contingent upon the economic utility of subjects, so that even if England's laboring poor retain an affective bond to the nation, this sentiment is not reciprocated by the nation itself, "that country that is so much out of love with them." Eburne estranges the familial metaphors of nationhood, later describing England as "rather a stepdame than a mother" to the laboring poor (121) and, in the passage just cited, portraying the national economy as a father unable to care for his superabundant children. In Eburne's formulation, nationhood is recast as a matter of "adoption," a process in which subjects must find other national homes or families "where you may best live and thrive." And, significantly, Eburne counters the intentions of anti-vagrant statutes by acknowledging the necessary mobility of labor within England. Thus, just as young laborers must often leave their parishes to find work, so too may they need to leave their country for economic survival.

Eburne's passage attests to the ways that an early history of capital formation transformed definitions of the national community so as to exclude the nation's most economically abject members. Yet, while the prospect of colonialism served as a means to literalize the expulsion of these subjects through their venting abroad, it also enabled the creation and maintenance of alternative nations through colonial migration. As Eburne states, "if you will needs live in England," then colonial migrants may create a virtual nation in the environment of a colonial diaspora. And even though Eburne places these colonies as economic dependents of England, his vision of colonial prosperity potentially disjoins colonial culture from its metropolitan roots. As Eburne concludes, "it be the people that makes the land English," an acknowledgment of the foundation of a nation's construction upon populist affective bonds. While the economic disruptions resulting from early modern capital formation led to an abstraction of the role of England's lower classes in the national body politic, Eburne offers a possibility for England's lower classes to recuperate their customary rights in the form of colonial "liberty." Eburne's passage thus marks a significant moment of historical transition, testifying to the ways in which the subjects who comprised early modern England's internal colonies increasingly served to constitute England's colonial classes.

NOTES

INTRODUCTION: INTERNAL COLONIALISM IN EARLY MODERN ENGLAND

1. Qtd. in Christopher Hill, "Puritans and 'the Dark Corners of the Land,'" *Change and Continuity in 17th-Century England* (London: Weidenfeld and Nicolson, 1974) 20.
2. *The Works of Michael Drayton*, ed. J. William Hebel (1932; Oxford: Blackwell, 1961) 3.208. In *New English Canaan* (1637), Thomas Morton renders the condition of the nation's underclass as more debased than that of indigenous cultures, denying that Amerindians lived as poorly as "our Beggers in England" (sig. G4).
3. David B. Quinn, ed., *The Roanoke Voyages, 1584–1590*, 2 vols. (London: Hakluyt Society, 1955) 1.204; *Calendar of State Papers, Colonial Series, America and West Indies, 1574–1660*, ed. W. Noel Sainsbury (London: Longman, 1862) 3.
4. Although I will use the term "domestic" most often in reference to the English national economy, this study also considers the implications of this term in relation to the gendered economy of the household: see chapter 1 and the conclusion. For an extended analysis of this issue, see Wendy Wall, *Staging Domesticity: Household Work and English Identity in Early Modern Drama* (Cambridge: Cambridge University Press, 2002) and Natasha Korda, *Shakespeare's Domestic Economies: Gender and Property in Early Modern England* (Philadelphia: University of Pennsylvania Press, 2002).
5. Here and throughout I self-consciously use the term "British Isles," despite its Anglocentric connotations, rather than J.P.A. Pocock's alternative but more obscure formulation of "the Atlantic archipelago": see Pocock's "British History: A Plea for a New Subject," *Journal of Modern History* 47 (1975): 606.
6. Benedict Anderson, *Imagined Communities: Reflections on the Origin and Spread of Nationalism* (1983; London: Verso, 1991) 149.
7. Edmund S. Morgan, *American Slavery, American Freedom: The Ordeal of Colonial Virginia* (New York: Norton, 1975).
8. Étienne Balibar and Immanuel Wallerstein, *Race, Nation, Class: Ambiguous Identities* (London: Verso, 1991) 210.

9. Michel Foucault, "Society Must Be Defended," in *Ethics: Subjectivity and Truth*, ed. Paul Rabinow (New York: The New Press, 1997) 59–65. For analysis of Foucault's essay, see Ann Laura Stoler, *Race and the Education of Desire: Foucault's History of Sexuality and the Colonial Order of Things* (Durham: Duke University Press, 1995).

10. See Theodore W. Allen, *The Invention of the White Race, Volume One: Racial Oppression and Social Control* (London: Verso, 1994) and *The Invention of the White Race, Volume Two: The Origin of Racial Oppression in Anglo-America* (London: Verso, 1997).

11. In addition, I wish to clarify that my analysis of the links between categories of class and race in this period does not overlook the distinctive trajectory of racial formations and the extent to which class groups were differentiated from racialized non-English populations. Among discussions of race in the early modern period, see Kim F. Hall, *Things of Darkness: Economies of Race and Gender in Early Modern England* (Ithaca: Cornell University Press, 1995) and Margo Hendricks and Patricia Parker, eds., *Women, "Race," and Writing in the Early Modern Period* (London and New York: Routledge, 1994).

12. Allen, *Invention of the White Race* 1.19.

13. For other examples, see Hill, "Puritans" 19–20.

14. In A.V. Judges, ed., *The Elizabethan Underworld* (London: George Routledge & Sons, 1930) 386, 396 ff. An earlier version of this analogy is found in Joseph Hall's *Mundus Alter et Idem* (1605), translated as *The Discovery of the New World* (1609).

15. See, e.g., William Fennor's *The Counter's Commonwealth or a Voyage Made to an Infernal Island Discovered by many Captains, Seafaring Men, Gentlemen, Merchants, and Other Tradesmen* (1617) (in Judges, *Elizabethan Underworld* 423–87); Thomas Dekker's *The Gull's Hornbook* (1609); John Earle's *Micro-Cosmographie* (1628).

16. *Ben Jonson*, ed. C.H. Herford and Percy and Evelyn Simpson, 11 vols. (Oxford: Clarendon, 1926–52). All further references to Jonson's plays, unless otherwise noted, are drawn from this edition.

17. Michel Foucault, *The Order of Things* (1970; New York: Vintage, 1994) 57.

18. Lisa Jardine and Anthony Grafton, "'Studied for Action': How Gabriel Harvey Read his Livy," *Past and Present* 129 (1990): 40–42.

19. D.B. Quinn, "Renaissance Influences in English Colonization," *Explorers and Colonies: America, 1500–1625* (London: Hambledon Press, 1990) 103–05.

20. Jane Ohlmeyer, "'Civilizinge of those Rude Partes': Colonization within Britain and Ireland, 1580s–1640s," in Nicholas Canny, ed., *The Oxford History of the British Empire, Volume One: The Origins of Empire: British Overseas Enterprise to the Close of the Seventeenth Century* (Oxford and New York: Oxford University Press, 1998) 137.

21. Ohlmeyer, "Civilizinge" 132.

22. David Armitage, *The Ideological Origins of the British Empire* (Cambridge: Cambridge University Press, 2000) 13.

23. D.B. Quinn, *The Elizabethans and the Irish* (Ithaca: Cornell University Press, 1966); Nicholas Canny, "The Ideology of English Colonization: From Ireland to America," *William and Mary Quarterly* 30 (1973): 575–98; *The Elizabethan Conquest of Ireland: A Pattern Established, 1565–76* (Hassocks, Sussex: Harvester, 1976); "The Permissive Frontier: The Problem of Social Control in English Settlements in Ireland and Virginia 1560–1650," in Kenneth Andrews et al., eds., *The Westward Enterprise: English Activities in Ireland, The Atlantic, and America, 1480–1650* (Detroit: Wayne State University Press, 1979) 17–44; *Kingdom and Colony: Ireland in the Atlantic World, 1560–1800* (Baltimore: Johns Hopkins University Press, 1988). For a critique of the Atlanticist approach, see Andrew Murphy, *But the Irish Sea Betwixt Us: Ireland, Colonialism, and Renaissance Literature* (Lexington: University of Kentucky Press, 1999) 3–7.

24. Karen Ordahl Kupperman, *Settling with the Indians: The Meeting of English and American Cultures in America, 1580–1640* (Totowa, NJ: Rowman and Littlefield, 1980). James Boon discusses the importance of class and status to early modern ethnography in *Other Tribes, Other Scribes: Symbolic Anthropology in the Comparative Study of Cultures, Histories, Religions, and Texts* (Ithaca: Cornell University Press, 1982) 154–77. For a critique of Kupperman, see Margo Hendricks, "Civility, Barbarism, and Aphra Behn's *The Widow Ranter*," in Hendricks and Parker, eds., *Women, "Race," and Writing*, esp. 228–29, 231–32.

25. V.I. Lenin, *The Development of Capitalism in Russia* (Moscow: Foreign Languages Publishing House, 1956) and *Imperialism: The Highest Stage of Capitalism* (1939; New York: International Publishers, 1977).

26. Antonio Gramsci, *The Modern Prince and Other Writings* (1957; New York: International Publishers, 1968) 28–51.

27. Qtd. in Gayatri Spivak, "Bonding in Difference, Interview with Alfred Arteaga," in *The Spivak Reader: Selected Works of Gayatri Chakravorty Spivak* (London: Routledge, 1996) 24.

28. Michael Hechter, *Internal Colonialism: The Celtic Fringe in British National Development, 1536–1966* (1975; New Brunswick, NJ: Transaction Publishers, 1999).

29. Ibid., 6–9, 81.

30. Immanuel Wallerstein, *The Modern World-System I: Capitalist Agriculture and the Origins of the European World-Economy in the Sixteenth Century* (New York: Academic Press, 1974) and *The Modern World-System II: Mercantilism and the Consolidation of the European World-Economy* (New York: Academic Press, 1980). John Michael Archer discusses the continued relevance of world-systems theory in *Old Worlds: Egypt, Southwest Asia, India, and Russia in Early Modern English Writing* (Stanford: Stanford University Press, 2001), esp. 5–11.

31. For a critique of the application of Wallerstein's model to the British archipelago, see Bernard Bailyn and Philip D. Morgan, eds., *Strangers Within the Realm: Cultural Margins in the First British Empire* (Chapel Hill: University of North Carolina Press, 1991) 1–31.

32. Canny, "The Origins of Empire: An Introduction," *Origins of Empire* 12.

33. For the classic discussion of this issue, see Quentin Skinner, *The Foundations of Modern Political Thought*, 2 vols. (Cambridge: Cambridge University Press, 1978), esp. 1.221–28. Among recent discussions of the body politic metaphor in early modern texts, see Jonathan Gil Harris, *Foreign Bodies and the Body Politic: Discourses of Social Pathology in Early Modern England* (Cambridge: Cambridge University Press, 1998); Andrew McRae, *God Speed the Plough: The Representation of Agrarian England, 1500–1660* (Cambridge: Cambridge University Press, 1996) 38–39, 55, 167; Claire McEachern, *The Poetics of English Nationhood, 1590–1612* (Cambridge: Cambridge University Press, 1996) 103–05; and Andrea Finkelstein, *Harmony and the Balance: An Intellectual History of Seventeenth-Century English Economic Thought* (Ann Arbor: University of Michigan Press, 2000) 15–25. For background on this topic, see Ernst Kantorowicz, *The King's Two Bodies: A Study in Mediaeval Political Theology* (1957; Princeton: Princeton University Press, 1997) and David Hale, *The Body Politic: A Political Metaphor in Renaissance English Literature* (The Hague: Mouton, 1971).

34. For analysis of this declaration, see Philip Corrigan and Derek Sayer, *The Great Arch: English State Formation as Cultural Revolution* (Oxford: Blackwell, 1985) 43 ff. and Armitage, *The Ideological Origins of the British Empire* 35.

35. Roger Mason, "The Scottish Reformation and the Origins of Anglo-British Imperialism," in Roger Mason, ed., *Scots and Britons: Scottish Political Thought and the Union of 1603* (Cambridge: Cambridge University Press, 1994) 161–86.

36. Armitage, "Literature and Empire," in Canny, ed., *Origins of Empire* 114. Nonetheless, Dee's vision of British imperial expansion was conceptualized as a "recovery" of territories formerly held in the nation's mythic past, from the Arthurian conquests of Iceland and Northern Europe to the Welsh prince Madoc's twelfth-century "possession" of America. Dee's construction of a British empire used overseas expansion merely as a means to reconsolidate the dynastic realm's territorial possessions. On Dee's use of British history to justify overseas colonial ventures, see William H. Sherman, *John Dee: The Politics of Reading and Writing in the English Renaissance* (Amherst: University of Massachusetts Press, 1995) 148–52, 182–92 and Lesley Cormack, "Britannia Rules the Waves?: Images of Empire in Elizabethan England," *Early Modern Literary Studies* 4.2 (September 1998): 10.1–20.

37. On the Jacobean Union of the Realms, see especially Brian P. Levack, *The Formation of the British State: England, Scotland, and the Union 1603–1707* (Oxford: Clarendon, 1987) and Bruce Galloway, *The Union of England and Scotland 1603–1608* (Edinburgh: John Donald, 1986). Jenny Wormald has dealt with this topic in several articles: "The Creation of Britain: Multiple Kingdoms or Core and Colonies?" *Transactions of the Royal Historical Society*, 6th ser., 2 (1992): 175–94; "The Union of 1603," in Mason, ed., *Scots and Britons* 17–40; "James VI, James I and the Identity of Britain," in Brendan Bradshaw and John Morrill, eds., *The British Problem, ca. 1534–1707: State Formation in the Atlantic Archipelago* (Basingstoke: Macmillan, 1996) 148–71; "The High Road from Scotland: One King, Two Kingdoms," in Alexander Grant and Keith J. Stringer, eds., *Uniting the Kingdom? The Making of British History* (London: Routledge, 1995) 123–32.

38. Hechter, *Internal Colonialism* 65.

39. Anderson, *Imagined Communities* 6.

40. Richard Helgerson, *Forms of Nationhood: The Elizabethan Writing of England* (Chicago: University of Chicago Press, 1992). Although most studies of nationalism focus on the nineteenth and twentieth centuries, a small number analyze the early modern period: see Liah Greenfeld, *Nationalism: Five Roads to Modernity* (Cambridge, MA: Harvard University Press, 1992); J.H. Elliot, "A Europe of Composite Monarchies," *Past and Present* 137 (1992): 48–71; McEachern, *The Poetics of English Nationhood*; Adrian Hastings, *The Construction of Nationhood: Ethnicity, Religion and Nationalism* (Cambridge: Cambridge University Press, 1997); and Colin Kidd, *British Identities Before Nationalism: Ethnicity and Nationhood in the Atlantic World, 1600–1800* (Cambridge: Cambridge University Press, 1999).

41. Pocock, "British History" 605.

42. Ibid., 605.

43. Ibid., 611.

44. Among recent anthologies analyzing the New British History, see Bailyn and Morgan, eds., *Strangers Within the Realm*; Grant and Stringer, eds., *Uniting the Kingdom?*; Steven G. Ellis and Sarah Barber, eds., *Conquest and Union: Fashioning a British State, 1485–1725* (London and New York: Longman, 1995); Brendan Bradshaw and John Morrill, eds., *The British Problem*; Brendan Bradshaw and Peter Roberts, eds., *British Consciousness and Identity: The Making of Britain, 1533–1707* (Cambridge: Cambridge University Press, 1998).

45. David J. Baker, *Between Nations: Shakespeare, Spenser, Marvell, and the Question of Britain* (Stanford: Stanford University Press, 1997); Willy Maley, *Salvaging Spenser* (London and New York: St. Martin's Press, 1997); Baker and Maley, eds., *British Identities and English Renaissance Literature* (Cambridge: Cambridge University Press, 2002). Also see Martin Butler, "The Invention of Britain in the Early Stuart Masque," in R. Malcolm Smuts, ed., *The Stuart Court and Europe*

(Cambridge: Cambridge University Press, 1996) 65–85; McEachern, *The Poetics of English Nationhood* 138–91; and Tristan Marshall, *Theatre and Empire: Great Britain on the London Stages under James VI and I* (Manchester: Manchester University Press, 2000).

46. On Smith's career, see Armitage, *Ideological Origins of the British Empire* 47–51; D.B. Quinn, "Sir Thomas Smith (1513–1577) and the Beginnings of English Colonial Theory," *Proceedings of the American Philosophical Society* 89 (1945): 543–60; Hiram Morgan, "The Colonial Venture of Sir Thomas Smith in Ulster, 1571–1575," *The Historical Journal* 28 (1985): 261–78; Mary Dewar, *Sir Thomas Smith: A Tudor Intellectual in Office* (London: Athlone Press, 1964) 156–70; Canny, *The Elizabethan Conquest of Ireland* 128–32.

47. John Norden, *The Svrveiors Dialogve* (1607; 3rd edition, 1618) sigs. D5, E7v.

48. Karl Marx, "The General Formula for Capital," *Capital: A Critique of Political Economy, Volume One*, trans. Ben Fowkes (London: Penguin and New Left Review, 1976) 247. All further references to volume one of *Capital* are from this translation.

49. Karl Marx, *Capital: A Critique of Political Economy, Volume Three*, trans. David Fernbach (London: Penguin and New Left Review, 1981) 444. All further references to volume three of *Capital* are from this translation. For a related discussion, see Barry Hindess and Paul Q. Hirst, *Pre-Capitalist Modes of Production* (London: Routledge & Kegan Paul, 1975) 261.

50. Robert Brenner, "The Origins of Capitalist Development: A Critique of Neo-Smithian Marxism," *New Left Review* 104 (July–August 1977): 33. For a similar point, see Balibar and Wallerstein, *Race, Nation, Class* 2.

51. Marx, *Capital* 1.874–75.

52. Ibid., 1.873n., 875. Also see Michael Perelman, *The Invention of Capitalism: Classical Political Economy and the Secret History of Primitive Accumulation* (Durham: Duke University Press, 2000).

53. On the significance of customary rights, see Garrett A. Sullivan, Jr., *The Drama of Landscape: Land, Property, and Social Relations on the Early Modern Stage* (Stanford: Stanford University Press, 1998).

54. For further analysis, see John E. Martin, *Feudalism to Capitalism: Peasant and Landlord in English Agrarian Development* (London: Macmillan, 1983), esp. 128–40 and R.H. Tawney, *The Agrarian Problem in the Sixteenth Century* (1912; New York: Harper, 1967).

55. On early modern vagrancy, see especially A.L. Beier, *Masterless Men: The Vagrancy Problem in England, 1560–1640* (London: Methuen, 1985).

56. Richard Halpern, *The Poetics of Primitive Accumulation: English Renaissance Culture and the Genealogy of Capital* (Ithaca: Cornell University Press, 1991) 69.

57. Ibid., 68. For further discussion of the "transitional" nature of early modern capital, see Hindess and Hirst, *Pre-Capitalist Modes of*

Production 266–71 and Louis Althusser and Étienne Balibar, *Reading Capital* (1970; London: NLB, 1977) 236–41.

58. Andrew McRae, *God Speed the Plough*; James Holstun, *Ehud's Dagger: Class Struggle in the English Revolution* (London: Verso, 2000); David Hawkes, *Idols of the Marketplace: Idolatry and Commodity Fetishism in English Literature, 1580–1680* (New York: Palgrave, 2001). On "moral economy," see E.P. Thompson, "The Moral Economy of the English Crowd in the Eighteenth Century," *Past and Present* 50 (1971): 76–136.

59. Marx, *Capital* 1.173; Williams, *The Country and the City* (New York: Oxford University Press, 1973) 9–12.

60. For Max Weber's distinction between classes and status groups, see *Economy and Society: An Outline of Interpretive Sociology*, ed. Guenther Roth and Claus Wittich (New York: Bedminster Press, 1968) 302–07. Among discussions of the advantages of classifications of "status" over "class," see Lawrence Stone, "Social Mobility in England, 1500–1700," *Past and Present* 33 (1966): 16–55; Alan Everitt, "Social Mobility in Early Modern England," *Past and Present* 33 (1966): 56–73; and Jonathan Barry, "Introduction" to *The Middling Sort of People: Culture, Society and Politics in England, 1550–1800*, ed. Jonathan Barry and Christopher Brooks (Basingstoke: Macmillan, 1994) 1–27. For recent defenses of the applicability of "class" as a category of analysis for the early modern period, see Holstun, *Ehud's Dagger* 96–106 and David Scott Kastan, *Shakespeare After Theory* (New York: Routledge, 1999) 149–51.

61. Raymond Williams, *Keywords: A Vocabulary of Culture and Society* (New York: Oxford University Press, 1976) 60–69.

62. E.P. Thompson, "Eighteenth-Century English Society: Class Struggle Without Class?" *Social History* 31 (1978): 149.

63. My analysis is influenced by the work of the Subaltern Studies Group: see, in particular, Ranajit Guha, "On Some Aspects of the Historiography of Colonial India," *Subaltern Studies I* (Delhi and Oxford: Oxford University Press, 1982) 4. However, throughout this study I attempt to problematize the category of the subaltern, keeping in mind the useful critique of this term provided by Gayatri Spivak in "Can the Subaltern Speak?" in Cary Nelson and Lawrence Grossberg, eds., *Marxism and the Interpretation of Culture* (Urbana: University of Illinois Press, 1988) 271–313 and "Subaltern Studies: Deconstructing Historiography," *Subaltern Studies IV* (Delhi and Oxford: Oxford University Press, 1985) 330–63.

1   "THE UNIVERSAL MARKET OF THE WORLD": CAPITAL FORMATION AND *The Merchant of Venice*

1. See Sir Albert Feaveryear, *The Pound Sterling* (Oxford: Clarendon, 1963); C.E. Challis, *The Tudor Coinage* (Manchester: Manchester

University Press, 1978); Challis, ed., *A New History of the Royal Mint* (Cambridge: Cambridge University Press, 1992).

2. According to Fernand Braudel, the value of the pound sterling remained stable from 1560 to the 1920s (*Civilization and Capitalism, 15th–18th Century, Volume III: The Perspective of the World* [Berkeley: University of California Press, 1992] 356).

3. On economic crisis and the seventeenth century, see Immanuel Wallerstein, *The Modern World System II*, esp. 2–9; Eric H. Hobsbawm, "The General Crisis of the European Economy in the Seventeenth Century," in Trevor Aston, ed., *Crisis in Europe* (New York: Anchor Books, 1967) 5–62; Barry Supple, *Commercial Crisis and Change in England, 1600–1642: A Study in the Instability of a Mercantile Economy* (Cambridge: Cambridge University Press, 1964); Jan De Vries, *Economy of Europe in an Age of Crisis, 1600–1750* (Cambridge: Cambridge University Press, 1976).

4. Andrew Sullivan, "There will always be an England," *New York Times Magazine* (February 21, 1999).

5. For discussion, see J.D. Gould, *The Great Debasement* (Oxford: Clarendon, 1970).

6. Sir Thomas Smith, *A Discourse of the Commonweal of this Realm of England*, first published as *A Compendious or Briefe Examination of Certayne Ordinary Complaints* (1581), ed. Mary Dewar (Charlottesville, VA: Folger Shakespeare Library, 1969) 86.

7. Smith's *Discourse* was attributed to Shakespeare by Charles Marsh, the editor of the 1751 edition of the text (Dewar, intro., *A Discourse of the Commonweal* xviii n.). Marx also notes the ascription of the text to Shakespeare (*Capital* 1.906n.).

8. Walter Cohen, "*The Merchant of Venice* and the Possibilities of Historical Criticism," *ELH* 49 (1982): 765–89, republished in *Drama of a Nation: Public Theater in Renaissance England and Spain* (Ithaca: Cornell University Press, 1985) 195–211; Thomas Moison, "'Which is the Merchant Here? And which the Jew': Subversion and Recuperation in *The Merchant of Venice*," in Jean E. Howard and Marion F. O'Connor, eds., *Shakespeare Reproduced: The Text in History and Ideology* (New York: Methuen, 1987) 188–206; Michael Nerlich, *Ideology of Adventure: Studies in Modern Consciousness, 1100–1750, Volume 1*, trans. Ruth Crowley (Minneapolis: University of Minnesota Press, 1987) 108–82; Lars Engle, "'Thrift is Blessing': Exchange and Explanation in *The Merchant of Venice*," *Shakespeare Quarterly* 37 (1986): 20–37, revised in *Shakespearean Pragmatism: Market of His Time* (Chicago: University of Chicago Press, 1993) 77–106; Michael Ferber, "The Ideology of *The Merchant of Venice*," *ELR* 20 (1990): 431–64.

9. Cohen, "*The Merchant of Venice* and the Possibilities of Historical Criticism" 771.

10. Fernand Braudel, *Civilization and Capitalism, 15th–18th Century, Volume II: The Wheels of Commerce*, trans. Sian Reynolds (1979; New

York: Harper & Row, 1982) 237; for a related discussion, see Brenner, "The Origins of Capitalist Development" 25–92.

11. Braudel, *Wheels of Commerce* 233. Robert S. DuPlessis discusses the etymology and applications of "capital" in the early modern period in "Capital Formations," in Henry S. Turner, ed., *The Culture of Capital: Property, Cities, and Knowledge in Early Modern England* (New York: Routledge, 2002) 27–49.

12. Karl Marx, *Grundrisse: Foundations of the Critique of Political Economy*, trans. Martin Nicolaus (London: Penguin and New Left Review, 1973) 103, 327.

13. On early modern mercantilism, see Eli F. Heckscher, *Mercantilism*, 2 vols. (1935; New York: Macmillan, 1955); Lars Magnusson, *Mercantilism: The Shaping of an Economic Language* (New York: Routledge, 1994); Finkelstein, *Harmony and the Balance*, esp. 247–66.

14. For a related discussion, see Jean-Christophe Agnew, *Worlds Apart: The Market and the Theater in Anglo-American Thought, 1550–1750* (Cambridge: Cambridge University Press, 1986) 9–10, 41–46 and Patricia Fumerton, *Cultural Aesthetics: Renaissance Literature and the Practice of Social Ornament* (Chicago: University of Chicago Press, 1991) 173–87.

15. The phrase is from John Maynard Keynes's critique of mercantilism; see E.E. Rich and C.H. Wilson, eds., *The Cambridge Economic History of Europe, Volume 4: The Economy of Expanding Europe in the Sixteenth and Seventeenth Centuries* (Cambridge University Press, 1967) 505.

16. *The Riverside Shakespeare*, ed. G. Blakemore Evans et al. (Boston: Houghton Mifflin, 1997). All further references to Shakespeare's plays are from this edition.

17. Craig Muldrew, "Interpreting the Market: The Ethics of Credit and Community Relations in Early Modern England," *Social History* 18, 2 (May 1993): 169.

18. Sandra K. Fischer, *Econolingua: A Glossary of Coins and Economic Language in Renaissance Drama* (Newark: University of Delaware Press, 1985) 80.

19. On the historical conditions prompting hoarding in the early modern period, see Marx, *Capital* 1.227–32.

20. Fischer, *Econolingua* 41.

21. For Elizabeth's contemporary statement on the recoinage, see R.H. Tawney and Eileen Power, eds., *Tudor Economic Documents* (London: Longmans, 1924) 2.195–99; Paul L. Hughes and James F. Larkin, eds., *Tudor Royal Proclamations, Volume II: The Later Tudors (1553–1587)* (New Haven: Yale University Press, 1969) 150–54.

22. William Camden, *Remains Concerning Britain*, ed. R.D. Dunn (Toronto: University of Toronto Press, 1984) 176; also see Camden's *The History of the Most Renowned and Victorious Queen Elizabeth Late Queen of England*, ed. Wallace T. MacCaffrey (Chicago: University of

Chicago Press, 1970) 57–58. The 1560 recoinage was even listed on Elizabeth's tomb among the primary accomplishments of her reign (Malcolm Gaskill, *Crime and Mentalities in Early Modern England* [Cambridge: Cambridge University Press, 2000] 125).

23. Feaveryear, *The Pound Sterling* 54, 84. Other estimates calculate Elizabeth's profit even higher, at £50,000 (Challis, *A New History of the Royal Mint* 248).

24. Fischer, *Econolingua* 25; Camden, *Remains* 175.

25. For discussion, see Gaskill, *Crime and Mentalities* 123–99. Among depictions of "coining" in early modern plays, see Jonson, *Eastward Ho!* 4.1.214–42 and *The Alchemist* 1.1.111–14 and 3.2.148–53.

26. Engle, "Thrift is Blessing" 23. On the early modern development of the idea of a "velocity of circulation," see Foucault, *Order of Things* 185. Although Thomas Gresham never formulated what has come to be known as Gresham's Law, that debased metals circulate faster, Elizabethan economic policies in many ways embodied this principle (see Foucault, *Order of Things* 171; Braudel, *Wheels of Commerce* 196 and *The Structures of Everyday Life*, volume 1 of *Civilization and Capitalism* [New York: Fontana Press, 1985] 460, 467; and E.E. Rich and C.H. Wilson, eds., *The Cambridge Economic History of Europe, Volume 5: The Economic Organization of Early Modern Europe* [Cambridge: Cambridge University Press, 1977] 291).

27. Compare 1.3.107 and 2.7.26.

28. According to Marx, "In the credit system, *man* replaces metal or paper as the mediator of exchange. However, he does this not as a man but as the *incarnation of capital and interest*...Money has not been transcended in man within the credit system, but man is himself transformed into *money*, or, in other words, money is *incarnate* in him" ("Excerpts from James Mill's *Elements of Political Economy*," qtd. in Theodore B. Leinwand, *Theatre, Finance and Society in Early Modern England* [Cambridge: Cambridge University Press, 1999] 23).

29. Braudel, *The Structures of Everyday Life* 439–40; for a similar point, see Agnew, *Worlds Apart* 9.

30. Theodore K. Rabb calculates that 1,200 gentlemen participated in overseas commercial ventures in this period (*Enterprise and Empire: Merchant and Gentry Investment in the Expansion of England* [Cambridge, MA: Harvard University Press, 1967] 27). Robert Ashton finds that 28 London aldermen serving in 1603 had overseas investments, 22 had investments in overseas trade, and 18 were involved in more than one branch of overseas trade (*The City and the Court 1603–1643* [Cambridge: Cambridge University Press, 1979] 35–85).

31. Marx, *Capital* 3.735.

32. This image is similarly used in Thomas Carew, *Coelum Britannicum* (1635) (*Court Masques: Jacobean and Caroline Entertainments, 1605–1640*, ed. David Lindley [Oxford: Oxford University Press,

1995] ll. 332–33) and *The Jew of Malta* 4.2.108 (*Christopher Marlowe: The Complete Plays*, ed. J.B. Steane [Harmondsworth: Penguin, 1969]). For other examples of this *topos*, see John Gillies, *Shakespeare and the Geography of Difference* (Cambridge: Cambridge University Press, 1994) 136 and Yves Peyré, "Marlowe and the Argonauts," in Jean-Pierre Maquerlot and Michèle Willems, eds., *Travel and Drama in Shakespeare's Time* (Cambridge: Cambridge University Press, 1996) 106–23. In addition, the Order of the Golden Fleece was the chief chivalric order of early modern Spain.

33. Henry Roberts, *The Trumpet of Fame: Or Sir Fraunces Drakes and Sir Iohn Hawkins Farewell* (1595) sig. A3.

34. On Frobisher, see Vilhjalmur Stefansson, ed., *The Three Voyages of Martin Frobisher*, 2 vols. (London: Argonaut, 1938), esp. 2.48–50.

35. For further discussion of this transition, see Nerlich, *Ideology of Adventure* 1.164; Helgerson, *Forms of Nationhood* 163–81; Leinwand, *Theatre, Finance and Society* 110–39; and Joan Pong Linton, *The Romance of the New World: Gender and Literary Formations of English Colonialism* (Cambridge: Cambridge University Press, 1998) 43 ff.

36. William Vaughan, a Welsh writer on colonization, additionally refers to the Newfoundland fishing industry as England's "golden fleece" in *The Golden Fleece* (1626). For discussion, see my article, "Writing Britain from the Margins: Scottish, Irish, and Welsh Projects for American Colonization," forthcoming in *Prose Studies*.

37. Ben Jonson, *The Complete Masques*, ed. Stephen Orgel (New Haven: Yale University Press, 1969). All further references to Jonson's masques are from this edition.

38. Marx, "Historical Material on Merchant's Capital," *Capital* 3.446.

39. Carol Leventen, "Patrimony and Patriarchy in *The Merchant of Venice*," in Valerie Wayne, ed., *The Matter of Difference: Materialist Feminist Criticism of Shakespeare* (New York: Harvester, 1991) 69.

40. Ibid., 62–65.

41. For a related discussion, see Raymond Williams, *Marxism and Literature* (Oxford: Oxford University Press, 1977) 11.

42. For recent analyses of the early modern household, see Wall, *Staging Domesticity* and Korda, *Shakespeare's Domestic Economies*.

43. See Karen Newman, "Portia's Ring: Unruly Women and Structures of Exchange in *The Merchant of Venice*," *Shakespeare Quarterly* 38 (1987): 31–32.

44. For further discussion, see Helgerson, *Forms of Nationhood* 181–91 and Jeffrey Knapp, *An Empire Nowhere: England, America, and Literature from Utopia to The Tempest* (Berkeley: University of California Press, 1992).

45. Sir Walter Raleigh, *Discoverie of Guiana*, qtd. in Knapp 198. Compare similar comments in Raleigh's "A Report of the Truth of the Fight About the Isles of Azores" (*Selected Writings*, ed. Gerald Hammond [Harmondsworth: Penguin, 1984] 75).

46. On "world money" (which Marx also terms "world coin"), see *Capital* 1.240–44, *Capital* 3.449, and *Grundrisse* 229.
47. Louis Adrian Montrose also discusses how codes of sexual conduct served to differentiate English colonialism from its Spanish rival in "The Work of Gender in the Discourse of Discovery," in Stephen Greenblatt, ed., *New World Encounters* (Berkeley: University of California Press, 1992) 177–217.
48. John Donne, *The Complete English Poems*, ed. A.J. Smith (Harmondsworth: Penguin, 1971) ll. 29–30. All further references to Donne's poems are from this edition.
49. Braudel, *Wheels of Commerce* 196.
50. In contrast to Donne's efforts to differentiate English commerce from Spanish currency, in 1601 the Royal Mint issued special coins that attempted to replicate the Spanish currency, the real, for use by the East India Company; however, Indian traders refused to accept these coins because they did not recognize the English images and inscriptions stamped on them (Challis, *The Tudor Coinage* 145–46).
51. Braudel, *Wheels of Commerce* 174–75.
52. See, e.g., John Payne, *The Royall Exchange* (1597) sigs. B2v-B3.
53. Theodor de Bry, *Americae Pars Quarta* (1594) illustration XX.
54. John Lyly, *Midas*, ed. Anne Begor Lancashire (Lincoln: University of Nebraska Press, 1969) 3.1.4; see esp. 2.1.95–115, 3.1.1–69, and 4.1.168–200.
55. Marx, *Grundrisse* 233–34.
56. Marx, "Historical Material on Merchant's Capital," *Capital* 3.455. For a similar point, see Marx, "Private Property and Labor," from *Economic and Philosophic Manuscripts of 1844*, trans. Martin Milligan (Amherst, NY: Prometheus Books, 1988) 96.
57. Marx, *Grundrisse* 227.
58. Ibid., 225.
59. Ibid., 234.
60. On the play's advocacy of an "ideology of risk," see Moison, "Which is the Merchant Here?" 197 and Ferber, "The Ideology of *The Merchant of Venice*" 446.
61. Adam Smith praised Mun's work as the model for European mercantilism (Rich and Wilson, eds., *The Cambridge Economic History of Europe* 4.503). Mun's *Discovrse of Trade*, published in 1621, also established the context for the ensuing pamphlet war in 1622–23 between Gerard de Malynes, who advocated the reestablishment of the intrinsic value of England's currency, and Edward Misselden, whose model of circulation and trade balance followed Mun's precedent. For discussions of Mun, see Mary Poovey, *A History of the Modern Fact* (Chicago: University of Chicago Press, 1998) 66–91; Joyce Oldham Appleby, *Economic Thought and Ideology in Seventeenth-Century England* (Princeton: Princeton University Press, 1978) 37–41 and *passim*; Fumerton, *Cultural Aesthetics* 173–87;

Supple, *Commercial Crisis and Change* 185–88, 211–21; Finkelstein, *Harmony and the Balance* 74–97; K.N. Chaudhuri, "The East India Company and the Export of Treasure in the Early Seventeenth Century," *Economic History Review* 16 (1963): 23–38.

62. L.C. Knights, *Drama and Society in the Age of Jonson* (London: Chatto & Windus, 1937) 54.

63. For proclamations and statutes on this issue, see Tawney and Power, eds., *Tudor Economic Documents* 2.177–78; James F. Larkin and Paul L. Hughes, eds., *Stuart Royal Proclamations, Volume 1: Royal Proclamations of King James I, 1603–1625* (Oxford: Clarendon, 1973) 158–61, 272–76, 436–39, 540–43.

64. *A Discovrse of Trade* (1621) sigs. D3-D3v. Mun also discusses the trade in Spanish coin and silver in *England's Treasure by Forraign Trade* (1664; Oxford: Basil Blackwell, 1933) 24. Citing Mun, Edward Misselden makes a similar argument in *The Circle of Commerce* (1623) sigs. F1v-F2v.

65. For a discussion of the links between capitalism and aescetic forms of Protestantism, see Max Weber, *The Protestant Ethic and the Spirit of Capitalism* (1904; London: Routledge, 1992).

66. For an excellent analysis of the sense of estrangement that accompanied the East India trade, see Fumerton, *Cultural Aesthetics* 169–206.

67. Marx, *Capital* 1.249–50.

68. Ibid., 1.250.

69. Agnew, *Worlds Apart* 22–23.

70. Marx, *Grundrisse* 226. Engels associates the emergence of the middleman with the rise of a depersonalized money economy ("The Origin of the Family and Private Property and the State," in *The Marx-Engels Reader*, ed. Robert C. Tucker [New York: Norton, 1978] 756).

71. For discussion of the Royal Exchange, see Ann Saunders, ed., *The Royal Exchange* (London: The London Topographical Society, 1997).

72. John Stow, *A Survey of London* (1603), ed. Charles L. Kingsford, 2 vols. (Oxford: Clarendon, 1908) 1.183, 193, 201.

73. Thomas Heywood, *If You Know Not Me You Know Nobody*, ed. Madeleine Doran (Oxford: Malone Society and Oxford University Press, 1935). Among recent discussions of the play, see Bruster, *Drama and the Market* 3–7; Leinwand, *Theatre, Finance, and Society* 24–31; Jean E. Howard, "Competing Ideologies of Commerce in Thomas Heywood's *If You Know Not Me You Know Nobody, Part II*," in Turner, ed., *The Culture of Capital* 163–82. The Royal Exchange also serves as the setting for Heywood's *Fair Maid of the Exchange* (ca. 1601–02); in contrast to the elite characters populating his later play, Heywood's comedy deals with shopkeepers at the Exchange (ed. Karl E. Snyder [New York: Garland, 1980]).

74. Payne, *The Royall Exchange* sigs. B4v, D3v.
75. Camden, *Remains Concerning Britain* 171.
76. Rich and Wilson, eds., *The Cambridge Economic History of Europe* 4.504.
77. For background on the New Exchange and Jonson's entertainment, see James Knowles, "Jonson's *Entertainment at Britain's Burse*," in Martin Butler, ed., *Re-Presenting Ben Jonson: Text, History, Performance* (New York: St. Martin's Press, 1999) 114–31. Knowles's edited version of the text is also included in the Butler collection (132–51).
78. Karen Newman, *Fashioning Femininity and English Renaissance Drama* (Chicago: University of Chicago Press, 1991) 131–43. Among references to the New Exchange in early modern plays, see Jonson, *Epicoene* 1.3.36–39 and 3.3.24–25, *The Alchemist* 4.4.48–49, and *Bartholomew Fair* 1.2.7; John Fletcher, *The Night Walker* 4.1.39 (*The Dramatic Works in the Beaumont and Fletcher Canon*, ed. Fredson Bowers, vol. 7 [Cambridge: Cambridge University Press, 1989]); and Philip Massinger, *The City Madam* (*The Selected Plays of Philip Massinger*, ed. Colin Gibson [Cambridge: Cambridge University Press, 1978]) 3.1.13.
79. See Craig Muldrew, "Interpreting the Market" 163–83; *The Economy of Obligation: The Culture of Credit and Social Relations in Early Modern England* (Basingstoke: Macmillan, 1998); and "'Hard Food for Midas': Cash and its Social Value in Early Modern England," *Past and Present* 170 (February 2001): 78–120.
80. Challis, *The Tudor Coinage* 280.
81. Gaskill, *Crime and Mentalities in Early Modern England* 127, 131, 187. For a discussion of counterfeiting in the early modern period, see Valerie Forman, "Marked Angels: Counterfeits, Commodities, and *The Roaring Girl*," *Renaissance Quarterly* 54 (2001): 1531–60.
82. Muldrew, "Hard Food for Midas" 90.
83. For further discussion of alternative economies of token money and copper coins used by the early modern poor, see Rich and Wilson, eds., *The Cambridge Economic History of Europe* 5.295; Braudel, *Wheels of Commerce* 423–26; Muldrew, "Hard Food for Midas" 100–03. For an example of the circulation of English coins from different reigns, all of which have a distinct value, see Jonson, *The Alchemist* 3.4.142–48.
84. One counterfeiter named John Powell even offered to lend his expertise to the Royal Mint in 1568, while a seventeenth-century Mint employee's surreptitious counterfeiting was discovered only because the counterfeit coins he produced were of higher quality than those issued by the Mint (Gaskill, *Crime and Mentalities in Early Modern England* 181, 137).
85. See Larkin and Hughes, eds., *Stuart Royal Proclamations* 1.287–90, 308–10, 350–51. Elizabeth I had attempted a similar, although less

mercenary, plan to mint base coins for use as small change: see Joan Thirsk and J.P. Cooper, eds., *Seventeenth-Century Economic Documents* (Oxford: Clarendon Press, 1972) 599–601 and Hughes and Larkin, eds., *Tudor Royal Proclamations* 3.222–24.

86. Qtd. in Gaskill, *Crime and Mentalities in Early Modern England* 129.

87. Elizabeth reduced the value of most coins by 25 to 50% (Tawney and Power, eds., *Tudor Economic Documents* 2.195–99).

88. Tawney and Power, eds., *Tudor Economic Documents* 2.203; Thirsk and Cooper, eds., *Seventeenth-Century Economic Documents* 602–03.

89. Challis, *The Tudor Coinage* 146–47, 268–74.

90. Moison, "Which is the Merchant Here?" 190; also see Cohen, "*The Merchant of Venice* and the Possibilities of Historical Criticism" 769.

91. For further discussion, see David C. McPherson, *Shakespeare, Jonson, and the Myth of Venice* (Newark: University of Delaware Press, 1990).

92. Thomas Coryat, *Crudities* (1611; Glasgow: MacLehose, 1905) 1.312.

93. Ibid., 1.314.

94. For a similar comment, see Giovanni Botero, *Relations, of the Most Famovs Kingdoms and Common-Weales Thorovgh the World* (1611) sig. Gg3v.

95. Cohen, "*The Merchant of Venice* and the Possibilities of Historical Criticism" 769–72; also see Ferber, "The Ideology of *The Merchant of Venice*" 451.

96. *A Garland for the New Royal Exchange: Composed of the Pieces of Divers Excellent Poets made in Memory of the First Opening Thereof on January the 23rd, Anno Dom. 1571* (London: J.D. White, 1845) 60.

97. Ibid., 21, 54.

98. See William Lithgow's comments in *The Totall Discourse of the Rare Adventures & Painefull Peregrinations of Long Nineteene Yeares Travayles* (1632; Glasgow: MacLehose, 1906) 35.

99. Lewes Roberts, *The Marchants Mapp of Commerce* sig. Gg3; for similar comments, see William Thomas, *The History of Italy* (1549), ed. George B. Parks (Ithaca: Cornell University Press, 1963) 69. Roberts also notes how the Venetians manipulate the exchange rate in order to defraud English merchants and privateers (sig. Gg2v).

100. Botero, *Relations, of the Most Famous Kingdoms and Common-Weales Thorovgh the World* (1608) sig. V and *An Historicall Description of the Most Famous Kingdomes and Common-Weales in the Worlde* (1603) sig. Q4v; for a similar comment, see Thomas, *The History of Italy* 69.

101. On early modern senses of "commodity" as "economic convenience," see Douglas Bruster, *Drama and the Market in the Age of Shakespeare* (Cambridge: Cambridge University Press, 1992) 41 and Fischer, *Econolingua* 57.

102. Among other examples, see Engle, *Shakespearean Pragmatism* 101 and Cohen, "*The Merchant of Venice* and the Possibilities of Historical Criticism" 774 and *Drama of a Nation* 205; for support of Shylock's accusations, see Engle, "Thrift is Blessing" 197; René Girard, "'To Entrap the Wisest': A Reading of *The Merchant of Venice*," in Edward Said, ed., *Literature and Society* (Baltimore: Johns Hopkins University Press, 1980) 112; Marc Shell, *Money, Language, and Thought: Literary and Philosophical Economies from the Medieval to Modern Era* (Berkeley: University of California Press, 1982) 68; Nerlich, *Ideology of Adventure* 160.

103. John Wheeler, *A Treatise of Commerce* (1601) sigs. B1v-B2.

104. See, among other examples, Agnew, *Worlds Apart* 88–89, Bruster, *Drama and the Market* 41–42, and Poovey, *History of the Modern Fact* 87–88; in each case, Wheeler's passage is taken at face value as an embrace of market relations.

105. Marx, *Capital* 1.131–37, 725–34. On Max Weber's definition of appropriation, see chapter 3.

106. Brenner, "The Origins of Capitalist Development" 27, 32–33, and 41.

107. Foucault, *The Order of Things* 166.

108. Elizabeth Fox-Genovese and Eugene Genovese, *Fruits of Merchant Capital: Slavery and Bourgeois Property in the Rise and Expansion of Capitalism* (New York: Oxford University Press, 1983) 4.

109. I should clarify my use of the term "abstracted labor": while Marx's labor theory of value is, of course, premised on the abstraction of the concrete labor of individuals into a generalized form of labor power, I wish to emphasize the material effects of this process of abstraction, particularly in an early period of capital formation. In addition, as I will discuss further in my analysis of Contarini, I wish to highlight the ramifications of the abstraction of labor in terms of an erasure of labor and the laboring classes from the representation of the national body politic. For a relevant discussion, see Marx, *Capital* 1.150, 308.

110. For insightful Marxist critiques of New Historicist approaches to issues of labor and economics, see Holstun, *Ehud's Dagger*, esp. 46–84; Scott Culter Shershow, "Idols of the Marketplace: Rethinking the Economic Determination of Renaissance Drama," *Renaissance Drama* 26 (1995): 1–27; and Christopher Pye, "The Theater, the Market, and the Subject of History," *ELH* 61 (1994): 501–22.

111. Harris, *Foreign Bodies and the Body Politic*.

112. In her edition of Smith's *De Republica Anglorum*, Mary Dewar concludes that Smith borrowed much of this section from William Harrison's discussion of English classes in "Of Degrees of People in the Commonwealth of England," from his *Description of England* (first published in Raphael Holinshed's *The Chronicles of England, Scotland, and Ireland* [1577, rev. 1587]) (158). Nonetheless, several important passages are unique to Smith, which is why I cite his version rather than Harrison's. Passages unique to Harrison's

version regarding the serving classes and the existence of slavery in England are discussed in chapter 3.

113. Sir Thomas Smith, *De Republica Anglorum*, ed. Mary Dewar (Cambridge: Cambridge University Press, 1982) 76. Laura Caroline Stevenson analyzes early modern representations of artisans in *Praise and Paradox: Merchants and Craftsmen in Elizabethan Popular Culture* (Cambridge: Cambridge University Press, 1984) 161–79.

114. Smith, *De Republica Anglorum* 57, 62.

115. Ibid., 77.

116. Everitt, "Social Mobility in Early Modern England" 57. For a discussion of the yeomanry as a "buffer" social group, see Allen, *The Invention of the White Race* 1.13, 23 and 2.13, 17.

2 A NATION OF PIRATES: PIRACY, CONVERSION, AND NATION SPACE

1. Paul Hentzner, *Travels in England* (1797) 63.

2. Fernand Braudel, *The Mediterranean* (New York: Harper & Row, 1972) 2.886–87.

3. See Alberto Tenenti, *Piracy and the Decline of Venice, 1580–1615* (Berkeley: University of California Press, 1967) 56–86 and Christopher Lloyd, *English Corsairs on the Barbary Coast* (London: Collins, 1981) 58–64.

4. See, e.g., *Calendar of State Papers, Domestic Series, James I, 1603–1610* [hereafter referred to as *CSP, Dom.*] 470.

5. Sir Godfrey Fisher, *Barbary Legend: War, Trade and Piracy in North Africa, 1415–1830* (1957; Westport, CT: Greenwood Press, 1974) 142.

6. See Larkin and Hughes, eds., *Stuart Royal Proclamations* 1.53–56. Yet, attesting to the inconsistencies of Jacobean policies toward piracy, Tompkins was not arrested until seven years after James's initial proclamation, and he defended himself by claiming that he had earlier paid 1,000 marks to procure a pardon. Tompkins was ultimately pardoned (perhaps after buying a pardon once more) but died in prison before his release (C.M. Senior, *A Nation of Pirates: English Piracy in its Heyday* [London: Newton Abbot, 1976] 40–41, 81–82; Evelyn Berckman, *Victims of Piracy: The Admiralty Court, 1575–1678* [London: Hamish Hamilton, 1979] 48).

7. Larkin and Hughes, eds., *Stuart Royal Proclamations* 1.54n.

8. Ibid., 1.30.

9. *The Complete Works of Captain John Smith*, ed. Philip L. Barbour, 3 vols. (Chapel Hill: University of North Carolina Press, 1986) 3.239.

10. Nottingham even received a payment of £1,000 resulting from Tompkins's seizure of the *Black Balbiano* (Senior, *A Nation of Pirates* 87).

11. Ibid., 17.

12. Qtd. in Michael Oppenheim, *A History of the Administration of the Royal Navy and of Merchant Shipping in Relation to the Navy* (1896; Hamden, CT: Shoe String Press, 1961) 187; Sir Henry Mainwaring, "Of the Beginnings, Practices, and Suppression of Pirates" (ca. 1616–17), *The Life and Works of Sir Henry Mainwaring*, ed. G.E. Manwaring, 2 vols. (London: Navy Records Society, 1920–22) 2.41. All further references to Mainwaring are from this edition.

13. Larkin and Hughes, eds., *Stuart Royal Proclamations* 1.108–11, 549–51.

14. Ibid., 1.570–72.

15. Ibid., 1.634–36.

16. Unemployed mariners were also included in Elizabeth's 1597 "Acte for Punyshment of Rogues, Vagabondes and Sturdy Beggars" (39 Elizabeth, c. 4): see Tawney and Power, eds., *Tudor Economic Documents* 2.355, 361–62.

17. Barbour, ed., *Complete Works* 3.128. Mary C. Fuller analyzes the trajectory of Smith's career and writings in *Voyages in Print: English Travel to America, 1576–1624* (Cambridge: Cambridge University Press, 1995) 85–140.

18. Thomas Heywood and William Rowley, *Fortune by Land and Sea*, ed. Herman Doh (New York: Garland, 1980). For a recent discussion of the play, see Barbara Fuchs, "Faithless Empires: Pirates, Renegadoes, and the English Nation," *ELH* 67 (2000): 52–57, reprinted in *Mimesis and Empire: The New World, Islam, and European Identities* (Cambridge: Cambridge University Press, 2001).

19. Braudel, *The Mediterranean* 2.866.

20. See Hughes and Larkin, eds., *Tudor Royal Proclamations*, 3 vols. (New Haven: Yale University Press, 1969).

21. [Thomas Heywood], *The True Relation, of the Lives and Deaths of the Two Most Famous English Pyrats, Purser, and Clinton* (1639) sig. C3. Jacques Lezra mentions this episode in *Unspeakable Subjects: The Genealogy of the Event in Early Modern Europe* (Stanford: Stanford University Press, 1997) 275–77.

22. The goods confiscated by privateers constituted 10–15% of England's total imports during the period. Kenneth Andrews estimates the value of Spanish prizes captured in 1589–91 at £400,000 (*Elizabethan Privateering: English Privateering during the Spanish War, 1585–1603* [Cambridge: Cambridge University Press, 1964] 128, 124).

23. Raphael Holinshed, *The Chronicles of England, Scotland and Ireland* (1587) 1354.

24. Senior, *A Nation of Pirates* 15–16, 36.

25. Marcus Rediker, *Between the Devil and the Deep Blue Sea: Merchant Seamen, Pirates, and the Anglo-American Maritime World, 1700–1750* (Cambridge: Cambridge University Press, 1987) 264.

26. On the association of piracy with egalitarian social relations, see Rediker, *Between the Devil and the Deep Blue Sea* and Christopher

Hill, *Liberty Against the Law: Some Seventeenth-Century Controversies* (London: Penguin, 1996) 114–22.

27. Rediker, *Between the Devil and the Deep Blue Sea* 118.

28. Heywood, *The True Relation, of … Purser, and Clinton* sig. A8v.

29. Rediker, *Between the Devil and the Deep Blue Sea* 264.

30. John Smith also includes Harris and Jennings in his list of Jacobean pirates in *The True Travels*. Among the captains noted by Smith, only those two were punished by English authorities (*Complete Works* 3.239).

31. For a relevant discussion of the classed valences of rhetorical "style," see Halpern, *The Poetics of Primitive Accumulation*.

32. Edward Arber, ed., *A Transcript of the Registers of the Company of Stationers of London 1554–1640*, 5 vols. (London: privately printed, 1875–94) 3.206b.

33. Muldrew, *The Economy of Obligation, passim*.

34. Senior, *Nation of Pirates* 13; Fischer, *Econolingua* 39.

35. Senior, *Nation of Pirates* 40.

36. Barry, author of *Ram Alley* (ca. 1608), was associated with Harris, Captain Bishop, and other pirates based in Ireland, and he was also involved in Raleigh's semi-piratical expedition to Guiana in 1617: see C. L'Estrange-Ewen, *Lording Barry, Poet and Pirate* (privately printed, 1938) 11, 15.

37. Berckman, *Victims of Piracy* 47.

38. *CSP, Dom., 1603–1610* 568.

39. John Stow, *The Annales, or Generall Chronicle of England* (1615) sig. Ffff3.

40. For details relating to this case, see Senior, *Nation of Pirates* 126–38.

41. *Clinton, Purser, & Arnold to Their Countrymen Wheresoever* (ca. 1583), Illustrations of Early English Popular Culture, ed. J. Payne Collier (London: privately printed, 1863). Lost earlier versions of these ballads include "Clintons lamentacyon," registered in 1583, and "The confession of 9 Rovers, Clinton and Purser beinge chief," entered into the Stationers' Company Registers in 1586 (Arber 2.197, 210b).

42. Heywood's *Fair Maid of the West* (part I, ca. 1604; part II, ca. 1631), set during the Islands' Voyage of 1597, provides the best example of Jacobean and Caroline nostalgia for Elizabethan maritime victories. On this topic, see Anne Barton, "Harking back to Elizabeth: Ben Jonson and English Nostalgia," *ELH* 48 (1981): 706–31 and A.J. Hoenselaars, *Images of Englishmen and Foreigners in the Drama of Shakespeare and His Contemporaries* (Rutherford, NJ: Farleigh Dickinson University Press, 1992) 216–36.

43. Charles Fitzgeffrey's poem, "Sir Francis Drake," notes: "Had he surviv'd, *Tempe* had beene our land, / And *Thames* had stream'd with *Tagus* golden sand" (*The Poems of Rev. Charles Fitzgeoffrey*, ed. Alexander Grosart [privately printed, 1881] 40).

44. David B. Quinn and A.N. Ryan, *England's Sea Empire, 1550–1642* (London: George Allen & Unwin, 1983) 123, 143.

45. On Elizabethan foreign policy toward Islamic cultures, see Nabil I. Matar, *Turks, Moors, and Englishmen in the Age of Discovery* (New York: Columbia University Press, 1999) 33.

46. Fisher, *Barbary Legend* 142. Gifford was mentioned by name as the captain of a pirate ship in a June 13, 1606 proclamation (Larkin and Hughes, eds., *Stuart Royal Proclamations* 1.146). Tried in Admiralty Court on December 8 of that year, Gifford was bailed in 1611; although still active as a pirate in 1615, he was later recommended for a baronetcy, ending his career on the Admiralty Commission (Larkin and Hughes 1.146n.; Fisher 172–73).

47. On senses of "doubleness" in formulations of nationhood, see Tom Nairn's discussion of "Janus-faced" nationalism in *The Break-Up of Britain: Crisis and Neo-Nationalism* (London: NLB, 1977) and Homi Bhabha's analysis of forms of "double-time" in "DissemiNation: Time, Narrative and the Margins of the Modern Nation," *The Location of Culture* (New York: Routledge, 1994) 139–70.

48. Michel Foucault, *Discipline and Punish: The Birth of the Prison*, trans. Alan Sheridan (1975; New York: Vintage, 1979) 48, 67. On practices of carnival and the carnivalesque, see Mikhail Bakhtin, *Rabelais and his World*, trans. Hélène Islowsky (Bloomington: Indiana University Press, 1984) and Peter Stallybrass and Allon White, *The Politics and Poetics of Transgression* (Ithaca: Cornell University Press, 1986).

49. Thomas Laqueur, "Crowds, Carnival and the State in English Executions, 1604–1868," in A.L. Beier et al., eds., *The First Modern Society* (Cambridge: Cambridge University Press, 1989) 340.

50. *Fortune* 3.4.1529–74; *True Relation, of... Purser, and Clinton* sig. C3.

51. *CSP, Dom., 1611–1618* 577. Raleigh was interviewed in the Tower by Sir Thomas Wilson, Keeper of Records and one of the main subjects of chapter 5. For Wilson's notes of his September 1618 talks with Raleigh, see Public Record Office, SP 14/99/ff. 172–73.

52. Another text, *Declaration of the Demeanor and Cariage of Sir Walter Raleigh* (1618), was written by Francis Bacon and published after Raleigh's execution in order to justify James's actions and counter popular sympathy for Raleigh: for analysis, see Fuller, *Voyages in Print* 57 ff. Other contemporary comments on Raleigh's execution include the ballad, "Sir Walter Rauleigh his lamentation" (1618), and Sir Lewis Stukeley, *The Humble Petition and Information* (1618), in which the vice-admiral of Devon responsible for Raleigh's apprehension defended his actions against popular criticism (*Harleian Miscellany* 3 [1809]: 388–95).

53. My discussion of the spectral forms of cultural memory is influenced by Jacques Derrida, *Specters of Marx: The State of the Debt, The Work of Mourning, and the New International*, trans. Peggy Kamuf (New York: Routledge, 1994).

54. For discussion, see Michael J. Braddick, *State Formation in Early Modern England c. 1550–1700* (Cambridge: Cambridge University Press, 2000) 16–20.

55. Janice E. Thomson, *Mercenaries, Pirates, and Sovereigns: State-Building and Extraterritorial Violence in Early Modern Europe* (Princeton: Princeton University Press, 1994) 7–20.

56. For discussion of the figure of the renegade, see Samuel Chew, *The Crescent and the Rose: Islam and England during the Renaissance* (New York: Oxford University Press, 1937) 347–62; Nabil I. Matar, "The Renegade in English Seventeenth-Century Imagination," *Studies in English Literature* 33 (1993): 489–505; Lois Potter, "Pirates and 'Turning Turk' in Renaissance Drama," Maquerlot and Willems 127–43; Daniel Vitkus, intro., *Three Turk Plays* (New York: Columbia University Press, 2000) 24–39; and Fuchs, "Faithless Empires" 45–69.

57. Larkin and Hughes, eds., *Stuart Royal Proclamations* 1.158–61. Showing a link with the economic anxieties discussed in the previous chapter, this proclamation associated travel with the illegal export of coin and bullion.

58. Ibid., 1.184–85. In 1608, the Privy Council also directed officers of the ports to remand to custody anyone refusing to take the oath of allegiance: see British Library Stowe MS 170. Edmondes Papers.Vol.V.f.26.

59. Ibid., 1.147–48. This proclamation specifically dealt with the travel of women and minors, groups associated with Catholic exiles and seminaries on the Continent. Despite a lack of travel accounts written by women in this period, Alison Games's study of port records has shown that women comprised 27% of travelers to the Continent in 1635 (*Migration and the Origins of the English Atlantic World* [Cambridge: Harvard University Press, 1999] 24). I discuss the correlation of Catholic exiles with travel in "The English Roman Life: Representing the English Catholic Diaspora in Early Modern Europe," in Ronald Corthell et al., eds., *Catholic Culture in Early Modern England* (Notre Dame: Notre Dame University Press, forthcoming).

60. For a list of travel advice texts, see Edward Cox's section on "Directions for Travelers," in *A Reference Guide to the Literature of Travel*, 3 vols. (Seattle: University of Washington Press, 1938) 2.320–31. For analysis of this genre, see George B. Parks, "Travel as Education," in *The Seventeenth Century*, ed. R.F. Jones (Stanford: Stanford University Press, 1951) 264–90.

61. Thomas Palmer, *An Essay of the Meanes How to Make Our Trauailes, into Forraine Countries, the More Profitable and Honourable* sig. A4v.

62. The French missionary Père Pierre Dan estimated the number of European renegades residing in North Africa as 8,000 in Algiers (of whom 1,000 to 1,200 were women), 3,000 to 4,000 male and 600 to 700 female converts in Tunis, 300 in Salé, and 100 in Tripoli (*Histoire de Barbarie et de ses Corsairs* [1637] 313–14, qtd. in Stephen Clissold, *The Barbary Slaves* [London: Paul Elek, 1977] 87).

63. Thirty-three of the 48 grand viziers in power in Constantinople from 1453 to 1623 were converts from Christianity, while in 1580, more than half of leading officials in Algiers (*qaids*) and 25 of the 33 naval commanders (*raïs*) were renegades (Clissold 86–87). See also John B. Wolf, *The Barbary Coast: Algiers under the Turks, 1500 to 1830* (New York: Norton, 1979) 164–65 and Nabil I. Matar, " 'Turning Turk': Conversion to Islam in English Renaissance Thought," *Durham University Journal* 86 (1994): 33–41.

64. Francis Knight, *A Relation of Seaven Yeares Slaverie Vnder the Turks of Argiere, Suffered by an English Captive Merchant* (1640) sig. B1v.

65. Sir Thomas Sherley, *Discours of the Turkes* (ca. 1606–07), ed. E. Denison Ross (London: Camden Miscellany, 1936) 4.

66. Ibid., 11. For a similar comment, see PRO, SP 14/70/f. 170v and *CSP, Dom., 1611–18* 149.

67. Richard Hakluyt, *The Original Writings and Correspondence of the Two Richard Hakluyts*, 2 vols., ed. E.G.R. Taylor (London: Hakluyt Society, 1935) 2.218.

68. See Matar, *Islam in Britain, 1588–1685* and *Turks, Moors, and Englishmen in the Age of Discovery*.

69. Edward Said, *Orientalism* (New York: Pantheon, 1978) 184 [italics in text].

70. Ibid., 215, 222–23.

71. For details, see notes 93 and 107–08.

72. David D. Hebb, *Piracy and the English Government, 1616–1642* (Brookfield, VT: Scolar Press, 1994) 138. On captivity narratives, see Nabil Matar, "English Accounts of Captivity in North Africa and the Middle East: 1577–1625," *Renaissance Quarterly* 54 (2001): 553–72 and "Introduction: England and Mediterranean Captivity, 1577–1704," in Daniel Vitkus, ed., *Piracy, Slavery, and Redemption: Barbary Captivity Narratives from Early Modern England* (New York: Columbia University Press, 2001) 1–52.

73. William Laud, *The Works of the Most Reverend Father in God, William Laud*, 7 vols. (1853; New York: AMS, 1975) 5.352. William Juxon, the bishop of London, Francis White, the bishop of Ely, and Matthew Wren, the bishop of Norwich, were all fellow Arminians, explaining the central role allotted to the priest in the reconversion ceremony (Hebb, *Piracy and the English Government* 167n.).

74. Laud, "A Form of Penance and Reconciliation of a Renegado or Apostate from the Christian Religion to Turcism, &c.," in *Works* 5.372–76.

75. Margo Todd, "A Captive's Story: Puritans, Pirates, and the Drama of Reconciliation," *The Seventeenth Century* 12 (1997): 37–56.

76. William Gouge, *A Recovery from Apostacy. Set out in a Sermon Preached in Stepny Church neere London at the Receiving of a Penitent Renegado into the Church, Octob. 21, 1638* (1639) sigs. B1-B1v.

77. Gouge, in casting apostasy as a departure from the Church (or father's house), repeats the language of the Book of Common Prayer's version of Psalm 68:6: "He is the God that maketh men to be of one mind in an house, and bringeth the prisoners out of captivity: but letteth the runagates continue in scarceness" (qtd. in Matar, *Islam in Britain* 63).

78. Bhabha, "DissemiNation," *The Location of Culture* 145.

79. Matar, *Islam in Britain* 65–66.

80. Todd, "A Captive's Story" 40. Gouge refers to this earlier ceremony in his sermon (sig. G1).

81. Edward Kellet and Henry Byam, *A Retvrne from Argier. A Sermon Preached at Minhead in the County of Somerset the 16 of March, 1627 at the Re-Admission of a Relapsed Christian into Our Chvrch* (1628).

82. Laud, *Works* 5.372; Gouge, *Recovery* sig. M1v.

83. For a similar comment, see Heywood's *The Fair Maid of the West, Part I* (ed. Robert K. Turner, Jr. [Lincoln: University of Nebraska Press, 1967] 5.2.130); Barbara Fuchs also discusses these passages in "Faithless Empires" 61–64. Robert S. DuPlessis notes that "caput" was an early term for "capital" ("Capital Formations," in Turner, ed., *The Culture of Capital* 31).

84. George Puttenham cites the precedents of Jack Cade and Captain Kett as rebels who used ambiguous language to stir their followers (*Arte of English Poesie* [1589] sigs. Ff3-Ff3v).

85. Steven Mullaney, *The Place of the Stage: License, Play, and Power in Renaissance England* (Chicago: University of Chicago Press, 1988) 118–25.

86. Paul Ricaut, *The Present State of the Greek and Armenian Churches* (1679) 289, qtd. in Matar, "The Renegade in English Seventeenth-Century Imagination" 501.

87. Valerie Forman, "Material Dispossessions and Counterfeit Investments: The Economies of *Twelfth Night*," unpublished paper, Shakespeare Association of America, 2001.

88. Ibid., 2.

89. Among depositions of returning captives, see PRO, SP 16/5/f. 39; SP 16/316/f. 100; SP 16/329/f. 46; SP 16/332/ff. 42–42v and 44–46. Nabil Matar also notes these documents in *Turks, Moors, and Englishmen* 210n.

90. John N. Wall, *Transformations of the Word* (Athens: University of Georgia Press, 1988) 23–34.

91. Charles Fitzgeffrey, *Compassion Towards Captives, Chiefly Towards our Brethren and Country-men Who are in Miserable Bondage in Barbarie ... Preached in Plymovth, in October 1636* (1637) sig. B1.

92. Kellet's sermon also makes the analogy between captivity and domestic social relations, likening conversion to servitude, in which the subject is as "a poore debtor, wrap't in Bands, worse then the Bonds

of Vsurers; in Bonds forfeited, and impossible to be satisfied" (*Retvrne from Argier* sig. C1).

93. A Turkish pirate ship had notoriously sailed up the Thames to Leigh in 1616; another Turkish vessel was captured on the Thames in October of the following year (*Letters of George Lord Carew to Sir Thomas Roe, 1615–1617*, ed. John Maclean [London: Camden Society, 1860] 61; *CSP, Dom., 1611–18* 427). For other records, see Chew, *Crescent and the Rose* 362–63.

94. *Calendar of State Papers Relating to English Affairs in Venetian Archives, 1603–1607* (Nendeln, Liechtenstein: Kraus, 1970) 149, 157; *CSP, Dom., 1625–1626* 83, 89; *CSP, Dom., 1640* 450.

95. See Henry Barnby, "The Sack of Baltimore," *Journal of the Cork Historical and Archaeological Society* 74 (1969): 101–29.

96. Ibid., 111. A 1636 report by a former captive warned that 870 English, Scottish, and Welsh captives in Salé, Morocco were plotting to take revenge on their nations unless they were ransomed (Matar, *Turks, Moors, and Englishmen* 63).

97. Among other examples, see Smith, *True Travels* (*Complete Works* 2.239) and the ballad, "The lamentable cries of at least 1500 Christians: most of them being Englishmen (now Prisoners in Argiers under the Turkes)" (C.H. Firth, ed., *Naval Songs and Ballads* [London: Navy Records Society, 1908] 31–33).

98. Mainwaring, *Life and Works* 2.40–49.

99. Henry Robinson, *Libertas, or Reliefe to the English Captives in Algier* (1642) sigs. B1v-B2.

100. Anthony Munday, *The Admirable Deliverance of 266. Christians by John Reynard Englishman from the Captiuitie of the Turkes* (1608) sig. A2.

101. For primary records, see the anonymous *Algiers Voyage* (1620) and John Dunton, *A Trve Iovrnall of the Sally Fleet* (1637). On the expeditions, see Hebb, *Piracy and the English Government* 21–135 and 237–65; on diplomatic relations with North Africa, see Hebb 173–97 and Fisher, *Barbary Legend* 169–228. Naval action against the Barbary States might have been more successful in generating popular support for efforts to suppress piracy than in accomplishing military objectives. As evidence of increasing populist sentiment for the state position on piracy, Nathaniel Knott, a West Country sea captain, dedicated to Archbishop Laud his manuscript treatise, "An Aduise of a Sea-man touchinge The Expedition intended against the Turkish Pyrates" (1634): see PRO, SP 16/279/ff. 199–264.

102. PRO, SP 14/95/f. 60-60v; *CSP, Dom., 1611–18* 516. For a comprehensive survey of records of Turks and Moors shipwrecked or captured in England, see Matar, *Turks, Moors, and Englishmen* 19–42.

103. Fuchs, "Faithless Empires" 48.

104. Mainwaring, *Life and Works* 2.15–16.

105. *The Naval Tracts of Sir William Monson*, ed. Michael Oppenheim (London: Navy Records Office, 1902) 3.65. The blurred identities of Mainwaring and Monson also reveal the interconnections between pirates and state officials in the economy of piracy, relationships that produced a consequent inversion of social roles. Captain Williamson, hired by the state to rid the Munster coast of pirates, seems to have developed close ties to pirate captains such as Jennings and Richard Bishop, who are recorded as having captured and entertained Williamson (Senior, *Nation of Pirates* 68).

106. Hebb, *Piracy and the English Government* 170.

107. In his recent article, "Counting European Slaves on the Barbary Coast," Robert C. Davis estimates the number of European captives as 27,000 in Algiers, 6,000 in Tunis, and 2,000 in Tripoli and other ports, or an average of 35,000 captives throughout the seventeenth century (*Past and Present* 172 [August 2001]: 106–08). For other estimates, see Lloyd, *English Corsairs* 113; Clissold, *Barbary Slaves* 146; and Hebb, *Piracy and the English Government* 139.

108. Although an estimated 600 English captives were redeemed, along with 600 more who returned from North Africa, more than two-thirds of captives never returned to England (Hebb, *Piracy and the English Government* 163). Davis estimates than only 2% of captives were ever redeemed ("Counting European Slaves" 114). On redemption efforts, see Hebb 157–63.

109. Matar, *Islam in Britain* 41–42.

3 VENTING TRINCULOS: *The Tempest* AND DISCOURSES OF COLONIAL LABOR

1. Among the few critical sources discussing this issue, see Abbot Emerson Smith, *Colonists in Bondage: White Servitude and Convict Labor in America, 1607–1776* (Chapel Hill: University of North Carolina Press, 1947) and Peter Wilson Coldham, *Emigrants in Chains* (Baltimore: Genealogical Publishing, 1992). Timothy J. Coates studies the Portuguese history of colonial transportation in *Convicts and Orphans: Forced and State-Sponsored Colonizers in the Portuguese Empire, 1550–1755* (Stanford: Stanford University Press, 2001).

2. Carole Shammas, "English Commercial Development and American Colonization, 1560–1620," in Andrews et al., eds., *The Westward Enterprise* 151–74.

3. Appleby, *Economic Thought and Ideology* 18; for a similar point, see Shannon Miller, *Invested with Meaning: The Raleigh Circle in the New World* (Philadelphia: University of Pennsylvania Press, 1998) 13.

4. E.A. Wrigley and R.S. Schofield, *The Population History of England, 1541–1871: A Reconstruction* (London: Edward Arnold, 1981) 531–32; D.M. Palliser, *The Age of Elizabeth*, 2nd edition (London: Longman, 1991) 40.

5. Robert Brenner, "Agrarian Class Structure and Economic Development in Pre-Industrial Europe," in T.H. Aston and C.H.E. Philpin, eds., *The Brenner Debate: Agrarian Class Structure and Economic Development in Pre-Industrial Europe* (Cambridge: Cambridge University Press, 1985) 11.

6. The figures are those of John F. Pound, qtd. in John McMullan, *The Canting Crew: London's Criminal Underworld, 1550–1700* (New Brunswick: Rutgers University Press, 1984) 29.

7. Peter Laslett, *The World We Have Lost* (New York: Scribner's, 1965) 20, 12. For a discussion of the status of servants in early modern England, see Frances Dolan, *Dangerous Familiars: Representations of Domestic Crime in England, 1550–1700* (Ithaca: Cornell University Press, 1994) and Mark Thornton Burnett, *Masters and Servants in English Renaissance Drama and Culture: Authority and Obedience* (New York: St. Martin's Press, 1997).

8. Paul Slack, *Poverty and Policy in Tudor and Stuart England* (London: Longman, 1988) 47.

9. For sources on this topic, see chapter 1, 3n. Periods of particular crisis included two failed harvests in 1596–98, which resulted in the death of an estimated 6% of the population, along with lesser crises in 1587 and 1622–23 (Slack, *Poverty and Policy* 49). Supple finds the worst economic conditions in 1622 (*Commercial Crisis* 56). Significantly, these years witnessed the first proposal of transportation (see below on the 1597 "An Acte for Punyshment of Rogues, Vagabondes and Sturdy Beggars" [39 Elizabeth, c. 4]) and the rise of an economy of indentured servitude, whose codification Theodore Allen situates around 1622 (*The Invention of the White Race* 2.98–99).

10. For a similar point, see Halpern, *Poetics of Primitive Accumulation* 312n.

11. On Virginia Company investors, see Wesley Frank Craven, *Dissolution of the Virginia Company: The Failure of a Colonial Experiment* (1932; Gloucester, MA: Peter Smith, 1964) and Robert Brenner, *Merchants and Revolution: Commercial Change, Political Conflict, and London's Overseas Traders, 1550–1653* (Princeton: Princeton University Press, 1993) 92–112.

12. Among examples, see the Company's second charter (ca. Feb. 1609), in Alexander Brown, ed., *Genesis of the United States*, 2 vols. (1890; New York: Russell & Russell, 1964) 1.248–49; William Crashaw, *A Sermon Preached in London Before the Right Honorable the Lord Lawarre…*(1610) sig. B4; Thomas West, Baron De La Warr, *The Relation of the Right Honorable Lord De-La-Warre* (1611) sig. C1v.

13. Andrew Fitzmaurice, "The Civic Solution to the Crisis of English Colonization, 1609–1625," *The Historical Journal* 42, 1 (1999): 25–51.

14. For discussion of Company labor practices, see Allen, *Invention of the White Race* and James Curtis Ballagh, *White Servitude in the Colony of Virginia: A Study of the System of Indentured Labor in the American Colonies* (New York: Burt Franklin, 1969).

15. Samuel Purchas, *Hakluytus Posthumus, or, Purchas his Pilgrimes* (1625) 20 vols. (Glasgow: MacLehose, 1906) 19.5–72. All references to Strachey's *True Report* are from this edition.

16. Robert Hitchcock, *A Pollitique Platt for the Honour of the Prince, the Great Profite of the Publique State, Relief of the Poore* (1580).

17. D.C. Coleman, "Labour in the English Economy of the Seventeenth Century," *Economic History Review* 8 (1956): 280–95.

18. William Carroll discusses Hitchcock's text in *Fat King, Lean Beggar: Representations of Poverty in the Age of Shakespeare* (Ithaca: Cornell University Press, 1996) 53–55.

19. For further analysis of the commonwealth tradition and its response to capital formation, see McRae, *God Speed the Plough*, esp. 23–57.

20. Sir Thomas More similarly expressed doubts about reform in Book 1 of *Utopia* (1516), the "dialogue of counsel," wherein Raphael critiques More's proposal to "influence policy indirectly" (trans. Robert M. Adams [New York: Norton, 1975] 26–27). Despite its place in the humanist tradition, the treatment of labor in *Utopia* anticipates the most severe of later anti-vagrant legislation as well as England's economy of colonial servitude in the following century.

21. Sir Humphrey Gilbert, *The Voyages and Colonizing Enterprises of Sir Humphrey Gilbert*, ed. D.B. Quinn (London: Hakluyt Society, 1940) 1.161.

22. Hakluyt, *Original Writings* 2.235.

23. Ibid., 2.316–17; Peckham makes a similar proposal in his *True Report* (Quinn, ed., *Voyages... of Sir Humphrey Gilbert* 2.462). For a discussion of the economy in "trifles," see Knapp, *An Empire Nowhere* 125.

24. Quinn, "Renaissance Influences in English Colonization," *Explorers and Colonies* 106.

25. Ibid., 107.

26. See Appleby, *Economic Thought and Ideology* 120–21.

27. For Hakluyt's comments, see *Original Writings* 2.343.

28. One earlier exception is John Hawkins's prefatory poem to Peckham's *True Report* (1583); it is perhaps appropriate that Hawkins, the first Englishman to be actively engaged in the slave trade, should also be associated with the idea of venting the poor: see *Voyages... of Sir Humphrey Gilbert* 2.438.

29. Hakluyt, *Original Writings* 2.343.

30. See, e.g., *The Riverside Shakespeare* 466n. Aside from numerous instances in which vent is used in the sense of "express," Shakespeare also links the term on several occasions to trade and exchange, having it refer to a traveler's knowledge and conversation (*As You Like It*

2.7.41; *All's Well That Ends Well* 2.3.202–03) and the circulation of scandalous ballads (*Cymbeline* 5.3.56).

31. Scott Shershow notes this passage in "Idols of the Marketplace" 1–2. I am indebted to Scott for reminding me of this reference.

32. Among other examples recommending colonial venting, see the tracts by the elder Hakluyt and Edward Hayes published in John Brereton's *Discovery of the North Part of Virginia* (1602).

33. See D.B. Quinn, *Set Fair for Roanoke: Voyages and Colonies, 1584–1606* (Chapel Hill: University of North Carolina Press, 1985) and *The Roanoke Voyages, 1584–1590.*

34. Morgan, *American Slavery, American Freedom* 24.

35. Tawney and Power, eds., *Tudor Economic Documents* 2.354–61.

36. Carroll, *Fat King, Lean Beggar* 26. For further discussion of this statute, see chapter 4.

37. Tawney and Power, eds., *Tudor Economic Documents* 2.357. As an alternative, vagrants could be assigned a life sentence of labor in galley ships (*Tudor Economic Documents* 2.357); for either punishment, their unlicensed return was punishable by death (2.357). Monetary penalties were also given for failing to enforce the law (10 shillings) as well as for harboring a vagrant (5 s.) (2.358).

38. Beier, *Masterless Men* 162; otherwise, there is no evidence found that the 1597 Act's stipulation of transportation and galley slavery was ever enforced (161).

39. Qtd. in Carroll, *Fat King, Lean Beggar* 111. On the early modern workhouse, see Carroll 108–24 and Joanna Innes, "Prisons for the Poor: English Bridewells, 1555–1800," in Francis Snyder and Douglas Hay, eds., *Labour, Law, and Crime* (London: Tavistock, 1987) 42–120.

40. Michel Foucault, *Madness and Civilization*, trans. Richard Howard (1961; New York: Vintage, 1973) 58.

41. See Innes, "Prisons for the Poor" and Braddick, *State Formation in Early Modern England* 111.

42. See Foucault, *Discipline and Punish* 25, 206, 219–21.

43. A.L. Beier, "Poverty and Progress in Early Modern England," in Beier et al., eds., *The First Modern Society* 201–39.

44. Hilary McD. Beckles, *White Servitude and Black Slavery in Barbados, 1627–1715* (Knoxville: University of Tennessee Press, 1989) xiv.

45. Ibid., 5–7.

46. Eric Williams, *Capitalism and Slavery* (Chapel Hill: University of North Carolina Press, 1944); Morgan, *American Slavery, American Freedom*; Beckles, *White Servitude and Black Slavery*; Allen, *The Invention of the White Race*; for a recent survey, see Robin Blackburn, *The Making of New World Slavery: From the Baroque to the Modern, 1492–1800* (London: Verso, 1997).

47. Allen, *The Invention of the White Race* 2.3.

48. On the 1547 statute, see C.S.L. Davies, "Slavery and the Protector Somerset: The Vagrancy Act of 1547," *Economic History Review* 19

(1966): 533–49; Allen, *The Invention of the White Race* 2.20–22; and Maurice Hunt, "Slavery, English Servitude, and *The Comedy of Errors*," *ELR* 27 (1997): 31–56. Despite the repeal of the 1547 Act, the Scottish Privy Council passed a similar statute in 1605 (*Register of the Privy Council of Scotland*, volume 7 [1604–07] [Edinburgh: H.M. General Register House, 1885] 56–57).

49. William Harrison, *Description of England*, ed. Georges Edelen (Ithaca: Cornell University Press, 1968) 118–19.

50. Ibid., 190.

51. For a survey of discussions of the Mediterranean contexts of *The Tempest*, see Goran V. Stanivukovic, "Recent Studies of English Renaissance Literature of the Mediterranean," *ELR* 32 (2002): 177–78.

52. Among discussions of *The Tempest* in the context of attitudes toward apprentices and servants, see Andrew Gurr, "Industrious Ariel and Idle Caliban," in Maquerlot and Willems, eds., *Travel and Drama* 193–208 and Dolan, *Dangerous Familiars* 64–71.

53. I have emended the Riverside Shakespeare's transcription of the phrase as "vild race." Jonathan Goldberg analyzes this passage as a precursor of Enlightenment discourses of race in "The Print of Goodness," in Turner, ed., *The Culture of Capital* 231–54.

54. Qtd. in Allen, *Invention* 2.12. For other examples, see Smith, *Colonists in Bondage* 3–25, 136–51.

55. *A True and Sincere Declaration* sig. A4; this text is reprinted in Brown, *Genesis of the United States* 1.337–53.

56. On the influence of the 1607 Midlands Rising on *Coriolanus*, see Annabel Patterson, *Shakespeare and the Popular Voice* (Oxford: Blackwell, 1989) 135–46.

57. Among other examples, see Thomas Dekker's *O Per Se O* (1612) (Judges, *Elizabethan Underworld* 377–78) and Samuel Rid's *Martin Markall* (1610) (Judges 395 ff.).

58. *Statute of Artificers* (1563), in Tawney and Power, eds., *Tudor Economic Documents* 1.338–50.

59. Qtd. in Maurice Dobb, *Studies in the Development of Capitalism* (New York: International Publishers, 1947) 233.

60. For an example of the paternalistic application of the context of household labor to domestic and colonial economies, see Richard Eburne's *A Plain Pathway to Plantations* (1624), which recommends "to place abroad your children into other houses, as it were into colonies, where they may be set awork" (36). For a discussion of paternalism in early modern economic and social relations, see E.P. Thompson, "Eighteenth-Century English Society: Class Struggle Without Class?" 133–37.

61. Northrup Frye associates the Romance with nostalgia in *Anatomy of Criticism* (Princeton: Princeton University Press, 1957) 200. On Romance and early modern colonialism, see David Quint, *Epic and Empire: Politics and Generic Form from Virgil to Milton*

(Princeton: Princeton University Press, 1993) 248–67. For a recent discussion of *The Tempest* as Romance, see Linton, *The Romance of the New World* 155–84.

62. The first instance of a vented laborer occurred in 1607, with a runaway dyer's apprentice who had stolen his master's goods (Beier, *Masterless Men* 161–62).

63. See Robert C. Johnson, "The Transportation of Vagrant Children from London to Virginia, 1618–1622," in *Early Stuart Studies*, ed. Howard S. Reinmuth, Jr. (Minneapolis: University of Minnesota Press, 1970) 137–51. Governor Thomas Dale of the Virginia colony expressed his support for conscripting vagrants and convicts as indentured servants in August 1611, contemporary to the play's initial performance, while James I is recorded as advocating this policy in January 1614 (Beckles, *White Servitude and Black Slavery* 59, 56–57).

64. This transition was reflected in the introduction of the legal mechanism enabling masters to "assign" their servants—and thereby transfer ownership through sale in cases of death, bankruptcy, or for profit—which became codified in Virginia Company indenture contracts in 1622. The concept of assign, previously unknown in English labor relations, served a crucial role in adapting definitions of servitude and labor to "capitalist categories of commodity exchange and free flow of capital" (Allen, *Invention of the White Race* 2.99; for a similar point, see Beckles, *White Servitude* 6).

65. John Pory, "Letter of John Pory to Dudley Carleton, 1619," in Lyon Gardiner Tyler, ed., *Narratives of Early Virginia, 1606–1625* (1907; New York: Barnes & Noble, 1952) 285.

66. Stephen Greenblatt, *Shakespearean Negotiations: The Circulation of Social Energy* (Berkeley: University of California Press, 1988) 142–63.

67. Morgan, *American Slavery, American Freedom* 45.

68. Ibid., 45. A key distinction between the charters resulted from the fact that the second charter allowed prospective colonists to accrue private profits from their land and crops yet denied them access to the "joint-stock" of the Company itself, reinforcing the distinction between investors and settlers.

69. Marx, "The Modern Theory of Colonization," *Capital* 1.931–40. An important counterargument to Marx's formulation is provided by Robert J. Steinfeld's *The Invention of Free Labor: The Employment Relation in English and American Law and Culture, 1350–1870* (Chapel Hill: University of North Carolina Press, 1991), which argues that both "free" and unfree labor relations coexisted in the early modern period and that the latter, in fact, remained the dominant form of contractual labor (6–7).

70. The figures are those of Theodore Rabb, qtd. in Linton, *Romance of the New World* 159.

71. Morgan, *American Slavery, American Freedom* 84. In seventeenth-century Virginia, 30.6% of emigrants were gentry and 27.6% were

merchants, while mariners and agricultural laborers made up only 4.4 and 3.2% of the white male population (James Horn, " 'To Parts Beyond the Seas': Free Emigration to the Chesapeake in the Seventeenth Century," in Ida Altman and James Horn, eds., *"To Make America": European Emigration in the Early Modern Period* [Berkeley: University of California Press, 1991] 92). Alison Games analyzes emigration patterns in *Migration and the Origins of the English Atlantic World*.

72. In an example of this problem, Barbara Fuchs interprets Stephano and Trinculo as general representatives of English colonialism, only casually noting the importance of their class status: see "Conquering Islands: Contextualizing *The Tempest*," *Shakespeare Quarterly* 48 (1997): 12n. 47. For readings of the play that link Stephano and Trinculo with the position of masterless men, see Paul Brown, " 'This thing of darkness I acknowledge mine': *The Tempest* and the Discourse of Colonialism," in *Political Shakespeare: New Essays in Cultural Materialism*, ed. Jonathan Dollimore and Alan Sinfield (Manchester: Manchester University Press, 1985) 56 and Curt Breight, " 'Treason doth never prosper': *The Tempest* and the Discourse of Treason," *Shakespeare Quarterly* 41 (1990): 17.

73. See Dekker, *Lantern and Candlelight* (1608), in Judges, *Elizabethan Underworld* 345.

74. Ann Rosalind Jones and Peter Stallybrass, *Renaissance Clothing and the Materials of Memory* (Cambridge: Cambridge University Press, 2000) 17. Jones and Stallybrass also demonstrate how clothing was often sold to pawnbrokers and used as an alternative currency by rich and poor alike (26–32, 181–93).

75. Pory, "Letter of John Pory to Dudley Carleton, 1619" 285.

76. Jones and Stallybrass, *Renaissance Clothing* 5.

77. John Rolfe, *Virginia in 1616* (1616), in *Virginia: Four Personal Narratives* (New York: Arno Press, 1972) 104.

78. Smith, *A True Relation* (1608) (*Complete Works* 1.35); *A Map of Virginia* (1612) (*Complete Works* 1.176). For analysis, see Fuller, *Voyages in Print* 85–140.

79. Robert Johnson, *The New Life of Virginea* (1612) sig. C1.

80. Some promotional texts described Gates's own men in these terms: as a "headlesse and vnbridled multitude" (*A True and Sincere Declaration* sig. C2; Brown, *Genesis* 1.347) and "so headie a multitude" (Strachey, *True Report* 46).

81. Ralph Hamor, *A Trve Discovrse of the Present State of Virginia* (1615) sig. D1.

82. For sources attributing Jamestown's failures to a lack of social distinctions in the colony, see Kupperman, *Settling with the Indians* 122n.

83. Relevant to my argument is Benedict Anderson's discussion of "creole nationalism" in *Imagined Communities* 47–65.

84. Donna B. Hamilton, *Virgil and The Tempest: The Politics of Imitation* (Columbus: Ohio State University Press, 1990) 55–66.

85. Brenner, *Merchants and Revolution* 199–239.
86. Qtd in Hamilton, *Virgil* 57. For similar comments, see Smith, *Description of New England* (*Complete Works* 1.349 and 1.360). William Wood, in *New England's Prospect* (1635), remarks: "there is as much freedom and liberty for servants [in the colonies] as in England and more too" (qtd. in David W. Galenson, *White Servitude in Colonial America* [Cambridge: Cambridge University Press, 1981] 10).
87. Walter Cohen notes the connection between the rhetoric of early promotional materials and later radical writers in *Drama of a Nation* 402.
88. Fitzmaurice, "The Civic Solution to the Crisis of English Colonization" 45.
89. After 1619, when Sir Edwin Sandys's "gentry party" wrested control of the Virginia Company from Sir Thomas Smythe's "merchant party," the leaders of the Company under the second charter were accused of having introduced a "slave" economy to Virginia: for discussion, see *CSP, Colonial Series, America and West Indies, 1574–1660* 39–40; Allen, *Invention of the White Race* 2.88 ff.; and Brenner, *Merchants and Revolution* 99 ff. Since the 1620s marked the ascendancy of an economy of indentured servants and vented laborers, the devastating effects of the Company's labor practices were elided through accusations against earlier officials such as Smythe, Gates, and Dale. During Sandys's tenure, the Company continued and even increased policies of transportation: for discussion, see Johnson, "Transportation."
90. See Greenblatt, "Martial Law" 149; Strachey, *True Report* 11.
91. *A Publication by the Counsell of Virginea, Touching the Plantation There* (ca. December 1609) [STC 24831.7]; *By the Counsell of Virginea* (publ. December 1610) [STC 24831.3]; *By the Counsell of Virginea* (publ. January 1611) [STC 24833.2]. These broadsides are reprinted in Brown, *Genesis of the United States* 1.354–56, 439, 445.
92. *A Publication by the Counsell of Virginea* (Brown, *Genesis of the United States* 1.355).
93. Although Smith's texts were often critical of Company leaders and at odds with official Company narratives, they seem to have been "neither resented nor disregarded" by company officials (Philip Barbour, *The Three Worlds of Captain John Smith* [Boston: Houghton Mifflin, 1964] 287). The Virginia Company even purchased copies of Smith's texts in 1623 (Barbour, *Complete Works of Captain John Smith* 1.125). Nonetheless, Smith repeatedly perceived himself as marginal, if not opposed, to Company policies: see, e.g., *A True Relation* (*Complete Works* 1.45).
94. Smith, *Complete Works* 1.176.
95. On Smith's ability to manipulate cultural codes, see Peter Hulme, *Colonial Encounters: Europe and the Native Caribbean, 1492–1797* (London and New York: Methuen, 1986) 153 ff. I borrow the term

"improvisation" from Greenblatt, *Renaissance Self-Fashioning* (Chicago: University of Chicago Press, 1980) 227–28.

96. For a discussion of gender and the Virginia colony, including the status of women transplanted to the colony, see Kathleen M. Brown, *Good Wives, Nasty Wenches, and Anxious Patriarchs: Gender, Race, and Power in Colonial Virginia* (Chapel Hill: University of North Carolina Press, 1996), esp. 80–104.

97. Smith, *The Proceedings of the English Colonie in Virginia* (1612) (*Complete Works* 1.238–39). The *Proceedings* was a text of corporate authorship; the chapter from which this passage is drawn is signed by Richard Wifflin, William Phettiplace, and Anas Todkill (238n.). Wifflin and Phettiplace are described as "gentlemen" in the text, while Todkill is classified as a carpenter, testifying to the cross-class alliances attempted by Company policy (208, 222).

98. Winthrop Jordan, *White over Black: American Attitudes toward the Negro, 1550–1812* (Chapel Hill: University of North Carolina Press, 1968) 53.

99. Kupperman, *Settling with the Indians* 139.

100. John Gillies, "Shakespeare's Virginian Masque," *ELH* 53 (1986): 679.

101. Peter Linebaugh and Marcus Rediker, *The Many-Headed Hydra: Sailors, Slaves, Commoners, and the Hidden History of the Revolutionary Atlantic* (Boston: Beacon Press, 2000) 22.

102. Knapp, *An Empire Nowhere* 221–22. On colonial husbandry, also see Linton, *Romance of the New World*, esp. 155–84.

103. Slack, *Poverty and Policy* 24.

104. Richard Eburne, *A Plain Pathway to Plantations*, ed. Louis B. Wright (Ithaca: Cornell University Press, 1962) 40.

105. Smith, *Complete Works* 1.347. Smith also adds: "here are no hard Landlords to racke us with high rents, or extorted fines to consume us" (1.332).

106. I will analyze another key example, Eburne's *A Plain Pathway to Plantations* (1624), in the conclusion.

107. Robert Johnson, *Nova Britannia* sig. D1v.

108. John White, *The Planters Plea* (1630) sig. F3.

109. Harris, *Foreign Bodies and the Body Politic* 13–14, 19–20.

110. John Donne, *The Sermons of John Donne*, 10 vols., ed. George R. Potter and Evelyn M. Simpson (Berkeley: University of California Press, 1962) 4.272.

111. Robert Gray, *A Good Speed to Virginia* sig. B3v. Patrick Copland borrows from this passage in his sermon, *Virginia's God be Thanked* (1622) sigs. E2v–E3.

112. Mary Poovey, *Making a Social Body: British Cultural Formation, 1830–1864* (Chicago: University of Chicago Press, 1995) 34.

113. Crashaw, *A Sermon Preached in London* sigs. E4v–F1.

114. By contrast, the Virginia Company's *A True and Sincere Declaration* (1610) feared that vented laborers would contaminate the colonial

environment: "and such as are the weedes and rancknesse of this land; who beeing the surfet, of an able, healthy, and composed body; must needes bee the poyson of one so tender, feeble, and yet vnformed" (sig. D3; Brown, *Genesis of the United States* 1.352).

115. Howard Mumford Jones, "The Colonial Impulse: An Analysis of the 'Promotion' Literature of Colonization," *Proceedings of the American Philosophical Society* 90 (1946): 133; Greenblatt, *Shakespearean Negotiations* 147.

116. There was a contemporary perception, in fact, that the market was glutted with promotional material: see, e.g., Brown, *Genesis of the United States* 1.321 and Hamor, *A True Discovrse of the Present Estate of Virginia* (1615) sig. A2.

117. A similar critique is made by Meredith Anne Skura in "Discourse and the Individual: The Case of Colonialism in *The Tempest*," *Shakespeare Quarterly* 40 (1989): 44.

118. Greenblatt, *Shakespearean Negotiations* 142–58. Greenblatt addresses issues of class struggle and rebellion much more directly in "Murdering Peasants: Status, Genre, and the Representation of Rebellion," in *Learning to Curse: Essays in Early Modern Culture* (New York and London: Routledge, 1990) 99–130.

119. For a similar point, see Richard Halpern's critique of New Historicist models of power in *The Poetics of Primitive Accumulation* 3.

120. Theodore Allen notes the frequency of changes in the terms of laborers' contracts of service (*The Invention of the White Race* 2.96–97), a contradiction of the protections ensured by the Statute of Artificers. The mutineers' fears concerning permanent detention in the Virginia colony were later realized, for until 1616 colonists were prohibited from returning voluntarily to England (Brown, *Genesis* 2.798).

121. Greenblatt's comments from his essay, "Invisible Bullets," exemplify the underlying limits to this argument, which fails to recognize the potential oppositionality or autonomy of class and cultural groups: "Thus the subversiveness that is genuine and radical . . . is at the same time contained by the power it would appear to threaten. Indeed the subversiveness is the very product of that power and furthers its ends" (*Shakespearean Negotiations* 30). For an insightful critique of the New Historicist emphasis on contained subversion, see Holstun, *Ehud's Dagger*, esp. 72–76.

122. Allen, *The Invention of the White Race* 2.107.

123. Qtd. in Morgan, *American Freedom* 128. Edward Maria Wingfield's "Discourse" (1608), a narrative account of the first year at Jamestown, similarly notes that "Wear this whipping, lawing, beating, and hanging in Virginia knowne in England I feare it would driue many well affected myndes from this honorable action of Virginia" (Philip Barbour, *The Jamestown Voyages Under the First Charter, 1606–1609*, 2 vols. [Cambridge: Cambridge University Press, 1969] 1.225).

124. Greenblatt, *Shakespearean Negotiations* 146; on Gates's pardoning of mutineers, see Strachey's *True Report* 30, 32, 37.

125. Brown, *Genesis of the United States* 2.1043. Promotional texts and Company records document a number of similar incidents. Strachey mentions near the end of his text a "Captain Davies" who had spread rumors about life in the Virginia colony (*True Report* 69). *A Publication by the Counsell of Virginea, Touching the Plantation There* (1610) reports how "unruly youths" sent to Virginia had stowed away and returned to England in November 1609: "(being of most leaud and bad condition) and such as no ground can hold" (Brown, *Genesis* 1.354). In *A Map of Virginia* (1612), Smith also attempts to counter the false reports circulated by elite adventurers who had returned to England (*Complete Works* 1.176).

126. Linebaugh and Rediker, *The Many-Headed Hydra* 356n.

127. Ibid., *passim.*

128. This text is published in Brown, *Genesis of the United States* 1.402–13.

129. No published text exists under this title. It is tempting to think that Strachey may be evading the issue by citing a phantom text. More likely, he is referring to the Company publication, *A True and Sincere Declaration* (Louis B. Wright, ed., *A Voyage to Virginia in 1609* [Charlottesville: University of Virginia Press, 1964] 65n.).

130. In Peter Force, ed., *Tracts and other Papers, Relating Principally to the Origin, Settlement, and Progress of the Colonies in North America*, volume 3 (Washington: William G. Force, 1844) 15. Derived from Strachey, this text, compiled by Sir Thomas Smythe and others, was entered for publication on November 8, 1610.

131. Compare, e.g., the images of georgic prosperity found in *The Tempest* 4.1.110–13 and Strachey, *True Report* 67–68.

132. Brown, "This thing of darkness" 64.

133. Among other accounts, see Hulme, *Colonial Encounters* 119; Brown, "This thing of darkness" 67; Greenblatt, "Martial Law" 144. As Knapp notes, the reapers constitute "the only image of laborers . . . in a Jacobean masque" (*An Empire Nowhere* 235).

134. Strachey, *True Report* 48; cf. "Letter of the Governor and Council of Virginia" (Brown, *Genesis of the United States* 1.410).

135. Texts written following the 1622 Virginia massacre, including those by Edward Waterhouse and Samuel Purchas, represent the Algonquians as violating their own land in order to negate their rights of possession (Hulme, *Colonial Encounters* 172–73; Linton, *Romance of the New World* 180–84).

136. Strachey, *True Report* 48; cf. "Letter of the Governor and Council of Virginia" (Brown, *Genesis* 1.410).

137. On "appropriation," see Max Weber, *The Theory of Social and Economic Organization*, ed. Talcott Parsons (New York: Oxford University Press, 1947) 40–45 and 139 ff. and *Economy and Society*

44, 75; for analysis, see John Torrance, *Estrangement, Alienation and Exploitation: A Sociological Approach to Historical Materialism* (New York: Columbia University Press, 1977) 163–64 and Beckles, *White Servitude* 76.

138. See, among other sources, Christopher Hill, *The Century of Revolution, 1603–1714* (New York: Norton, 1966) 43–46 and C.B. Macpherson, *The Political Theory of Possessive Individualism* (Oxford: Clarendon, 1962).

4 "COUNTERFEIT EGYPTIANS" AND IMAGINED BORDERS: JONSON'S *The Gypsies Metamorphosed* AND THE UNION OF THE REALMS

1. All references to *The Gypsies Metamorphosed* are from *Ben Jonson: The Complete Masques*, ed. Orgel.

2. On vagrancy and poverty in early modern England and Scotland, see especially Beier, *Masterless Men* and Paul Slack, *Poverty and Policy in Tudor and Stuart England* and *The English Poor Law, 1531–1782* (London: Macmillan, 1990). Linda Woodbridge surveys the critical controversies surrounding early modern vagrancy in *Vagrancy, Homelessness, and English Renaissance Literature* (Urbana: University of Illinois Press, 2001) 1–37 and 267–84.

3. On the Jacobean regulation of the Borders, see *The Register of the Privy Council of Scotland*, volumes 7–13 (Edinburgh: H.M. General Register House, 1885–96); Penry Williams, "The Northern Borderlands under the Stuarts," in H.E. Bell and R.L. Ollard, eds., *Historical Essays 1600–1750* (London: Adam & Charles Black, 1963) 1–17; Maurice Lee, Jr., *Government by Pen: Scotland under James VI and I* (Urbana: University of Illinois Press, 1980) 45–47, 72–74, 207–09; Levack, *The Formation of the British State* 190–93; Galloway, *The Union of England and Scotland* 65–68, 84–86, 142–43; George MacDonald Fraser, *The Steel Bonnets: The Story of the Anglo-Scottish Border Reivers* (London: Barrie and Jenkins, 1971) 357–81; Howard S. Reinmuth, Jr., "Border Society in Transition," *Early Stuart Studies* (Minneapolis: University of Minnesota Press, 1970) 231–50; Dennis Hay, "England, Scotland and Europe: The Problem of the Frontier," *Transactions of the Royal Historical Society*, 5th ser., 25 (1975): 77–91; Gordon Donaldson, "Foundations of Anglo-Scottish Union," in S.T. Bindoff et al., eds., *Elizabethan Government and Society* (London: Athlone Press, 1961) 282–314; D.H. Wilson, "King James I and Anglo-Scottish Unity," in W.H. Aiken and B.D. Henning, eds., *Conflict in Stuart England* (New York: New York University Press, 1960) 43–55.

4. Orgel gives the following casting: Captain (Buckingham); Second Gypsy (William, Baron Feilding, Buckingham's brother-in-law); Third Gypsy (the courtier Endymion Porter); Fourth Gypsy (John,

Viscount Purbeck, Buckingham's eldest brother); Fifth Gypsy (Sir Gervase Clifton, a baronet from a nearby Nottinghamshire family) (*Complete Masques* 495–96n.).

5. Dale B.J. Randall, *Jonson's Gypsies Unmasked* (Durham: Duke University Press, 1975).

6. Martin Butler, "'We are one mans all': Jonson's *The Gipsies Metamorphosed*," *Yearbook of English Studies* 21 (1991): 255. Jonson was paid an extraordinary £100 by Buckingham in advance of the performances and hoped to use Buckingham's patronage to earn a knighthood.

7. Ibid., 258. For a recent discussion of Jonson's masque in the context of the status of gypsies in early modern England, see Bryan Reynolds, *Becoming Criminal: Transversal Performance and Cultural Dissidence in Early Modern England* (Baltimore: Johns Hopkins University Press, 2002) 23–63.

8. Harrison, *Description of England* 183–84. Beier estimates that the number of vagrants rose from 15,000 in 1560 to 25,000 in 1640 (*Masterless Men* 16).

9. Jonathan Goldberg, *James I and the Politics of Literature*, rev. ed. (Stanford: Stanford University Press, 1989) 130.

10. For critical sources on the Jacobean Union of the Realms, see the introduction, note 37.

11. For sources on early modern nationhood, see the introduction, note 40.

12. Anderson, *Imagined Communities* 6.

13. Ibid., 7, 19. Claire McEachern similarly assesses the applicability of Anderson's thesis to the Union of the Realms in *The Poetics of English Nationhood* 158.

14. For example, see the counter-objections made by Thomas Egerton, Lord Ellesmere concerning the naturalization of the Scots (1609) as well as James's own remarks before Parliament (1607), in *Cobbett's Collection of State Trials*, ed. T.B. Howell (London: T.C. Hansard, 1816) 2.690, 120.

15. On Scottish nationalism, see Arthur H. Williamson, *Scottish National Consciousness in the Age of James VI* (Edinburgh: John Donald, 1979) and "Scotland, Antichrist and the Invention of Great Britain," in John Dwyer et al., eds., *New Perspectives on the Politics of Culture of Early Modern Scotland* (Edinburgh: John Donald, 1983) 34–58; C.V. Wedgwood, "Anglo-Scottish Relations, 1603–40," *Transactions of the Royal Historical Society* 32 (1950): 31–48.

16. Elliot, "A Europe of Composite Monarchies" 48–71.

17. Anderson, *Imagined Communities* 19. These questions were brought up particularly in *Calvin's Case*, which questioned whether the *post-nati*, Scots born after James's accession to the English throne, could inherit property in England: see Richard Marienstras, *New Perspectives on the Shakespearean World*, trans. Janet Lloyd (Cambridge: Cambridge University Press, 1985) 99–125 and McEachern, *The Poetics of English Nationhood* 148–55.

18. "A Proclamation for the uniting of England and Scotland" (May 19, 1603), in Larkin and Hughes, eds., *Stuart Royal Proclamations* 1.18.

19. "A Proclamation charging all Actors or partners in the incursion on the Borders, to resort to the Kings Commissioners at a day limited" (May 17, 1603), ibid., 1.16–18.

20. *Somers Tracts*, ed. Walter Scott, 13 vols. (London: T. Cadell and W. Davies, 1809) 2.62.

21. Ibid., 2.131.

22. Sir Francis Bacon, "A Draught of a Proclamation Touching his Majesty's Stile, prepared not used" (1604) (*Works*, ed. James Spedding, Robert Leslie Ellis, and Douglas Denon Heath, 14 vols. [London: Longmans, 1857–74] 10.236) and "Certain Articles or Considerations touching the Union of the Kingdoms of England and Scotland" (1604) (*Works* 10.223).

23. Ibid., 10.237.

24. Ibid., 10.221.

25. James I, *His Majesties Speech to both the Houses of Parliament, in his Highnesse great Chamber at Whitehall . . . the last day of March, 1607* (*Somers Tracts* 2.125–26).

26. Bacon, *Works* 10.228; on the terms "North-Britain" and "South-Britain," see 10.225.

27. On James's 1617 Progress to the North Country and Scotland, see R.T. Spence, "A Royal Progress in the North: James I at Carlisle Castle and the Feast of Brougham, August 1617," *Northern History* 27 (1991): 41–89.

28. Campion's masque, "The Ayres that were Sung and Played at Brougham Castle in Westmerland, in the Kings Entertainment" (1617), is reprinted in *The Works of Thomas Campion*, ed. Walter R. Davis (New York: Norton, 1970) 464–71.

29. Thomas Carew's *Coelum Britannicum* (1634) testifies to the continuing influence of Campion's depiction of gypsies, for the text also includes an antimasque of gypsies, who are presented as surprisingly docile and amenable to changes in fortune (Lindley, ed., *Court Masques* ll. 572–82).

30. Spence, "A Royal Progress" 84–85.

31. For discussion of Jonson in Scotland, see *The Register of the Privy Council of Scotland*, volume 11 [1616–19] (Edinburgh: H.M. Register House, 1894) clxii–clxv and *Ben Jonson*, ed. Herford and Simpson 1.73–74, 143, 150. Jonson refers to his lost travel narrative, "Discovery," in *The Underwood* 43: "An Execretion upon Vulcan" (*Ben Jonson*, ed. Herford, Simpson, and Simpson 8.207, 11.78). John Taylor, the water poet, had also visited Scotland in 1618, writing his text, *Taylors Penniless Pilgrimage*, based on his travels (*All the Workes of Iohn Taylor The Water Poet* [1630] sigs. M1v-N4v).

32. *Ben Jonson*, ed. Herford and Simpson 1.74n. and *Conversations* ll. 644–45 (Herford and Simpson 1.150).

33. Jonson had also written a poem, "On the Vnion," included among his *Epigrammes*: see *Ben Jonson*, ed. Herford, Simpson, and Simpson 8.28. Jennifer Brady argues that Jonson's early Jacobean writings show the influence of James's speeches on the Union, while his writings following the 1617 Progress demonstrate a hardening of his attitude toward the monarch: see "Jonson's 'To King James': Plain Speaking in the *Epigrammes* and the *Conversations*," *Studies in Philology* 82 (1985): 380–99.

34. Qtd. in Galloway, *The Union of England and Scotland* 40.

35. Marienstras, *New Perspectives on the Shakespearean World* 24.

36. For references to peripheral regions of Britain as colonized cultures, see Hill, *Change and Continuity* 3–47.

37. David MacRitchie, *Ancient and Modern Britons*, 2 vols. (London: Kegan Paul, Trench & co., 1884) 2.133. For a further discussion of James's policies toward regions of Scotland, see Ohlmeyer, "Civilizinge of those Rude Partes," in Canny, ed., *The Origins of Empire* 124–47.

38. James I, *The Political Works of James I*, ed. Charles Howard McIlwain (1918; Cambridge: Harvard University Press, 1965) 22.

39. The Statutes attempted to induce a gradual assimilation of the region by limiting retainers, suppressing the protection of vagrants and bards, and stipulating that leaders' children be educated in lowland Scotland; responsibility for the enforcement of these clauses, however, was left to the regional chiefs themselves (Maurice Lee, Jr., *Great Britain's Solomon: James VI and I in His Three Kingdoms* [Urbana: University of Illinois Press, 1990] 216; also see Ohlmeyer, "Civilizinge" 133).

40. On Jacobean policies toward the Highlands and Hebrides, see *Register of the Privy Council of Scotland*, volume 7 [1604–07] (Edinburgh: H.M. General Register House, 1885) lxxvii–lxxix and volume 8 [1607–10] (Edinburgh: H.M. General Register House, 1887) liii–lxvii; Lee, *Government by Pen* 10–12, 44–45, 75–82 and *Great Britain's Solomon* 196–232; Ohlmeyer, "Civilizinge" 124–47.

41. James I, *Political Works* 22.

42. In the first year of the Borders Commission, Scottish officials executed 59 persons (including 27 executed by Dunbar), banished 15, and outlawed 140; English officials executed 52 and outlawed 45 Borderers (Lee, *Government* 46).

43. Galloway, *The Union of England and Scotland* 65–68.

44. Williams, "The Northern Borderlands" 11–14.

45. Levack, *The Formation of the British State* 190.

46. Robert Pont, *Of the Union of Britayne* (1604), in Bruce Galloway and Brian Levack, eds., *The Jacobean Union: Six Tracts of 1604* (Edinburgh: Scottish Historical Society, 1985) 21–22. For a similar comment, see John Russell, *A Treatise of the Happie and Blessed Union* (1604) (Galloway and Levack 116–17).

47. *A Treatise about the Union of England and Scotland* (1604) (Galloway and Levack 61).

48. Qtd. in Lee, *Government* 73.

49. Said, *Orientalism* 226.

50. *Register of the Privy Council of Scotland* 8.86, 243.

51. Qtd. in Fraser, *The Steel Bonnets* 368.

52. *Register of the Privy Council of Scotland* 7.286.

53. Ibid., 8.278, 471, 846.

54. Larkin and Hughes, eds., *Stuart Royal Proclamations* 1.18–19.

55. Ibid., 1.64–66; quoted passage on 1.65. For discussion of the earl of Cumberland's motives, see Williams, "The Northern Borderlands" 6–7.

56. On the Grahams, see Williams, "The Northern Borderlands" 7–9; Fraser, *The Steel Bonnets* 366–73; Lee, *Great Britain's Solomon* 211–12.

57. "A Proclamation conteining the Kings Majesties pleasure concerning the apprehension of the Greames," July 22, 1614 (Larkin and Hughes, eds., *Stuart Royal Proclamations* 1.310–12).

58. "A Proclamation for the better and more peaceable government of the middle Shires of Northumberland, Cumberland, and Westmerland," December 23, 1617 (ibid., 1.374–80; quoted passage on 1.378).

59. See Angus Fraser, *The Gypsies* (Cambridge, MA: Blackwell, 1992) 140 and David MacRitchie, *Scottish Gypsies under the Stewarts* (Edinburgh: David Douglas, 1894) 100. This group had been apprehended by William Sinclair and pardoned only after their male leaders were executed; see notes 97–98.

60. Fraser, *The Gypsies* 118; MacRitchie, *Scottish Gypsies* 39. James may have given Faw this power only to ensure that some form of authority was maintained over the gypsies, disburdening the Scottish court from having to exercise control over these groups. The compromise was short-lived, though, for James revoked all privileges the following year (Fraser 119).

61. MacRitchie, *Scottish Gypsies* 51.

62. Judges, intro., *The Elizabethan Underworld* xxv.

63. Fraser, *The Gypsies* 133.

64. Randall, *Jonson's Gypsies Unmasked* 48.

65. Rid, *Martin Markall* (1610) (in Judges, *The Elizabethan Underworld* 421).

66. For analysis of Fletcher's play, see Rosemary Gaby, "Of Vagabonds and Commonwealths: *Beggars' Bush, A Jovial Crew,* and *The Sisters,*" *SEL* 34 (1994): 401–24.

67. For a similar example, see Rid's *Martin Markall* and its depiction of the realm of "Thievingen," discussed in the introduction.

68. *Register of the Privy Council of Scotland* 11.34.

69. See Larkin and Hughes, eds., *Stuart Royal Proclamations* 1.408, 434–35.

70. On James's correlation of absolutist monarchy with mobility, see Julie Robin Solomon, "Going Places: Absolutism and Movement in Shakespeare's *The Tempest,*" *Renaissance Drama* 22 (1991): 3–45. Jeffrey Knapp discusses the association of the post-Reformation

English nation with vagrancy in *Shakespeare's Tribe: Church, Nation, and Theater in Renaissance England* (Chicago: University of Chicago Press, 2002) 61–79.

71. Marienstras, *New Perspectives on the Shakespearean World* 24–25.

72. Judges, *The Elizabethan Underworld* 344.

73. Fraser, *The Gypsies* 137.

74. John Cowell, *The Interpreter: Or Booke Containing the Signification of Words* (1607) sig. Bb1.

75. Bacon, "A Speech used by Sir Francis Bacon, in the Lower House of Parliament, concerning the Article of Naturalization" (1607), *Works* 10.317. For analysis, see Marienstras, *New Perspectives on the Shakespearean World* 116.

76. For a discussion of local governance, see Braddick, *State Formation*.

77. On regulation of the Marches, see Steven G. Ellis, *Tudor Frontiers and Noble Power: The Making of the British State* (Oxford: Clarendon, 1995). The charter of the semiautonomous Palatinate of Durham served as the model for the government of the Maryland colony (Braddick, *State Formation* 40). For a discussion of palatinates and borderlands in early modern Ireland, see Baker, *Between Nations* 80–85.

78. See McEachern, *The Poetics of English Nationhood* 140–41 and Galloway, *The Union of England and Scotland* 82–84.

79. *Register of the Privy Council of Scotland* 7.381. This prohibition was repeated in 1620 (Wedgwood, "Anglo-Scottish Relations" 34).

80. Ibid., 7.544.

81. Richard Brome, *A Jovial Crew*, ed. Ann Haaker (Lincoln: University of Nebraska Press, 1968) 3.1.143.

82. *The Roxburghe Ballads*, ed. William Chappell (Hertford: Ballad Society, 1869 and 1875) 1:1.137–41 and 3:1.323–28; the quoted passage is from 3:1.327. In William Bullein's *A Dialogue...Against of the Fever Pestilence* (1573), a beggar from Northumberland describes how he was helped by a beadle, a fellow Northumbrian, upon his arrival in London (Andrew McRae, "The Peripatetic Muse: Internal Travel and the Cultural Production of Space in Pre-Revolutionary England," in Gerald Mclean et al., eds., *The Country and the City Revisited: England and the Politics of Culture, 1550–1850* [Cambridge: Cambridge University Press, 1997] 50).

83. Francis Osborne, *Traditional Memoyres on the Raigne of King James the First* (1658) 1.143, 254, 252, 254. Similar comments are made in another commonwealth-era anti-Jacobean text, Sir Anthony Weldon's "A Perfect Description of the People and Country of Scotland" (1659) (reprinted along with Osborne in *Secret History of the Court of James I*, ed. Walter Scott, volume 1 [Edinburgh and London: James Ballantyne and Co., 1811]). On James's Scottish courtiers in England, see Keith M. Brown, "The Scottish Aristocracy, Anglicization and the Court, 1603–38," *The Historical Journal* 36 (1993): 543–76.

84. Titus Tatius [pseudonym for Sir J. Skinner], *Rapta Tatio* (1604) sig. D4.

85. Among other Jacobean-era examples, a ballad of "Poor Sisley" described a woman's Scottish suitor, "a poor Scot that can do nought but beg," while another ballad commented, "Our Scottishmen are beggars yet" (C.H. Firth, "The Ballad History of the Reign of James I," *Transactions of the Royal Historical Society*, 3rd ser., 5 [1911]: 24). Firth cites other ballads, including those repeated by Osborne, in "Ballads Illustrating the Relations of England and Scotland During the Seventeenth Century," *Scottish Historical Review* 6 (1908–09): 113–28. For other examples, see Donna B. Hamilton, "*The Winter's Tale* and the Language of Union, 1604–1610," *Shakespeare Studies* 21 (1993): 243–44.

86. *State Trials* 2.640.

87. Randall, *Jonson's Gypsies Unmasked* 48.

88. For a list of statutes, see J. Thomas Kelly, *Thorns on the Tudor Rose: Monks, Rogues, Vagabonds, and Sturdy Beggars* (Jackson: University of Mississippi Press, 1977) 148–60 and C.J. Ribton-Turner, *A History of Vagrants and Vagrancy* (1887; Montclair, NJ: Patterson Smith, 1972) 677–80, 687–88.

89. See Fraser, *The Gypsies* 114–15 and Beier, *Masterless Men, passim*. Statutes specifically targeting gypsies were passed in England in 1530, 1554, and 1562 (Kelly, *Thorns on the Tudor Rose* 148–50).

90. Ribton-Turner, *A History of Vagrants and Vagrancy* 90. On the 1547 statute, see chapter 3, note 36.

91. See MacRitchie, *Scottish Gypsies* 63–85 and Ribton-Turner, *A History of Vagrants and Vagrancy* 344, 687.

92. Brian Vesey-Fitzgerald, *The Gypsies of Britain* (London: the Country Book Club, 1951) 21; Fraser, *The Gypsies* 112–13, 118.

93. Father Richard Augustine Hay, *Genealogie of the Saintclares of Rosslyn*, qtd. in MacRitchie, *Scottish Gypsies* 56.

94. MacRitchie, *Scottish Gypsies* 57. On popular appropriations and subversive uses of the Robin Hood legend in the early modern period, see Hill, *Liberty Against the Law* 71–82.

95. Donaldson, "Foundations of Anglo-Scottish Union" 301.

96. For early examples and records associating gypsies with the Morris dance, see MacRitchie, *Scottish Gypsies* 25–26.

97. *The Register of the Privy Council of Scotland*, volume 13 [1624] (H.M. General Register House, 1896) 295, 813.

98. MacRitchie, *Scottish Gypsies* 94, 99; *Register of the Privy Council of Scotland* 13.410 and volume 10 [1616] (H.M. General Register House, 1891) 655.

99. Peter Roberts explores the relation of anti-vagrant legislation to the emerging professionalization of English players in "Elizabethan Players and Minstrels in the Legislation of 1572 Against Retainers and Vagabonds," in Anthony Fletcher and Peter Roberts, eds., *Religion, Culture, and Society in Early Modern Britain* (Cambridge: Cambridge University Press, 1994) 29–55.

100. Qtd. in Fraser, *The Gypsies* 117.

101. Leah Marcus, *The Politics of Mirth: Jonson, Herrick, Milton, Marvell, and the Defense of Old Holiday Pastimes* (Chicago: University of Chicago Press, 1986) 25.

102. The 1597 Act largely repeats an earlier proclamation, "An Acte for the Punishement of Vacabondes, and for Releif [*sic*] of the Poore and Impotent" (14 Elizabeth, c. 5) (1572). Whereas the earlier statute had set an important precedent by recasting the need of the poor as "counterfeit," I have quoted from the 1597 Act because it more specifically targets gypsies as a counterfeit identity: see Tawney and Power, eds., *Tudor Economic Documents* 2.355.

103. Patricia Fumerton, "London's Vagrant Economy: Making Space for 'Low' Subjectivity," in Lena Cowen Orlin, ed., *Material London, ca. 1600* (Philadelphia: University of Pennsylvania Press, 2000) 206–25.

104. A comparable example is provided by Shakespeare's Pistol, who declares his intention following Henry's campaign in France to return to England and become, alternately, a bawd, a cutpurse, and a beggar with counterfeit war injuries (5.1.85–89). Deprived of his (often illegal) income as a soldier, and having lost his wife and friends, Pistol likewise demonstrates an ability to adapt as a result of necessity.

105. Tawney and Power, eds., *Tudor Economic Documents* 2.355. As will be discussed later, gypsies could similarly evade punishment by entering the service of a nobleman.

106. Ibid., 2.355. For a similar comment, see Samuel Rid, *The Art of Jugling or Legerdemaine* (1612) sig. B2.

107. Jean Baudrillard, *Simulations* (New York: Semiotext(e), 1983) 5. On "simulation" and "dissimulation" in relation to the status of sturdy beggars, see Carroll, *Fat King, Lean Beggar*.

108. Ibid., 83–92.

109. Tawney and Power, eds., *Tudor Economic Documents* 2.328; for analysis, see Barbara A. Mowat, "Rogues, Shepherds, and the Counterfeit Distressed: Texts and Intracontexts of *The Winter's Tale* 4.3," *Shakespeare Studies* 22 (1994): 65. This legislation supports what A.L. Beier has described as the "desanctification" of the poor (*Masterless Men* 4–7); for a related discussion, see Mark Koch, "The Desanctification of the Beggar in Rogue Pamphlets of the English Renaissance," in David G. Allen and Robert A. White, eds., *The Work of Dissimilitude* (Newark: University of Delaware Press, 1992) 91–104.

110. The anthropologist Judith Okely similarly notes the widespread self-differentiation among late twentieth-century gypsies between those born as travelers, those with a gorgio (non-gypsy) parent, and those who joined gypsy society ("Gypsies Travelling in Southern England," in Farnham Rehfisch, ed., *Gypsies, Tinkers and other Travellers* [London: Academic Press, 1975] 60–66; also see Okely's *The Traveller-Gypsies* [Cambridge: Cambridge University Press, 1983]).

111. Rid's chronology is supported by discussions of proto-capitalist social relations in the late medieval period: see Wallerstein, *The Modern World-System* 1.15–63 and Robert Brenner, "The Agrarian Roots of European Capitalism," in *The Brenner Debate* 213–327.

112. Judges, *The Elizabethan Underworld* 420–21.

113. The first reference to Cock Lorel (or Cock-lorrel) occurs in Wynkyn de Worde's *Cocke Lorelles Bote* (ca. 1510), in which he is described as neither a vagrant or gypsy. Giles Hatcher first appears as a vagrant—not a gypsy—in Awdeley's *Fraternity of Vagabonds* (1575), while the name Kit Callot might have an even earlier origin, perhaps derived from a conflation of the names of Piers's wife and daughter in *Piers Plowman* (Randall, *Jonson's Gypsies Unmasked* 58–60; Judges, *Elizabethan Underworld* 34n. 516–17).

114. For an expanded discussion of the connection of gypsies with personal liberties, see Christopher Hill, *Liberty Against the Law* 131–41.

115. *The Works of Thomas Middleton*, ed. A.H. Bullen, volume 6 (New York: AMS Press, 1964) 2.1.6–11, 38–39. All further references to Middleton's plays are from this series.

116. Beier notes that most of those arrested for vagrancy before 1620 traveled singly or in pairs (*Masterless Men* 57). For a contrary argument analyzing the existence of a criminal subculture in early modern England, see Reynolds, *Becoming Criminal.*

117. MacRitchie, *Scottish Gypsies* 80; also see *Register of the Privy Council of Scotland* 10.656. The Act of June 1609 ratified a 1603 Privy Council decision; for analysis, see Randall, *Jonson's Gypsies Unmasked* 55–56.

118. *Register of the Privy Council of Scotland*, volume 12 [1619–22] (Edinburgh: H.M. Register House, 1895) 3–4.

119. Ibid., 13.415.

120. Ibid., 13.410.

121. J.A. Sharpe, *Crime in Early Modern England 1550–1750*, 2nd edition (1984; London: Longman, 1999) 146.

122. *Register of the Privy Council of Scotland* 7.434.

123. Lindley, ed., *Court Masques* 1. 75.

124. *Register of the Privy Council of Scotland* 7.749.

125. MacRitchie, *Scottish Gypsies* 80

126. *Register of the Privy Council of Scotland* 10.656–57. This statute was reinforced in 1620, when the Privy Council began to institute forms of surveillance against the gentry, employing informers and commissioners to oversee those among their own officers who refused to act against the gypsies (*Register* 12.312–15).

127. Ibid., 7.372, 712.

128. Ibid., volume 9 [1610–13] (Edinburgh: H.M. General Register House, 1889) 171, 205. MacRitchie cites a late seventeenth-century document that erroneously notes Faw's execution in July 1611 (*Scottish Gypsies* 84).

129. MacRitchie, *Scottish Gypsies* 101.

130. Qtd. in *Register of the Privy Council of Scotland* 7.xxxviii. Piggot also distances James from his Scottish origins, describing how "our king hath hardly escaped" his Scottish assassins and, by extension, his native countrymen in general (xxxviii). Regardless of this defense of James, Piggot was expelled from the House of Commons and his seat declared vacant (xxxix).

131. For representations of the supposedly polygamous sexual customs of gypsies, see Thomas Harman's *A Caveat for Common Cursitors* (1566) (Judges, *Elizabethan Underworld* 70, 94, 98, 99, 105, 107, 108) and Thomas Dekker's *Lantern and Candlelight* (1608) (Judges 346).

132. For a discussion of gypsies in relation to this play, see Charles Whitney, "Charmian's Laughter: Women, Gypsies, and Festive Ambivalence in *Antony and Cleopatra*," *The Upstart Crow* 14 (1994): 67–88.

133. Judges, *Elizabethan Underworld* 100, 101–05. For a discussion of images of vagrant women inverting these exploitative social relations, see Pamela Brown, "Laughing at the Cony: A Female Rogue and 'The Verdict of the Smock,'" *ELR* 29 (1999): 201–24.

134. Randall, *Jonson's Gypsies Unmasked* 69.

135. *Tom Tell-Troath*, in *Harleian Miscellany* 2 (1809): 435.

136. On the association of homosexuality with counterfeiting, see Will Fisher, "Queer Money," *ELH* 66 (1999): 1–23; on the link to *Basilikon Doron*, see Fisher 2.

137. Alan Bray, "Homosexuality and the Signs of Male Friendship in Elizabethan England," *History Workshop* 29 (1990): 1–19.

138. As evidence of the text's anti-Jacobean potential, William Drummond later used the refrain from this song in an attack on the king entitled "The Five Senses"; the poem remained unpublished until 1711 (*Ben Jonson*, ed. Herford, Simpson, and Simpson 10.631n.).

139. Randall, *Jonson's Gypsies Unmasked* 69n., 40–41, 12.

140. MacRitchie, *Scottish Gypsies* 73 [italics in text].

141. Judges, *The Elizabethan Underworld* 344.

142. Sir Thomas Browne, "Of Gypsies," *Pseudodoxia Epidemica* (1646) 6.13 (*The Works of Sir Thomas Browne*, vol. 2, ed. Geoffrey Keynes [Chicago: University of Chicago Press, 1964] 481–82).

143. Coryat, *Crudities* 1.200.

144. Hakluyt, *Principal Navigations*, 3 vols. (1598–1600), rpt. 8 vols. (New York: Dent, 1927) 3.324.

145. George Abbot, *A Briefe Description of the Whole Worlde* (1634) sig. G8v. For other examples demonstrating how gypsies' exotic appearance was believed to be counterfeit—and potentially imitated by English vagrants through blackface—see Fynes Moryson, *Itinerary* (1617; Glasgow: MacLehose, 1907) 1.79, 422–23; Middleton, *More Dissemblers Besides Women* (1615) 4.1.214; and *The Spanish Gypsy* (1623) 2.1.6–9.

146. David Lindley, "Embarrassing Ben: The Masques for Frances Howard," *ELR* 16 (1986): 357.

147. Bhabha, "DissemiNation," *The Location of Culture* 139.

148. Ibid., 150.

149. Victor Turner, *Dramas, Fields, and Metaphors: Symbolic Action in Human Society* (Ithaca: Cornell University Press, 1974) 232.

150. Mary Douglas, *Purity and Danger: An Analysis of Concepts of Pollution and Taboo* (New York: Praeger, 1966) 96.

151. Ibid., 122.

152. Bacon, "A Draught of a Proclamation Touching his Majesty's Stile, prepared not used" (1604) (*Works* 10.238).

5 FORGETTING THE ULSTER PLANTATION:
JOHN SPEED'S *The Theatre of the Empire of Great Britain* (1611) AND THE COLONIAL ARCHIVE

1. PRO, SP 45/20/ff. 62–66; *Calendar of State Papers, Relating to Ireland, of the Reign of James I, 1603–1606* (Nendeln, Liechtenstein: Kraus, 1974) xx–xxi [hereafter referred to as *CSP, Ire.*].

2. PRO, SP 45/20/f. 73; *CSP, Ire., 1603–1606* xxi.

3. PRO, SP 45/20/f. 56. Also see W. Noel Sainsbury, ed., "Calendar of Documents Relating to the History of the State Paper Office to the Year 1800," *Annual Report of the Deputy Keeper of the Public Records* (London, 1869) 212, 229.

4. See Thomas Powell, *Direction for Search of Records Remaining in the Chancerie. Tower. Exchequer, with the Limne Thereof* (1623) and Powell and Arthur Agard, *The Repertorie of Records* (1631). Spenser cites a document from Tower records in *A View of the Present State of Ireland* (ca. 1596, publ. 1633), ed. Andrew Hadfield and Willy Maley (Oxford: Blackwell, 1997) 67.

5. See F. Smith Fussner, *The Historical Revolution: English Historical Writing and Thought, 1580–1640* (New York: Routledge and Paul, 1962) 77 and 92 and John Kenyon, *The History Men: The Historical Profession in England since the Renaissance* (London: Weidenfeld and Nicolson, 1983) 89–92.

6. The most detailed account of the Ulster plantation remains George Hill's *An Historical Account of the Plantation in Ulster at the Commencement of the Seventeenth Century, 1608–1620* (1877; Shannon: Irish University Press, 1970). Useful general accounts also include Aidan Clarke, "Pacification, Plantation, and the Catholic Question, 1603–23," in T.W. Moody et al., eds., *A New History of Ireland, Volume 3: Early Modern Ireland, 1534–1691* (Oxford: Clarendon Press, 1984) 187–232; Philip Robinson, *The Plantation of Ulster* (New York: St. Martin's Press, 1984); Richard Bagwell, *Ireland under the Stuarts*, volume 1 (1908; London: Holland Press, 1963); Jonathan Bardon, *A History of Ulster* (Belfast: Blackstaff Press, 1992) 115–47.

7. On the use of historical memory to consolidate class relations and a racialized separation of communities in Northern Ireland, see Nairn, *The Break-Up of Britain* 216–55 and Allen, *The Invention of the White Race* 1.115–35.

8. The Ulster plantation remains omitted from many state-sponsored narratives of Ulster history, including the Ulster Museum, the self-described "national museum for Northern Ireland," which barely mentions the early plantation era (Richard Kirkland, *Literature and Culture in Northern Ireland Since 1965: Moments of Danger* [New York: Longman, 1996] 1–3).

9. Pocock, "British History: A Plea for a New Subject" 611.

10. On Munster, see Michael MacCarthy-Morrogh, *The Munster Plantation: English Migration to Southern Ireland, 1583–1641* (Oxford: Oxford University Press, 1986).

11. On Spenser's influence on English colonialism in the seventeenth century, see Nicholas Canny, "Identity Formation in Ireland: The Emergence of the Anglo-Irish," in Nicholas Canny and Anthony Pagden, eds., *Colonial Identity in the Atlantic World, 1500–1800* (Princeton: Princeton University Press, 1987) 159–212; Willy Maley, "How Milton and Some Contemporaries Read Spenser's *View*," in Brendan Bradshaw, Andrew Hadfield, and Willy Maley, eds., *Representing Ireland: Literature and the Origins of Conflict, 1534–1660* (Cambridge: Cambridge University Press, 1993) 191–208, reprinted in his *Salvaging Spenser* 118–35; and Baker, *Between Nations* 116–23.

12. Bacon, "Certain Considerations Touching the Plantation in Ireland, Presented to His Majesty, 1606," in *Works* 11.123. Lord Deputy Sir Arthur Chichester made a similar comment to support the "seriousness" of the Ulster plantation: "I had rather labour with my hands in the plantation of Ulster, than dance or play in that of Virginia" (*CSP, Ire., 1608–1610* 520).

13. This passage is taken from the first English translation of Camden's *Britannia*, entitled *Britain, or A Chorographicall Description of the Most Flourishing Kingdomes, England, Scotland, and Ireland, and the Ilands Adioyning, out of the Depth of Antiqvitie*, trans. Philemon Holland (1610) sig. ¶4.

14. Camden dismisses such myths of origin as England's Brutus (*Britain* sig. A4) and Scotland's Scota (sigs. A4, K4). For positive appraisals of Camden's pragmatic historical methodology, see Fussner, *Historical Revolution* 230–52 and Hugh Trevor-Roper, *Queen Elizabeth's First Historian: William Camden and the Beginnings of English "Civil History"* (London: Jonathan Cape, 1971).

15. *Britain* sig. ¶4. Like Camden, Speed reproduces Roman coins and inscriptions in the narrative companion volume to his *Theatre*, *The Historie of Great Britaine* 172–77.

16. Michel Foucault, *The Archaeology of Knowledge and the Discourse on Language*, trans. A.M. Sheridan Smith (New York: Pantheon, 1972) 7.

17. Ibid., 7 [italics in text]. My discussion of how emergent forms of knowledge production displaced an emphasis on historical memory is influenced by Frances A. Yates, *The Art of Memory* (Chicago: University of Chicago Press, 1966), esp. 368–89. For an analysis of memory and early modern cartography, see Rhonda Lemke Sanford, *Maps and Memory in Early Modern England: A Sense of Place* (New York: Palgrave, 2002).

18. Michel de Certeau, *The Writing of History*, trans. Tom Conley (New York: Columbia University Press, 1988) 5 [italics in text].

19. For a similar argument, see Michel-Rolph Trouillot, *Silencing the Past: Power and the Production of History* (Boston: Beacon Press, 1995) 52.

20. My discussion is indebted to Dominick LaCapra, *Rethinking Intellectual History: Texts, Contexts, Language* (Ithaca: Cornell University Press, 1983) 31 and Gayatri Chakravorty Spivak, "The Rani of Sirmur," in *Europe and its Others, Volume One*, Francis Barker et al., eds. (Colchester: University of Essex Press, 1985) 130. Among other discussions of the archive and knowledge production, see Thomas Richards, *The Imperial Archive: Knowledge and the Fantasy of Empire* (London: Verso, 1993); Jacques Derrida, *Archive Fever: A Freudian Impression* (Chicago: University of Chicago Press, 1996); and Siân Echard, "House Arrest: Modern Archives, Medieval Manuscripts," *Journal of Medieval and Early Modern Studies* 30 (2000): 185–210.

21. Although I follow conventional usage by giving the date of Speed's texts as 1611, the title pages of Books III and IV of the *Theatre* are dated 1612, when Speed's texts were finally published, while Speed's maps of Ireland were engraved in 1610: see R.A. Skelton, *County Atlases of the British Isles, 1579–1850* (1970; Folkstone, Kent: Dawson, 1978) 31–33.

22. Speed himself frequently acknowledges his debt to Camden: see *The Theatre of the Empire of Great Britain* sig. ¶3 and *Historie of Great Britaine* 897.

23. For discussions of Speed and early modern cartography, see J.H. Andrews, *Shapes of Ireland: Maps and Their Makers, 1564–1839* (Dublin: Geography Publications, 1997) 89–117; Bernhard Klein, *Maps and the Writing of Space in Early Modern England and Ireland* (New York: Palgrave, 2001) 105–11, 122; Christopher Ivic, "Mapping British Identities: Speed's *Theatre of the Empire of Great Britaine*," in Baker and Maley, eds., *British Identities and English Renaissance Literature* 135–55; E.G.R. Taylor, *Late Tudor and Early Stuart Geography, 1583–1650* (London: Methuen, 1934) 49–51; and R.V. Tooley, *Maps and Map-Makers*, 6th ed. (London: Batsford, 1978) 52, 68–70, 84, 92–93. On Speed and Renaissance historiography, see D.R. Woolf, *The Idea of History in Early Stuart England* (Toronto: University of Toronto Press, 1990) 64–72; Stan A.E. Mendyk, *Speculum Britanniae: Regional Study, Antiquarianism, and Science in Britain to 1700* (Toronto: University of Toronto Press,

1989) 78–81; and F.J. Levy, *Tudor Historical Thought* (San Marino, CA: Huntington Library, 1967) 196–99.

24. See James R. Akerman, "The Structuring of Political Territory in Early Printed Atlases," *Imago Mundi* 47 (1995): 138–54.

25. "A Proclamation concerning the Kings Majesties Stile, of King of Great Britaine, &c." (October 20, 1604), in Larkin and Hughes, eds., *Stuart Royal Proclamations* 1.97.

26. Speed, *Theatre* sig. A2v. Speed's maps are reproduced in Alasdair Hawkyard, ed., *The Counties of Britain: A Tudor Atlas by John Speed*, intro. Nigel Nicolson (London: Pavilion, 1988). Spenser discusses Edward the Bruce's status as king of Ireland, thus acknowledging precedents for Irish unity, in *A View of the Present State of Ireland* 25–28.

27. For further discussion of the use of Roman colonization as a precedent for English colonial policy, see the introduction.

28. William Strachey, *The Historie of Travell into Virginia Britania* (1612), ed. Louis B. Wright and Virginia Freund (London: Hakluyt Society, 1953) 24.

29. Camden, *Britain* (1610) sig. Ffff3v.

30. De Certeau, *The Writing of History* 4.

31. For a similar construction of memory and forgetting, see Ernest Renan's "What is a Nation?" (1882), in *The Nationalism Reader*, Omar Dahbour and Micheline R. Ishay, eds. (Atlantic Highlands, NJ: Humanities Press, 1995) 145. Anderson analyzes Renan's essay in *Imagined Communities* 199–201.

32. Bhabha, "DissemiNation," *The Location of Culture* 145.

33. Part of the fashioning of James's "British" kingdom also emphasized the Gaelic roots of his title; for discussions, see Michael J. Enright, "King James and His Island: an Archaic Kingship Belief?" *Scottish Historical Review* 55 (1976): 29–40 and Breandán Ó Buachalla, "James our True King: The Ideology of Irish Royalism in the Seventeenth Century," in *Political Thought in Ireland Since the Seventeenth Century*, ed. D. George Boyce, Robert Eccleshall, and Vincent Geoghegan (New York: Routledge, 1993) 11.

34. *OED* notes the contemporary use of both of these senses of "ancient": "belonging to time past" (I.1.a) and "of early origin or formation" (II.4.a).

35. Knapp, *An Empire Nowhere, passim.*

36. On the multiple affiliations of "British" subjects, see McEachern, *The Poetics of English Nationhood* 138–91 and Baker, *Between Nations.*

37. Mason, "The Scottish Reformation and the Origins of Anglo-British Imperialism," in Mason, ed., *Scots and Britons* 161–86; Armitage, "Literature and Empire," in Canny, ed., *The Origins of Empire* 113–14.

38. Canny discusses the incomplete nature of this assimilation, analyzing how Scottish undertakers segregated themselves within their own enclaves in Ulster ("The Origins of Empire: an Introduction," in

The Origins of Empire 1–32). On Scottish immigrants in Ulster, see M. Perceval-Maxwell, *The Scottish Migration to Ulster in the Reign of James I* (London: Routledge & Kegan Paul, 1973) and Raymond Gillespie, *Colonial Ulster: The Settlement of East Ulster, 1600–1641* (Cork: Cork University Press, 1985).

39. Renan, "What is a Nation?" 145.
40. For a discussion of the role of Ulster in Anglo-Scottish relations, see David Armitage, "Making the Empire British: Scotland in the Atlantic World, 1542–1707," *Past and Present* 155 (1997): 34–63. On early modern connections between Ulster and Scotland, see Maley, *Salvaging Spenser* 136–62; Spenser notes the historical foundations of this link in *A View of the Present State of Ireland* 45, 110–11.
41. Eric Hobsbawm, "Introduction: Inventing Traditions," in Hobsbawm and Terence Ranger, eds., *The Invention of Tradition* (Cambridge: Cambridge University Press, 1983) 1–14.
42. Ernest Gellner, *Nations and Nationalism* (Oxford: Blackwell, 1983) 49.
43. Hechter, *Internal Colonialism* xxi.
44. Speed's main sources were Camden's *Britannia* (1586), Mercator's *Ultoniae orientalis pars* (1595), and, especially, the manuscript maps of Francis Jobson, who was commissioned to survey central Ulster in 1590–91 following O'Neill's surrender at the end of the Desmond Rebellion of 1584–89 (Andrews, *Shapes of Ireland* 103, 107, 109).
45. See Andrews, *Shapes of Ireland*, chapters 2–3. For discussions of the Irish maps that preceded Speed's, see Klein, *Maps and the Writing of Space* and "Partial Views: Shakespeare and the Map of Ireland," *Early Modern Literary Studies* 4, 2 (September 1998): 5.1–17; Mercedes Maroto Camino, " 'Methinks I see an Evil Lurk Unespied': Visualizing Conquest in Spenser's *A View of the Present State of Ireland*," *Spenser Studies* 12 (1998): 169–94.
46. Andrews, *Shapes of Ireland* 89, 103; Hawkyard, *Counties of Britain* 269. On Bartlett's maps of Ulster, see G.A. Hayes-McCoy, *Ulster and other Irish Maps, c. 1600* (Dublin: Irish Manuscripts Commission, 1964); for analysis, see Michael Neill, *Putting History to the Question: Power, Politics and Society in English Renaissance Drama* (New York: Columbia University Press, 2000) 393–96 and Klein, *Maps and the Writing of Space* 125–27.
47. *CSP, Ire., 1608–1610* 280. In a 1609 letter to the earl of Salisbury, Davies described Ulster as "heretofore as unknown to the English here as the most inland part of Virginia is yet unknown to our English colony there" but through recent maps now "laid open to all posterity" (*Calendar of the Manuscripts of the Most Honourable the Marquess of Salisbury Preserved at Hatfield House, Part XXI (1609–1612)* [London: H.M. Stationery Office, 1970] 121).
48. On the Nine Years' War in the context of Irish politics, see Hiram Morgan, *Tyrone's Rebellion: The Outbreak of the Nine Years War in*

Tudor Ireland (Woodbridge, Suffolk: Boydell Press, 1993); on the war's effect on England, see John McGurk, *The Elizabethan Conquest of Ireland: The 1590s Crisis* (Manchester: Manchester University Press, 1997).

49. Qtd. in Ó Buachalla, "James our True King" 10. James Ware uses similar language in his 1633 preface to Spenser's *A View of the Present State of Ireland* (6).

50. Ó Buachalla, "James our True King" 9.

51. As Andrews notes, these forts, many of which were built from 1600–03, are the most contemporary details recorded by Speed (*Shapes of Ireland* 107). In Spenser's *View*, the plans for the military occupation of Ulster are famously outlined through reference to a map of Ireland (96).

52. Morgan, *Tyrone's Rebellion* 139–66.

53. British Library, Cotton MS. Augustus I.ii.39.

54. Michel Foucault, "Questions on Geography," *Power/Knowledge: Selected Interviews and Other Writings, 1972–1977*, ed. Colin Gordon (New York: Pantheon, 1980) 69.

55. Quinn includes plates of another of Thomas's sketches, of a battle at Ballyshannon in 1593, in *The Elizabethans and the Irish*, plates 20, 24.

56. Historians of cartography have previously noted Speed's debt to Thomas's sketch and attributed this influence to Speed's consultation of Cotton's library: see R.A. Skeleton, "Tudor Town Plans in John Speed's *Theatre*," *Archaeological Journal* 108 (1951): 113 and J.H. Andrews, *Shapes of Ireland* 30n. 116.

57. See Wilson's letter to Cotton, ca. 1611–12, asking for the return of materials (British Library, Cotton MS. Julius.C.III. f.87). On Cotton's collecting habits, see Kevin Sharpe, *Sir Robert Cotton, 1586–1631: History and Politics in Early Modern England* (Oxford: Oxford University Press, 1979) 65, 80, 92 and *Annual Report of the Deputy Keeper* 226, 237–38, 240.

58. Fussner, *The Historical Revolution* 77; *Annual Report of the Deputy Keeper* 229.

59. On the Society of Antiquaries, see Joan Evans, *A History of the Society of Antiquaries* (Oxford: Oxford University Press, 1956) 1–32 and Linda Van Norden, "Sir Henry Spelman on the Chronology of the Elizabethan College of Antiquaries," *Huntington Library Quarterly* 13/14 (1949/50): 131–60. On Cotton's role in the Society and his patronage of Speed, see Sharpe, *Sir Robert Cotton* 37–39, 54. For a discussion of the Society's influence on Spenser's writings on Ireland, see Bart Van Es, "Discourses of Conquest: *The Faerie Queene*, the Society of Antiquaries, and *A View of the Present State of Ireland*," *ELR* 32 (2002): 118–51.

60. Speed, *Historie of Great Britaine* [1241]; Speed's letters to Cotton are reproduced in Sir Henry Ellis, ed., *Original Letters of Eminent Literary Men* (London: Camden Society, 1843) 108–13.

61. *CSP, Ire., 1603–1606* xxxix.

62. For a contemporary account, see *Later Newes from Ireland. Concerning the Late Treacherous Action, and Rebellion, of Sir Carey Adoughertie* (1608).

63. Sir Niall Garve O'Donnell, the Tyrconnell heir, was imprisoned in the Tower after Irish juries refused to convict him of treason; he died in prison in 1626. Tyrone's brother, Sir Cormac O'Neill, left as custodian of Tyrone's lands after the Flight of the Earls, was imprisoned despite informing Chichester of Tyrone's self-imposed exile. Tyrone's son, Con O'Neill, was actually seized from Eton and taken to the Tower (Hill, *Plantation in Ulster* 60–64).

64. On the London companies' plantation, see T.W. Moody, *The Londonderry Plantation, 1609–1641: The City of London and the Plantation in Ulster* (Belfast: Mullan, 1939) and James Stevens Curl, *The Londonderry Plantation, 1609–1914* (Chichester, Sussex: Phillimore, 1986); documents relating to the plantation are reprinted in T.W. Moody and J.G. Simms, eds., *The Bishopric of Derry and the Irish Society of London*, 2 vols. (Dublin: Irish Manuscripts Commission, 1968) and *Londonderry and the London Companies, 1609–1629. Being a Survey and Other Documents Submitted to King Charles I by Sir Thomas Phillips* (Belfast: H.M. Stationery Office, 1928).

65. Moody, *A New History of Ireland* 3.223; Hill, *Plantation in Ulster* 37 and 51–52.

66. Moody, *A New History of Ireland* 3.202. Of the 280 Irish landowners who were granted estates, only 26 of these individuals received 1,000 acres or more, estates comparable in size to those granted to English and Scottish undertakers. But these lands were most often not in grantees' home districts, enabling the English government to resettle O'Donnells and O'Neills far from Tyrconnell and Tyrone. Many of these leases also expired with the death of the grantee, allowing for future legal expropriation of additional territory. This latter practice demonstrates an early example of what came to be known as the "Ulster custom," restrictions in Catholic leasing that abetted the geographic segregation of the province (Robinson, *The Plantation of Ulster*, 75–77; for a list of Irish grantees, see Robinson 199–201 and Allen, *The Invention of the White Race* 1.121–24, 129–33).

67. See J.H. Andrews, *Plantation Acres: An Historical Study of the Irish Land Surveyor and His Maps* (Belfast: Ulster Historical Foundation, 1985). For discussions of practices of surveying in England, see McRae, *God Speed the Plough* 169–97; Sullivan, *The Drama of Landscape*; Klein, *Maps and the Writing of Space* 42–60; and Henry S. Turner, "Plotting Early Modernity," in Turner, ed., *The Culture of Capital* 85–127.

68. On the "scientific" claims of cartography, see Howard Marchitello, *Narrative and Meaning in Early Modern England* (Cambridge: Cambridge University Press, 1997) 77 and Bernhard Klein, "The Lie

of the Land: English Surveyors, Irish Rebels and *The Faerie Queene*,"
Irish University Review 26, 2 (1996): 211.

69. See J.B. Harley, "Silences and Secrecy: The Hidden Agenda of
Cartography in Early Modern Europe," *Imago Mundi* 40 (1988):
57–76.

70. Hill, *Plantation in Ulster* ii. Contemporary surveys underestimated the
size of the Ulster plantation by as much as eight times, an erroneous
figure often cited by historians (J.S. Brewer and William Bullen, eds.,
*Calendar of the Carew Manuscripts, preserved in the Archiepiscopal
Library at Lambeth* [1873; Nendeln, Liechtenstein: Kraus Reprint,
1974] xxxii and 235; Bagwell, *Ireland under the Stuarts* 1.75).

71. The quoted passage is Harley's helpful paraphrase of a section from
Foucault's preface to *The Order of Things* (xxi–ii): see "Silences and
Secrecy" 59.

72. Ibid., 61.

73. See Gilles Deleuze and Félix Guattari, *Anti-Oedipus: Capitalism and
Schizophrenia* (Minneapolis: University of Minnesota Press, 1983) 225.

74. Ibid., 195.

75. Anthony Giddens, *A Contemporary Critique of Historical Materialism,
Vol. 1: Power, Property and the State* (Berkeley: University of California
Press, 1981) 94.

76. PRO, SP 14/94/f. 192.

77. For other discussions of early modern European state apparatuses and
control over the dissemination of geographical knowledge, see
J.B. Harley, "Silences and Secrecy" 57–76 and "Maps, Knowledge,
and Power," in Denis Cosgrove and Stephen Daniels, eds., *The
Iconography of Landscape* (Cambridge: Cambridge University Press,
1988) 277–312; Chandra Mukerji, *From Graven Images: Patterns of
Modern Materialism* (New York: Columbia University Press, 1983)
79–130; and Peter Barber, "England II: Monarchs, Ministers, and
Maps, 1550–1625," in David Buisseret, ed., *Monarchs, Ministers, and
Maps: The Emergence of Cartography as a Tool of Government in Early
Modern Europe* (Chicago: University of Chicago Press, 1992) 57–98.

78. Richard Rambuss, *Spenser's Secret Career* (Cambridge: Cambridge
University Press, 1993).

79. Conyers Read, *Mr Secretary Walsingham and the Policy of Queen
Elizabeth*, 3 vols. (Oxford: Clarendon Press, 1925) 1.428–29. For a
discussion of Beale's treatise, see Swen Voekel, " 'Upon the Suddaine
View': State, Civil Society and Surveillance in Early Modern England,"
Early Modern Literary Studies 4, 2 (September 1998): 2.1–29.

80. *CSP, Ire., 1606–1608* cxxi.

81. *Letters from Sir Robert Cecil to Sir George Carew*, ed. John Maclean
(London: Camden Society, 1864) vi; *Annual Report of the Deputy
Keeper* 212, 225. As further evidence of the association of his position
with secrecy, Wilson had directed Salisbury's correspondence with
agents on the Continent while in his service (*CSP, Ire., 1606–08* cxxi

and 655–56; Historical Manuscripts Commission, *Calendar of the Manuscripts of the . . . Marquess of Salisbury . . . , Part XIX (A.D. 1607)* [London: H.M. Stationery Office, 1965] 15–17, 249–51).

82. Qtd. in Fussner, *The Historical Revolution* 77. On Wilson, see A.F. Pollard's entry in *The Dictionary of National Biography*, volume 21; *Annual Report of the Deputy Keeper* 212–23; and R.B. Wernham, "The Public Records in the Sixteenth and Seventeenth Centuries," in Levi Fox, ed., *English Historical Scholarship in the Sixteenth and Seventeenth Centuries* (London: Oxford University Press, 1956) 21–22.

83. *CSP, Ire., 1615–1625* 202; Wilson wrote to the earl of Middlesex with a plan to maintain 4,000 soldiers (*Fourth Report of the Royal Commission on Historical Manuscripts. Part I. Report and Appendix* [London: H.M. Stationery Office, 1874] 284).

84. F.J. Fisher has edited "On the State of England A.D. 1600" in *Camden Miscellany* 16 (1936): v–vii. Although "Booke on the State of Ireland" may have been written by Henry Cuffe, secretary to the earl of Essex, Wilson claims authorship of it within his other text (*CSP, Ire., 1598–1599* 505 ff.; Wilson, "On the State of England" 18). On Wilson's unfinished treatise, see *Annual Report of the Deputy Keeper* 217 and 231; *CSP, Dom., 1623–1625* 555.

85. For apologist accounts of Chichester's career, see Cyril Falls, *The Birth of Ulster* (1936; London: Constable, 1996) and John McCavitt, *Sir Arthur Chichester: Lord Deputy of Ireland 1605–1616* (Belfast: Queen's University, 1998). On Davies's manipulation of legal mechanisms, see Hans S. Pawlisch, *Sir John Davies and the Conquest of Ireland: A Study in Legal Imperialism* (Cambridge: Cambridge University Press, 1985) and Baker, *Between Nations* 91–100, 117–20.

86. For a further discussion of gaps in knowledge in early modern maps, see Harley, "Silences and Secrecy" 57–76.

87. On the 1609 survey, see J.H. Andrews, "Maps of the Escheated Counties of Ulster, 1609–10," *Proceedings of the Royal Irish Academy* 74 (1974): 133–70.

88. Hill, *Plantation in Ulster* 67–71, 118–21.

89. Norden's map is catalogued as British Library, Cotton MS. Augustus I.ii.44. Andrews speculates that alongside the set sent to Salisbury and later reproduced by Norden, another version of the 1609 survey remained in Ireland to assist in administering the plantation ("Maps of the Escheated Counties" 159, 163–64).

90. For other examples attesting to the increasing popularity of maps and atlases among elite "armchair travelers," see Victor Morgan, "The Cartographic Image of 'the Country' in Early Modern England," *Transactions of the Royal Historical Society*, 5th ser., 29 (1979): 144–47 and Barber, "England II" 43, 58–84.

91. In his pamphlet's most famous passage, Blenerhassett casts the feminized figure of "depopulated Vlster" as a damsel in distress, recently

freed from "the vsurping tyrannie of Traytors," and proposes that the exportation of England's surplus population will ameliorate the condition of Ulster, where "there remayneth nothing but ruynes and desolatio[n]" (*A Direction for the Plantation of Ulster* sig. A2).

92. Andrews, *Shapes of Ireland* 113. Carew had seen the Ulster plantation firsthand, having been appointed by James to lead a commission to check on initial settlement in 1610–11 (Hill, *Plantation in Ulster* 447). On Carew's collection, see William O'Sullivan, "George Carew's Irish Maps," *Long Room* 26–27 (1983): 15–25 and Brewer and Bullen, eds., *Calendar of the Carew Manuscripts* vii–xlix.

93. [Richard Hadsor], *Advertisements for Ireland, Being a Description of the State of Ireland in the Reign of James I, Contained in a Manuscript in the Library of Trinity College Dublin*, ed. George O'Brien (Dublin: Royal Society of Antiquaries of Ireland, 1923) 3. For background on Hadsor, see Victor Treadwell, "Richard Hadsor and the Authorship of 'Advertisements for Ireland,' 1622/3," *Irish Historical Studies* 30, no. 119 (May 1997): 331–36.

94. Moody, *A New History of Ireland* 3.197.

95. This practice helped transfer half the county of Fermanagh from the Maguires to undertakers in 1605 (Bardon, *History of Ulster* 116).

96. "A Chronicle of Lord Chichester's Government of Ireland" [ca. 1615], in John Lodge, ed., *Desiderata Curiosa Hibernica: Or a Select Collection of State Papers*, 2 vols. (Dublin, 1772) 1.249, 266–67. Spenser similarly mentions this problem in *A View of the Present State of Ireland* (31). The English state also employed officials to hunt for concealed lands in England, testifying to the use of colonial practices within the domestic body politic: see Braddick, *State Formation* 42–43.

97. In the 1613 Parliament, Ulster put forward 38 of the added 84 seats to the lower house; only one of the province's 64 seats was represented by a Catholic. For details, see Moody, *A New History of Ireland* 3.210–19; Bagwell, *Ireland under the Stuarts* 1.108–38; Falls, *Birth of Ulster* 203–10. On the influence of the Irish Parliament on Jonson's *Irish Masque at Court*, see Lindley, "Embarrassing Ben" and James M. Smith, "Effaced History: Facing the Colonial Contexts of Ben Jonson's *Irish Masque at Court*," *ELH* 65 (1998): 297–321. Francis G. James, in *Lords of the Ascendancy: The Irish House of Lords and Its Members, 1600–1800* (Dublin: Irish Academic Press, 1995), finds a surprising degree of accommodation among Gaelic Irish and Old English elites to the Protestant Ascendancy.

98. For example, Farmer encourages the crown to claim one-fourth to one-third of the revenue earned from changes in tenure ("Chronicle of Lord Chichester's Government" 1.266–67).

99. Speed's *Theatre* was republished several times in the seventeenth century: 1616, 1623, 1627, 1632, 1646, 1650 (with four editions from 1651–54), 1665, and 1676; beginning in 1627, the *Theatre* was

published together with Speed's *Prospect*. In addition, a Latin version of the *Theatre* was published in 1616, 1621, and 1646. As evidence of the increasing popularity of Speed's maps, they were also reengraved in a more accessible and cheaper octavo ("pocketbook") format and published under the title *England, Wales, and Ireland described* in 1627, 1632, 1646, 1662, 1665, 1666, 1668, and 1676; with the exception of 1666, editions from 1646 onwards were published together with an octavo version of Speed's *Prospect*: see Skelton, *County Atlases* 30–44 and *passim*; R.V. Tooley, "John Speed: a Personal View," *Map Collector* 1 (1977): 1–9; Rodney W. Shirley, *Early Printed Maps of the British Isles: a Bibliography, 1477–1650* (London: Holland Press, 1980) 102.

100. Andrews, *Shapes of Ireland* 114; Tooley, *Maps and Map-Makers* 93.

101. Andrews, *Shapes of Ireland* 114; Tooley, *Maps and Map-Makers* 80, 93. For examples of other late seventeenth- and eighteenth-century atlases based on Speed, see Rodney W. Shirley, *Printed Maps of the British Isles, 1650–1750* (London: Map Collector Publications, 1988).

102. Tooley, *Maps and Map-Makers* 93. Petty's text, *Hiberniae delineatio* (1685), has been reproduced with an introduction by J.H. Andrews (Shannon: Irish University Press, 1969). For a discussion of Petty, see Andrews, *Shapes of Ireland* 118–52 and Poovey, *History of the Modern Fact* 120–38.

103. The 1676 edition of Speed's *Prospect* added four other maps of England's American colonies: Virginia and Maryland; New England and New York; Jamaica and Barbados; Carolina (Tooley, "John Speed" 7).

104. Edward Lynam, *The Mapmaker's Art* (London: Batchworth Press, 1953) 118. As a sign of its importance, Norwood's map was also reproduced in John Smith's *The Generall Historie of Virginia, New-England, and the Summer Isles* (1624). For Norwood's biography and his personal account of his time in Bermuda, see Wesley Frank Craven and Walter B. Hayward, eds., *The Journal of Richard Norwood* (New York: Scholars, 1945). Rebecca Ann Bach discusses Norwood's map in *Colonial Transformations: The Cultural Production of the New Atlantic World, 1580–1640* (New York: Palgrave, 2000) 99–106, 110–12.

105. By contrast, Richard Ligon's 1657 map of Barbados features a number of images within the interior of the island that illustrate the dependence of its sugar industry upon slave labor, including two escaping slaves being pursued by an overseer as well as African slaves leading pack animals, evidence of an acknowledgment of the island's slave economy: see "A Topographicall Description and Admeasurement of the Yland of Barbados," a foldout map in *A Trve & Exact History of the Island of Barbados* (1657) sig. A4v.

106. Harley, "Silences and Secrecy" 68. For other discussions of the cartographic effacement of labor, see Helgerson, *Forms of Nationhood* 109

and Mary Hamer, "Putting Ireland on the Map," *Textual Practice* 3 (1989): 184–201.

107. The first survey of Ulster, from the summer of 1608, simply listed territories opened up for confiscation. Bodley's team surveyed the six escheated Ulster counties from July–October 1609 (Andrews, "Maps of the Escheated Counties" 139, 142).

108. Sir Josias Bodley, "Survay of Ye Undertakers and Servitors Planted in Ulster Between the 2 of February 1612 [1613] and the 25 April 1613," Hastings Collection, Huntington Library, San Marino, CA. Bodley's initial September 1613 survey of the areas of Coleraine that had been granted to the London companies is no longer extant (Moody, *Londonderry Plantation* 159).

109. Hill, *Plantation in Ulster* 447–48n.

110. This passage is taken from Bodley's 1614 survey of the Londonderry plantation (qtd. in Moody, *Londonderry Plantation* 162). Spenser uses similar language to describe the failures of the Munster plantation in *A View of the Present State of Ireland* 121.

111. Karl Marx, *Capital*, trans. Samuel Moore and Edward Aveling (New York: International Publishers, 1967) 1.716. (I have chosen to use Moore and Aveling's translation of this passage rather than Fowkes's, cited earlier.)

112. Moody, *Londonderry Plantation* 159–65, 177–78; Perceval-Maxwell, *Scottish Migration* 161, 163; Hill, *Plantation in Ulster* 449; Curl, *Londonderry Plantation* 63–64, 70.

113. Hill, *Plantation in Ulster* 153n.

114. Davies had grounds either to suppress or neglect Bodley's findings: Bodley, as the king's servant, could potentially undercut the power and autonomy of colonial officials in Ireland. Colonial officials and undertakers, in fact, accused royal commissioners of giving unfavorable reports of the plantation so as to force the king to revoke undertakers' leases and thereby claim the confiscated holdings for themselves (Moody, *Londonderry Plantation* 178; Curl, *Londonderry Plantation* 64). For discussions of the complicated power relations between the English court and colonial officials in Ireland, see Maley, *Salvaging Spenser* 99–117 and Christopher Highley, *Shakespeare, Spenser, and the Crisis in Ireland* (Cambridge: Cambridge University Press, 1997) 40–66.

115. For a critique of competing Protestant and Catholic mythologizations of Ulster history, see John Montague's poetic sequence *The Rough Field* (1972; Winston-Salem: Wake Forest University Press, 1989).

116. For a list of collections, see *CSP, Ire., 1603–1606* xxxi–cix.

117. Foucault, *The Archaeology of Knowledge* 129.

118. Ibid., 130.

119. Ibid., 131.

120. For a general discussion of the role of cultural memory in contemporary Northern Ireland, see Kirkland, *Literature and Culture in*

Northern Ireland Since 1965. On Foucault's discussion of counter-memory, see "Nietzsche, Genealogy, History," in *Language, Counter-Memory, Practice: Select Essays and Interviews* (Ithaca: Cornell University Press, 1977) 160.

121. Paul Ricoeur, "Memory and Forgetting" and "Imagination, Testimony and Trust: a Dialogue with Paul Ricoeur," in *Questioning Ethics: Contemporary Debates in Philosophy*, ed. Richard Kearney and Mark Dooley (New York: Routledge, 1999) 9, 16. For a critique of the use of memory as a category of analysis, see Kerwin Lee Klein, "On the Emergence of Memory in Historical Discourse," *Representations* 69 (Winter 2000): 127–50.

Conclusion: The Unmaking of English Working Class

1. E.P. Thompson, *The Making of the English Working Class* (1963; New York: Pantheon, 1964).
2. Thompson discusses the eighteenth century in several studies, including "The Moral Economy of the English Crowd" and "Class Struggle Without Class?" Among assessments and critiques of Thompson's work, see Perry Anderson, *Arguments Within English Marxism* (London: NLB and Verso, 1980), esp. 30–49 and Dipesh Chakrabarty, *Rethinking Working-Class History: Bengal 1890–1940* (Delhi and Oxford: Oxford University Press, 1996) 221–23.
3. Thompson, *Making of the English Working Class* 194.
4. Ibid., 194.
5. Thompson, "The Moral Economy of the English Crowd"; for a similar argument, see David Underdown, *Revel, Riot and Rebellion: Popular Politics and Culture in England, 1603–1660* (New York: Oxford University Press, 1985).
6. Laslett, *The World We Have Lost* 16–21.
7. Nancy Armstrong and Leonard Tennenhouse, *The Imaginary Puritan: Literature, Intellectual Labor, and the Origins of Personal Life* (Berkeley: University of California Press, 1992) 69–88. Also see Christopher Hill's critique of Laslett in *Change and Continuity* 205–18.
8. For a relevant discussion, see Anderson, *Imagined Communities* 7.
9. Eric Hobsbawm, *Nations and Nationalism since 1780* (Cambridge: Cambridge University Press, 1990) 10. Hobsbawm critiques the approach to nationalism, perhaps exemplified by Ernest Gellner's *Nations and Nationalism*, which views nationalism as generated primarily by state power.
10. For a related discussion, see David Lloyd, "Nationalisms against the State," in *The Politics of Culture in the Shadow of Capital*, ed. Lisa Lowe and David Lloyd (Durham: Duke University Press, 1997) 173–97.

11. Helgerson, *Forms of Nationhood* 107–47; McEachern, *The Poetics of English Nationhood* 138–91. In addition, Helgerson's consideration of the laboring classes is limited to an analysis of the exclusion of these groups from representations of the nation (*Forms of Nationhood* 10–11). He therefore confines his discussion of these classes to their depiction in dramatic texts, analyzing the progressive marginalization of populist concerns in the early modern public theater.

12. For a discussion of the relation between elite and popular expressions of nationhood, see David Underdown, *A Freeborn People: Politics and Nation in Seventeenth-Century England* (Oxford: Clarendon, 1996).

13. For a discussion of cottagers, see Tawney, *Agrarian Problem* 277–80; Roger B. Manning, *Village Revolts: Social Protest and Popular Disturbances in England, 1509–1640* (Oxford: Clarendon, 1988) 170–78; and Christopher Hill, *The World Turned Upside Down: Radical Ideas During the English Revolution* (London: Temple Smith, 1972) 35, 42.

14. *The Agrarian History of England and Wales*, volume 4, ed. H.P.R. Finberg (Cambridge: Cambridge University Press, 1967) 420. In early modern Essex, the larger group of agricultural laborers and weavers of which cottagers formed the most destitute part constituted 35–40% of the population (William Hunt, *The Puritan Moment: The Coming of Revolution in an English County* [Cambridge: Harvard University Press, 1983] 21).

15. Hunt, *The Puritan Moment* 4.

16. For a discussion of manufacture as a transitional mode of production, see Marx, *Capital* 1.455–91; for analysis, see Althusser and Balibar, *Reading Capital* 236–41, 302–08.

17. Among the few contemporary references to the position of cottagers in the English social system, see Smith, *Discourse of the Commonweal* 50–51; Harrison, *Description of England* 216, 257–58; and Wilson, *The State of England* 19–20.

18. King estimated a population of 364,000 laborers and outservants and 400,000 cottagers and paupers; based on King's figures, cottagers would have comprised around 24 percent of England's total population (*Seventeenth-Century Economic Documents*, ed. Thirsk and Cooper 781).

19. Halpern, *Poetics of Primitive Accumulation* 74.

20. Sir Francis Bacon appropriately described cottagers as "but hous'd beggars" in his comments on enclosure in *The Reign of Henry VII*, a passage that Marx cites in *Capital* (1.881n.).

21. Norden, *The Svrveiors Dialogve* (1618 edition) sigs. H7–H7v.

22. Slack, *Poverty and Policy* 43. See also Natasha Korda's discussion of gender, poverty, and labor in *Shakespeare's Domestic Economies*, esp. 160–61, 176–91.

23. Peter Burke discusses this early nineteenth-century nostalgia for pre-industrial social relations, and the rising interest in "popular" and

"folk" culture, in *Popular Culture in Early Modern Europe* (London: Temple Smith, 1978) 3–22. Williams notes a similar phenomenon in *Country and the City* 9–12.

24. Eburne, *A Plain Pathway to Plantations* 92.

25. Slack, *Poverty and Policy* 63. A 1589 statute (31 Elizabeth, c. 8) had prohibited the construction of unlicensed buildings on commons as well as cottages with less than four acres of adjoining land. This law remained on the statute books until the late eighteenth century (Hunt, *The Puritan Moment* 70).

26. See Hill, *Change and Continuity* 219–38. It should be noted, though, that even many radicals excluded servants and the landless poor from the category of "freeborn Englishmen" (Hill 223).

INDEX

merchants, foreign/resident alien, 18–19, 20, 36–39, 42, 43
Middleton, Thomas: *More Dissemblers Besides Women*, 255 n145; *The Spanish Gypsy*, 158, 163, 255 n145
Midlands Rising, the, 107, 239 n56
Moison, Thomas, 20, 42, 222 n60
Molin, Nicolo, 53
money: currency manipulation, 18, 23–25, 37–41, 220 n25, 224 n81, 224 n83–84; "farthing tokens," 40–41; Irish recoinage (1601), 41
Monson, Sir William, 89, 235 n105
Montague, John, 267 n115
Montaigne, Michel de, 122
Montrose, Louis Adrian, 222 n47
"moral economy," 13, 97, 103, 109, 202, 207, 217 n58
More, Sir Thomas, 237 n20
Morgan, Edmund S., 3, 101, 104
Morton, Thomas, 211 n2
Moryson, Fynes, 255 n145
Mountjoy, Charles Blount, Lord, 41, 181
Muldrew, Craig, 23, 39, 63, 224 n79, 224 n83
Mullaney, Steven, 84
Mun, Sir Thomas, 19, 20, 33–35, 36, 38, 46, 222 n61
Munday, Anthony, 88
Munster plantation, 173, 257 n10, 267 n110

Nairn, Tom, 230 n47, 257 n7
nationhood: and colonial migration, 2–5, 93–94, 99–101, 124–27, 134, 208–10; and gender, 30, 203, 209, 211 n4; and historical narrative, 175–79; and laborers, 47–50, 95–100, 123–27, 201–10; and national economy, 7–9, 13, 17–20, 21–23, 28–30, 32–39, 41, 47–50, 95–100, 103–04, 123–27, 207–08; and

nostalgia, 67, 71–72, 202, 208, 229 n42, 269 n23; performativity of, 81, 137–38, 166, 168–70; populist expressions of, 67, 72, 202–03, 210, 269 n11; and sexuality, 30, 164–65, 222 n47; theories of, 215 n40. *See also* body politic; British identity; commonwealth
Navy, the Royal, 54–55, 88, 234 n101
Nerlich, Michael, 20, 221 n35
Netzloff, Mark, 221 n36, 231 n59
New British History, 10, 215 n44–45. *See also* British identity
New Exchange, The, 36, 39, 42, 224 n77–78
Newfoundland, 5, 60, 92, 93, 98, 100, 221 n36
New Historicism, 129, 226 n110, 244 n121
Newman, Karen, 39
Norden, John, 11, 190, 205–09, 264 n89
Norton, Thomas, 82
Norwood, Richard, 192–95, 266 n104

O'Cahan, Donal, 181, 185
O'Doherty, Sir Cahir, 181, 185, 262 n62
O'Donnell, Hugh Roe, 181
O'Donnell, Rory, earl of Tyrconnell, 181, 185
Ó hEodhasa, Eochaidh, 181
Okely, Judith, 253 n110
O'Neill, Hugh, earl of Tyrone, 181, 182, 185, 196
Orientalism, 78–79
Osborne, Francis, 150, 251 n83, 252 n85
Ottoman Empire, 56, 67, 77, 78

Paine, Henry, 130
Palmer, Thomas, 74–76
Patterson, Annabel, 239 n56